Implementing Triple Bottom Line Sustainability into Global Supply Chains

Implementing Triple Bottom Line Sustainability into Global Supply Chains

EDITED BY LYDIA BALS AND WENDY TATE

Greenleaf
PUBLISHING

© 2016 Greenleaf Publishing Limited

Published by Greenleaf Publishing Limited
Aizlewood's Mill
Nursery Street
Sheffield S3 8GG
UK
www.greenleaf-publishing.com

The right of Lydia Bals and Wendy Tate to be identified as Editors of this Work has been asserted
by them in accordance with sections 77 and 78 of the Copyright, Designs and Patents Act 1988.

Cover by LaliAbril.com.
Printed and bound by Printondemand-worldwide.com, UK.

British Library Cataloguing in Publication Data:
 A catalogue record for this book is available from the British Library.

 ISBN-13: 978-1-78353-351-0 [hardback]
 ISBN-13: 978-1-78353-352-7 [PDF ebook]
 ISBN-13: 978-1-78353-374-9 [ePub ebook]

Contents

Methodology

Education

1

The journey from triple bottom line (TBL) sustainable supply chains to TBL shared value chain design[1]

Lydia Bals
University of Applied Sciences Mainz, Germany; Copenhagen Business School, Denmark

Wendy L. Tate
University of Tennessee, USA

While sustainable supply chain management (SSCM) research has become significantly more relevant and rigorous, there is still much to be learned about how to truly implement triple bottom line (TBL; economic, environmental and social) sustainability into global supply chains. Most of the research to date focuses on some, but not all, of these three dimensions. This book is a compilation of work that addresses various aspects of the TBL. This introductory chapter provides an overview on the different chapters contained within the four sections of the book, but also proposes future research suggestions to stimulate research in this field. It closes with an outlook on how TBL sustainable supply chain design might evolve to TBL shared value chain design.

---

1 The editors would like to thank all authors for their contributions, Greenleaf Publishing for the fantastic collaboration on this project and Anne Synnatschke for all her support as a student assistant.

1.1 Introduction: expanding the sustainability scope

The call to think and act differently in sustainable supply chain management (SSCM) is becoming increasingly louder. In the *Journal of Supply Chain Management* 50th anniversary issue, Pagell and Shevchenko (2014, p. 44f.) spelled out a clear need for future research into the issues of "how to create truly sustainable supply chains" and "what new practices and processes are needed to create truly sustainable supply chains".

In response to this, the idea behind this edited collection was to introduce innovative cases, approaches and concepts that show how to successfully implement all three dimensions of triple bottom line (TBL) sustainability into supply chains. It particularly targeted chapters that take a true TBL (economic, environmental and social; Elkington, 1998) perspective and/or offer specific insights into implementation of different aspects of the TBL, for example by incorporating innovative case studies. There is recognition that research has mostly focused on the environmental and economic dimension of the TBL, but the social dimension is still relatively under-researched (Seuring and Müller, 2008). Therefore, papers that include the social dimension were of particular interest for this collection. Noting that this interface of environmental, economic and social aspects in supply chain management is not yet well covered, it also sought to address the call for further research concerning the base of the pyramid (BoP) business models that address the sustainability needs of the global poor (e.g. Karnani, 2007; Hahn, 2009).

Another target of the call for contributions was to learn more regarding the role of social entrepreneurs in transforming supply chains according to TBL criteria, e.g. by establishing social businesses that are economically and environmentally sustainable. From these businesses' inception, the entrepreneur is focused on building sustainability into their supply chain or supply network. The goal of these types of entrepreneur is to convince social investors of the return on investment in all three pillars. This allows them to creatively consider the business model upfront and establish sustainable and innovative business models. For sustainable business models we follow the definition of Boons and Lüdeke-Freund (2013), where the firm creates value through balancing economic, ecological and social elements, by promoting equitable relationships among the stakeholders and adopting a fair revenue model. Linking such models to SCM, as stated by Seuring and Gold (2013, p. 5), "could help us to address aspects that are so far weakly developed, such as the social dimension of sustainability management".

Concerning the actual implementation, additional insights into how (social) businesses can successfully build TBL effective business models was solicited, as these will be playing an increasing role in global business. It is estimated that by 2020 about US$500 billion will be allocated to impact investing initiatives (World Economic Forum, 2013). Therefore, aspects such as what makes them successful and/or what can be learned from failures holds tremendous potential for advancing this trend and furthering sustainable practices.

The following sub-sections of this introductory chapter follow the overall structure of the book and provide an overview on how the respective chapters fit together and help the subject of TBL sustainability emerge. Each section is followed by an outlook and suggestions for future research based on the fruitful discussions and materials that the compilation of this edited book brought together.

1.2 The importance of TBL sustainability in global supply chains

In the initial section, there are some thought-provoking chapters that challenge one of the basic assumptions in current research: Western countries know what is good for the rest of the world. Examining this, Touboulic and Ejodame (Chapter 2: "Are we really doing the "right thing"? From sustainability imperialism in global supply chains to an inclusive emerging economy perspective") adopt Griggs *et al.*'s (2013) representation of TBL sustainability, draw inspiration from the international development and poverty literature and apply Maslow's hierarchy of needs as a theoretical lens. They suggest a multilevel and systemic view of the issue and articulate a number of propositions to guide future research. This is followed by Bellow (Chapter 3: "Supply chain resilience"), who investigates the importance from a risk perspective as he focuses on supply chain resilience and proposes that in order for a supply chain to be resilient it must be able to anticipate and adapt to risk, based on several examples. Then Meutcheho (Chapter 4: "A mixed-methods analysis of the effect of global sustainable supply chain management on firm performance") turns towards importance from a performance perspective and analyses how professionals perceive the contribution of SSCM to a company's environmental, social and economic performance based on survey responses of 242 professionals from a diverse range of industries.

These chapters set the stage for additional research questions that might help move the field forward and increase the importance and visibility of the topic of TBL SSCM:

1. What can be learned about the dynamics between the three TBL objectives from an emerging-market perspective? There are many locations around the globe facing extreme challenges economically, socially and environmentally. For example, Haiti was destroyed by an earthquake in 2010 and even today there are people who have not been able to rebuild their homes so have to live in temporary structures and face extreme poverty. To make matters even worse, only 1% of the natural forests remain—creating environmental and social issues. There are many other areas in the world facing extreme conditions that could use insights from both theory and practice to help make their communities more liveable, productive and hygienic.

2. Which stakeholders, beyond direct supply chain partners, are important in implementing TBL sustainability? Identifying all of the stakeholders and taking a systems perspective and understanding the interrelationships between those stakeholders is critical for TBL outcomes. The stakeholders vary across countries and across different types of business—governments, professional associations, competitors, customers and community members may all have different roles. Also, the impact investors and social business ventures play a key role in success.

3. How do (human and financial) resource constraints affect SSCM decision-making? The financial support chain is critical to these sustainability models from the idea stage to implementation and delivery. The financial chain is quite extensive and complicated—because TBL means economic sustainability as well as social and environmental, there has to be "proof" of profitability. Investors and other stakeholders demand economic viability.

4. Is resilience becoming more intertwined with sustainability in a scenario of increasing climate change issues? The looming supply chain disruption implications of climate change pose threats, but also opportunities for functions such as purchasing and supply management to help companies navigate through these (Bals, 2012). Increasing companies' supply chain resilience in light of scenarios such as hurricanes and floods might become an approach both for corporate survival as well as potentially gaining competitive advantage for those doing it successfully (e.g. because of floods in Thailand some automotive companies were able to continue production with their local suppliers while others had to stop production).

1.3 Enabling TBL sustainability by fostering transparency, having appropriate methodologies and a shift in business education

This section focuses on the enablers of TBL sustainability, starting with transparency, then methodology and concluding with education. Opening on the area of having the necessary transparency in order to further improve sustainability, Ellram and Tate (Chapter 5: "Mapping networks and the influence on the natural environment") start with their chapter on how network analysis can support one in gaining an overview about the network positions or roles and importance (based on dollars of spending) of various network members, based on data by the Global Reporting Initiative (GRI). This determines the embeddedness of an organization and identifies sub-groups or clusters to which the focal firm has to gain access in order to share its position on TBL sustainability and pass on information. The focal firm has the opportunity to use brokers as intermediaries between, among and with the sub-groups. Using network mapping tools, organizations can identify the types of brokers and how to best position themselves to share the most information and get the best TBL results. Next, providing a comprehensive overview of such data sources such as GRI, Abe and Chee (Chapter 6: "Integrating sustainability reporting into global supply chains in Asia and the Pacific") show their results of an analysis of 121 sustainability reporting initiatives at both global and regional levels to develop and propose a sustainable global supply chain (GSC) reporting framework in Asia and the Pacific.

Continuing with methodological requirements, Steinberg (Chapter 7: "The sustainability blind spot: Identifying and managing climate risk in global supply chains") turns towards the area of risk management in supply chains and presents the case for why reduction of climate risk in the supply chain and business-led community risk reduction are complementary to each other, outlining a method for identifying risk and prioritizing supplier and community engagement opportunities. This is followed by Halog and Nguyen (Chapter 8: "Evaluating supply chain networks by incorporating the triple dimensions of sustainability paradigm"), who develop mathematical-programming-based efficiency metrics under the headline of "sustainable network operational efficiency" (SNOE), targeted at assessing supply chain performance and evaluating possible design configurations of a global supply chain. Finally, Moxham and Kauppi (Chapter 9: "The valorization of social sustainability: Using quality seals to drive continuous improvement in global supply chain management") present their examination of quality seals: standards, certifications, codes of conduct and labelling, which they use as proxies for socially sustainable supply chain management.

Closing the section on enablers, London (Chapter 10 "The role of business schools in developing leaders for TBL sustainability") turns towards the role of higher education and how business schools in particular can facilitate the journey towards TBL sustainable supply chains. He states that based on the large numbers of students attending a wide variety of programmes—and business schools' capacity for creating events that will attract discussion of these issues—they are uniquely positioned to move the topic forward as a central curriculum item and educate students on good business practice, rather than positioning such content as "nice to have".

Adding to this, the following future research questions come to mind:

1. How can we gain transparency in particularly complex supply networks (e.g. multi-tier and sub-contractor prone supply chains such as in the electronics, automotive and garment industry)? Transparency and information sharing are largely aligned. Understanding how to access and to validate the information in complex networks is very challenging.

2. How can we map a TBL network that includes all of the different stakeholders and use this information to better design both the financial and information supplementary chains? There are a number of calls for work in network

design and sustainability; understanding how to disseminate the necessary information or change a network structure is crucial for TBL success.

3. Are quality seals becoming more globally trusted by consumers or does negative coverage of one also affect the others negatively? The multitude of different seals still poses a barrier to improved consumer decisions and whenever a seal makes the headlines as "untrustworthy" anecdotal evidence suggests that consumers see the trustworthiness of other seals decline, too. To provide an illustration of such trust breaches, in Germany the media has covered practices such as adding unsustainable ingredients to partially balance recipes (for example, a case where some fair-trade sugar and cocoa was added to a product otherwise containing non-fair-trade sugar and cocoa) and labelling this "mass balance" on the packaging's fine print. Such practices can undermine consumer trust in such labels.

4. How can sustainability be embedded into business school curricula beyond specific domains (e.g. business ethics)? Why is sustainability often still just a "module" within specific content domains, such as marketing, supply chain management or human resources management? How could it become not optional but required learning for all business operations within modern higher education curricula?

1.4 Practical insights from cases on how TBL sustainability can be achieved

This section focuses on the implementation aspect of TBL sustainability and has a number of cases that discuss this aspect. What are some of the keys to success? What are some of the barriers that need to be overcome? What are some of the intended and unintended consequences of focusing on TBL sustainability?

Camacho and Vázquez-Maguirre (Chapter 11: "Sustainable supply chain in a social enterprise") start by developing a framework that focuses on the introduction of sustainability into a supply chain and present a social enterprise that focuses on community well-being through value creation and sustainability. This is followed by Sahasranamam and Ball (Chapter 12: "Sustainable procurement in social enterprises: Comparative case studies from India and Scotland"), who compare two social enterprises, one from the developing-country context of India and the other from the developed-country context of Scotland. Through these case studies they illustrate how social enterprises integrate TBL aspects into their procurement in the two contexts.

Continuing with a focus on the social angle, Eisenmeier (Chapter 13: "Sustainable supply chain management and the role of trust at the base of the pyramid [BoP]: An exploratory case study") presents an explorative case study following the BoP 2.0

approach, which argues that poverty can be alleviated by integrating the base of the global income pyramid actors, such as producers and suppliers, into global supply chains. Based on a specific BoP project conducted in Peru, the chapter concludes that there is low mutual interpersonal trust between farmers and suppliers at the BoP, which leads to a low level of association and organization. Turning towards the construction industry as one of the world's greatest CO_2 emission generators, Jervis, Meehan and Moxham (Chapter 14: "Addressing the triple bottom line: Lowering construction emissions through the implementation of collaborative supply chains") highlight how moving away from technological solutions to environmental problems and towards an integrated supply chain approach would be beneficial in future. This is followed by a closer look into the Ready Made Garment (RMG) industry by Heuer (Chapter 15: "Value chain connectedness as a framework for sustainability governance"), who illustrates the implications of value chain governance, particularly involving relationships between developed-country lead firms and suppliers in developing countries. This section concludes with a look at legal boundaries and guidelines on how to implement sustainability. Next, Phillips (Chapter 16: "Sustainable bio-based supply chains in light of the Nagoya Protocol") explores the impact of national legal, regulatory and policy measures on access and benefit-sharing measures envisaged by the Nagoya Protocol and their impact on global supply chains in bio-based industries (e.g. agriculture, botanicals, cosmetics, industrial biotechnology and pharmaceuticals).

Adding to this, the following future research questions come to mind:

1. Which practices from developed-country contexts may be transferable to emerging markets contexts and vice versa? While some practices that involve high-tech solutions and related high budgets may be more applicable to solve issues in the Western world—such as having water for agriculture (e.g. water desalination plants)—emerging markets might need more nimble and affordable solutions, which are easy to obtain, operate, maintain and repair (such as moving back to traditional planting of certain trees, bushes and crops in groups to give each other shade, protection and thus minimize external water needs).

2. How could intermediaries (such as NGOs) facilitate dissemination of best practices? NGOs are still evolving towards a more mainstream stakeholder group, although they are in a unique position to help disseminate best practices across firms and whole industries. In these regards, social business investors such as Yunus Social Business are increasingly working together with NGOs to engage them in nurturing sustainable businesses.

3. What are the intended and unintended consequences of TBL sustainable global supply chains? It is well known that the TBL dimensions are potentially conflicting. Therefore, optimizing one might be to the detriment of the other. Although this certainly is not intended deliberately in SSCM (e.g. that a company raises the prices it pays for a raw material to improve farmers'

situations, but thereby makes the product completely unaffordable for the local population), when have such intended consequences occurred and what can we learn from them?

4. Can multinational organizations retrofit their supply chain networks to become more TBL sustainable? So far, the retrofit approach in many cases has challenged multinational organizations in varying degrees of CSR because their networks are diverse and constantly changing. The main approach taken is to focus primarily on cause-based issues for a particular region (usually by generating donations). Still, the business of business is business, to make money, and some of the TBL outcomes require investment without a guaranteed return on investment. Many of the "social" aspects focus internally on issues such as worker safety, lack of child labour and hours of service for employees. These internally focused issues do not address some of the major social concerns such as widespread poverty, lack of clean drinking water, general hygiene issues or even education. In many situations, a thorough and innovative redesign of their operations is needed. A first step is to realize that movement into these more emerging environments may not mean a cut and paste from other operational designs.

1.5 Terminological and methodological clarity for future research

The book concludes with three chapters that advance terminological clarity and provide methodological suggestions for future research.

First, Bartczek, Semeijn and Quintens (Chapter 17: "Promoting socially responsible purchasing [SRP]: The role of Transaction Cost Economics dimensions") investigate how Transaction Cost Economics can be utilized in the context of socially responsible purchasing (SRP), developing a conceptual model to investigate the role of supplier behavioural uncertainty, buyer-specific investments and transaction frequency for buyer and supplier SRP. Next, terminological clarity is advanced by Lüdeke-Freund, Gold and Bocken (Chapter 18: "Sustainable business model and supply chain conceptions: Towards an integrated perspective") as they compare the main characteristics of sustainable supply chains (SSCs) and sustainable business models (SBMs) from the current academic literature and investigate conceptual similarities, differences and areas where both can actually complement each other. This part of the book concludes with the chapter by Saunders, Tate, Zsidisin and Miemczyk (Chapter 19: "A network perspective on the TBL in global supply chains"), who provide a network perspective on TBL sustainability in global supply chains, using two illustrative examples to demonstrate how social network variables interact in the networks of large multinational organizations.

Adding to this, the following future research questions in relation to network analysis come to mind:

- How do brokers play a role in management of TBL sustainability across a multinational and multilevel network?

- How does public opinion and personal opinion influence buying behaviour in international networks?

- What role do incentives play in designing for TBL sustainability?

- Can TBL sustainability be designed into supply chains and supply networks? If so, what is it that we need to know?

- Is TBL sustainability with its three dimensions a sufficient conceptualization in today's complex stakeholder networks?

1.6 A far-reaching outlook: towards shared value chain design and the circular economy

Taking up the last two research questions above on global supply chain network aspects, a specific area for future research relates to supply chain structure and design. In line with the latest on supply chain theory (Carter *et al.*, 2015), the physical chain and support chain(s) should be differentiated. In the former, the physical products move from supplier to focal firm to customer, whereas the support supply chain concerns the information and financial flows. In order to arrive at sustainable supply chains, the editors of this book suggest that the design of all three flows should be in the scope of future research.

Moreover, in terms of supply chain design, it still focuses on the more traditional metrics of economic performance, leading to a narrow scope. This is no surprise as the majority of the literature on supply chain modelling during the 1990s focused on costs (e.g. Lee *et al.*, 1997; Tzafestas and Kapsiotis, 1994; Beamon, 1998), but even in more current SCM research typically there are, at most, two dimensions of the TBL considered together, mostly economic and environment (e.g. Sarkis, 2006; Srivastava, 2007; Vachon and Klassen, 2006;) or economic and social (e.g. Xia *et al.*, 2015). There is still considerable opportunity to encompass broader design parameters. Here, we would like to propose to expand the scope towards designing for "TBL shared value".

The concept of shared value is defined as the policies and operating practices that enhance competitiveness of a company while simultaneously advancing the economic and social conditions in the communities in which it operates (Porter and Kramer, 2006, 2011). Shared value is the alignment of different actors across the value chain (Sink, 1991). It is the alignment of these actors (or stakeholders) that improves TBL performance. Moreover, as a contextual research variable, in the emerging market context the supply chain design takes place under severe financial, human resources and environmental constraints.

In terms of how that shared value might be delivered, Porter and Kramer (2011, p. 65) define three basic ways that companies can create shared value opportunities:

- By reconceiving products and markets
- By redefining productivity in the value chain
- By enabling local cluster development.

The actual implementation of these three models has not had much research focus to date (Spitzeck and Chapman, 2012). To study how this might correspond to SSCM is suggested for further research.

In conclusion, in order to achieve SSCM, it is suggested that the design stage is central and that incorporating all three flows as well as both the supply-side and demand-side considerations would pave the way for shared value chain design. Although the two terms "supply chain" and "value chain" are often used interchangeably, they actually differ in that the supply chain centres on transferring products or materials to a final point without necessarily adding value while so doing, whereas a value chain adds value at various points (Gereffi *et al.*, 2005). Therefore, in order to get to a very comprehensive understanding of what to design and how, we consider "TBL shared value chain design" to be a topic of increasing interest. The challenge of the future will be to find ways to close the loop for the flows involved and further advance the idea of a circular economy.

References

Bals, L. (2012). Climate change's impact on procurement: Risks and opportunities. In J. Stoner & C. Wankel (Eds.), *Managing Climate Change Business Risks and Consequences: Leadership for Global Sustainability* (pp. 101-119). Basingstoke, UK: Palgrave-Macmillan.

Beamon, B.M. (1998). Supply chain design and analysis: Models and methods. *International Journal of Production Economics*, 55(3), 281-294.

Boons, F., & Lüdeke-Freund, F. (2013). Business models for sustainable innovation: State-of-the-art and steps towards a research agenda. *Journal of Cleaner Production*, 45 (April), 9-19.

Carter, C.R., Roger, D.S., & Choi, T.Y. (2015). Toward the theory of the supply chain. *Journal of Supply Chain Management*, 51(2), 89-97.

Elkington, J. (1998). *Cannibals with Forks*. Gabriola Island, BC: New Society Publishers.

Gereffi, G., Humphrey, J., & Sturgeon, T. (2005). The governance of global value chains. *Review of International Political Economy*, 12(1), 78-104.

Griggs, D., Stafford-Smith, M., Gaffney, O., Rockström, J., Öhman, M.C., Shyamsundar, P., Steffen, W., Glaser, G., Kanie, N., & Noble, I. (2013). Sustainable development goals for people and planet. *Nature*, 495, 305-307.

Hahn, R. (2009). The ethical rational of business for the poor: Integrating the concepts bottom of the pyramid, sustainable development, and corporate citizenship. *Journal of Business Ethics*, 84(3), 313-324.

Karnani, A.G. (2006). Mirage at the bottom of the pyramid. William Davidson Institute, Working Paper Number 835, 1-27.

Lee, H.L., Padmanabhan, V., & Whang, S. (1997). Information distortion in a supply chain: The bullwhip effect. *Management Science*, 43(4), 546-558.

Pagell, M., & Shevchenko, A. (2014). Why research in sustainable supply chain management should have no future. *Journal of Supply Chain Management*, 50(1), 44-55.

Porter, M.E., & Kramer, M.R. (2011). Creating shared value. *Harvard Business Review*, 89(1/2), 62-77.

Porter, M.E., & Kramer, M.R. (2006). Strategy and society. The link between competitive advantage and corporate social responsibility. *Harvard Business Review*, 84(12), 78-92.

Sarkis, J. (2006). *Greening the Supply Chain*. New York: Springer Verlag.

Seuring, S., & Gold, S. (2013). Sustainability management beyond corporate boundaries: From stakeholders to performance. *Journal of Cleaner Production*, 56(1), 1-6.

Seuring, S., & Müller, M. (2008). From a literature review to a conceptual framework for sustainable supply chain management. *Journal of Cleaner Production*, 16(15), 1,699-1,710.

Spitzeck, H., & Chapman, S. (2012). Creating shared value as a differentiation strategy: The example of BASF in Brazil. *Corporate Governance: The International Journal of Business in Society*, 12(4), 499-513.

Srivastava, S., (2007). Green supply-chain management: A state-of-the-art literature review. *International Journal of Management Reviews*, 9(1), 53-80.

Tzafestas, S., & Kapsiotis, G. (1994). Coordinated control of manufacturing/supply chains using multi-level techniques. *Computer Integrated Manufacturing Systems*, 7(3), 206-212.

Vachon, S., & Klassen, R.D. (2006). Extending green practices across the supply chain: The impact of upstream and downstream integration. *International Journal of Operations & Production Management*, 26(7), 795-821.

Xia, Y., Zu, X., & Shi, C. (2015). A profit-driven approach to building a "people-responsible" supply chain. *European Journal of Operational Research*, 241(2), 348-360.

Lydia Bals is Professor of Supply Chain and Operations Management at the University of Applied Sciences Mainz, Germany and a Visiting Professor at the Department for Strategic Management and Globalization at Copenhagen Business School, Denmark. Prior to that she was a visiting scholar at Wharton and Columbia Business School. From 2008 to 2013 she worked in industry full-time in managerial positions before returning to academia in 2014. Her main research areas are Sustainable Supply Chain Management, Offshoring and Procurement Organization. She has published in the *Journal of Supply Chain Management*, *Journal of International Management*, *Industrial Marketing Management*, *Journal of Purchasing & Supply Management* and other academic outlets.

Wendy Tate is an Associate Professor of Supply Chain Management Department of Marketing and Supply Chain Management at the University of Tennessee. Her research can be broadly classified under the umbrella of purchasing but focuses primarily on two different types of business problems. The first is in the area of services purchasing including outsourcing and offshoring. This area of research has recently expanded into "reshoring", or bringing manufacturing back to the home country. The second area is on environmental business practices and trying to understand how these initiatives can be diffused across a supply chain and a supply network. She presents at many different venues including both academic- and practitioner-oriented conferences. She has published research in many top-tier academic journals including the *Journal of Operations Management*, *Journal of Supply Chain Management*, *California Management Review* and others.

Part I
**TBL global supply chains:
why are they important?**

2

Are we really doing the "right thing"?

From sustainability imperialism in global supply chains to an inclusive emerging economy perspective

Anne Touboulic
Cardiff University, UK

Ehimen Ejodame
Nigerian Air Force

This chapter suggests a deficiency in the understanding of the complex realities in emerging economies in global supply chains. We question the underlying assumptions that drive current approaches to sustainability in global supply chains. Sustainability as currently defined and approached by large multinational corporations, a large group of NGOs and international institutions attempts to define a normative pathway to improvement that primarily relies on Western values and in some parts is rooted in the vested interests of a minority of players. The chapter draws on a discussion of existing literature and insights from a developing country. It specifically adopts Griggs et al.'s (2013) representation of TBL of sustainability, gets inspiration from international development and poverty literature, and applies Maslow's hierarchy of needs as a theoretical lens. We suggest a multilevel and systemic view of the issue and articulate a number of propositions to guide future research.

2.1 Introduction

It has become evident for both the private and public sector that there is a need to develop sustainable production and consumption systems (Lebel and Lorek, 2008). However, there is a notable gap between vast theoretical desires and actual implementation practice. The drawback situation exists in every part of the world with remarkable evidence of poor social and environmental practices in emerging economies. But why is this the case? And how can we improve the situation?

Understanding sustainability from an emerging economy perspective requires questioning the underlying assumptions that drive current approaches to sustainability in global supply chains. Central to our argument is the view that sustainability, as defined by large multinational corporations, a large group of NGOs and international institutions, attempts to define a normative pathway to improvement that primarily relies on Western values and in some part is rooted in the vested interests of a minority of players. A common premise for sustainability practices in developed economies places a premium on the standard of regulatory bodies and the consciousness and influence of stakeholders. In contrast in emerging economies, regulatory bodies are often non-existent or inherently incapacitated. In situations where emerging economy stakeholders are directly affected by environmental concerns, they are often voiceless or silenced by the hierarchical structure and high power distance. In this chapter, we suggest a deficiency in understanding the complex realities in the emerging economies who are rated the least capable of managing social and environmental issues.

The chapter seeks to explore the phenomenon of progressing towards sustainability from an emerging economy perspective by exposing the shortcomings of current research, offering some exploratory evidence and building on relevant conceptual lenses to suggest propositions. This therefore enables the identification of promising avenues for future research. We attempt to address the following research question: How can we conceptualize global supply chain sustainability from the perspective of emerging economies?

Empirically we draw from the extensive work experience of the first author in related fields in an African country who has collected primary evidence on the issue. Theoretically, we propose a multilevel, systemic view of the issue and draw specifically on capability development from an international development perspective (Sen, 1990) and Maslow's hierarchy of needs theory (1970) to understand the implications and ability to deal with environmental and social issues in supply chains involving emerging economies.

The remainder of the chapter is structured as follows. First, we provide some background to the questions of corporate sustainability and sustainable supply chain management (SSCM). In this section we identify the key challenges in current SSCM research in relation to addressing sustainability in an emerging economy context, which we call the "imperialism problem". Second, we present the methodology adopted and some empirical insights gained in Africa. Third, we introduce our theoretical background and discuss the relevance of the lenses adapted to our problem. Finally, we discuss the multilevel practical and research implications of attempting to develop a multilevel and systemic view of global supply chain sustainability from an emerging economy perspective.

2.2 Sustainability, sustainable supply chains and the "imperialism problem"

2.2.1 The concepts of corporate sustainability and CSR: biased and narrow views?

There are diverse interpretations of the concept of sustainability; however the triple bottom line (TBL) approach has been widely adopted by researchers and businesses to operationalize sustainability. This constitutes the environmental, economic and social dimensions (Seuring and Müller, 2008). Dyllick and Hockerts (2002) framed these three dimensions of sustainability as the business case (economic), the natural case (environmental) and the societal case (social).

The usual representation of the TBL is three interconnected circles of equal size, each representing a dimension of sustainability. This is in line with the business case for sustainability that views the sustainable development challenge as providing greater business opportunities for creating value and gaining competitive advantage (Carroll, 1979; Hart, 1995; Markley and Davis, 2007). In this sense, corporate sustainability is associated with specific measures looking to improve the social and environmental conditions in which businesses operate while maintaining a certain level of profitability (Carter and Rogers, 2008).

This approach has been criticized by authors such as Griggs *et al.* (2013) who instead propose an ecocentric view of sustainability, placing the earth's life-support systems at the core of their definition. Their representation of the three dimensions of sustainability uses concentric circles to show how the economy and society are embedded within, and ultimately depend upon, the preservation of the natural system. The argument against the three equal circles is that it makes it appear addressing each dimension is optional, as all of them carry the same weight.

Another recent conceptualization of corporate sustainability reasserts the necessity to adopt a systemic and ecocentric view. In this sense sustainability is about envisioning a prosperous future within planetary boundaries (Whiteman *et al.*, 2013) and the framework proposed by the authors calls for an assessment and a re-embedding of corporate activities' impact within socio-ecological systems. From this perspective, companies are viewed as operating within society and the natural environment and therefore must take into account a broader network of actors within their strategy and not only focus on satisfying the economic interests of their shareholders. According to the authors, understanding firms' impacts on planetary boundaries is a first step to take action, and they encourage a change-and-action approach to sustainability research.

The persistent ambiguity of the notion of corporate sustainability is largely due to the fact that it has been developed and evolved in a context dominated by an economistic view of the firm (Angus-Leppan *et al.*, 2010) or technocentric paradigm as described by Gladwin *et al.* (1995). In particular, despite the proliferation of corporate attempts to address sustainability challenges, the primacy of a narrow stakeholder capitalist framework is obvious. The phrase "as long as it makes business sense" is not uncommon when discussing sustainability with business employees. Whether this is a reflection of their personal values or simply of the system they find themselves in is another debate entirely.

The question is not new, in the international development literature in particular. For example, Joseph Stiglitz (2002) is very critical of the ideological foundations of institutions such as the IMF and the World Bank, and openly questions the credibility of their policies that promote a development that is damaging for ecosystems and favours investors.

Beyond the context in which the concept of corporate sustainability has emerged and evolved, there is also a concern about the interests that it is serving. Going back to early work on sustainable development such as the report by the Brundtland Commission (WCED, 1987) reveals that individuals and society are key protagonists in this development, in order to ensure that future generations can satisfy their own needs. However, this concern about the role of individuals and society seems to fade when considering corporations as central agents of sustainability. Much emphasis in the corporate sustainability literature has been put on incremental improvements and green metrics (Hassini *et al.*, 2012). In many cases, the major human and change implications of sustainability are underplayed and "sustainability initiatives" seem implemented from the top to the bottom with little concern about and consultation with those that it is supposed to affect.

2.2.2 Sustainable supply chains: a tale of control and compliance

In line with current debates regarding the definition of corporate sustainability, Pagell and Shevchenko (2014) argue that current SSCM research primarily reflects a narrow shareholder view and overly focuses on the economic (i.e. profit) implications of being sustainable. In addition, they argue that much research has focussed on investigating how supply chains (SC) could be more sustainable rather than how they could become truly sustainable.

In spite of the growing demands to implement social and environmental issues in supply chains there is a notable gap between the theoretical desires and actual implementation in practice (Andersen and Skjøtt-Larsen, 2009; Bowen *et al.*, 2001). This gap is apparently more evident in the emerging economies where the focus is more about using available resources to meet the needs of the present rather than considerations about sustainability for future generations to meet their own needs (Linton *et al.*, 2007). There are particular references to countries in Africa

(Amaeshi *et al.*, 2008). This is because the African continent is highly dependent on natural resources, such as precious minerals and fossil fuel; hence issues relating to business and environment are often linked in a complex manner. The continent is widely accepted as the most vulnerable to social and environmental sustainability issues and also rated as probably the least in capacity to manage these issues (Webersik and Wilson, 2008). This research therefore considers it a worthy option to explore the phenomena focusing on the African continent. This has been echoed by other authors in the field of sustainability, who view the African context as particularly interesting to:

- Understand how to deal with complex and interconnected issues of environmental degradation and societal development, and

- Move beyond the predominant Western rationalist and disciplinary approach to sustainability (Banerjee, 2003; Spence and Rinaldi, 2014; Valente, 2012).

The dearth of contributions related to the interests of developing countries or emerging economy stakeholders is actually quite striking. When research deals with a developing country context it is very much from a top down compliance approach and looks at suppliers' "misbehaviours". Examples include studies that explore the introduction of codes of conducts or implementation of certification programs by large multinationals in their global supply chains (SCs) (e.g. Alvarez *et al.*, 2010; Huq *et al.*, 2014; Jiang, 2009). A mechanistic view of sustainability implementation in global SCs prevails and it seems that the underlying assumption of all studies is the existence of a "sustainability imperative" which justifies interventions, and taking responsibility for the behaviour of the least advantaged players.

Nonetheless, there are many examples that discuss sustainability initiatives in the Chinese context (Miao *et al.*, 2012; Qinghua *et al.*, 2005; Shi *et al.*, 2008). It remains debatable whether China can be considered an emerging economy as such. Interestingly most of these studies focus on green/environmental initiatives and remain fairly quantitative. The social inequalities and issues in Chinese SCs also remain relatively under-explored.

Amid the growing literature on SSCM issues, there are few examples of studies that specifically address the question of sustainability from the perspective of the "least advantaged players". These include Hall and Matos's study (2010) that explores the integration of impoverished communities in sustainable SCs in Brazil; and Huq *et al.*'s (2014) recent paper that specifically focuses on social sustainability in Bangladesh and reveals that differences in cultural practices and social priorities affect ability of suppliers to comply with Western buyers' requirements. Ojo *et al.*'s (2013) study analysing green SC management in South Africa and Nigeria corroborates the lack of understanding of the realities in the emerging economies and therefore calls for further research.

Currently, methodologically speaking, most research reports on organizational activities related to sustainability and limits itself to providing accounts about the control mechanisms that are put in place by large organizations to address the "misconducts" of their suppliers (Pagell and Shevchenko, 2014; Touboulic and Walker, 2015). This distanced and mostly rationalist approach to research very much goes hand-in-hand with the theoretical bias towards top-down SSCM. There is a dearth of research that seeks a deeper exploration of these issues and in particular that engages with the relevant stakeholders in attempts to change the situation (Pagell and Shevchenko, 2014).

From this brief discussion of the literature on sustainable global SCs it is questionable whether or not corporations' practices go beyond paying lip service as most of them do not seem to take into consideration the complex socioeconomic context in which their suppliers are operating when developing and implementing their sustainability policies. One of the major shortcomings of current SSCM literature noted by a number of different authors (Ashby *et al.*, 2012; Carter and Easton, 2011; Pagell and Shevchenko, 2014; Touboulic and Walker, 2015) is the predominance of a large buyer firm perspective, to which we could add Western.

It is quite striking that much of the SC sustainability literature seems to remain centred on issues that are viewed as priorities in developed economies despite evidence that stakeholders in developed and developing countries do not actually perceive the urgency of these issues in the same way (Hall and Matos, 2010; Walsh, 2011). This point is very relevant when considering global SCs, which straddle national boundaries and bring together multiple actors in different socioeconomic contexts (Alvarez *et al.*, 2010; Park-Poaps and Rees, 2010).

2.2.3 Connecting North and South: aspects of global SC sustainability

It is valuable to turn to the literature related to geography, international development and global value chains in order to explore further the connection between North and South on sustainability in global SCs. In particular this can enable understanding more specifically what progressing towards sustainability in global SCs may entail.

Having established the top-down and power-driven approach to sustainability in SCs (Spence and Rinaldi, 2014), it is important to note that global SCs often connect the demands of consumers in the North to suppliers in the global South (Tencati *et al.*, 2010). In this case, large corporations do act as the intermediaries through which requirements filter (Gereffi, 1994). A global view of SC sustainability therefore implies an interconnected network of actors in different geographical areas, facing different levels of development and different needs.

The perspective taken on the upstream end of global SCs has often been one of interventionism in order to promote international development and increased fairness (Jenkins, 2005). Market initiatives tackling issues of poverty and inequality are particularly interesting in this context as they are often proposed in response to a lack of sufficient and appropriate local public infrastructures. Fair-trade, for instance, has been viewed as a way to address such issues in global SCs by specifically providing a premium to producers upstream. From this perspective ethical consumption in the North is hence linked to development in the South.

Arguably however, such initiatives do still reflect a fairly narrow understanding of the perspective of the weakest players in the chain and are often reduced to bureaucratic certification processes (Tencati *et al.*, 2010). Voluntary standards addressing social and environmental issues in global SCs have become increasingly viewed as new modes of governance of North-South relations on sustainable development (Henson, 2006; Henson and Humphrey, 2010). Authors have warned of the limits of market-driven approaches to sustainable development in a global context (Fridell, 2007).

It is evident that current surveillance and monitoring approaches to sustainability are a clear reflection of the exercise of power in global SCs and of the era of SC capitalism (Kanngieser, 2013). There are important geo-economic and political questions to the idea of global SC sustainability, which need to be taken into account by researchers in the field of SSCM. Concerns about fairness and justice are also an intrinsic part of relations between actors in the North and suppliers in the South (Boyd *et al.*, 2007; Hornibrook *et al.*, 2009).

2.3 Methodology: insights from an African case study

Having established the lack of understanding of an emerging economy perspective on the question of sustainability in global SCs, in this section we present some empirical insights from Africa that can serve to enrich our discussion.

2.3.1 Research context and motivation

The investigation essentially follows the current growing interest for studies about SCs in developing new economies (Hsu *et al.*, 2013). There is evidence in the literature that emerging economies such as China, India, Mexico and Brazil are in fact growing faster than some other established industrial economies of the world (Guillén and Garcia-Canal, 2009). This is in spite of the physical, social and cultural conditions in emerging economies where managing SCs has proved to be more challenging than in advanced economies (Sahay, Gupta and Mohan, 2006). Emerging economies are faced with the situation of how to manage SCs, coordinate information flows with multiple partners while tackling the associated prevalent socioeconomic challenges. At the same time there are expectations to contribute to the social and economic status of the country using SCM concepts and practices (Shi *et al*, 2011). However, it is worth noting that some emerging countries, particularly in the African continent, have been significantly latent in the discussion (Msimangira, 2003). This is not withstanding that Nigeria has been identified among the key emerging markets in the world and that their public procurement will almost triple by 2030, contributing to a £452 billion economy. Nigeria is ranked first in Africa and eighth in the world of the emerging markets after China, Saudi Arabia, South Korea, Brazil, Poland, India and the United Arab Emirates.

Several studies on Nigeria have been justified by the relative dearth of study and shortcomings of management practices observed in the country (Adebanjo *et al.*, 2013). The recognition of the strategic role of Nigeria in the African sub-region is another notable rationale that has made it the focus of study. This includes the responsibility of providing leadership and direction to other African nations in areas of technological advancement, improved business and SC management practices as well as security and other socioeconomic development.

The country's oil reserves have played a major role in its growing wealth and influence. Following the rebasing of her Gross Domestic Product (GDP) from 1990 to 2010, Nigeria became the largest economy in Africa and the 26th largest in the world (AfDP, 2013). The recalculation and rebasing process in April 2014 was supported by the African Development Bank, World Bank and the IMF providing technical assistance to ensure that the results were credible, reliable and in line with best global practices. The country's GDP increased by 89.2% from $285.56 billion to $509.9 billion; its GDP per capita almost doubled from $1,437 to $2,688. There are enthusiastic reports supporting this statistical indicator championing Nigeria's economic might (Sanusi, 2012). However, some have warned that the statistics should not be viewed as a precise appraisal of economic life in Nigeria. The argument is that 90% of her earnings are dependent on oil export; the nation has not diversified its economy despite its enormous human, agricultural and largely untapped mineral resources. Even though the nation's economy has improved sharply, the general population does not feel the impact. Most of the nation's wealth is concentrated among a small class of people with 63% of its population still living below the poverty line with corruption commonly adduced as the primary reason for the manifestation of this situation (Imhonopi and Ugochukwu, 2013).

The issues about corruption have generated several debates in Nigeria due to its perceived impact and underlying hindrances to socioeconomic development. A simplified definition depicted by the Laws of Nigeria describes corruption as including such acts as "bribery, fraud and other related offences" (The Corrupt Practices and other Related Offences Act, 2000). There is political or "government" corruption, which refers to practices like embezzlement, where government officials exploit their official capacity for personal gains. Corruption, however, exists in different scales. There is the "petty corruption", which occurs at the lower scale, and the "grand corruption", which occurs at high levels of government. Corruption in the Nigerian context is often described as endemic (or systemic). Endemic (or systemic) corruption weakens organizational processes. The situation in Nigeria has reflected several of the factors responsible for endemic corruption: lack of transparency, a culture of impunity, conflicting incentives as well as discretionary and monopolistic use of power (Imhonopi and Ugochukwu, 2013). While there are arguments that Nigeria lacks funds to execute the critical developmental projects, there remains evidence of misappropriated funds by way of corrupt practices. What is certain is that there is economic potential, which is indicative of the nation's capability to join the array of advanced economies in attaining technological prowess. However, its economic situation also reflects an enormous gap between such aspirations and the realities on the ground.

2.3.2 Research approach and data collection

The insights reported in this chapter are those gathered through a preliminary enquiry and are also based on the author's extensive experience in the field. The preliminary enquiry aimed to explore and define the problem situation to facilitate the main study. The rationale for this preliminary study was to surface some of the challenges in the field and confront them with our understanding of the literature.

The methodological approach combines a study process "on" stakeholders involved with the phenomenon as well as an enquiry process "with" stakeholders. The preliminary study is akin to an action research-collaborative inquiry considering the position of the inquirer who is involved in the situation with experiences in varied capacity: as a pilot, engineer and procurement officer as well. This approach is consistent with principles of action research. It offers the opportunity to explore the phenomenon within its context, using different data sources (Heron, 1996; Reason and Bradbury, 2001). This flexible and rigorous approach facilitates the development of theory as well as the capture of rich insights.

In addition to the author's perspective, the study involved interviews with six stakeholders in the public sector organization. The stakeholders interviewed are practitioners in a public sector aviation industry in Nigeria. The six stakeholders include two pilots, two engineers and two procurement officers who are key stakeholders in the operations and SCM functions in the organization, all with over ten years working experience and a minimum of two years international experience in institutions of developed economies. This choice was to ensure reflexive input from the participants considering their years of experience and their exposure to the workings of developed economies. The participants were asked an open-ended questions which sought to get input about their perception of SC sustainability practices in their local context. The broad questions in the interviews sought to find their views about the sustainability challenges, to describe their personal experiences in relation to the phenomenon as well as elicit information about strategies aimed at addressing the observed challenges.

2.4 Insights from stakeholders

The views from the participants who took part in the preliminary enquiry were similar to those echoed in previous research (Hall and Matos, 2010; Ojo *et al.*, 2013), highlighting various shortcomings about sustainability practices. There was a scorching remark calling for the need to redefine sustainability concept from the perspective of the emerging economies. An illustration relating to local means of water distribution involving boys using water jerry cans carried in locally-made carts was highlighted. The participant asserts that while this may not be considered a sustainable approach from the perspective of the mechanized developed economies, the local approach was however noted to be void of gas emission and other environmentally damaging problems and perhaps was a more sustainable environmental practice. The proposed idea to redefine SC sustainability practices from the perspective of the emerging countries was seen as a potentially viable idea hence this illustration was documented for further review. Other notable remarks from the stakeholders were comments bothered about the conduct of the research. A stakeholder believed that the project was an uphill task, which could clash with the interests of the political/leadership class. Another remark emphasized that it was unfortunate that they (stakeholders) were not particularly aware or bothered about crucial environmental issues. A third notable remark was that the proposed study was particularly relevant in the prevailing situation. This was followed by a question from the interviewee; "but where do we start from?". The question posed by the interviewee underpins the sense of helplessness and inability to cope with the sustainability challenge.

2.5 Towards a needs and capability framework for global SC sustainability

As mentioned previously, the notions of sustainability and sustainable development are contentious and there is much debate on their meanings and scope. It is particularly complex to try and establish a definition which can encompass both North and South perspectives. The findings from our preliminary enquiry confirm that sustainability and sustainable development may indeed hold different meanings in an emerging economy context where priority is given to issues that seem most critical locally and where infrastructures and systems may be very different from those in developed economies.

2.5.1 Background on Maslow's theory of needs

In light of our discussion above, we propose to draw on Maslow's hierarchy of needs theory (1970) to theoretically make sense of the question of the sustainability in global SCs. We were motivated to explore this theory in more depth, as it appeared to help us conceptualize the prioritization differential between developing versus developed economies. In addition, we feel that there is a need in SSCM research to further explore the interaction between the national, organizational and individual levels of analysis in order to grasp the complexity of moving towards sustainability.

This has already been suggested by a number of authors in the field (Carter and Easton, 2011; Touboulic and Walker, 2015). Maslow's framework, emerging from psychology, represents a starting point in our attempt to move towards this more multilevel understanding. Furthermore, it can potentially be a step forward in reflecting about the question of perception, values and ethics, and reintroducing the notion of change in SSCM research. A number of authors have already considered the fit of Maslow's theory to the question of sustainability (Datta, 2013; Walsh, 2011). In particular these contributions highlight that the theory can be adapted beyond the individual to encompass the community and broader society. In his contribution, Datta (2013) shows that there may be an additional level of needs—transcendent needs—when taking an ecological view of Maslow's theory. He views this level as the final highest level, which corresponds to the needs to care beyond oneself and have a need to address the concerns of the local, national and global communities as embedded in the natural environment.

Maslow suggests that all individuals face different levels of need from basic to more advanced. He argues that unless the most basic of needs are catered for, individuals will not develop and feel the other needs and will not respond to them. Hence, there is a hierarchy of needs. Beyond needs identification, Maslow's theory provides insights into motivational aspects of human behaviour in view of needs satisfaction. Figure 2.1 depicts a typical Maslow pyramid of needs.

Figure 2.1 Maslow's hierarchy of needs
Source: adapted by the authors

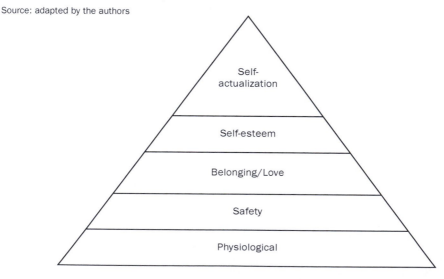

There are five levels of needs according to Maslow, and the pyramid can be viewed as a stage model. The first level corresponds to basic physiological needs such as air, food, shelter, drink, warmth, sex and sleep. The second level relates to safety needs and the need to feel protected, have security, order, law, stability and freedom from fear. The third level corresponds to belonging and love and includes aspects such as friendship, intimacy, affection from family, friends, etc. The fourth level is esteem needs such as achievement, mastery, independence, status, prestige, self-respect and respect from others. Finally, the fifth level relates to self-actualization needs and the realization of personal potential and self-fulfilment.

Maslow's hierarchy of needs theory (Maslow, 1970) can be particularly valuable to understand the motivational implications and ability to deal with environmental and social issues in an emerging economy context and at different levels of global SCs. If we consider the development and implementation of sustainability policies from Maslow' lens we may be able to make sense of why some practices are successful and others fail as they do not address the needs of those at which they are targeted. In other words, it is difficult to expect individuals in very poor communities in an emerging economy to care for climate change, as it may seem a very distant issue compared to their immediate needs to feed their families. This means that this theoretical perspective can be valuable in mapping the gaps between different levels of the SC. In parallel, Maslow's theory may be valuable in understanding how corporations may fulfil a critical role in addressing the needs of the local communities they work with or on which they have an impact as, for example, described by Pulver (2007). Finally, Maslow's theory calls for an exploration of the individual and community levels of analysis when addressing the question of sustainability in global SCs.

2.5.2 The capability approach to sustainable development in global SCs

By definition an SC is about the connection between different organizations and actors and about the flow of material, money and information (Carter and Rogers, 2008; Seuring and Müller, 2008). While we have established that much research has explored the role of SC in achieving top-down sustainability, there has been little exploration of the role of SC networks in addressing the concerns of marginalized communities (Yawar and Seuring, 2015).

In recent years, there have been significant developments on the notion of business for the poor in fields such as marketing and strategy, exemplified by the concepts of shared value (Porter and Kramer, 2011) and Bottom of the Pyramid (BoP) (Karnani, 2005; Karnani, 2006; Prahalad, 2012; Prahalad and Hammond, 2002). These have been subject to strong criticism notably for their simplistic view of the poor as consumers and for excluding important power dynamics (Karnani, 2006).

Hence, we draw on work in political economics that has considered how to address global development issues such as poverty rather than the BoP. In particular, Amartya Sen's contributions on questions of ethics, justice and poverty (Sen, 1999) have certainly moved the international development debate forward. His ideas have served to question the value of commonly adopted international indicators such as the Human Development Index.

It is widely accepted that inequality is not only defined by objective factors related to wealth distribution but also by normative aspects and ethical concerns that cannot be readily measured objectively (Sen, 1973). Sen has introduced a capability perspective to the development, human rights and poverty (Sen, 1990, 2005), which constitutes a fruitful lens for global SC sustainability.

The capability perspective enables reintroducing the notion of opportunity to achieve valuable activities for human and ecological flourishing. While opportunity alone focuses largely on the means that are at the disposal of actors, the notion of capability enables making the subtle distinction between means and ability to achieve the opportunities (Sen, 1990, 2005). While Sen applies this notion to the micro level of individuals, it is possible to see its relevance in the context of global SCs that connect actors at the macro-, meso- and micro-levels.

Drawing further on Sen's work (Sen, 1990, 2005), we can propose a set of possible reasons as to why there exist differences in the capability of actors in the global SC, which hence impairs the advancement towards sustainability:

- Inherent characteristics of the actors (whether individuals or organizations, such as physical differences, size, etc.)

- Variation in external resources (such as the nature of public infrastructures, degree of social cohesion, community support)

- Environmental diversities (e.g. climatic conditions, varying threats from epidemic disease or crime), and

- Different relative positions within the network in connection with other actors.

Understanding these circumstances can enable a more inclusive view of how to achieve sustainable development goals that are relevant to the actors involved. The four reasons described above can easily be viewed as potential levers for change as well as conditional elements. It is possible to link this additional capability perspective to Maslow's theory in attempting to provide potential explanations as to why actors may find themselves at different levels of the pyramid across global SCs. Addressing the four identified dimensions above may provide a way to bridge the gaps.

2.6 Discussion: multilevel practical and research implications

2.6.1 Multilevel research implications

In light of our discussion of the literature, the preliminary findings presented earlier and Maslow's framework, we propose that advancing sustainability in the context of global SCs necessitates a multilevel and systemic understanding of the salient issues at these various levels. We do not prescribe a "one-size-fits-all" but rather to better contextualize sustainability practice and research. This leads to our first proposition:

> **Proposition 1**: *The more significant the difference between the contexts in which sustainability initiatives are developed in contrast to where they are implemented, the higher the likelihood of gaps and discrepancies emerging in global SCs.*

We have noted the importance of going beyond the Western buying firm level and valuing the perspective of emerging economies' actors in global SC sustainability, in particular as their circumstances are significantly at odds with those of the downstream actors with which they are connected. Existing local knowledge and solutions may constitute fruitful ways forward. We suggest the following proposition:

> **Proposition 2**: *Exploring the perspectives of supplier firms, in particular developing country suppliers, is critical to shed light on under-explored aspects of sustainability and stimulate learning from emerging economy practices.*

The capability perspective combined with the theory of needs puts particular emphasis on the need to understand the contextual situations of actors and adopt a bottom-up approach to sustainability. It also emphasizes the connection between the different actors in global SCs. Several theoretical lenses may be valuable to explore the relation between relationships between actors in a global context and capabilities development for sustainability. Social capital for examples has been viewed as fruitful means through which to enable capabilities development for communities affected by poverty, inequality and dire environmental conditions (Ansari *et al.*, 2012; Asadi *et al.*, 2008; Kwon and Adler, 2014). There has been much research in SCM that has considered the development and importance of social capital (Matthews and Marzec, 2012), hence this is a promising lens for future research. We have the following propositions:

> **Proposition 3**: *Considering the interactions between the individual, organizational and national levels of analysis will positively impact on the way in which sustainability issues are addressed and implemented in global SCs.*

> **Proposition 4**: *Making sense of sustainability in global SCs through a needs and capability framework enables a more inclusive and systemic perspective to emerge.*

Considering the interconnection between North and South actors in the global SC even further, it is possible to see how tensions between different levels of needs and capabilities are bound to exist as well as tensions between the different sustainability issues (Hahn *et al.*, 2014). We argue that these tensions must be embraced in future research. This leads to our fifth proposition:

> **Proposition 5**: *Tensions between different sustainability issues as well as levels of needs and capabilities of different actors signifi-cantly affect the progression towards sustainability in global SCs.*

Finally, we contend that our chapter does not simply interrogate what we research but how we do research. Our argument is in line with Pagell and Shevchenko's (2014) as we see value in adopting more qualitative, participative and innovative research approaches to explore sustainability issues in global SCs.

> **Proposition 6a**: *Qualitative grassroots research approaches can allow developing an emerging economy perspective of sustainable development in global SCs.*

> **Proposition 6b**: *Participative research approaches can enable the development of innovative SC designs for sustainability that are inclusive of an emerging economy perspective.*

2.6.2 Theoretical and practical contributions

This chapter has drawn on Maslow's theory of needs and Sen's capability perspec-tive to support the argument that considerations for the position and perspective of local people and communities is critical in advancing sustainability in global SCs. This theoretical grounding is particularly original in the field of sustainable SCM and hence this chapter makes an interesting theoretical contribution.

There are strong implications for practice. In particular, considering the chal-lenges that managers face in going beyond compliance and low-hanging fruits, an emerging economy perspective is topical and pertinent. While top-down approaches may be more straightforward to implement, there is value in consider-ing what a more inclusive and contextualized approach to sustainability may look like in global SCs. Businesses operating on a global scale may seek the support of local communities and actors to ensure that their approaches make a meaningful impact.

2.7 Conclusion

This chapter aims to pave the way for research that seeks to enhance our under-standing of global SC sustainability practices and in particular from an emerg-ing economy perspective. We suggest that existing conceptual frameworks in the literature are built on perceptions from the developed economies, which are at odds with the realities of emerging economies and do not capture pertinent realities of the complex and inherent dynamics of sustainability issues in this context. As such, existing concepts are considered deficient to drive progress towards sustainability in global SCs. We encourage research to seek inspiration from literature in other fields such as politics, international development and economics.

The chapter is clearly limited by its exploratory nature and further research is needed to support the proposed framework. An obvious avenue for future research would be to explore the propositions that we have suggested. Further work is needed to refine our theoretical contribution and explore more systematically the connection and relevance of a needs and capability theory to sustainability in global SCs.

References

Adebanjo, D., Ojadi, F., Laosirihongthong, T., & Tickle, M. (2013). A case study of supplier selection in developing economies: a perspective on institutional theory and corporate social responsibility. *Supply Chain Management: An International Journal*, 18(5), 553-566.

AfDB, O. E. C. D. (2013). UNDP, & ECA.(2013). *African Economic Outlook* 2013-Structural Transformation and Natural Resources.

Alvarez, G., Pilbeam, C., & Wilding, R. (2010). Nestlé Nespresso AAA sustainable quality program: An investigation into the governance dynamics in a multi-stakeholder supply chain network. *Supply Chain Management: An International Journal*, 15(2), 165-182. doi: 10.1108/13598541011028769

Amaeshi, K.M., Osuji, O.K., & Nnodim, P. (2008). Corporate social responsibility in supply chains of global brands: A boundaryless responsibility? clarifications, exceptions and implications. *Journal of Business Ethics*, 81(1), 223-234. doi: 10.1007/s10551-007-9490-5

Andersen, M., & Skjoett-Larsen, T. (2009). Corporate social responsibility in global supply chains. *Supply Chain Management: An International Journal*, 14(2), 75-86. doi: 10.1108/13598540910941948

Angus-Leppan, T., Benn, S., & Young, L. (2010). A sensemaking approach to trade-offs and synergies between human and ecological elements of corporate sustainability. *Business Strategy and the Environment*, 19(4), 230-244. doi: 10.1002/bse.675

Ansari, S., Munir, K., & Gregg, T. (2012). Impact at the 'bottom of the pyramid': The role of social capital in capability development and community empowerment. *Journal of Management Studies*, 49(4), 813-842. doi: 10.1111/j.1467-6486.2012.01042.x

Asadi, A., Akbari, M., Shabanali Fami, H., Iravani, H., Rostami, F., & Sadati, A. (2008). Poverty alleviation and sustainable development: The role of social capital. *Journal of Social Sciences*, 4(3), 202-215.

Ashby, A., Leat, M., & Hudson-Smith, M. (2012). Making connections: A review of supply chain management and sustainability literature. *Supply Chain Management: An International Journal*, 17(5), 497-516.

Banerjee, S.B. (2003). Who sustains whose development? Sustainable development and the reinvention of nature. *Organization Studies*, 24(1), 143-180.

Bowen, F.E., Cousins, P.D., Lamming, R.C., & Faruk, A.C. (2001). Horses for courses. *Greener Management International*, (35), 41.

Boyd, D.E., Spekman, R.E., Kamauff, J.W., & Werhane, P. (2007). Corporate social responsibility in global supply chains: A procedural justice perspective. *Long Range Planning*, 40(3), 341-356. doi: 10.1016/j.lrp.2006.12.007

Carroll, A.B. (1979). A three-dimensional conceptual model of corporate performance. *Academy of Management Review*, 4(4), 497-505.

Carter, C.R., & Easton, P.L. (2011). Sustainable supply chain management: Evolution and future directions. *International Journal of Physical Distribution & Logistics Management*, 41(1), 46-62. doi: 10.1108/09600031111101420

Carter, C.R., & Rogers, D.S. (2008). A framework of sustainable supply chain management: Moving toward new theory. *International Journal of Physical Distribution & Logistics Management*, 38(5), 360-387.

Datta, Y. (2013). Maslow's hierarchy of basic needs: An ecological view. *Oxford Journal: An International Journal of Business & Economics*, 8(1).

Dyllick, T., & Hockerts, K. (2002). Beyond the business case for corporate sustainability. *Business Strategy and the Environment*, 11(2), 130-141. doi: 10.1002/bse.323

Fridell, G. (2007). *Fair trade coffee: The prospects and pitfalls of market-driven social justice* (Vol. 28). Toronto: University of Toronto Press.

Gereffi, G. (1994). Capitalism, development and global commodity chain. In L. Sklair (Ed.), *Capitalism and Development* (pp. 211-231). London: Routledge.

Gladwin, T.N., Kennelly, J.J., & Krause, T.-S. (1995). Shifting paradigms for sustainable development: Implications for management theory and research. *The Academy of Management Review*, 20(4), 874-907.

Griggs, D., Stafford-Smith, M., Gaffney, O., Rockström, J., Öhman, M.C., Shyamsundar, P., Steffen, W., Glaser, G., Kanie, N., Noble, I. (2013). Sustainable development goals for people and planet. *Nature*, 495(7441), 305-307.

Guillén, M. F., & García-Canal, E. (2009). The American model of the multinational firm and the "new" multinationals from emerging economies. *The Academy of Management Perspectives*, 23(2), 23-35.

Hahn, T., Pinkse, J., Preuss, L., & Figge, F. (2014). Tensions in corporate sustainability: Towards an integrative framework. *Journal of Business Ethics*, 127(2), 297-316. doi: 10.1007/s10551-014-2047-5

Hall, J., & Matos, S. (2010). Incorporating impoverished communities in sustainable supply chains. *International Journal of Physical Distribution & Logistics Management*, 40(1/2), 124-147. doi: 10.1108/09600031011020368

Hart, S.L. (1995). A natural resource-based view of the firm. *Academy of Management Review*, 20(4), 986-1014.

Hassini, E., Surti, C., & Searcy, C. (2012). A literature review and a case study of sustainable supply chains with a focus on metrics. *International Journal of Production Economics*, 140(1), 69-82. doi: 10.1016/j.ijpe.2012.01.042

Henson, S. (2006). *The role of public and private standards in regulating international food markets*. Paper presented at the IATRC Summer Symposium "Food Regulation and Trade: Institutional Framework, Concepts of Analysis and Empirical Evidence", Bonn, Germany.

Henson, S., & Humphrey, J. (2010). Understanding the complexities of private standards in global agri-food chains as they impact developing countries. *Journal of Development Studies*, 46(9), 1628-1646.

Heron, J. (1996). *Co-operative inquiry: Research into the human condition*. London: Sage.

Hornibrook, S., Fearne, A., & Lazzarin, M. (2009). Exploring the association between fairness and organisational outcomes in supply chain relationships. *International Journal of Retail & Distribution Management*, 37(9), 790-803. doi: 10.1108/09590550910975826

Hsu, C.-C., Tan, K. C., Zailani, S. H. M., & Jayaraman, V. (2013). Supply chain drivers that foster the development of green initiatives in an emerging economy. *International Journal of Operations & Production Management*, 33(6), 656-688. doi: 10.1108/ijopm-10-2011-0401

Huq, F.A., Stevenson, M., & Zorzini, M. (2014). Social sustainability in developing country suppliers: An exploratory study in the ready made garments industry of Bangladesh. *International Journal of Operations & Production Management*, 34(5), 610-638. doi: 10.1108/IJOPM-10-2012-0467

Imhonopi, D., & Ugochukwu, M.U. (2013). Leadership crisis and corruption in the Nigerian public sector: An albatross of national development. *Journal of the African Educational Research Network*, 13(1), 78-87.

Jenkins, R. (2005). Globalization, corporate social responsibility and poverty. *International Affairs*, 81(3), 525-540.

Jiang, B. (2009). Implementing supplier codes of conduct in global supply chains: Process explanations from theoretic and empirical perspectives. *Journal of Business Ethics*, 85(77-92).

Kanngieser, A. (2013). Tracking and tracing: Geographies of logistical governance and labouring bodies. *Environment and Planning D: Society and Space*, 31(4), 594-610.

Karnani, A.G. (2006). Mirage at the bottom of the pyramid.

Karnani, A.G. (2005). Misfortune at the bottom of the pyramid. *Greener Management International*, 2005(51), 99-111.

Kwon, S.-W., & Adler, P.S. (2014). Social capital: Maturation of a field of research. *Academy of Management Review*, 39(4), 412-422.

Lebel, L., & Lorek, S. (2008). Enabling sustainable production-consumption systems. *Annual Review of Environment and Resources*, 33(2008), 241-275.

Linton, J., Klassen, R., & Jayaraman, V. (2007). Sustainable supply chains: An introduction. *Journal of Operations Management*, 25(6), 1075-1082. doi: 10.1016/j.jom.2007.01.012

Markley, M.J., & Davis, L. (2007). Exploring future competitive advantage through sustainable supply chains. *International Journal of Physical Distribution & Logistics Management*, 37(9), 763-774. doi: 10.1108/09600030710840859

Maslow, A.H. (1970). *Motivation and Personality* (2nd ed.). New York, NY: Harper & Row.

Matthews, R.L., & Marzec, P.E. (2012). Social capital, a theory for operations management: A systematic review of the evidence. *International Journal of Production Research*, 50(24), 7081-7099.

Miao, Z., Cai, S., & Xu, D. (2012). Exploring the antecedents of logistics social responsibility: A focus on Chinese firms. *International Journal of Production Economics*, 140(1), 18-27. doi: 10.1016/j.ijpe.2011.05.030

Msimangira, K. A. (2003). Purchasing and supply chain management practices in Botswana. *Supply chain management: An international journal*, 8(1), 7-11.

Ojo, E., Akinlabi, E.T., & Mbohwa, C. (2013). *An analysis of green supply chain management in South Africa and Nigeria: A comparative study*. Paper presented at the International Conference on Integrated Waste Management and Green Energy Engineering, Johannesburg, South Africa.

Pagell, M., & Shevchenko, A. (2014). Why research in sustainable supply chain management should have no future. *Journal of Supply Chain Management*, 50(1), 44-55.

Park-Poaps, H., & Rees, K. (2010). Stakeholder forces of socially responsible supply chain management orientation. *Journal of Business Ethics*, 92(2), 305-322. doi: 10.1007/s10551-009-0156-3

Porter, M.E., & Kramer, M.R. (2011). Creating shared value. *Harvard Business Review*, 89(1/2), 62-77.

Prahalad, C.K.(2012). Bottom of the pyramid as a source of breakthrough innovations. *Journal of Product Innovation Management*, 29(1), 6-12.

Prahalad, C.K., & Hammond, A. (2002). Serving the world's poor, profitably. *Harvard Business Review*, 80(9), 48-59.

Pulver, S. (2007). Introduction: Developing-country firms as agents of environmental sustainability? *Studies in Comparative International Development*, 42(3-4), 191-207. doi: 10.1007/s12116-007-9011-7

Qinghua, Z., Joseph, S., & Yong, G. (2005). Green supply chain management in China: Pressures, practices and performance. *International Journal of Operations & Production Management*, 25(5/6), 449.

Reason, P., & Bradbury, H. (Eds.) (2001). *Handbook of Action Research: Participative Inquiry and Practice*. London: Sage.

Sahay, B. S., Gupta, J. N., & Mohan, R. (2006). Managing supply chains for competitiveness: the Indian scenario. *Supply Chain Management: An International Journal*, 11(1), 15-24.

Sanusi, L. S. (2012). Banking reform and its impact on the Nigerian economy. *CBN Journal of Applied Statistics*, 2(2), 115-122.

Sen, A. (2005). Human rights and capabilities. *Journal of Human Development*, 6(2), 151-166.

Sen, A. (1999). *Development as freedom*. New York, NY: A.A. Knopf.

Sen, A. (1990). Development as capability expansion. *Human Development and the International Development Strategy for the 1990s*, 1.

Sen, A. (1973). *On economic inequality*. Oxford: Oxford University Press.

Seuring, S., & Müller, M. (2008). From a literature review to a conceptual framework for sustainable supply chain management. *Journal of Cleaner Production*, 16(15), 1699-1710. doi: 10.1016/j.jclepro.2008.04.020

Shi, H., Peng, S.Z., Liu, Y., & Zhong, P. (2008). Barriers to the implementation of cleaner production in Chinese SMEs: Government, industry and expert stakeholders' perspectives. *Journal of Cleaner Production*, 16(7), 842-852. doi: 10.1016/j.jclepro.2007.05.002

Spence, L.J., & Rinaldi, L. (2014). Governmentality in accounting and accountability: A case study of embedding sustainability in a supply chain. *Accounting, Organizations and Society*, 39(6), 433-452.

Stiglitz, J.E. (2002). *Globalization and its Discontents*. New York, NY: Norton.

Tencati, A., Russo, A., & Quaglia, V. (2010). Sustainability along the global supply chain: The case of Vietnam. *Social Responsibility Journal*, 6(1), 91-107.

Touboulic, A., & Walker, H. (2015). Theories in sustainable supply chain management: A structured literature review. *International Journal of Physical Distribution & Logistics Management*, 45(1/2), 16-42.

Valente, M. (2012). Theorizing firm adoption of sustaincentrism. *Organization Studies*, 33(4), 563-591.

Walsh, P.R. (2011). Creating a "values" chain for sustainable development in developing nations: Where Maslow meets Porter. *Environment, Development and Sustainability*, 13(4), 789-805. doi: 10.1007/s10668-011-9291-y

World Commission on Environment and Development (WCED) (1987). *Our common future*. Oxford: Oxford University Press.

Webersik, C., & Wilson, C. (2008). Environment for African: A sustainable future through science and technology; *United Nations University Institute of Advanced Studies Report*.

Whiteman, G., Walker, B., & Perego, P. (2013). Planetary boundaries: Ecological foundations for corporate sustainability. *Journal of Management Studies*, 50(2), 307-336. doi: 10.1111/j.1467-6486.2012.01073.x

Yawar, S.A., & Seuring, S. (2015). Management of social issues in supply chains: A literature review exploring social issues, actions and performance outcomes. *Journal of Business Ethics*, 1-23.

Anne Touboulic is a lecturer at Cardiff Business School, Cardiff University, UK. Her research interests lie at the intersection of sustainable development and operations management with a primary focus on implementing sustainable inter-organizational relationships and driving change for sustainability in production and consumption networks. She is particularly interested in the links between micro-individual behaviours and inter-organizational practices for sustainability. She is passionate about engaged and innovative approaches to research, which enable collaborating with stakeholders and changing practice. Her research has so far been published in *Decision Sciences, Human Relations, International Journal of Physical Distribution and Logistics Management* and *Journal of Purchasing and Supply Management.*

Ehimen Ejodame is a serving military logistician with the rank of Wing Commander in the Nigerian Air Force. He holds a Bachelor in Engineering from the Nigerian Defence Academy and Masters in Transport and Logistics from the Nigerian Institute of Transport Technology, Zaria (best graduating student in 2007). He obtained a PhD in the area of Supply Chain Management and Information Systems from the University of Sheffield, UK. Some roles held in service include Officer Commanding Supply Squadrons, Grade 1 Logistics Staff Officer and Air Assistant to Air Officers Commanding Tactical and Training Commands. He has also taught logistics and SC modules, as a Directing Staff in the Armed Forces Command and Staff College Jaji-Nigeria and as lecturer at Nottingham Business School, UK, and the Air Force Institute of Technology (AFIT), Nigerian Air Force, where he is currently the Head of the Supply Management Department.

3

Supply chain resilience

Edgar Bellow
NEOMA Business School, France

The world is a complex place. No longer does a company survive and remain profitable based on a stream of customers from the local area. In a world of globalized shopping, supply and demand, there are many inputs into developing a supply chain (SC) that is not only adequate, but effective and resilient. The concept of the triple bottom line (TBL) was developed to leverage the environment, economy and impact on society into the SC. In order for a SC to be resilient, or able to withstand the stress of change, it must be able to anticipate and adapt to risk. A sustainable chain will be able to maintain and persist. The people, the place and the price all factor into the development of a resilient and sustainable SC. The combination of these factors can be used to develop a SC that is resilient and responsive and can lead a company to sustainability, as long as the company understands that the SC is part of the overall system that provides products and services to the customers or clients.

3.1 Introduction

Today, many factors go into the development of a resilient and sustainable SC. Resilient SCs are those that are able to be sustained through risks and upheaval because they are strong and flexible (Wieland and Wallenberg, 2013). Resilient chains have also been defined as having "the ability of a system to absorb disturbances and still retain [its] basic function and structure" (Walker and Salt, 2006, p. 1), and having "the capacity to change in order to maintain the same identity" (Folke *et al.*, 2010). Primary among those factors is the concept of the TBL, or the key areas of the environment, the economy and the impact on society. The combination of these three factors, sometimes referred to as the 3Ps of people, profit and planet (Fisk, 2010) are linked together. A change in one factor results in change in another. In order to be successful the company has to pay attention to each of the factors. The company must be persistent, or sustainable (Folke *et al.*, 2010), with a SC that is resilient, or able to recover from disruption (Ponis and Koronis, 2012). Resilience provides the framework for sustainability (Walker and Salt, 2006). A sustainable SC will be able to produce goods and deliver them while avoiding environmental and resource depletion (Reid, 2013). In a successful company, resilience and sustainability are linked and the TBL is a tool which supports them (Pisano, 2012). Profit, or the ability to make money, is why all companies exist. Even non-profit organizations which exist to provide services must make money, or bring in enough money from donations, to stay fiscally viable (Foster and Bradach, 2005). Whether or not non-profit organizations should actively seek to make a profit to ensure that they have money "in the bank" in order to remain sustainable is a different matter. Foster and Bradach (2005) suggested that this is one of the most hotly debated ethical and fiscal issues today. Non-profits are considered in the context of sustainability in TBL initiatives. The purpose of this qualitative research is to determine how SC resilience can be developed through implementation of TBL initiatives of people, profit and planet. When people, profit and planet intersect, sustainability results (Elleithy *et al.*, 2010). However, resilience must also be addressed with different cultures in different countries, because these different cultures will have different needs. The research is conducted within the context of systems theory (Pisano, 2012). The following research questions support that purpose and were developed to investigate the TBL initiatives of resilient SC management in order to make recommendations for improved SC functioning in cultures with a variety of needs. How can SC management facilitate successful implementation of TBL-focused initiatives? How can SC management overcome the significant barriers to efficient development and delivery of necessary goods and services in different cultures with very different needs? There were several objectives of this chapter. One objective was to determine what the TBL is, and how it can be developed for sustainability. It was also important to understand the demand chain, because it underlies the SC, as well as to understand how culture impacts on demand. Finally, the chapter sought to understand how these barriers can be overcome in order to successfully implement TBL-focused initiatives.

3.2 The TBL of people, profit and planet

Turning towards the aspect of people, society is comprised of human rights, education, labour regulations, access to various products, access to services, health of customers, employees and people in general, the impact on the community and diversity issues (Christopher, 2012). Mena *et al.* (2014) suggest that issues of employment, labour standards, fair-trade, diversity, equality, corruption and bribery fall into the general area of dealing with people.

Christopher (2012) points out that in considering profit, impact on the gross domestic product or GDP of a nation should be of concern, as well as the return on investment (ROI) of the people associated with the company. In TBL, social value, or the importance of people in the company as well as customers, is used in ROI consideration (Fauzi and Rahman, 2008). The company will pay taxes, which should be considered both in terms of profit levels of the organization and the possible input to the government that receives the taxes. Whether or not the company contributes to the alleviation of poverty must be considered, as well as whether or not the company has policies that will allow it to avoid corrupt actions (Porter and Kramer, 2006). The company's employment policies should be considered, as well as wage levels and their impact on employees and the community in general (Kaine and Greene, 2013). Finally, the impact of the corporate ethical stance should be considered. Mena *et al.* (2014) report that issues of cost, efficiency, value, risk and innovation are issues of profit, or economy.

The last aspect is that of the planet or environmental impacts. The energy-use levels of the company need to be considered, not only from the perspective of cost to the company, but to the impact on people and the possible changes they will develop in the environment (Slaper and Hall, 2011). Water usage, biodiversity and the impacts of chemicals, toxins, and air pollution are of utmost importance. In the long term, the impact of ozone depletion impacts on everyone (Slaper and Hall, 2011). Mena *et al.* (2014) add that waste issues, considerations of greenhouse gas (GHG) emissions and overall depletion of resources must be considered in determining both SC resilience and how the SC management can facilitate successful implementation of TBL-focused initiatives.

In Figure 3.1, the intersection of people, planet and profit is the target area of sustainability (Talbot and Venkataraman, 2011). Segal-Horn and Faulkner (2010) pointed out that the three areas "are conceptualized separately but overlap in practice" (p. 308). Figure 3.1 provides a graphic representation of this overlap. Other areas of overlap represent areas where people and profit are considered, where profit and the planet is considered, or where the planet and people are considered.

While the intersection of two of the three criteria represents an effort at making the SC responsive and flexible, it is only the intersection of the three criteria that will truly form a sustainable SC focus on the TBL.

Figure 3.1 Researcher's representation of intersection of people, planet and profit

Source: Adapted from Talbot and Venkataraman, 2011, p. 34

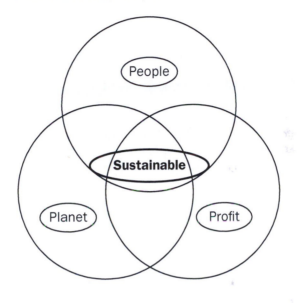

3.3 TBL and the resilient, sustainable SC

Ahi and Searcy (2015) argued that it is difficult to build sustainability into the SC because there are so many factors that can either help the implementation or hinder it. In addition, they believe that in order for sustainability (or resilience) to be implemented, the TBL approach of concentrating on the importance of people, profit and the planet must be implemented. They suggest that a mathematical model can be developed that helps determine how easy it would be to access elements of sustainability in any given chain. The model proposed by Ahi and Searcy (2015) is based on the concept that it is possible to account for factors related to sustainability by using probability in the model.

In most disciplines, it is understood that there are key characteristics that lead to success in an endeavour. They are commonly known as key success factors (KSFs) (Daniel, 1961; Rockart, 1979). Beske and Seuring (2014) argue that the SC should be no different; there are practices that are related to sustainability that result in high sustainability performance. Since sustainability or resilience is focused on the TBL, the categories of importance, or KSFs, are also related to SCs. Beske and Seuring (2014) assert that there are five KSFs in SC resilience. First, the company must orient itself towards SC management, resilience and sustainability. Second, continuity is the key. Collaboration is a key factor all along the SC. Risk management is a high level success factor and some organizations and businesses will face more risk than others. Finally, being positioned to be able to take proactive steps to sustain the SC is critical. These key categories or KSFs represent key points in sustainable SC management (SSCM). Beske and Seuring make the assumption that if SSCM is implemented, more businesses would be able to achieve SC resilience, particularly in the TBL areas. Beske *et al.* (2014) report that even in the food industries, when sustainability practices are utilized, it becomes easier to trace and track products and supplies and to ensure that customer needs are met.

Cleaner SC management, or the management of the company to emphasize the planet (Romm, 1994), may also be one way to increase levels of resilience (Subramanian and Gunasekaran, 2015). Through more intense planning, better product and service designs, efficient purchasing, production and distribution, less pollution and environmental damage occurs. At the same time, better human resources and information technology departments or organizations can lead to a more definitive method of directing operations and thus to clearer frameworks for performance. If this is achieved, the organization is likely to achieve a higher level of competitiveness and is more likely to become, and remain, resilient (Subramanian and Gunasekaran, 2015).

While Beske and Seuring (2014) asserted that there are five basic KSFs, Walker *et al.* (2014) reflected that resilience and sustainability in the SC may extend from emphasizing corporate social responsibility (CSR) as part of operations management (OM). They see OM as the pursuit of a number of environmental, social and economic objectives. This is typically referred to as the TBL. TBL includes not only the actions of the firm but the SC and the communities (Walker *et al.* 2014). Sustainable and resilient systems are not a solid, static items, rather they are constantly changing. Walker *et al.* (2014) suggest that part of the interest in effective and resilient SCs developed from the desire to be "green" in terms of making resource utilization more effective and more efficient. If companies could gain profit or competitive advantage from doing so, then it would be a value-added facet of the business.

One of the more controversial assertions in the sustainable OM literature is that companies who do not recognize the value, capabilities and ability to promote their employees will generally fail to maintain sustained business performance, including SC development (Walker *et al.*, 2014). Yet it can be argued that companies such as McDonald's, which has been at the forefront of fast food production for two generations (Skarlicki and Kulik, 2004), and Walmart, the world's largest retailer, are famous for neglecting employees, providing them with low salaries, and artificially suppressing working hours (Fishman, 2006). The counterpoint to this would be that now, the poor employee treatment has caught up with the companies, and their names are in the news reflecting employees' demands for decent treatment.

The argument that ill treatment of employees will reflect poorly on a company's reputation is important, particularly if SC resilience is being addressed in terms of people, planet and profit.

Another question that has been recently asked is whether the TBL approach is a new one, or whether it is merely a rehashing of existing management theory (Vanclay, 2004). Glavas and Mish (2014) researched whether firms that utilize the TBL use different methods to achieve economic competitive advantage than firms that use a more traditional resource-based view (RBV) of operations. They found that companies which utilize TBL emphasize the maintenance, or sustainability, of resources rather than having a supply of resources. The net effect is that since sustainable resources in a resilient SC are imitable, they can be more readily found and are generally substitutable, they do not carry the power that resources in the RBV do. From an ethical standpoint, the company that uses TBL is more transparent than is a company which uses the RBV. They must, however, be more people- and HR-oriented simply because they spend more time on maintaining and sustaining the resource capabilities (Lawler and Boudreau, 2015). Glavas and Mish (2014) conclude that companies that seek SC sustainability and resilience focus on collaborative advantage, while a more traditional approach focuses on competitive advantage. Taken to its logical conclusion, this would mean that companies who utilize TBL have redefined the concept of value overall and linked it with the TBL of people, price and planet.

Not all researchers agree, of course. Isaksson *et al.* (2015) disagree with the concept that the TBL is effective. They suggest that the indicators of people, planet and price actually clash and can be harmful if one truly intends to measure sustainability, as they pointed out, when indicators of people are included in the TBL, the utility value changes. When researchers consider sustainability, they typically refer to sustainability issues affecting what the main stakeholders feel to be important. As an example, if the company's stakeholders value keeping a low product price, then the importance of people in the TBL would be downplayed, because the people's price demands would be a factor of less importance than the overall stakeholder values. People are only part of the TBL insofar as their utility can be related to both harm and value in the venue of sustainability or resilience (Isaksson *et al.*, 2015). Along these lines, Eriksson and Svensson (2015) suggest that when considering the overall resilience of the social responsibilities relative to SCs, the elements that affect the SC need to be classified into broad categories. Their suggestion is that elements be considered either as drivers, facilitators or inhibitors in terms of social responsibility and SCs. If it can be determined what elements improve social responsibility, then companies that wish to use the TBL can concentrate on these elements (Eriksson and Svensson, 2015).

Empirical research by Pagell *et al.* (2010) and by Saunders *et al.* (2015) showed an unexpected result relating to supplier integration inside the SC. While Pagell *et al.* (2010) concentrated on studies in environmental sustainability regarding suppliers, Saunders *et al.* (2015) concentrated on general integration with an emphasis on social sustainability outcomes. While the results were similar, it is important to note the base concentration was different. Pagell *et al.*'s 2010 work found that suppliers who were engaged in integration with firms early in the lifecycle of the products were not as strategically important as had been generally assumed. Similarly, Saunders *et al.* (2015) found that suppliers who are involved early in the process are not the ones who turn out to have a strategic purpose as suppliers. These suppliers ended up being categorized as leverage suppliers, who have specialized knowledge and can generally help the company increase sustainable outcomes that will end up giving them a market advantage. Again, the results are similar, but the emphasis is different. Early suppliers are used as leverage (Pagell *et al.*, 2010), while later suppliers are more closely related to sustainability outcomes (Saunders *et al.*, 2015). While the difference may seem indistinguishable to the end-user, it is a key point in developing strategy.

Earlier, it was suggested that collaboration along the SC might offer a more effective approach to resilience, especially if sustainable SC management was utilized. One of the issues with this suggestion is that empirical studies that have been carried out have concentrated on the impact of cooperation on the economic bottom line of the company but did not assess the impact on sustainability or resilience. It would be quite possible for an action to positively impact the bottom line in the short term, but have no, or even a negative, impact on sustainability in the long term (Hollos *et al.*, 2012). Hollos *et al.* (2012) set out to study whether or not consistent and supportive supplier cooperation over the long-term would differ from what they called one-dimensional supplier cooperation. Sustainable cooperation adds in the impact of green performance and social performance. The authors do note that even when studies concentrate on different areas, there will be elements of the studies that overlap, since some of the activities that support these elements support both types of activities (Hollos *et al.*, 2012).

The researchers concluded that integrating procurement with the company's strategy is important to the TBL perspective. They also found that green behaviours are linked to sustainable cooperation by suppliers. If the buying firm cooperates with suppliers on environmentally friendly practices and also uses its own efforts, it makes it possible to exploit resources within the buyer's firm while using socially and ecologically responsible practices (Hollos *et al.*, 2012). Still, not all green initiatives will make a positive impact on the firm's economic performance. Some will; some will not. The Hollos *et al.* (2012) study did not find any impact based on social practices. However, as the researchers pointed out, social practices did not increase costs, so it is possible that other positive social practice impacts should be considered given that many firms now seem to be using social practices from a moral, rather than economic, standpoint (Phillips and Reichart, 2000). It seems unlikely they would do this without some form of reinforcement; Phillips and Reichart (2000) argue that companies may do this from the perspective of fairness, or they may do this from some type of ulterior motive.

Malik *et al.* (2015) found that when SCs are modelled and assessed for TBL performance, it is important that there are no finite limits placed on the chain. If both top-down assessments and bottom-up assessments are combined at the same time, an analysis of the inputs and outputs on the chain may be useful (Malik *et al.*, 2015). This process is a form of modelling. A more involved method of modelling can be utilized by companies within an industry to model the entire industry, so that it is possible to use relatively few parameters to get an idea which companies will do what and how the industry as a whole will operate at any given point in time (Malik *et al.*, 2015). The more details that can be entered into the model, the better the TBL assessment. They also suggest that TBL assessments by the government can be used to help the government plan, for example in situations where the state of the oil or gas market may be a concern. This implies that TBL assessments are relatively accurate. In general, companies doing this type of assessment will focus on close suppliers in the chain, but nevertheless this offers an interesting use for the company's data and also may offer some social value-added considerations, such as the ability to plan one's fuel use in advance (in the case of the governmental calculations), to acquire alternate fuel sources, or to increase one's savings for the winter. The same type of considerations would be available to clients of private companies. For example, a low-income customer who may need a refrigerator might like to have information that would help him or her make the choice to buy, or defer the purchase.

3.4 Social networks in SC resilience

Just as technology and sociology have changed over the years, business has responded. Today, social networks are utilized in dealing with SCs. O'Leary (2011) explained both how, and why, social networking enhances SC resilience. With complex SCs, there is no way that one person can gather, sort, store and access all of the information and knowledge that is needed in order to make a typical SC operate at its best capacity; one company may not be able to handle all the information. The utilization of social networking in SC management may have begun as an offshoot of customer relationship management (CRM) (Fiorito *et al.*, 2010). What the literature refers to as CRM once controlled a great deal of the information that is now utilized in managing the SC. Consider, for example, the club card or customer card at grocery stores. The value card was aimed at getting information from the customer. As the customer used the card, it tracked demographics, what each customer liked to buy, how often the customer bought it, what other products they bought at the same time and even brands and sizes. Taken individually the company was able to develop an effective picture of each customer's ordering habits (Hassan and Parves, 2013). Examined collectively, card data allowed individual stores to examine overall buying habits and to control stock levels by ordering based on the same day last year, on local festivals or tourism patterns and so on (Hassan and Parves, 2013). Stores that are able to accurately plan and order have better, but leaner, stock levels; the store benefits but so do the customers. As a result, the SC reaps the benefit and is better able to withstand changes that may occur. Tesco is a prime example of this process (Hassan and Parves, 2013). With a stronger SC, the company is more likely to survive financial upheaval from the economy and other external factors.

Companies today have refocused their loyalty programmes to encompass social media. Using social media in a variety of forms allows companies to gather a different type of data than is allowed by the use of club cards. Social media on Twitter and Facebook is a multidimensional communication (O'Leary, 2011). The card allows data transmission from the customer to the company in the form of invisible electronic record transmissions. The data from the card transmission was private; no one but the company knew what the customer was buying. Social media communications go back and forth, from a customer or potential customer to the company. The company can see the post and respond. However, social media has an additional benefit. It is multidirectional; other social media readers can post comments and the company will be able to access not only the original comment but the responses that show how other people feel about the first post. As a result, a customer who writes to a cereal company and says they like their product may cause dozens of responses that the cereal is fabulous, or that it is awful, that it would be better with a chocolate filling, or that it should be individually packaged. Walmart, Amazon and other companies now commonly have an area on their websites for reviews, comments and feedback (Saravanakumar and Suganthalakshmi, 2012). The feedback to the company is invaluable. Multiplicities of companies now use social media to communicate not only with the customer but with the individuals who happen to see the media postings (O'Leary, 2011). Although this feedback can contribute to the company's ability to gauge supply and demand, its worth goes well beyond this; it allows the company to plan for supply flux and to keep the entire supply line more flexible than it would be if a certain number of items was produced on a regular schedule. The attributes of the products can be changed more easily and the TBL is improved by the lean delivery system.

Since social media can be utilized to gather general information about what customers like, or do not like, in near real time, the data can then be used to make SC predictions, or even to design products. An example of this occurs with Holy-Clothing, which has accounts on Facebook, Pinterest, Instagram, and Twitter. Holy-Clothing "designs, manufactures and markets a wide range of handmade Gothic, Renaissance, Bohemian, Boho and Gypsy Clothing at affordable prices" (Holy-Clothing, 2015, Company overview). HolyClothing produces women's clothing sized small to 5X, in these styles. HolyClothing combines requests for customer feedback with plenty of contests, which may run monthly, weekly or daily. Visitors to the site who sign up for emailing lists get an extra contest entry; they are asked to "Like/Comment to Enter to Win" (Facebook, 2015). Companies that acquire data directly from customers are more likely to be able to meet their needs, run a leaner supply line and have a more resilient and sustainable SC (PricewaterhouseCoopers, 2014). They are less likely to find themselves with a warehouse full of products that are not popular for one reason or another.

If HolyClothing needs clarification they ask for it. In the case of the Ashlee Sun Dress, the company asks customers "Do you like Cotton for Summer? Or another type of fabric?" (Facebook, 2015). Links to the company's online ordering process are included, but if the customer clicks the picture of the dress to get a better look, they are also taken to the online ordering process. Once customers receive their product, they are asked to review it. The reviews provide extra information for potential customers. For example, one Ashlee Sun Dress review states that "The quality of the fabric and the beautiful details are worthy of honourable mention as well. I am 5 feet tall and fairly voluptuous. This gown is long but in a pair of heels, I will be just fine" (HolyClothing, 2014, Utterly Gorgeous). Another reviewer comments that "I usually wear a 28 in pants and a 3X in shirts. I ordered a 3X in this dress, and like I've said, LOVED the fit! Very worth the price!" (HolyClothing, 2014, Great Buy). By finding out exactly what customers like and do not like, the company can produce designs that are likely to sell, without investing excess inventory in materials or designs that will not sell. These factors contribute to the ability to run a tighter supply line and improve the company's TBL. It is a model that has proven to be imminently successful for other companies as well, including Walmart and Amazon (Harris and Rae, 2009).

If the reviewers had left negative comments, then the company would know to review their clothing (or a particular style) for fit, colour, price or whatever a group of customers spoke about negatively. These types of interactions allow the company to see whether or not a particular product is likely to become a best seller or has peaked and will face retirement. The benefits to the SC are immense (O'Leary, 2014; PricewaterhouseCoopers, 2014; Saravanakumar and Suganthalakshmi, 2012). O'Leary (2011) points out that this type of information also allows the company to judge how their SC is doing. If customers are dissatisfied with the type of material, or have noted a difference in the quality of the lace, this is a SC issue. Again, these types of issues, particularly if persistent, allow the company to predict and address SC issues. Social media can be used to gather information that might not otherwise be available (O'Leary, 2011); customers considering a purchase might be thinking that the lace does not looks as good as it once did, but they are unlikely to pick up the phone to call. However, with Twitter messages about the product, combined with the need to comment on the HolyClothing page in order to get a chance to win, the customer is far more likely to take that step and point out that they still like the clothing but the lace is not as good as it was. Knowing that customers dislike a particular product (before hundreds are manufactured) allows the company to be very selective in future productions that might have been planned, to utilize the feature that customers report finding to be negative. Decreasing waste makes it easier for the company to achieve its TBL (Mena *et al.*, 2014).

Another advantage to using social media is that it quickly becomes obvious to the company how long it would take them to pass around information in an emergency. Emergencies do occur in business, whether they are something as simple as a delay in receiving the Silver Angel fabric to make dresses, or whether the dye in Royal Burgundy runs and will ruin a wash, which might prompt the company to tweet that customers should please return any merchandise coloured Royal Burgundy. This type of ability to communicate can distinguish a company among its competitors. O'Leary (2011) pointed out that the information which a company needs to operate is never in one place at one time. Given that the company's economy depends on moving products and services, having the information available easily and in an easy-to-access format can result in leveraged advantage to the organization. Social media utilization allows the company to access information, and contact customers in a way that was unheard of even a generation ago and collects information that a club card could not, much more rapidly (O'Leary, 2011; Saravanakumar and Suganthalakshmi, 2012). The information is then used to guide company initiatives that decrease waste of product, and thus decrease the cost of production and the pollution caused in the manufacturing process (Mena *et al.*, 2014).

Perhaps the best possible example of the SC interdependencies and ways they have been used to enhance customer fulfilment is the online giant Amazon, which not only uses social media to hype posts for products that might otherwise not have received much publicity, but also to deliver books and media electronically, bypassing bricks and mortar and even paper and ink completely. As an example, googling "Amazon social media funny reviews" leads to nearly 11 million hits, all of them talking about Amazon and representing free advertising! Free advertising in turn increases customer traffic and sales (Harris and Rae, 2009) while at the same time decreasing planned costs and increasing profit, decreasing stress to the planet and allowing better utilization of employees (people). The impact is on all three parts of the TBL triad.

The brilliance of this concept may be best expressed by Narula (2014) when she characterizes Goodreads, an Amazon subsidiary, as "millions of people reading alone, together, the title slogan". Goodreads and Amazon have managed to combine a SC and a social media outlet and the result has been the ability to fulfil wishes all over the world, while telling people things that they may wish for, but never knew about, and for free, while readers do all the work. Certainly this would be the fantasy of nearly every company imaginable. The network extends well past media, as well; shoppers have a variety of locations to choose from and a variety of companies to choose from as well as a range of shipping choices. Companies and individuals who use this service essentially set up their own SC based on their needs and what is available at the time. When a SC reflects exactly what the customer wants, it is far more likely to be resilient and sustainable (Flint *et al.*, 2011). It can provide more products at less cost and with less waste from both the environmental and financial perspectives.

3.5 Impact of culture and demand

Culture undeniably impacts on demand. The products that one culture likes may in no way be related to the products another culture enjoys. This is not only from the perspective of supply and demand but because the social ties of the parties are important (Hofstede *et al.*, 2010). The importance of cultural competence cannot be underestimated because the understanding and interface between the cultures is integral to the way that the SC can operate. Using HolyClothing as an example, individuals of one culture may find particular styles to be offensive, while others may find particular styles to be desirable. Care must be taken to ensure that one group of buyers or suppliers do not define the company's market or its resources. According to Gereffi and Lee (2012), small supplier groups tend to be subservient to the needs of the buyers. This concept is particularly important in the global environment, where the items supplied by suppliers in one country may not be considered acceptable by customers in another society.

An example of this, highly publicized, comes from interchanges with China. Some foods that China supplies are considered unacceptable on the American market for reasons of adulteration. In recent years, toys from China have been banned because they are painted with lead-based paint (Story & Barboza, 2007). Milk has been filled with melamine; seafood has been contaminated with bacteria (Foster, 2011) and pet foods have killed American pets. While it is unclear whether these products are acceptable in China (and rejected by America) or whether the products are banned in China but sent to the US, the result is the same. The actions are acceptable to China, but not to the United States. Both organizational and national culture plays a significant role in sustainability (Linnenluecke and Griffiths, 2010). The tourist industry has understood this for generations.

3.6 Adapting SC to different cultures and needs

Jüttner *et al.* (2007) support the idea that the best way to adapt the SC between nations (and thus cultures) is to recognize the concept of supply and demand. By only supplying what the customer demands, and supplying it only when they need it, a great deal of waste is prevented and the process is more environmentally sound. Thus, it is important to understand what issues in a culture may drive the demand chain. It would be folly, for example, to believe that Muslim nations will have the same demand for pork as nations with a small Muslim and Jewish population. The reality is that, with any given culture, different industries will have different drivers (Zhu and Sarkis, 2006). The company itself will have a business culture and an employee culture; these lead to ways of thinking that may be significantly different from the cultures of the suppliers and customers (Fawcett *et al.*, 2008).

Among multi-national companies this can be complicated by differing management cultures in the varying offices and nations.

Even gender attitudes will change from culture to culture, company to company and nation to nation (Blowfield and Evans, 2005). This can lead to a difference in product demands, as well as to demand for style difference in products. The result is the need to make adaptations in the SC if it is to be resilient, so that the SC is able to accommodate not only current demand for particular products, but be flexible enough to quickly adapt to different product demands without hiring additional people, stressing the environment or stressing the company's economy. Lee's (2004) interpretation of the "triple A" SC is that the SC needs to be ever-changing and ever-adapting. It is not something that is done once and is completed. In order to meet the demands of cultures that have very different needs, the standard SC needs to come to an end (Matthyssens and Vandenbempt, 2008). Instead, the new SC, based on TBL, will help develop and reinforce resilience.

3.7 Methodology

This qualitative study utilized available academic journals, books, websites and media materials as a basis of study. Books, journals and websites (including professional blogs) constituted the majority of the materials. Study materials were not limited to samples of materials from the United States, in part because other nations have also developed robust literature on SC resilience and in part because two of the objectives were to understand how culture impacts on demand as well as how barriers, including cultural barriers, can be overcome in order to successfully implement TBL-focused initiatives.

3.7.1 Philosophical approach

The philosophical approach is also called the research paradigm (Saunders *et al.*, 2012). The philosophical approach to this research is based in the constructionist approach to teaching and learning. Constructivist teaching is based on the concept that learning is an active process that best occurs when the learners are actively involved in the process of developing meaning and knowledge (Tam, 2000). It is one thing to sit in a classroom and be the passive recipient of imparted knowledge; it is quite another to step into the process of knowing and meaning construction. All learning is social; students learn as a group (Vygotsky, 1978). Thus, knowledge is constructed socially and is not developed simply because the learner is lectured to (Maphosa and Kalenga, 2012). As a result, knowledge can change as situations continue to grow and evolve. This is a particularly salient point given that the state of the modern SC is rapidly changing. Thus, what was once adequate knowledge is now dated and may no longer be correct.

Learning builds on prior learning and knowledge, in a process called scaffolding (Bruner, 1996). Thus, the ability to collect materials, analyze them, reach conclusions and contribute to knowledge development is based on information that has been developed throughout the career of the student, now developed into a researcher.

3.7.2 Literature review as a methodology

Search terms were developed and later used to collect information that initially appeared to be within the bounds of the research. As the collection of data progressed it was clear that some data would be included, while other data would be excluded. Qualitative, quantitative and mixed methodology studies were considered for inclusion, as well as governmental and commercial information relating to SC and its resilience, particularly regarding culture. In general, papers or information gathered before 2006 were excluded, although seminal information dated before 2006 was considered for inclusion.

3.7.3 Search terms

Initial search terms were developed to research the general topic of SC resilience. Initial combination of terms included SC culture, global SC, SC innovation, and resilience supply. Each set of terms and resulting documents led to more ideas for searches. Not all searches were productive or seemed relevant, however. The general pattern of discovery is illustrated in Figure 3.2, the author's depiction of his search process.

Figure 3.2 Development of search terms

Source: author

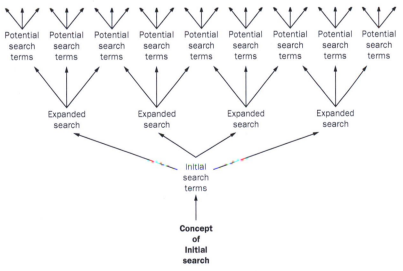

The data was first appraised and then it was synthesized. An organized and structured approach was needed to accomplish this process.

3.7.4 Extracting and appraising data

As potential search terms were utilized and potential data selected, the information contained in the data was analyzed. Identification of the data was made. As the data was extracted the researcher took notes; the notes were considered relating to the way they described the areas under investigation and what type of information they might add to the knowledge database (Easterby-Smith, 2008).

Initially, data was rated to be included or excluded. Once data had been initially sorted, data that was rated to be included had to be carefully evaluated to be certain that it really met the needs of the research. The researcher considered how the authors of the materials in question reached their conclusions and whether or not there were any underlying themes. The author's education and qualifications were considered and whether or not the work itself followed the method that the researcher had specified would be used in the development of the study (Hofstee, 2006). Whether or not the information would inform the research was considered, as well as how the information might contribute to existing evidence. The possibility that the evidence was superfluous or an outlier was considered, as well as potential contribution to the development of new theories or of existing explanations to existing practice (Easterby-Smith, 2008).

3.7.5 Synthesis of the data

Once the data was extracted and examined for applicability, it was placed in the context of the discipline (in this case, business and specifically SCs). The research questioned how the context shaped the findings and whether or not the data could be triangulated by other data that was collected. The findings were organized into general themes. Care was taken to understand the ethical issues that might surround the data, as well as economic issues that could impact on adoption or rejection of the findings (Easterby-Smith, 2008). All of the materials that are referenced are concepts originally developed by other authors or researchers, using data they, or someone else, had collected. There was no ethical concern with using attributed data. Had original research been conducted, privacy concerns would have been an issue. Some of the information, particularly information from websites, was recent. In using examples from current websites, the researcher took care to attribute the information correctly.

3.8 The final process

The final part of the process was to determine if the evidence seemed trustworthy and whether or not it was appropriate to answer the research questions. Future research possibilities were considered and recommendations for research were developed (Hofstee, 2006). The results of the research were compared against the researcher's personal opinion and research and from these comparisons the conclusions and recommendations were developed. The recommendations extend not only to the current state of knowledge but also to recommendations for future research and practice (Easterby-Smith, 2008).

3.8.1 The "social" SC

Companies that have been successful at harnessing SC information and interdependencies include Amazon and Walmart. Interdependencies between SC and customer needs and desires can be harnessed to help fulfil the customer's desires to acquire goods and services. Both Amazon and Walmart have been particularly successful at setting up vast SCs that can acquire nearly any product from a variety of distributors. Amazon even allows the customer to choose the distributor (rather than having a single distributor per product). Given that the prices are not equal for each of the distributors Amazon even posts the price from individual distributors, the shipping cost, the shipping information and any pertinent supply information, so that purchasers can make their decisions based on any (or all) of these criteria.

Consider the search for "frixion erasable pens", the researcher's secret pleasure. The search for "frixion erasable pens" on Amazon listed 1,537 results. The variety, colours and styles of these erasable pens were intimidating. The researcher has a particular favourite style, so the search was narrowed to "frixion ball erasable gel pens" taking the selections to a more manageable 776 results. The true pen aficionado may have further requirements. The search was narrowed further; in this case, the search was now "frixion ball erasable gel pens .07", reflecting that the ball was a fine, but not ultrafine, point. There were 227 products that met this requirement. The researcher uses purple erasable gel to make personal notes, so that factor was added into the search. After adding in the colour, only 18 products remained to be examined. It was immediately obvious that the "clacker" pens should be rejected, as the researcher likes a different style. The best value appeared to be "Pilot FriXion Ball Erasable Gel Pens, Fine Point, 8-Pack Pouch, Black/Blue/Red/Pink/Purple/Orange/Lime/Brown Inks" (Amazon, 2015a). The packet contained only one purple but the other colours were acceptable as the cost was less expensive per pen and the website showed that the Prime membership could be used to get free shipping. This meant that the pens would arrive at the researcher's home or office within two days. All of this information was readily available on the website.

By clicking either "new" or "used" under "More Buying Choices" on the screen illustrated above, the researcher was taken to the page with alternative purchase and shipping possibilities.

3.8.2 Implications for sustainability and resilience

Other online retailers have similar programmes. The same item may now come from a variety of suppliers, and be sold at a variety of retailers, for different price levels. Yet the SC is strengthened for each retailer, and becomes more resilient as the number of ways to sell the product increases. The net effect is that the supplier's level of sustainability increases. This applies to both the original supplier and to the larger supplier (for example, Amazon). In the next section, the importance of the social network to this type of merchandising and supply scheme is discussed.

3.8.3 Illustration of the application of the "social" SC

Amazon also has an advanced rating system: all purchasers are urged to rate products. Frixion pens, at the time of writing, had been reviewed 1,128 times, and been awarded on average a 4.5 star rating. By hovering the mouse on the Amazon page with the Frixion listings, one can see that 89% of the ratings were ether four or five stars. Once the user went to the review page, they could click to see the best reviews, the worst, or any level in between. The one star reviews ranged from complaints that none of the pens worked or that they were not retractable, to comments that the ink disappeared when it was hot and reappeared when it was cold. Interestingly, some of the reviewers considered this to be a negative point; others loved the mystique of disappearing ink. The negative reviews did show the suppliers where changes were needed: the ink needs to last longer, it dries out too quickly and the pens sometimes simply do not work. The positive reviews showed clearly what the customers did like, however: they wrote smoothly, the colours were fabulous, the pens were great for crafts, the pens erase well, the pens wrote in all sorts of places and were "a very unexpected pleasure" (Amazon, 2015b, Schwarz). On the website, customers were allowed to click whether or not a review was helpful, further informing the SC.

3.9 SC interrelationships: a systems perspective

Throughout the research, the idea was reinforced that sales, promotions, supply, demand, culture and strategic development of the organization's marketing are all interrelated. As Fiksel (2006) pointed out, effective pursuit of SC sustainability requires a systems approach. A decision in one part of the chain may have implications in another part of the chain. Consideration of the TBL requires consideration of "broader questions of energy, transportation, climate change, and urban planning" (Fiksel, 2006, p. 14). Fiksel (2006) advocated exploring sustainability issues within an integrated model and this stance was adopted for the research in this chapter. One of the key questions, as Fiksel (2006) pointed out, is to ask how systems can achieve short-term continuity, but at the same time maintain long-term integrity. Fiksel specifically relates this question to the area of ecology, or the area of planet in the TBL. Sustainability requires resilience and the ability to surpass the model of business which suggests that as long as the company is functioning and the status quo is being maintained, everything is fine (Fiksel, 2006). Instead, companies need to continue to develop ways to improve their TBL and one way to do this is to make SCs both sustainable and resilient. The multi-agent SC being used by Amazon and other online retailers has been very successful at accomplishing a strong level of resilience and sustainability. The next step may be to define a model of business which defines a specific system of TBL in SC sustainability.

In this study, the literature review showed that culture plays a large role in what products are demanded and the form or style in which they are demanded. The use of social media to inform SC and management decisions relating to SC can make a tremendous difference in how well the company receives the appropriate information and is able to integrate it into the company's operations without undue waste. In short, the better the organization is able to tap into the customers—and potential customers—wants and needs or demands, the earlier the company will be able to meet them. Thus, understanding the company and having a responsive SC leads to customers who are happier with the company. A resilient SC is integral to the company's survival from both an economic and social perspective.

3.10 Conclusions

Response to the research questions and objectives are presented below. The responses to the questions are the conclusions of this chapter. The first question asked *How can SC management facilitate successful implementation of TBL-focused initiatives?* The research showed that considering the people, the planet and the profit could be best accomplished by maintaining close contact with customers and potential customers. The examples in the research showed that companies who have been the most successful at doing this (for example, Amazon) are also the companies that are the most successful overall. Amazon and Walmart, two of the world's largest companies, also have some of the most active social interaction capacities in their vast websites. Customers literally integrate into the SC and become pseudo-employees, giving advice on purchasing, operating practices and value. In turn, the companies are able to respond more quickly to customer complaints, to needed redesigns of products and to distribution issues raised by customers. Customers become part of the corporate chain. At the same time, cutting down on the amount of extraneous stock and excess production contributes to environmental objectives. By doing away with distribution from a central warehouse to store and to customer and instead ensuring that suppliers ship direct to customer, shipping costs for the company are reduced to a negligible point. The same model has been adopted by Walmart, Target and other socially conscious retailers (Lang and Klein, 2015). Even more importantly, the environment benefits from the reduced levels of shipping and reshipping. Amazon, for example, has an active initiative to evaluate packaging materials (Amazon, 2015c). After a product arrives, customers are asked to evaluate if there was enough packaging, or too much, and whether the product would have been better packed in a single container (or put in separate containers). In this way, the company's environmental impact on planet can be carefully tailored from the packaging perspective.

Another example was given in the website of HolyClothing, which has an account on nearly every social web giant, and maintains very close contact not only with customers but with individuals who might wish to become customers at some point. HolyClothing is perhaps the best example of utilizing supply chain management to facilitate successful implementation of TBL-focused initiatives because it has done such a successful job of tying together social media to determine customer and potential customers' wants and needs to the company's ability to change designs and materials. By regularly offering the opportunity to win clothing that the company designs, supporters are encouraged to visit the Facebook page or the website and give feedback on existing designs and colours as well as proposed designs, colours and sizes. As soon as it is determined that a requisite percentage of customers support a proposed change or design, the prize can be awarded and suppliers can immediately engineer the desired changes. The result is a dynamic, living, resilient system in which the customer is kept happy, stylish and contributing to the company's coffers. Perhaps more importantly, HolyClothing has been able to own and operate a factory in India, which hires only workers age 18 and over who are given Sunday off, pays above average salaries and provides breaks for lunch and tea. The company does not require overtime and has a working environment that is safe and clean. In addition, the company does not discriminate based on religion or gender and points out that it has a large number of employees who are Sikhs, Muslims or Hindu (HolyClothing, 2006). Keeping the product popular and customers happy has resulted in an excellent TBL and the ability to develop a stronger and more resilient SC.

By working together with customers to develop better descriptions of desirable products, the number and volume of undesirable products is reduced. The impact on the environment is lessened and costs are kept low. The net effect is that the company becomes more sustainable.

The second research question asked *How can SC management overcome the significant barriers to efficient development and delivery of necessary goods and services in different cultures with very different needs?* The short version of the answer is that by innovating a collaborative supplier relationship, SC management can overcome the barriers. Overcoming the barriers contributes to the company's TBL.

Acknowledging that culture drives demand is critical. Thus, having cultural competence with both customers and suppliers is necessary. Having an excellent social media commitment can help inform management as to the relative beliefs and positions of customers. While the examples in this research concentrated on Holy-Clothing and Amazon, the acknowledgement is made that, in countries with prominent sub-populations and cultural groups, this issue is particularly critical. Vegans will not want leather goods; Muslims and Jews will not want pork products; different national cultures have pronounced differences in what they consider home-style foods to be. Selling "chilli" in one part of the United States will be a completely different product than the "chilli" sold on the other side of the United States. In New Mexico the product may have potatoes, pork and green chillies; in Cincinnati, it will have a tomato sauce, ground beef and spaghetti; and in West Virginia chilli may be relatively bland and contain beans and ground beef. These same considerations apply to staff; while HolyClothing, Walmart and Amazon all point out on their websites that their staff are varied and hiring is done without discrimination, Holy Clothing took the step of hiring their own suppliers and ensuring cultural diversity and sensitivity. Walmart and Amazon both have guidelines for ethical supplier actions. The TBL improves when there is less risk and ensuring that all employees, suppliers and customers are treated fairly and in a culturally-appropriate manner lowers risk to the company. Respecting cultural considerations affects the companies positively, from a systems perspective. In particular, the ability of customers to provide feedback on products is crucial.

Culture undeniably impacts on demand. Developing and preserving social ties between customers, potential customers, management or administration and suppliers is crucial to the developing resilience of the SC. If the company truly understands the concept of demand, it will be better situated to deal with the SC. In addition, the company needs to be aware that it has its own culture and that culture can impact on supply. Having a responsive SC, and a way to inform that chain, is the best way to develop resilience. Utilizing a TBL approach to balance the SC helps develop and maintain both resilience and sustainability. This chapter began with the contention that when people, profit and planet intersect, sustainability results. Respecting the culture of customers and employees alike, or considering the social facets of the TBL, is one way to ensure that demand remains high. Having an active social media presence allows the company to operate on a leaner supply basis, so that the environmental stress is less. With fewer excess products to be stored and maintained, the company's overall carbon footprint is lower.

Finally, the barriers that exist can be overcome in order to successfully implement TBL-focused initiatives. The research showed that the easiest and most effective way to overcome these barriers is to develop a close relationship with the customer through social media, and then to leverage that relationship to drive supply initiative in developing SC resilience. Future research should be established to determine the most effective ways of driving supply initiative. The research focuses on a strong and resilient SC. Thus, strengthening that chain is critical to the company's TBL. However, having strong and resilient SCs can contribute to a stronger national economy. Thus, this is a facet of the TBL from the systemic perspective. Further strengthening supply is one way to advance the resilience and sustainability of the chain. The Amazon example showed that suppliers can partner with more than one organization in the drive to sell their products. At present, the sub-suppliers partner with each major supplier (Amazon, Walmart and so forth) separately. The idea of a more formal supplier and sub-supplier system should be considered for future research.

References

Ahi, P., & Searcy, C. (2015). Assessing sustainability in the supply chain: A triple bottom line approach. *Applied Mathematical Modelling*, 39(10), 2,882-2,896

Amazon (2015a). Frixion. Retrieved from http://www.amazon.com/s/ref=nb_sb_noss_2?url=search-alias%3Doffice-products&field-keywords=frixion

Amazon (2015b). Frixion customer reviews. Retrieved from http://www.amazon.com/Pilot http://www.amazon.com/s/ref=sr_pg_1?rh=i%3Aaps%2Ck%3Afrixion+ball+erasable+gel+pens+.07+purple&keywords=frixion+ball+erasable+gel+pens+.07+purple&ie=UTF8&qid=1437604382

Amazon (2015c) Enter your packaging feedback. Retrieved from http://www.amazon.com/gp/help/customer/display.html?nodeId=201117470&pop-up=1

Beske, P., Land, A., & Seuring, S. (2014). Sustainable supply chain management practices and dynamic capabilities in the food industry: A critical analysis of the literature. *International Journal of Production Economics*, 152, 131-143. doi:10.1016/j.ijpe.2013.12.026

Beske, P., & Seuring, S. (2014). Putting sustainability into supply chain management. *Supply Chain Management: An International Journal*, 19(3), 322-331.

Blowfield, M., & Frynas, J.G. (2005). Editorial, Setting new agendas: Critical perspectives on corporate social responsibility in the developing world. *International Affairs*, 81(3), 499-513.

Bruner, J. (1996). *In Search of Pedagogy: The Selected Works of Jerome S. Bruner*. New York, NY: Routledge.

Christopher, M. (2012). *Logistics and Supply Chain Management*. New York: Pearson.

Daniel, D.R. (1961). Management information crisis. *Harvard Business Review*, 39(5), 111-21.

Easterby-Smith, M. (2012). Doing a literature review. In M. Easterby-Smith, R. Thorpe & P.R. Jackson (Ed.), *Management Research*. London: Sage.

Elleithy, K., Sobh, T., Iskander, M., Kapila, V., Karim, M.A., & Mahmood, A. (Eds.). (2010). *Technological Developments in Networking, Education and Automation*. Berlin: Springer Science & Business Media.

Eriksson, D., & Svensson, G. (2015). Elements affecting social responsibility in supply chains. *Supply Chain Management: An International Journal*, 20(5), 561-566.

Facebook (2015). HolyClothing, Ashlee sun dress. Retrieved from https://www.facebook.com/holyclothingfan/timeline

Fauzi, H., & Abdul Rahman, A. (2008). The role of control system in increasing corporate social performance: The use of levers of control. *Issues in Social and Environmental Accounting*, 2(1), 131-144.

Fawcett, S.E., Magnan, G.M., & McCarter, M.W. (2008). Benefits, barriers, and bridges to effective supply chain management. *Supply Chain Management: An International Journal*, 13(1), 35-48.

Fiksel, J. (2003). Designing resilient, sustainable systems. *Environmental Science & Technology*, 37(23), 5,330-5,339.

Fiorito, S.S., Gable, M., & Conseur, A. (2010). Technology: Advancing retail buyer performance in the twenty-first century. *International Journal of Retail & Distribution Management*, 38(11/12), 879-893.

Fishman, C. (2006). *The Wal-Mart Effect: How an Out-of-Town Superstore Became a Superpower*. London: Allen Lane.

Fisk, P. (2010). *People Planet Profit: How to Embrace Sustainability for Innovation and Business Growth*. London: Kogan Page Publishers.

Flint, D.J., Golicic, S.L., & Signori, P. (2011, June). Sustainability through resilience: The very essence of the wine industry. In Conference Proceedings, The Faces of Wine Sustainability.

Folke, C. (2006). Resilience: The emergence of a perspective for social-ecological systems analyses. *Global Environmental Change*, 16, 253-267. doi: 10.1016/j.gloenvcha.2006.04.002

Foster, P. (2011) Top 10 Chinese food scandals. *The Telegraph*, 27 April 2011. Retrieved from http://www.telegraph.co.uk/news/worldnews/asia/china/8476080/Top-10-Chinese-Food-Scandals.html

Foster, W., & Bradach, J. (2005). Should non-profits seek profits? *Harvard Business Review*, February 2005. Retrieved from https://hbr.org/2005/02/should-nonprofits-seek-profits

Gereffi, G., & Lee J. (2012). Why the world suddenly cares about global supply chains. *Journal of Supply Chain Management*, 48(8), 25-32.

Glavas, A., & Mish, J. (2015). Resources and capabilities of triple bottom line firms: Going over old or breaking new ground? *Journal of Business Ethics*, 127(3), 623-642.

Harris, L., & Rae, A. (2009). Social networks: The future of marketing for small business. *Journal of Business Strategy*, 30(5), 24-31.

Hassan, A., & Parves, M. (2013). A comparative case study investigating the adoption of customer relationship management (CRM): The case of Tesco and Sainsbury's. *International Journal of Managing Value and SCs*, 4(1), 1.

Hofstede, G. (2011). Dimensionalizing cultures: The Hofstede model in context. *Online Readings in Psychology and Culture*, 2(1), 8. doi.org/10.9707/2307-0919.1014

Hofstede, G., Hofstede, G.J., & Minkov, M. (2010). *Cultures and Organizations: Software of the Mind* (3rd ed.). New York, NY: McGraw-Hill.

Hofstee, E. (2006) Constructing a good dissertation: A practical guide to finishing a Masters, MBA or PhD on schedule. *Exactica*. Retrieved from http://www.exactica.co.za/book-chapters.php

Hollos, D., Blome, C., & Foerstl, K. (2012). Does sustainable supplier co-operation affect performance? Examining implications for the triple bottom line. *International Journal of Production Research*, 50(11), 2,968-2,986. doi: 10.1080/00207543.2011.582184

HolyClothing (2006). Like ethical companies? Sept. 2006, we moved to our current Ethically Managed Factory. 15 September 2006. Retrieved from https://www.facebook.com/44383001500/posts/10150664130911501/?comment_tracking=%7B%22tn%22%3A%22O%22%7D

HolyClothing (2014). Ashlee Bohemian ruffles peasant Gypsy cotton corset sun dress. Retrieved from http://holyclothing.com/index.php/review/product/list/id/2464

HolyClothing (2015). About HolyClothing. Retrieved from https://www.facebook.com/holyclothingfan/info?tab=page_info

HolyClothing (2006). Like ethical companies? Sept. 2006, we moved to our current Ethically Managed Factory. Retrieved from https://www.facebook.com/44383001500/posts/10150664130911501/?comment_tracking=%7B%22tn%22%3A%22O%22%7D

Isaksson, R.B., Garvare, R., & Johnson, M. (2015). The crippled bottom line: Measuring and managing sustainability. *International Journal of Productivity and Performance Management*, 64(3), 334-355. doi: 10.1108/IJPPM-09-2014-0139

Jüttner, U., Christopher, M., & Baker, S. (2007). Demand chain management: Integrating marketing and supply chain management. *Industrial Marketing Management*, 36(3), 377-392.

Kaine, S., & Green, J. (2013). Outing the silent partner: Espousing the economic values that operate in not-for-profit organizations. *Journal of Business Ethics*, 118(1), 215-225.

Lang, S., & Klein, L. (2015). Walmart's sustainability initiative. *The Routledge International Handbook of the Crimes of the Powerful*, 197.

Lawler, E., & Boudreau, J. (2015). *Global Trends in Human Resource Management: A Twenty-Year Analysis*. Stanford, CA: Stanford University Press.

Lee, H.L. (2004). The triple-A SC. *Harvard Business Review*, 82(10), 102-113.

Lee, H.L., Peleg, B., Whang, S., & Zou, Y. (2008). Supply chain management in the presence of secondary market. In C.S. Tang, C.P. Teo & K.K. Wei (Eds.), *Supply Chain Analysis: A Handbook on the Interaction of Information, System and Optimization* (pp. 147-168). New York: Springer Science.

Linnenluecke, M.K., & Griffiths, A. (2010). Corporate sustainability and organizational culture. *Journal of World Business*, 45(4), 357-366.

Malik, A., Lenzen, M., & Geschke, A. (2015). Triple bottom line study of a lignocellulosic biofuel industry. *GCB Bioenergy*. doi: 10.1111/gcbb.12240

Maphosa, C., & Kalenga, R.C. (2012). Displacing or depressing the lecture system: Towards a transformative model of instruction for the 21st century university. *The Anthropologist*, 14(6), 555-563.

Matthyssens, P., & Vandenbempt, K. (2008). Moving from basic offerings to value-added solutions: Strategies, barriers and alignment. *Industrial Marketing Management*, 37(3), 316-328.

Mena, C., Christopher, M., & Van Hoek, T. (2014) *Leading Procurement Strategy: Driving Value through the SC*. London: Kogan Page Publishers

Narula, S. (2014, 12 February). Millions of people reading alone, together: The rise of Goodreads. *The Atlantic*. Retrieved from http://www.theatlantic.com/entertainment/archive/2014/02/millions-of-people-reading-alone-together-the-rise-of-goodreads/283662

O'Leary, D.E. (2011). The use of social media in the SC: Survey and extensions. *Intelligent Systems in Accounting, Finance and Management*, 18(2-3), 121-144.

Pagell, M., Wu, Z., & Wasserman, M.E. (2010.) Thinking differently about purchasing portfolios: An assessment of sustainable sourcing. *Journal of SC Management*, 46 (1), 57-73.

Phillips, R.A., & Reichart, J. (2000). The environment as a stakeholder? A fairness-based approach. *Journal of Business Ethics*, 23(2), 185-197.

Pisano, U. (2012). Resilience and sustainable development: Theory of resilience, systems thinking and adaptive governance. *European Sustainable Development Network (ESDN)*, Quarterly Report, 26, 50.

Ponis, S.T., & Koronis, E. (2012). SC resilience: Definition of concept and its formative elements. *Journal of Applied Business Research* (JABR), 28(5), 921-930.

Porter, M.E., & Kramer, M.R. (2007). The link between competitive advantage and corporate social responsibility. *Harvard Business Review*, December, 78-92.

PricewaterhouseCoopers (2014). Sustainable SCs: Making value the priority. *APICS Foundation*. Retrieved from https://www.pwc.com/us/en/operations-management/publications/assets/sustainable_supply_chain.pdf

Reid, D. (2013). *Sustainable Development: An Introductory Guide*. London: Routledge.

Rockart, J.F. (1979). Chief executives define their own data needs. *Harvard Business Review*, 81-93.

Romm, J.J. (1994). *Lean and Clean Management: How to Boost Profits and Productivity by Reducing Pollution*. Tokyo, Japan: Kodansha International.

Saravanakumar, M., & Suganthalakshmi, T. (2012). Social media marketing. *Life Science Journal*, 9(4), 4,444-4,451.

Saunders, L.W., Kleiner, B.M., McCoy, A.P., Lingard, H., Mills, T., Blismas, N., & Wakefield, R. (2015). The effect of early supplier engagement on social sustainability outcomes in project-based SCs. *Journal of Purchasing and Supply Management*, 21(4), 285-295.

Saunders, M., Lewis, P., & Thornhill, A. (2012). *Research Methods for Business Students* (6th ed.). New York: Pearson.

Segal-Horn, S., & Faulkner, D. (2010). *Understanding Global Strategy*. Cengage Learning EMEA.

Skarlicki, D.P., & Kulik, C.T. (2004). Third-party reactions to employee (mis) treatment: A justice perspective. *Research in Organizational Behavior*, 26, 183-229.

Slaper, T.F., & T.J. Hall (2011). The TBL: What is it and how does it work? *Indiana Business Review*, 4-8.

Story, L., & Barboza, D. (2007). Mattel recalls 19 million toys sent from China. *The New York Times*, 15 August 2007. Retrieved from http://strategy.sauder.ubc.ca/nakamura/c498_sept2007/mattel_recalls_and_china_aug2007.pdf

Subramanian, N., & Gunasekaran, A. (2015). Cleaner supply-chain management practices for twenty-first-century organizational competitiveness: Practice-performance framework and research propositions. *International Journal of Production Economics*, 164, 216-233. doi:10.1016/j.ijpe.2014.12.002

Talbot, J., & Venkataraman, R. (2011). Integration of sustainability principles into project baselines using a comprehensive indicator set. *International Business & Economics Research Journal (IBER)*, 10(9), 29-40.

Tam, M. (2000). Constructivism, instructional design, and technology: Implications for transforming distance learning. *Journal of Educational Technology & Society*, 3(2), 50-60.

Vanclay, F. (2004). The triple bottom line and impact assessment: How do TBL, EIA, SIA, SEA and EMS relate to each other? *Journal of Environmental Assessment Policy and Management*, 6(03), 265-288. doi: 10.1142/S1464333204001729

Vygotsky, L.S. (1978). Mind in Society: *The Development of Higher Psychological Processes*. Cambridge: MA, Harvard University Press.

Walker, B., & Salt, D. (2006). *Resilience Thinking: Sustaining Ecosystems and People in a Changing World*. Washington, DC: Island Press

Walker, P.H., Seuring, P.S., Sarkis, P.J., & Klassen, P.R. (2014). Sustainable operations management: Recent trends and future directions. *International Journal of Operations & Production Management*, 34(5). doi: 10.1108/IJOPM-12-2013-0557

Wieland, A., & Wallenburg, C.M. (2013). The influence of relational competencies on SC resilience: A relational view. *International Journal of Physical Distribution & Logistics Management*, 43(4), 300-320. doi: 10.1108/IJPDLM-08-2012-0243

Zhu, Q., & Sarkis, J. (2006). An inter-sectoral comparison of green SC management in China: Drivers and practices. *Journal of Cleaner Production*, 14(5), 472-486.

Edgar Bellow is Associate Professor at NEOMA Business School in France where he lectures in international management and geopolitics. Edgar's research interests are broadly in the area of geography and business environment, sustainable business, business ethics, supply chain resilience and risk management (risk preparedness) in international business and international management.

4

A mixed-methods analysis of the effect of global sustainable supply chain management on firm performance

Jean-Paul Meutcheho
Lawrence Technological University, USA

While many companies focus on their own internal sustainability initiatives there are a growing number of initiatives focused on promoting sustainability across the supply chain. The resulting Sustainable Supply Chain Management (SSCM) has to justify its contribution to the focal company's performance. Based on survey responses of 242 professionals from the automotive, aerospace, electronics and telecommunications industries and using a mixed-methods methodology this study analyses how professionals perceive the contribution of SSCM to a company's environmental, social and economic performance. The study also looks into the moderating effect of regulations on the relationship between SSCM and a company's performance.

Survey respondents were from NAFTA-based companies and were mainly supply chain, SSCM and sustainability professionals. The results of the quantitative analysis using multiple regression and factorial plot analysis in Minitab 17 showed that SSCM is statistically significant to focal company's environmental, social and economic performance. Likewise the regulatory framework was found to be a moderator of the SSCM–performance relationship. Thematic analysis showed SSCM's benefits, challenges and ways to overcome the challenges at the levels of the company, industry

and country. This study provides corporate leaders and professionals with meaningful business rationale for embarking on SSCM initiatives.

4.1 Introduction

Companies around the world are facing increasing pressure to address the environmental and social consequences of their business decisions. Pressures to adopt sound sustainability principles and practices have come from external stakeholders such as non-governmental organizations (NGOs), academia and governments (Ageron *et al.*, 2012; Marrewijk and Were, 2003; Steger *et al.*, 2007; UNGC, 2010). The pressure has also come from competitive forces within the industry (Svensson, 2009) or from the views and values of leaders within companies (Larkin, 2006; Laszlo, 2008). Addressing the environmental and social consequences of their actions raises risks and costs for companies. However, some recognize that addressing these challenges also presents strategic opportunities for companies (Rao and Holt, 2005). Effectively balancing the costs and benefits of addressing environmental and social concerns could be a source of long-term competitive advantage for organizations (Shi *et al.*, 2012).

The complexity of tackling environmental and social issues has been magnified by companies' increasing reliance on global supply chain networks to produce quality products at lower cost (Christopher *et al.*, 2011; Lai *et al.*, 2008; Zhu *et al.*, 2008). Beyond the increased supply chain logistical distance (SC-LD) different members of the integrated supply chain may have divergent views of the need to address environmental and social issues, different strategies for addressing these issues and different capabilities in comparison to the focal company. A focal company is the supply chain participant whose supply chain is being studied (Catalan and Kotzab, 2003; Pfeffer and Salancik, 1978; Wolf, 2014); it manages the supply chain and is often an original equipment manufacturer (OEM) as noted by Seuring (2008). Effectively addressing environmental and social issues typically requires a focal company to develop a comprehensive supply chain management (SCM) strategy that aligns, coordinates, and integrates the actions of suppliers throughout the chain (Carter and Rogers, 2008; Morali and Searcy, 2013). Among the recent evolutions of SCM, sustainable supply chain management (SSCM), defined as the integrated management of environmental, social and economic issues associated with the supply chain, is being turned into a source of competitive advantage by some companies (Laszlo and Zhexembayeva, 2011; Wong, 2013). Ford Motor Company, Hewlett Packard (HP) and Walmart are reported to have leveraged SSCM as a strategic tool (Ford Sustainability Report, 2013; HP, 2013). These reports of strategic SSCM are still to be satisfactorily proven.

With declining natural resources and growing demands, threats of climate change and concerns about air and water pollution, toxic wastes, fair treatment of socially disadvantaged groups, adverse community impact and growing requests for more corporate transparency, the need to integrate sustainability into SCM should be widely accepted (Laszlo and Zhexembayeva, 2011). However, the scarcity of empirical evidence of SSCM's contribution to corporate profitability has generated reticence from OEMs, suppliers and other stakeholders. The result is that, with a few exceptions, the business world has not enthusiastically embraced SSCM.

4.2 Background and theoretical foundation

Gibson's (2001) call to integrate the environmental, social and economic dimensions of business, or the triple bottom line (TBL), is increasingly being urged on corporations despite the lack of clear consensus or compelling empirical evidence that SSCM contributes to long-term competitive advantage. The underlying philosophical perspective of the TBL was developed by Brundtland and the World Commission on Environment and Development (WCED) (1987). They advocated satisfying today's needs without compromising the needs of future generations.

The term TBL itself was pioneered by Elkington (1997, 1998). TBL suggests that corporations should minimize the harm resulting from their activities and foster holistic growth by optimizing their environmental, social and economic goals. Corporations should avoid a narrow focus on profit to the detriment of environmental and social concerns (Carter and Rogers, 2008; Robins, 2006; Norman and MacDonald, 2004). Subsequently, authors like Shi *et al.* (2012) argue that SSCM practices built on the three legs of TBL will eventually lead to favourable financial performance. Shi *et al.*'s argument is supported by a number of theories suggesting that substantial benefits can be derived from a TBL approach to SCM. Incorporating sustainable business practices into SCM based on the TBL is the essence of SSCM (Morali and Searcy, 2013). Among others the following theories have been used to conceptualize SSCM.

The new development paradigm (NDP) is a theory that focuses on the environmental, social and economic impact of multinational firms (Dunning and Fortanier, 2007). The NDP's framework is macroeconomic and is reflected in global initiatives like the United Nations Millennium Development Goals. Another theory that emphasizes the role of MNCs in a global and interconnected economy is the base of the pyramid (BoP) theory which seeks to address the problem of social exclusion. BoP scholars argue for an alternative business model that includes impoverished communities in the modern economic systems (Hall and Matos, 2010; Prahalad and Hart, 2002).

The sustainability framework (SF) is another conceptual approach to SSCM that attempts to bring together a set of distinct but complementary SCM theories that could be leveraged to enact effective SSCM. Among them the resource dependence theory (RDT) which finds its origin in the work of Pfeffer and Salancik (1978) argues that organizations are dependent on other stakeholders for their survival. The resulting multiple dependencies will create relationships between the focal company (firm) and its stakeholders. Suppliers represent a set of such stakeholders with whom the focal company has mutual dependencies that are developed to reduce risks.

Customer-supplier relationships are governed by contracts as posited by the transaction cost economics (TCE). TCE theory finds its root in the work of Williamson (1975, 1985, 1991) and has been the dominant theory for analyzing transactions risks and associated contractual solutions (Leiblein, 2003). At a high level, TCE examines the comparative advantages of alternative types of contracts (market or hierarchical contracts) for governing buyer–supplier transactions (Williamson, 2002).

However, not all supply chain participants are linked by contracts and yet they are often interdependent when it comes to matters of SSCM compliance. Thus, and unlike the TCE the resource advantage (RA) theory provides a theoretical foundation to the claim that competitiveness can be enhanced in some circumstances by social structures and trust-based governance (Hunt and Arnett, 2003) rather than contracts. Along the same lines, the resource-based view (RBV) theory de-emphasizes the focus on transactions and contracts, and focuses on alternate means to create or enhance the competitive advantage of the organization (Priem and Swink, 2012). In his work on purchasing potential contribution to competitive advantage, Ramsay (2001) points out that RBV, or the Resource Based Perspective (RBP) as he calls it, is perhaps the most widely accepted view of corporate strategy.

These theories are rooted in the social sciences (primarily sociology, political science and economics), strategic management and the theory of competitive advantage (Carter and Rogers, 2008). SF, for example, borrows from all these theories to devise a context in which transactions, contractual obligations, access to resources and collaboration between the focal company and its supply chain are optimized by a TBL mindset. This is particularly relevant to SSCM for which collaboration is needed beyond contracting parties including sub-tier suppliers. These theories are evidence that conceptually, SSCM is relevant to performance.

However, there are at least two opposing camps in the debate about SSCM's contribution to corporate performance. Some researchers suggest that, to avoid negative consequences of companies narrow focus on profit, the environmental and social legs of the TBL should be integrated into business policies and practices to support societal goals (Brown, 2000; Elkington, 1997, 1998, Gibson, 2001). Other researchers argue that integrating environmental and social considerations into business or SCM should be considered only if there is evidence that this supports the economic goals of the company (Friedman, 1970; Norman and MacDonald, 2004; Robins, 2006). This study seeks to answer the following question: does SSCM contribute to company's performance in practice?

4.3 SSCM and performance

Drawing from stakeholders' theory and channel relational reciprocity literature, Luo and Zheng (2013) conclude that "joint CSR strength of both buyers and sellers positively influences channel relationship performance" (p. 210). Approaching the issue of channel performance from a similar angle, Hall *et al.* (2011) say that reaping the performance benefit of SSCM requires collaboration with suppliers because the sustainability of a company is tributary to that of its supplier chain.

The contribution of SSCM to environmental performance can be considered evident. In fact the environmental leg is considered to be the most covered in SSCM literature. The literature review points out that sustainability is at times regarded as synonymous with environmental issues in the field of SCM. Most articles deal in some way with the topic of the physical or natural environment, sometimes referred to as green supply chain management (GSCM), as noted by Shi *et al.* (2012) and Steger *et al.* (2007). This is corroborated by the prominence of ISO 14001 certification, which dominates the field of manufacturing as a standard certification for environmental compliance. Also, governmental agencies like the Environmental Protection Agency (EPA) in the United States and ministries in other nations are mandated with caring for, and making sure business practices and operations are protective of, the physical environment, and they do so via different schemes such as Corporate Average Fuel Economy (CAFE) and carbon trading initiatives. These agencies often rely on major OEMs to help propagate GSCM requirements their influence on their suppliers (Zhu *et al.*, 2008).

SSCM contribution to social performance is also evident given that SSCM can be leveraged to turn impoverished people into consumers (Calvano, 2007) by making them part of the supply chain enterprise through the global market system (Kandachar and Halme, 2007). But although called out in terms like CSR and human rights, which are at the core of sustainability, only a minority of articles deal directly with social issues. The most mentioned social standard Social Accountability 8000 (SA 8000) was referenced only a few times in the literature, moreover it is not widely used by businesses. This is not to say that businesses are ignoring the social aspect of TBL, but they tend to deal with it internally rather than externally (i.e. in collaboration with others including competitors and suppliers). Some businesses prefer to design and conduct their own social (working conditions) audit rather than rely on cross-sectors and cross-industries' standards. This could be explained at least in part by the non-standard nature of working conditions issues as opposed to the aforementioned environmental issues that are, for the most part, known and common. Next the contribution of SSCM to economic performance is reviewed. This study analyzes economic performance as made of operational, reputational and financial performance. These three dimensions of performance are thought to be the most relevant to SSCM.

Operational performance is defined as performance focused on business aspects related to operational efficiency, such as cost, quality, flexibility and speed (Golicic and Smith, 2013). SSCM is thought to influence operations-based performance; the commanding role of the focal company is envisioned to create a ripple effect throughout the supply chain. As Ramsay (2001) puts it, suppliers that are in sync with the customer on business initiatives including SSCM requirements are more likely to better contribute to improved speed to market, product quality and cost efficiency initiatives.

SSCM also contributes to reputational performance. SSCM is sometime seen as the aspect of CSR that involves the supply chain. CSR initiatives like SSCM are often associated with the idea of "doing good", as a reference to improved corporate image expressed in terms of "enhanced brand attributes and value leading to greater customers attraction, retention and trust, and new marketing opportunities" (Mason and Simmons, 2014, p. 820). CSR activities also improve internal reputation in the eyes of employees (Glavas and Godwin, 2013).

According to Tate *et al.* (2010) corporations used CSR and SSCM reports to reassure investors, customers, NGOs and governments that their environmental and social performance expectations are being met. This risk mitigation exercise can also be an image booster for companies whose SSCM actions can be viewed as deliberate attempts to influence public opinion. This reputation may also correlate to long-term performance and "can act as an intangible inimitable resource for the firm" (p. 22) thus creating market advantage and barrier to entry. SSCM is particularly beneficial to the image of companies in "the manufacturing sectors like automotive, consumer-products and electronics where 70% of the organization value added may be purchased from other organizations" (p. 27). In the words of Wang and Bansal (2012), the sustained legitimacy that results from SSCM could provide the focal company with the ability to charge premiums for products and/ or services, recruit and retain employees and attract investors or capital providers.

Companies who engage in SSCM and practice socially responsible supplier selection (SRSS) could enjoy financial performance advantage over rivals (Thornton *et al.*, 2013). There is compatibility between the ethical principles of SSCM and the profit-seeking goal of business (Mason and Simmons, 2014). But Golicic and Smith (2013) note that SSCM's effects are less pronounced on accounting and financial performance than on operational performance. Tate *et al.* (2010) actually observe that SSCM contribution to financial performance is indirect and goes through the mediation of operational performance or access to low cost of capital: lenders are more inclined to grant favourable loan terms to a company that is part of an SSCM scheme, because of the perceived lower risk that comes with SSCM. Delmas *et al.* (2013) corroborate this when they postulate that in the area of SSCM, financial performance is associated with process, not outcome, and has a high positive effect on stock price and access to capital markets.

Other authors, as they will be acknowledged in the following sentences, are more nuanced in their assessment of SSCM contribution to financial performance. Barnett and Salomon (2012) argue that the relationship between SSCM and financial performance is contingent on management of the focal company's ability to leverage their accrued stakeholder influence capacity (SIC) to turn the reputational and operational dividends of SSCM into financial benefits. McGuire *et al.* (1988) find that prior firm performance is a better predictor of its commitment to sustainability, thus financial performance could be the antecedent of corporate commitment to social responsibility in different functions including SCM. They also suggest that sustainability "may influence various aspects of corporate performance in different ways" (p. 869). On the other hand, Wang and Bansal (2012) posit that CSR actions will procure economic benefit if they are coupled with a long-term orientation, which will "positively moderate the relationship between CSR activities and financial performance" (p. 1,147). These three studies establish a contingent relationship between sustainability activities and financial performance, although not directly called out in this study, the role of factors such as SIC, past financial performance and long-term orientation is indeed critical for SSCM actions to impact financial performance. This study is focused on the regulatory framework as a moderator of the SSCM–performance relationship.

4.4 SSCM effects on performance and moderating variable

SSCM is more complex because it involves two dimensions of complexity, namely the coordination of supply chain members and the interactions among environmental, social and economic elements (Hall *et al.*, 2011; Perera *et al.*, 2013). This complexity could be further complicated by the effect of the regulatory framework which could moderate the SSCM-performance relationship.

The regulatory framework is part of the set of external pressures susceptible to significantly and positively influence SSCM adoption (Liu *et al.*, 2012). This is supported by the effect that the Organisation for Economic Cooperation (OECD) Due Diligence Guidance for Responsible Supply Chains of Minerals from Conflict-Affected and High-Risk Areas combined with Section 1502 of the US Dodd-Frank Act and the related Security and Exchange Commission (SEC) rules had on companies and industry efforts to rid their supply chains of minerals mined in conditions that contributed to armed conflicts and violence in mining communities. In this study, the regulatory framework is seen as a catalyst for enhanced SSCM contribution to a firm's performance: if a company SSCM agenda is supported by a legal mandate it is less likely to put the company in an unfavourable competitive position. Furthermore, an SSCM agenda based on a regulation is likely to provide first adaptors' advantage to leading companies and enhance their performance.

4.5 Research methodology and data collection

Mixed methods design was adopted as the research design for this study. "Mixed methods research is a research that combines qualitative and quantitative data collection and data analysis within a single study" (Piano, 2005 cited by Azorin and Cameron, 2010, p. 96). Mixed methods design was selected mainly because of the thoroughness of analysis and depth of understanding it provides (Creswell and Clark, 2006; Golicic and Davis, 2012; Venkatesh *et al.*, 2013; Zachariadis *et al.*, 2013).

The unit of analysis for this study was made of professionals dealing primarily with the topics of sustainability, SCM and corporate strategy. Other participants came from fields like marketing and product development. Quantitative and qualitative data was collected using a 48-question online survey designed for a dissertation. Following the Institutional Review Board approval, the survey was administered between September 2014 and January 2015.

Professionals from the North American Free Trade Area (NAFTA) were invited to take a 24 questions survey (including two open-ended questions) on SurveyMonkey. Of the 410 invitees who opened the survey link, 242 answered questions after providing their Informed Consent. As presented in Tables 4.1 and 4.2, reliability of the study was evaluated in Minitab 17 via Cronbach's alpha test of internal consistency reliability (Cronbach, 1951). Content validity (Fowler, 1995) was evaluated by asking the dissertation committee to check the face validity of the questionnaire items and by conducting a pilot survey with 14 professionals. Construct validity was evaluated by assessing the convergent validity of the scales in the questionnaire through the average variance extracted (AVE) reported in Tables 4.1 and 4.2.

Table 4.1 Reliability of the 13 items measuring Sustainable Supply Chain Management (SSCM)

SSCM items	Mean[1]	SD[2]	Alpha[3]	AVE[4]
SSCM (13 items)	3.28	1.06	0.953	
Environmental sustainability (6 items)	3.24	1.13	0.911	0.663
Extent of collaboration to address ES	3.61	1.33		
Extent of monitoring suppliers' performance for ES	3.31	1.32		
Extent of setting standards for ES	3.25	1.41		
Extent of rewarding suppliers for ES	2.45	1.30		
Extent of requiring cascading of ES Standards	2.86	1.34		
Extent of legal/regulatory influence on ES	3.88	1.26		

SSCM items	Mean[1]	SD[2]	Alpha[3]	AVE[4]
Social sustainability (7 items)	3.31	1.07	0.914	0.618
Extent of collaboration to address SS	3.61	1.32		
Extent of monitoring suppliers' performance for SS	3.30	1.33		
Extent of setting standards on SS	3.34	1.35		
Extent of rewarding suppliers for social performance	2.48	1.30		
Extent of requiring cascading of SS standards	2.92	1.38		
Extent of legal/regulatory influence on SS	3.80	1.24		
Extent of recruiting from disadvantaged groups	3.61	1.33		

Note: Psychometric properties conducted on data from N = 242 study participants; SSCM = Sustainable Supply Chain Management; ES = Environmental Sustainability; SS = Social Sustainability

1 Mean of items within scale where each item is measured on a 5-point Likert scale; 1 = not at all, 2 = some extent, 3 = moderate extent, 4 = considerable extent, 5 = great extent

2 Standard deviation

3 Cronbach's alpha reliability measure of internal consistency

4 Average variance extracted (AVE)

The quantitative data, collected through the first 22 questions of the survey, was analyzed using inferential statistics (multiple regressions) to identify relationships between SSCM and focal company's performance. Second, moderating variables were added to the regression to assess their impact on the relationship between the independent and dependent variables.

Table 4.2 Reliability of seven items measuring company performance

Company performance items	Mean[1]	SD[2]	Alpha[3]	AVE[4]
Firm performance (10 items)			0.96	
Environmental performance			0.85	0.735
Extent of influence by SC ES policy/practice				
Extent of influence by SC SS policy/practice				
Social performance			0.87	0.765
Extent of influence by SC ES policy/practice				
Extent of influence by SC SS policy/practice				
Economic performance			0.93	
Operational performance			0.88	0.780
Extent of influence by SC ES policy/practice				
Extent of influence by SC SS policy/practice				
Reputational performance			0.81	0.657
Extent of influence by SC ES policy/practice				
Extent of influence by SC SS policy/practice				
Financial performance			0.89	0.792

Company performance items	Mean[1]	SD[2]	Alpha[3]	AVE[4]
Extent of influence by SC ES policy/practice				
Extent of influence by SC SS policy/practice				

Note: Psychometric properties conducted on performance data from N = 242 study participants; SC = supply chain; ES = environmental sustainability; SS = social sustainability

1 Mean of items within scale where each item is measured on a 5-point Likert scale; 1 = not at all, 2 = some extent, 3 = moderate extent, 4 = considerable extent, 5 = great extent

2 Standard deviation

3 Cronbach's alpha reliability measure of internal consistency

4 Average variance extracted (AVE)

Qualitative data, collected through two open-ended questions at the end of the survey instrument, was analyzed using thematic analysis. The thematic analysis of the qualitative data aims at providing a deeper understanding and insights into the relationship between SSCM and a firm's performance. Finally, triangulation was used to integrate the quantitative and qualitative analysis.

4.6 Hypotheses testing and thematic analysis

This section reviews the results of the two main hypotheses tested in the study (Fig. 4.1). The following hypotheses were tested to determine the effect of SSCM on performance:

- *H1: SSCM (environmental sustainability and social sustainability in the supply chain) is a positive predictor of a firm's performance*

  - H1a: SSCM is a positive predictor of company's environmental performance
  - H1b: SSCM is a positive predictor of company's social performance
  - H1c: SSCM is a positive predictor of company's economic performance

- *H2: The regulatory framework moderates the impact of SSCM on company's performance*

Figure 4.1 Conceptual model with hypotheses

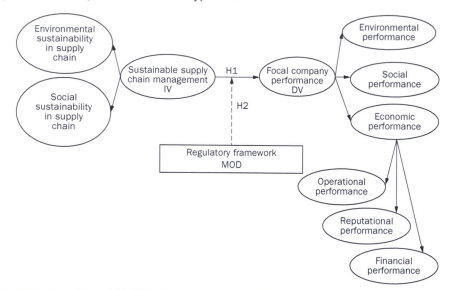

Note: IV = independent variable; DV = dependent variable; MOD = moderator, H1 = Hypothesis 1; H2 = Hypothesis 2.

This section presents the results of regression analyses used to test H1: testing indicates that there is a significant relationship between SSCM and performance. First, results of regressing SSCM on performance are presented. These results are further validated by conducting the regression at the level of the constitutive elements of SSCM (i.e. environmental sustainability—ES and social sustainability—SS). Next, dimensions of performance—PE, i.e. environmental performance—EnP, social performance—SoP, and economic performance—Ecp were shown to be reliably predictable by SSCM, hence justifying the adoption of performance as the higher level dependent variable.

Table 4.3 shows the results of performance regressed on SSCM. The regression had a Standard Error of the Estimate (S) of 0.64. This smaller S (≤ 2.5) indicates that there is a stronger linear relationship between SSCM and performance—PE. The regression had an R-squared (R2) of 66.52%, indicating that 66.52% of change in performance is explained by its relationship to SSCM. R2 is the percentage of variation in the response variable that is explained by its relationship with the predictor, the higher the R2 the better. The regression output also showed R-squared adjusted (R-sq adj) of 66.37%, it is used to assess the effect of the number of predictors in the model and will be discussed in the next paragraph. The model showed an R-squared predicted (R-sq pred) of 65.97%, very close to R2 of 66.52%, indicating that the model provides valid predictions for new observations. Larger values of R-sq (pred) indicate models of greater predictive ability. The regression showed that SSCM had a p-value of less than 0.01, which supports H1 and indicates that SSCM is statistically significant to, and is a predictor of, performance. Also the model had a coefficient (β) of 0.85 which implies that for every unit of increase in SSCM, there is a corresponding positive change of .85 units of mean performance. Given that this model had only one predictor, the variance inflation factor (VIF) of one confirms the absence of multicollinearity (correlation between predictors).

Table 4.3 Performance regressed on SSCM

Model summary						
	S	R-sq	R-sq(adj)	R-sq(pred)		
	0.636	66.52%	66.37%	65.97%		
Coefficients						
	Term	Coef	SE Coef	T-value	P-value	VIF
	Constant	0.44	0.14	3.24	0.00	
	SSCM	0.85	0.04	21.29	0.00	1.00
Regression equation						
	Performance = 0.444 + 0.8464 SSCM					

Note: N = 242

Table 4.4 shows the results of the regression with performance regressed on the two components of SSCM (i.e. ES and SS). Given that their t-values were less than 0.01, ES and SS were deemed statistically significant to, and were predictors of, performance. However, the lower t-value of SS (4.84) compared to ES's (5.55) indicates that the latter is a better predictor of performance; this observation is of minor relevance given that the p-value analysis had confirmed the statistical significance of both independent variables.

Table 4.4 Performance regressed on environmental sustainability and social sustainability

Model summary						
	S	R-sq	R-sq(adj)	R-sq(pred)		
	0.641	66.10%	65.80%	65.16%		
Coefficients						
	Term	Coef	SE Coef	T-value	P-value	VIF
	Constant	0.47	0.14	3.37	0.00	
	ES	0.44	0.08	5.55	0.00	4.33
	SS	0.40	0.08	4.84	0.00	4.33
Regression equation						
	Performance = 0.469 + 0.4377 ES + 0.4023 SS					

Note: N = 242

Contrasting the regression of performance on SSCM (Table 4.1) with that of the egression of performance on ES and SS (Table 4.2) indicated the following:

1. The smaller S value of 0.636 for the first regression indicates a stronger linear relationship SSCM and performance than there is between ES and SS, and performance.

2. The R2 for the first regression was higher, making it a better model in terms of explaining the response variable change due to the predictor(s).

3. The higher R-sq (adj) of 66.37% for the first model compared to 65.8% for the second, despite the higher number of predictors for the second model, showed that the model with SSCM provided a better explanation of changes in the dependent variable (performance).

4. The higher R-sq (pred) for the first model (65.97%) indicated that it had a better ability of prediction for new observations.

5. Finally the second regression showed identical VIF of 4.33. This implies the existence of moderate collinearity (correlation between predictors) in the regression analysis.

These results justify conducting other analyses based on SSCM as the predictor. Table 4.5 shows a summary of all measures of performance regressed on SSCM. It indicated that the model with PE as outcome variable was better than the other models based on the following:

1. An S score of 0.636 compares to 0.743, 0.712, and 07.26 for EnP, SoP and EcP respectively.

2. An R2 of 66.52% that was higher than that of EnP, SoP and EcP of 64.05%, 63.73% and 57.77% respectively.

3. For all regressions, SSCM had a p-value of ≤ 0.01 indicating that SSCM was statistically significant to and a predictor of PE as well as EnP, SoP and EcP.

4. SSCM explained less of EcP that it explained EnP and SoP based on their respective R2 of 57.77%, 64.05% and 63.73%.

5. SSCM had a positive β for all regressions thus confirming its positive relationship performance.

6. Taken separately the three factors of EcP, i.e. operational performance—OpP, financial performance—FiP and reputational performance—ReP), had R2 of 44.61%, 43.69%, and 61.56%. They all scored lower than EcP (57.77%) except for ReP. This indicates that the impact of SSCM on reputational performance is comparable to its impact on environmental and social performance.

Testing of the second hypothesis, H2, will be based exclusively on EP as the dependent variable and SSCM as the predictor.

Table 4.5 Performance's dimensions regressed on SSCM

Firm Performance items	S	R-sq (%)	Coef	SE Coef	T-value	P-value	VIF
PE	0.636	66.52					
Constant			0.444	0.137	3.24	0.00	
SSCM			0.846	0.039	21.29	0.00	1.00
EnP	0.743	64.05					
Constant			0.181	0.160	1.13	0.26	
SSCM			0.936	0.046	20.06	0.00	1.00
SoP	0.712	63.73					
Constant			0.353	0.154	2.29	0.02	
SSCM			0.891	0.044	19.93	0.00	1.00
EcP	0.726	57.77					
Constant			0.559	0.157	3.57	0.00	
SSCM			0.801	0.045	17.58	0.00	1.00
OpP	0.942	44.61					
Constant			0.401	0.204	1.97	0.05	
SSCM			0.798	0.059	13.46	0.00	1.00
FiP	0.933	43.69					
Constant			0.486	0.202	2.41	0.01	
SSCM			0.755	0.058	13.21	0.00	1.00
ReP	0.695	61.56					
Constant			0.790	0.150	5.27	0.00	
SSCM			0.830	0.043	19.02	0.00	1.00

Note: PE = Performance; SSCM = Sustainable Supply Chain Management; EnP = Environmental performance; SoP = Social performance; EcP = Economic performance; OpP = Operational performance; FiP = Financial performance; ReP = Reputational performance; $P < 0.01$; N = 242

H2: The effect of SSCM on performance is moderated by the regulatory framework. This was tested using multiple regression and factorial plot in Minitab 17. As reported in Table 4.6 the regulatory framework (reg/framework) and its interaction terms with SSCM (SSCM*reg/framework) were added to the regression model to assess the ability of reg/framework to moderate the effect of SSCM on performance. The regression model showed S, R2, R-sq (adj) and R-sq (pred) within ranges comparable to those of the regression of Performance on SSCM. The p-value of the interaction term, SSCM X reg/framework, indicated that it was statistically significant to the regression, implying a meaningful relationship with performance.

Table 4.6 Regulatory framework as a moderator of SSCM's effect on performance

Model summary						
	S	R-sq	R-sq(adj)	R-sq(pred)		
	0.63	67.36%	66.92%	66.12%		
Coefficients						
	Term	Coef	SE Coef	T-value	P-value	VIF
	Constant	1.12	0.36	3.12	0.00	
	SSCM	0.56	0.15	3.77	0.00	13.92
	Reg/Framework	-0.18	0.10	-1.86	0.06	7.73
	SSCM*Reg/ Framework	0.07	0.03	2.09	0.04	30.33

Note: N = 242

Furthermore, analysis of the relationship among these variables using a factorial plot (Fig. 4.2) showed that the lines for high and low reg/framework were nonparallel, suggesting that an interaction occurred and that there is an impact of reg/framework on the effect of SSCM on performance. The statistical significance of the relationship on the plot is reflected by the greater divergence of the two nonparallel lines past their point of interaction.

Figure 4.2 Factorial plot of the effect of regulatory framework on the relationship between SSCM and performance

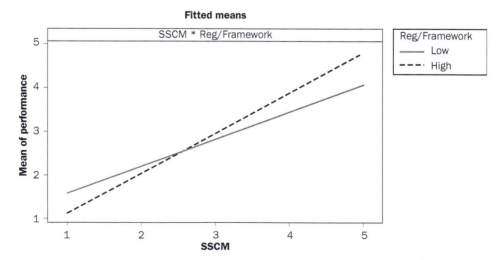

Thematic analysis of qualitative data was the second step in the data analysis strategy for this study. It consisted in analyzing responses to the following two

open-ended questions asked at the end of the survey to explore respondents' perception of the benefits, challenges and solutions to challenges of environmentally and socially sustainable SCM:

- Question 1: what are the major benefits and challenges to environmentally sustainable supply chain management? How can the challenges be overcome?

- Question 2: what are the major benefits and challenges to socially sustainable supply chain management? How can the challenges be overcome?

As presented in Table 4.5, themes developed from analyzing responses were grouped into the categories of major benefits, major challenges and solutions to challenges. The analysis followed Boyatzis' (1998) five-step framework and its data-approach (inductive) method.

Responses to each question were reviewed on four different occasions. The first review sought to identify key words in each response. The second review used the keywords to develop thematic labels and assign the themes to either major benefits (risk mitigation, competitive advantage and societal good), major challenges (cost, enforcement and implementation difficulties, and lack of common vision), or solutions to challenges (creation of tools for implementation, leadership, collaboration and proper regulations). The third review validated the themes' assignment and provided a count for the occurrence of each theme in any individual response. The fourth and final review repeated the preceding steps to ensure process consistency.

Table 4.7 Thematic analysis of responses for environmental and social
sustainability

Question 1 and 2 (Questions 23 and 24 of survey instrument)
What are the major benefits and challenges to environmentally (or socially) sustainable supply chain management? How can the challenges be overcome?

	Business or micro level	Societal or macro level	Solution to challenges
Major benefits	Risk mitigation and reputation · Stable supply chain · Risk management tool · Facilitate compliance with regulation · Tool to enhance or protect corporate **Competitive edge** · Leadership in meeting the demands of increasingly sophisticated customers · Contribution to innovation · Guarantor of safer products · Appeal to sustainability conscious investors	· Evidence of good CSR · Altruism · Promote long-term availability of natural resources* · Attraction of diversity-conscious employees** · Promotion of respect for Human Rights** · Social ascension opportunity for persons from socially disadvantaged groups**	

	Business or micro level	Societal or macro level	Solution to challenges
Major challenges	**Cost** · Cost hardly justifiable and risk of driving companies into unfavourable competitive position · Long-term horizon of perceived but diffuse benefits		· Create tools to translate perceived benefits into tangible metrics and quantifiable gains
	Enforcement and implementation · Hard to enforce and embed into business operations · Length and complexity of supply chain: lack of contract with non-direct suppliers make enforcement difficult · Plethora of environmental initiatives and standards of compliance · Difficulty in enacting cross-industries and cross-sectors collaboration		· Take a leadership role in training and educating suppliers · Promote industry and sector levels collaboration
	Lack of common vision and alignment · Lack of, or insufficient, suppliers' awareness and goodwill · Lack of alignment between the focal company vision and the cultural and regulatory framework of suppliers · Green washing		· Complement corporate initiatives with laws and regulations · Enactment of related laws and regulations

Note: * Environmental sustainability only. ** Social sustainability only

For question one on environmentally SSCM, applying the ten themes developed to the 88 responses as presented in Figure 4.3 yielded a total of 247 occurrences (not all respondents addressed each theme). Based on the thematic analysis, CSR and societal good stood out as the major benefit whereas perceived cost, enforcement and difficult implementation appeared to be the major challenges. Proper laws and regulations were the most reported solution to challenges.

Figure 4.3 Themes identified for question one on environmental sustainability

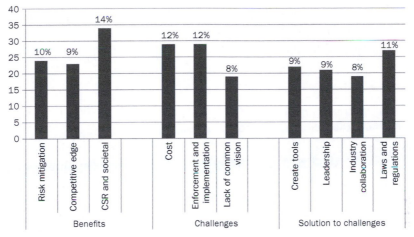

Note N = 247 (88 responses checked on ten themes, not all respondents addressed each theme).

For question two on socially SSCM, applying the ten themes developed to the 78 responses as presented in Figure 4.4 yielded a total of 230 occurrences (not all respondents addressed each theme).

CSR and societal good stood out as the major benefit in a higher proportion than was the case for environmental sustainability discussed above. Enforcement and difficult implementation appeared to be the major challenge. Corporate leadership coupled with proper laws and regulations were the most reported solutions to challenges.

Figure 4.4 Themes identified for question two on social sustainability

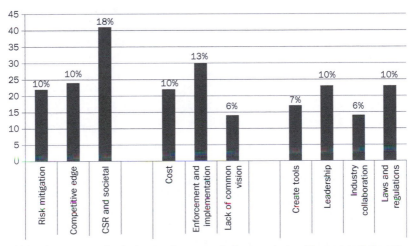

Note: N = 230 (78 responses checked on ten themes, not all respondents addressed each theme).

4.7 Summary and conclusion

This study was based on the analyses of the 242 responses to the 22 quantitative questions, 88 responses to the first qualitative question and 78 responses to the second qualitative question. The analyses helped answer the following research questions:

- Does SSCM contribute to the focal company's performance?

- Does the regulatory framework moderate the relationship between SSCM and the focal company's performance?

Answering these research questions provided an understanding of the relationship between SSCM and a firm's performance, and the impact that the regulatory framework had on the relationship between SSCM and performance.

The data analysis confirmed hypothesis H1: SSCM has a positive relationship with company's performance. This confirmation was also validated when the hypothesis was tested based on the two elements of SSCM. This is supported by views of authors like Luo and Zheng (2013) and Hall *et al*. (2011). H1 was supported and the literature review confirmed the qualitative analysis finding that SSCM contributed to operational performance (Golicic and Smith, 2013), reputational performance (Mason and Simmons, 2014; Glavas and Godwing, 2013) and financial performance (Delmas *et al*., 2013, Barnett and Salomon, 2012; McGuire *et al*., 1998).

Finally, for the test of moderation with H2 the interaction term, reg/framework X SSCM, was significant in the multiple regression analysis. This was confirmed by the factorial plot which showed that the paths for low and high regulatory framework were non parallel. Thus the claim of Liu *et al*. (2012) that the regulatory framework acts as catalyst and has a multiplier effect on the relationship between SSCM and performance was verified.

The thematic analysis yielded ten themes around which respondents explored the benefits, challenges and solutions to the challenges of SSCM. CSR, risk mitigation and enhanced reputation, and creation of a competitive edge were reported as the major benefits for SSCM. Perceived cost, difficult enforcement and implementation, and lack of common vision came out as the major challenges to SSCM. When asked to suggest solutions to these challenges respondents called out for the creation of effective tools, leadership, collaboration and sound laws and regulations.

Triangulation of the quantitative and qualitative analysis showed that the quantitative finding that SSCM had a positive relationship to performance was corroborated by the qualitative findings that the benefits SSCM were elements of reputational and CSR performance. Also, respondents perceived that SSCM could help the focal company mitigate risk and create a competitive edge by attracting sustainability-conscious stakeholders (customers, employees and investors). Based on R2 SSCM could explain no more than 67% of performance. The missing 33% could be due, at least in part, to the challenges (cost, difficult implementation and lack of common vision) evoked in the qualitative analysis. Solutions to these challenges included, among others, the need for more industry collaboration which was found to be a significant moderator of the relationship between SSCM and performance.

This mixed methods study provided empirical evidence to support the contribution of SSCM to corporate performance. It also validated the moderating effect of the regulatory framework on the relationship between SSCM and the performance of the focal company. These empirical findings complement the growing body of literature that has presented theories like BoP and SF as solid foundation for a TBL approach to SCM.

One limit of this study is that it relied on the perceptions of professionals in lieu of objective data on corporate performance, but such data seldom exists or is made public in a form that was suited for this study. Another apparent limitation of the study is its focus on the focal company performance, but singling out the focal company was more conceptual than substantial. In fact the network of supply chains is such that a customer for one product could well be a tier one or sub-tier supplier for another product.

Future research could look into the challenges of multiple, and sometime conflicting, regulations for MNCs as they promote and implement SSCM across multiple countries with their respective jurisdiction. A second research project could investigate contrasting the impact of SSCM on performance to the impact of other performance factors like quality and cost. This could provide a better view of how SSCM compares to these other factors and an insight into how and when to prioritize the adoption of an SSCM agenda, given how those other performance factors compare to SSCM.

References

Ageron, B., Gunasekaran, A., & Spalanzani, A. (2012). Sustainable supply chain management: An empirical study. *International Journal of Production Economics*, 140(1), 168-182.

Azorin, J.M., & Cameron, R. (2010). The application of mixed methods in organizational research: A literature review. *The Electronic Journal of Business Research Methods*, 8(2), 95-105.

Barnett, M.L., & Salomon, R.M. (2012). Does it pay to be really good? Addressing the shape of the relationship between social and financial performance. *Strategic Management Journal*, 33, 1340-1320.

Boyatzis, R. (1998). *Transforming Qualitative Information*. London, UK: Sage.

Brown, R.L. (2006). *Plan B 2.0: Rescuing a Planet under Stress and a Civilization in Trouble.* New York, NY: Earth Policy Institute.

Brundtland, G.H., & WCED (World Commission on Environment and Development) (1987). *Our Common Future: Report of the World Commission on Environment and Development.* Oxford, UK: Oxford University Press.

Calvano, L. (2007). Multinational corporations and local communities: A critical analysis of conflict. *Journal of Business Ethics*, 82, 793-805.

Carter, C., & Rogers, D. (2008). A framework of sustainable supply chain management: Moving toward new theory. *International Journal of Physical Distribution & Logistics Management*, 38(5), 360-387.

Catalan, M., & Kotzab, H. (2003). Assessing the responsiveness in the Danish mobile phone supply chain. *International Journal of Physical Distribution and logistics Management*, 33(8), 663-685.

Christopher, M., Mena, C., Khan, O., &Yurt, O. (2011). Approaches to managing global sourcing risk. *Supply Chain Management: An International Journal*, 16(2), 67-81.

Creswell, J.W., Clark, V.P. (2006). *Designing and Conducting Mixed Methods Research*. Thousand Oaks, CA: Sage.

Cronbach, L. (1951). Coefficient alpha and the internal structure of tests. *Psychomerika*, 16, 297-334.

Delmas, M.A., Etzion, D, & Nairn-Birch, N. (2013). Triangulating environmental performance: What do corporate social responsibility ratings really capture? *The Academy of Management Journal*, 27(3), 255-267.

Dunning, A., & Fortanier, F. (2007). Multinational enterprises and the new development paradigm: Consequences for the host country development. *Multinational Business Review*, 15(1), 25-45.

Elkington, J. (1998). Partnership from cannibals with forks: The triple bottom line of the 21st-century business. *Environmental Quality Management*, Autumn 1998, 37-51.

Elkington, J. (1997). *Cannibals with Forks: The Triple Bottom Line of the 21st Century Business*. Oxford, UK: Capstone.

Ford Motor Company. (2012/2013). Ford go further sustainability report 2012/2013. Retrieved from http://corporate.ford.com/microsites/sustainability-report-2012-13/default

Fowler, F.J. (1995). *Improving Survey Questions*. Thousand Oaks, CA: Sage.

Friedman, M. (1970, September 13). The social responsibility of business is to increase its profits. *The New York Times Magazine*.

Glavas, A., & Godwin, L.N. (2013). Is the perception of goodness good enough? Exploring the relationship between perceived corporate social responsibility and employee organizational identification. *Journal of Business Ethics*, 114, 15-27.

Gibson, R. (2001). Specification of sustainability-based environmental assessment decision criteria and implications for determining "significance" in environmental assessment. [Online publication]. Retrieved from http://www.sustreport.org/downloads/SustainabilityEA.doc

Golicic. S.L., & Davis, D.F. (2012). Implementing mixed methods research in supply chain management. *International Journal of Physical distribution & Logistics Management*, 42 (8/9), 726-741.

Golicic, S.L., & Smith, C. (2013). A meta-analysis of environmentally sustainable supply chain management practices and firm performance. *Sustainable SCM practices and performance*, 49(2), 78-95.

Hall, J., & Matos, S. (2010). Incorporating impoverished communities in sustainable supply chains. *International Journal of Physical Distribution & Logistics Management*, 40(1/2), 124-147.

Hall, J., Matos, S., & Silvestre, B. (2011). Understanding why firms should invest in sustainable supply chains: A complexity approach. *International Journal of Production Research*, 50(5), 1332-1348.

Hunt, S.D., & Arnett, D.B. (2003). Resource-advantage theory and embeddedness: Explaining R-A theory's explanatory success. *Journal of Marketing Theory and Practice*, Winter, 1-17.

Kandachar, P.V., Halme, M. (2007). An exploratory journey towards the research and practice of the base-of-the-pyramid. *Greener Management International*, 51, June, 3-17.

Lai, J., Harjati, A., McGinnis, L., Zhou, C., & Guldberg, T. (2008). An economic and environmental framework for analyzing globally sourced auto parts packaging system. *Journal of Cleaner Production*, 16(15), 1632-1646.

Larkin, J. (2006). Bill Ford interview. *Automotive Industry*, 186(4), p. 73.

Laszlo, C. (2008). *Sustainable Value: How the World's leading Companies are Doing Well by Doing Good*. Stanford, CA: Stanford University Press.

Laszlo, C., Zhexembayeva, N. (2011). *Embedded Sustainability: The Next Big Competitive Advantage*. Stanford, CA: Stanford University Press.

Leiblein, M.J. (2003). The choice of organizational governance form and performance: Prediction from transaction cost, resource-based, and real options theories. *Journal of Management*, 29(6), 937-961.

Liu, X., Yang, J., Qu, S., Wang, L., Shishime, T., & Bao, C. (2012). Sustainable production: Practices and determinant factors of green supply chain management of Chinese companies. *Business Strategy and the Environment*, 21, 1-16.

Luo, X., & Zheng, Q. (2013). Reciprocity in corporate social responsibility and channel performance: Do birds of a feather flock together? *Journal of Business Ethics*, 118, 203-213.

Marrewijk, M., & Were, M. (2003). Multiple levels of corporate sustainability. *Journal of Business Ethics*, 44, 107-119.

Mason, C., & Simmons, J. (2014). Embedding corporate social responsibility in corporate governance: A stakeholder system approach. *Journal of Business Ethics*, 119, 77-86.

McGuire, J.B, Sundgren, A., & Schneeweis, T. (1988). Corporate social responsibility and firm financial performance. *Academy of Management Journal*, 31(4), 854-872.

Morali, O., & Searcy, C. (2013). A review of sustainable supply chain management practices in Canada. *Journal of Business Ethics*, 117, 635-658.

Norman, W., & MacDonald, C. (2004). Getting to the bottom of "triple bottom line". *Business Ethics Quarterly*, 14(2), 243-262.

Perera, P.S., Perera, H.S., & Wijesinghe, T.M. (2013). Environmental performance evaluation in supply chain. *Vision*, 17(1), 53-61.

Pfeffer, J., & Salancik, G.R. (1978). *The External Control of Organizations: A Resource Dependence Perspective*. New York, NY: Harper & Row.

Prahalad, C.K., & Hart, S.L. (2002). The fortune at the bottom of the pyramid. *Strategy and Business*, 26(1), 54-67.

Priem, R.L., & Swink, M. (2012). A demand-side perspective on supply chain management. *Journal of Supply Chain Management*, 48(2), 7-13.

Ramsay, J. (2001). The resource based perspective, rents, and purchasing contribution to sustainable competitive advantage. *The Journal of Supply Chain Management*, Summer, 38-47.

Rao, D., & Holt, D. (2005). Do green supply chains lead to competitiveness and economic performance? *International Journal of Operations and Production Management*, 25(9), 898-916.

Robins, F. (2006). The challenge of TBL: A responsibility to whom? *Business and society review* 111(1), 1-14.

Seuring, S. (2008). Assessing the rigor of case study in research in supply chain management. *Supply Chain Management: An International Journal*, 13(2), 128-137.

Shi, V.G., Koh, S.C., Baldwin, J., & Cucchiella, F. (2012). Natural resource based green supply chain management. *Supply Chain Management: An International Journal*, 17(1), 54-67.

Steger, U., Ionescu-Somers, A., & Salzmann, O. (2007). The economic foundations of corporate sustainability. *Corporate Governance*, 7(2), 162-177.

Svensson, G. (2009). The transparency of SCM ethics. Conceptual framework and empirical illustrations. *Supply Chain Management: An International Journal*, 14(4) 259-269.

Tate, W., Ellram, L., & Kirchoff, J. (2010). Corporate social responsibility reports: A thematic analysis related to supply chain management. *Journal of Supply Chain Management*, 46(1), 19-44.

Thornton, L.M., Autry, C.W., Glicor, D.M., & Brik, A.B. (2013). Does socially responsible supplier selection pay off for customer firms? A cross cultural comparison. *Journal of Supply Chain Management*, 49(3), 66-89.

UNGC (United Nations Global Compact). (2010). *How to do Business with Respect for Human Rights: A Guidance Tool for Companies.* The Hague: Global Compact Network Netherlands.

Venkatesh, V., Brown, S.A., & Bala, H. (2013). Bridging the qualitative-quantitative divide: Guidelines for conducting mixed methods research in information systems. *MIS Quarterly*, 20(1), 21-54.

Wang, T., & Bansal, P. (2012). Social responsibility in new ventures. *Strategic Management Journal*, 33, 1135-1153.

WCED (World Commission on Environment and Development) (1987). *Our Common Future.* New York, NY: Oxford University.

Williamson, O.E. (2002). The theory of the firm as governance structure: From choice to contract. *Journal of Economic Perspectives*, 16(3), 171-195.

Williamson, O.E. (1991). Comparative economic organization: The analysis of discrete structural alternatives. *Administrative Science Quarterly*, 36, 269-296.

Williamson, O.E. (1985). *The Economic Institutions of Capitalism: Firms, Markets, Relational Contracting.* New York, NY: Free Press.

Williamson, O.E. (1975). *Markets and Hierarchy: Analysis and Antitrust Implications.* New York, NY: Free Press.

Wolf, J. (2014). The relationship between sustainable supply chain management, stakeholders' pressure and corporate sustainability performance. *Journal of Business Ethics*, 119, 317-328.

Wong, C. (2013). Leveraging environmental information integration to enable environmental management capability and performance. *Environmental Information Integration*, 49(2), 114-136.

Zachariadis, M., Scott, S., & Barrett, M. (2013). Methodological implications of critical realism for mixed methods research. *MIS Quarterly*, 37(3), 855-879.

Zhu, Q.H., Sarkis, J., & Lai, K.H. (2008). Confirmation of a measurement model for green supply chain management practices implementation. *International Journal of Productions Economics*, 111(2), 261-273.

Jean-Paul Meutcheho holds a Doctorate in Business Administration from Lawrence Technological University and has research interest in SC management and sustainability. He holds an MBA from the University of Detroit Mercy, and Bachelors and Masters Degrees in Business Economics from the Catholic University of Central Africa.

Between 1998 and 2012 he worked for Ford Motor Company where he held many positions in the corporate purchasing organization in the US and Mexico. He is currently the Director of Sourcing and Corporate Sustainability at Global Advanced Metals in Boyertown, PA, USA. On multiple occasions he has briefed the European Commission and US congressional staffs on their legislative processes for conflict minerals.

He has held leadership roles as: chairperson of the Conflict Minerals Workgroup at the Automotive Industry Action Group (AIAG); steering committee member of the Organisation for Economic Co-operation and Development (OECD) Workgroup for Responsible Supply of Minerals; governance committee member of the Public Private Alliance (PPA) for Responsible Minerals Trade; and governance committee member of the Conflict Free Sourcing Initiative (CFSI) of the Electronic Industry Citizenship Coalition (EICC).

Part II
Enablers:
what helps in the process?

Transparency

5

Mapping networks and the influence on the natural environment

Lisa M. Ellram
Farmer School of Business, Miami University, USA

Wendy L. Tate
University of Tennessee, USA

Using empirical data, this chapter presents the results of an exploratory analysis of two focal companies and their suppliers. The focal major first-tier and second-tier suppliers are mapped. Data is gathered regarding the Global Reporting Initiative (GRI) reporting of all members of the network and the relationship between focal firm GRI reporting and GRI reporting of key network members is explored. No relationship is found between the relative importance of the members in the network and their GRI reporting. Based on the mapping, the network positions or roles and importance (based on dollars of spending) of various network members are identified and discussed, along with the potential power of key network members.

5.1 Background and introduction

With many products and processes outsourced, firms are increasingly held accountable for their own actions and the environmental practices of their suppliers (Bacallan, 2000). In fact, the environmental performance of a firm consists of the environmental performance of its material, logistics and service suppliers (Mollenkopf *et al.*, 2010; Tate *et al.*, 2011). As more regulations are being introduced, more organizations are devising ways to implement, track and report on environmental impact; this includes the environmental performance of their suppliers and other network members. Organizations want to be perceived as environmentally friendly and are devising ways to influence their supply chain and network members to adopt good environmental practices.

The challenge is in developing and implementing consistent, effective environmental practices that can be assessed, implemented and managed both internally and across a global network of goods and services suppliers. Many companies self-report on environmental performance (their own) and do not consider the overall environmental performance of their supply chain or network. They often select measures that have data that is easy to collect, they report inconsistently year over year and in units of measure that are not comparable over time or between organizations. This inconsistency makes it challenging to try to influence other members of their network, largely because they need to get their own house in order before suggesting changes to others.

The Global Reporting Initiative (GRI) is a non-profit organization that works towards a sustainable global economy by providing sustainability reporting guidelines (GRI, 2015), partially alleviating some of the inconsistency inherent in reporting and standardizing measures. The GRI developed a comprehensive sustainability reporting framework that is increasingly used in organizations around the world. Data from the GRI has been used by multiple researchers to understand global and industry trends in sustainability reporting and implementation (Alonso-Almeida *et al.*, 2014). The framework enables organizations to measure and report their economic, environmental, social and governance performance on a standardized and consistent basis year-on-year.

GRI data is also linked to the Bloomberg Professional financial news and information service. Bloomberg has an integrated platform that incorporates a host of financial and other performance data related to companies around the world (Bloomberg, 2013). Even though the GRI data is published, its use in assessing actual environmental performance of an organization and its network has been limited and understanding the performance of supply chain members has not been addressed.

Being able to translate environmental metrics into a meaningful format is important in achieving positive performance in the environmental space across the network in which the firm operates. The Carbon Disclosure Project (CDP) estimates that 10% of the world's largest companies produce 73% of greenhouse gases (CDP,

2015). This exploratory research will provide recommendations about how an organization can improve the performance of its overall network. Social network structures and variables will be applied to provide insight into how organizations can influence network members in their adoption of environmental processes and environmental reporting practices to better track performance across multiple organizations.

5.2 What is the relationship between the network and the environment?

Networks represent inter-organizational relationships or "ties" between organizations. In theory, the network structure constrains and, at the same time, is shaped by a firm's actions (Granovetter, 1973; Burt, 1992). The network effect indicates that the behaviour of one party in the network, often a central party, influences the behaviour of others in the network. Current network research on the adoption of environmental practices indicates that relational and structural embeddedness influences the environmental responses of the members (Tate *et al.*, 2013). Structural embeddedness refers to the impersonal aspects of network structure whereas relational embeddedness looks at the interpersonal aspects and how information and resources are shared. Both types of embeddedness metrics have different implications on networks and are therefore relevant to discussions related to carbon and environmental performance (Gulati and Gargiulo, 1999).

The way in which a focal firm is embedded in the network determines the strength of ties between other network members and clusters. For example, a focal firm may have both direct ties to a supplier (i.e. first-tier supplier) as well as many indirect ties to suppliers (such as suppliers to the first-tier supplier, NGOs or industry associations). By understanding these network ties, the focal firm may be able to identify those network members that can help broker information related to its environmental priorities across the network. The focal firm has to reach across the entire network to achieve its intended environmental results. How can information about the environmental targets and goals of the focal firm be conveyed to organizations that are members of the network but do not have direct ties to the focal firm? How can the focal firm influence those indirectly connected organizations or clusters?

The idea behind this research is to begin to understand the relationship between the environment and the network structure. The environmental goals of the focal firm in the network have implications for the overall environmental performance of the network. Specifically, is the environmental disclosure, activities and performance of a central player (focal firm) in a network related to the environmental disclosure, activities and performance of its key network members? By understanding the relationships/ties in the network, can supply chain network structure be leveraged by the focal firm to influence the overall environmental performance of the network?

This research uses the Bloomberg Professional database to look upstream two tiers in the supply base of two organizations: IBM and Praxair. Bloomberg has a supply chain feature that specifically highlights key upstream and downstream trading partners of companies, as well as their relative financial dependencies, which may be viewed as a proxy of influence. Thus, after providing a brief literature review on network orientation and social network theory, the methodology is then presented. The data collected is used to provide an initial look at "mapping" a supply chain to understand the interrelationships in the network. Using financial dependencies in the network as a proxy for influence, we test whether there is a relationship between the importance of the firm in the focal network and its adoption of environmental sustainability practices. We also explore the specific social networks' relationships to see where influence may exist and how it might be impactful. Network orientation and the tenets of social network theory are introduced below.

5.3 Network orientation

Inter-organizational relationships are increasingly recognized for the role they play in ensuring any organization's success (Ritter, 1999). Every organization has multiple relationships with other organizations; suppliers, customers or other types of organizations such as NGOs; these relationships are often interconnected in a network of relationships that change and evolve over time (Ritter and Gemünden, 2003). Management of the network of organizations with which an organization is involved requires a certain level of competence (Ritter, 1999) as well as a basic recognition of the systemic, strategic implications of the activities involved in managing the various material and service flows across a largely distributed network (Mentzer *et al.*, 2001). Taking a broader network approach is required to manage environmental and energy issues for improved supply chain performance.

All networks consist of an interconnected set of stakeholders that are internal and external to the organization with both indirect and direct influence on the product/service flows. Stakeholders are those that have an interest, a legal or moral right, or ownership in an organization (Carroll, 1991), often with both similar and dissimilar interests. Some stakeholders may even have multiple "stakes" in an issue. For example, a company can be both a buyer and a seller to a given organization. A network orientation helps to structure multiple stakeholders as an organization attempts to implement strategic, overarching initiatives related to environmental improvements or energy conservation that require decision makers to manage the flows of products, services, finances, knowledge and information across multiple organizations over an extended time period.

A network orientation helps to better frame and manage these multiple and often conflicting "stakes" within the complex and dynamic web of people and groups that surround any organization (Madsen and Ulhøi, 2001). The behaviours, attitudes and preferences within and across the various groups of stakeholders are not static, but instead in a constant state of flux (Madsen and Ulhøi, 2001). These stakeholders have different methods of influence including both formal and informal control and communication mechanisms. While organizations typically focus on the material and information flows related to the products they manage, recognition of the influence and decisions of both internal and external stakeholders provides the foundational rationale for a network orientation. The various stakeholders can have a profound impact on the decisions that organizations make and the way they manage material and information flows, as well as the subsequent environmental consequences (Seuring, 2004). In order to improve the environmental performance of its network, an organization must make efforts to understand its network. It can achieve this understanding by first mapping its network to determine the influential members. Next, it can leverage the influential nodes to communicate its goals and objectives across the network and improve the environmental performance of the network.

5.4 Social network theory: relationships and characteristics

Social networks often exist among individuals who are boundary spanners across functions and even between or among organizations (Galaskiewicz, 2011). The idea is that actors (or participants) are embedded in networks of interconnected social relationships that offer opportunity for, and constraints on, behaviour (Brass *et al.*, 2004; Borgatti and Li, 2009). The network perspective views any system as a set of interrelated actors or nodes.

These types of social relationships are critical in explaining why inter-organizational networks are formed, disintegrate and succeed or fail (Galaskiewicz, 2011). Social network analysis focuses on different types of social relationships and how they provide context for action (Borgatti and Li, 2009). This research will focus specifically on two focal firms with very different networks: IBM and Praxair. The initial analysis includes their 12 first-tier suppliers that account for the largest percentage of their cost of goods sold, and up to 12 of the suppliers to the first tier that account for the highest cost of goods sold for each of those organizations. The way that these networks perform may be related to the strength of the ties between actors, the embeddedness of the focal firm within its network and the clusters of actors not directly linked to the focal firm (Tate *et al.*, 2013), and the brokers that represent them.

In social networks, the transfer of information and the focus on a common goal is dependent upon the trust and strength of ties that exist within the network (Borgatti and Li, 2009). Also, organizational goals and barriers encountered in achieving these goals vary depending on the project and the activity. This adds complexity and confounds the success of the network and the integration efforts. Having a common goal or understanding of key initiatives is critical for successful implementation of any initiative, especially environmental initiatives.

A significant management problem in working with networks is how to design a network that facilitates trust and therefore information sharing among network members (Borgatti and Li, 2009). One way to do this is to acculturate functionally interdependent nodes in the network into clusters and use representatives (brokers) to help develop or facilitate the relationship between the focal firm and its indirect or distant ties. In network research, clusters form among direct and indirect nodes in the network and are locally clustered and a bit distant from other members of the network (Scott, 2012; Watts and Strogatz, 1998). These clusters arise because of the embeddedness of the focal firms, they have strong ties to each other, maybe suppliers of a particular component or commodity, based on location, industry or a particular community of stakeholders with a specific mindset. There are challenges for a focal firm in reaching these clusters, creating the need for information brokers to bridge the structural hole with the focal firm.

Due to the dynamic nature of networks, new ties among actors are constantly formed and old ties are broken. So, maintaining the ties and trust is challenging. In research it is important to recognize the underlying shared expectations among those in social relationships are actually the key to developing trust and ensuring that network members deliver on their promises (Galaskiewicz, 2011). There is no single organization that controls all the resources or knowledge to bring about effective environmental or energy conservation results. The network must be managed to capture the knowledge and innovative approaches across multiple organizations and then facilitate coordinated efforts to seek outcomes that enhance network performance.

Knowledge and information sharing accompanied by learning is critical in the adaptation of any organization to its environment (Argote, 1999). Understanding the sustainability goals of the focal organization and how the focal firm, in this case IBM and Praxair, is embedded within its networks will help to understand how and if the network is organized to help meet these goals. If a supplier is not sustainable in its own right, how can a focal firm be sustainable? If a supplier has no direct connections to the focal firm, how does it learn about the practices of the focal firm? Networks provide efficient mechanisms for accessing and integrating new knowledge, especially in complex or highly volatile environments (Eisenhardt and Santos, 2000).

5.5 Methodology

The researchers selected two industries to use as initial test cases for exploring the Bloomberg data and creating networks. To date there is limited supply chain research that uses the Bloomberg data. The first industry selected was the electronics industry because it has been very visible and proactive in embracing and creating environmental standards by which it operates, such as the introduction and implementation of the Electronics Industry Citizenship Coalition (EICC) code of conduct. Most of the large electronics companies exceed existing U.S. regulations in their take-back and waste management policies, complying with or even exceeding the tougher EU take-back standards in the US operations. Companies that are leaders in their industry in terms of GRI compliance and CSR reporting were selected, as these would likely be the ones to expect their suppliers to also be CSR-conscious. The company within the electronics industry that was selected was IBM because it has been formally reporting its results through an environmental/CSR report since approximately 1991, longer than any other company in that industry and perhaps longer than any other US headquartered company. It is also consistently in the top quartile of the electronics industry since it began formally reporting to the GRI standards. IBM also has initiated environmental programmes to track the performance of their suppliers.

The other industry selected was the speciality chemical industry, due to the toxic nature of the materials it uses. The chemical industry was noted as one of the top ten most toxic polluting industries in the world in a 2012 report, behind industries we would suspect as being highly toxic such as battery recycling, lead smelting, mining and ore processing, municipal dumps and tanneries (Blacksmith Institute, 2012). Here, Praxair was selected. Praxair was also the company that had issued voluntary CSR/environmental reports for the longest time of those among the top quartile of GRI compliance in that industry in environmental performance.[1]

The Bloomberg Supply Chain Function was utilized to capture each of these companies' top 12 reported suppliers (by spending) in the category of cost of goods sold (COGS), and then their top 12 suppliers. COGS was chosen because these are generally manufactured items or materials, not services, so would be more likely to create significant emissions issues. Companies have focused most on engaging suppliers of COGS items regarding environmental issues because they generally have a larger environmental footprint (Tate *et al.*, 2009).

The data related to the amount the focal company spends with these suppliers, as well as the percentage of its total spend was collected for each recognized supplier for both of the focal firms. For each supplier, importance of the focal/buying firm in terms of percentage of the supplier's total revenue was captured. This process was followed to encompass the top cost of goods sold suppliers of each of these top twelve suppliers, dependent on the availability of the data. Then a custom template

---

1   According to Corporate Register, a repository for CSR reports.

was created to specify the data needed from Bloomberg, such as each company's market cap, country, industry sector, GRI compliance score, environmental disclosure score and more. The template was then populated with all the names of the first- and second-tier suppliers included in the network. This was the basis for the data analysis.

The tenets of social network theory helped to provide insight into the relationship between the focal firm and its network actors. The data gathered from Bloomberg helped to demonstrate the strength of relationships between actors and the clusters of relationships within the network. Financial data, such as percentage of costs and percentage of revenue accounted for between actors in the network, were used to establish a proxy of dependence in relationships. This approach is not perfect, in that Bloomberg does not have data on all companies, nor does it necessarily have complete data on each of the suppliers. However, this was the most complete data source of this type available. UCInet version 6.501 was used to create the network relationships and begin the data analysis.

5.6 The networks

The networks for both IBM and Praxair are presented below (Figs. 5.1 and 5.2). These figures show the basic relationship between the network members based on the percentage of cost of goods sold between the network members. The darker, thicker lines (also referred to as links) are indicative of the amount that the buying firm in each case spends with the supplier. Visually inspecting the figures shows that these two networks vary significantly in number of connections, strength of the connections and other leading indicators. Visually assessing the two networks shows that IBM has a much denser network than Praxair. IBM looks like a ball of rubber bands twisted together whereas Praxair has much more "space" between its network members. Keep in mind that both IBM and Praxair are leaders in their industry in terms of environmental reporting, practices and performance.

IBM has a very highly integrated and dense network where some suppliers are more embedded within the network than IBM (for example, Hon Hai and Samsung). The embeddedness of these suppliers influences the power between IBM and its other network members, especially those network members without direct connections to IBM. Also, IBM has been working with suppliers to help promote environmental sustainability since the early days of their reporting (tight compliance auditing for hazardous materials, suppliers) and have established environmental reporting metrics for its key suppliers.

Praxair's more distributed network is also interesting. The Praxair focal network consists of companies from many different industries supplying products and services. IBM is in a much more "focused" industry where many participants are primarily members of the electronics industry and are thus aligned on certain environmental metrics and reporting due to the EICC. Praxair's network appears to be made up of a number of independent clusters that each have their own centralized/embedded "core". These core members are those with the connections to others in the network. Also it appears that the clusters form because of location or because of commonality of purpose. It is interesting to note that IBM and Praxair share Samsung as an influential member in their individual networks.

5.6.1 Bonacich power

Because the network of the focal firm is the object of study, we would assume that this player would have the most power within its own network. Centrality is a common measure of power in network theory; the more well-connected the network, the higher the closeness centrality. Bonacich noted that closeness centrality is not enough to create power. While it may appear somewhat counterintuitive, he proposed that connections to others that are not well connected may make one powerful because these less connected actors become dependent on you. Well-connected actors are not reliant on you (Hanneman and Riddle, 2005).

Each of these types of Bonacich power has different implications. To make this analysis more interesting, each of the network ties was weighted according to the percentage of its revenue for which the connecting network player accounts. First, considering connections with lesser connected players as a source of power, weighted by the percentage of its total revenue accounted for by that company, IBM has some interesting results (Table 5.1). Hon Hai Precision (8.103) has significantly more power with those less well connected in the first two tiers of the supply network than does IBM (4.156).[2]

---

2   Bonacich recommends using a beta of -0.5 to note that those with more connections provide less power; when looking at centrality, the beta used is 0.

Figure 5.1 IBM network: top 12 COGS suppliers with second tier

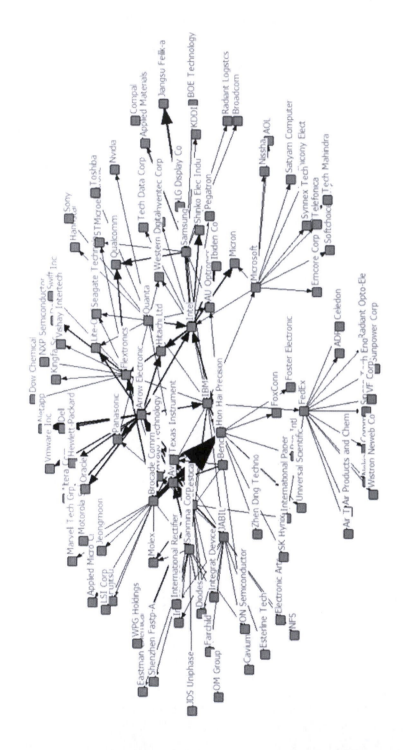

Figure 5.2 Praxair top 12 COGS suppliers with second tier

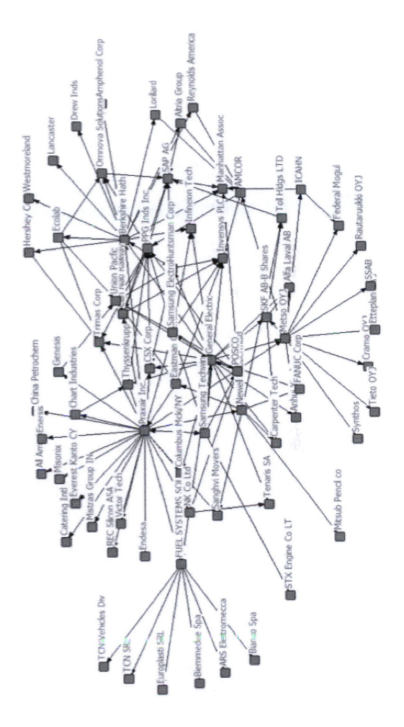

Table 5.1 IBM network revenue adjusted Bonacich power derived from
dependency of network neighbours

Company	Power	Normalized
Arrow Electronic	68.071	1.534
Brocade Communication	-26.711	-0.602
Celestica	-65.256	-1.470
FedEx	111.940	2.522
Flextronics	-123.537	-2.783
Hon Hai Precision	359.678	8.103
IBM	184.485	4.156
Intel	-27.822	-0.627
JABIL	17.990	0.405
Microsoft	7.833	.0176
Quanta	64.617	1.456
Samsung	26.964	0.607
Sanmina Corp.	4.270	0.096

Figure 5.3 shows Hon Hai's distinctive ego sub-network, illustrating its unique and powerful connections. It has a number of connections to network members that are not directly connected to IBM.

Figure 5.3 Hon Hai revenue Ego network

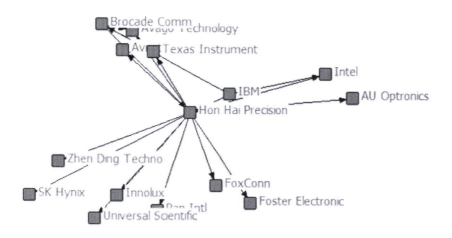

Note: Hon Hai and Foxconn merged in 2014 making this subnetwork even more important.

Because of Praxair's more distributed network, numerous actors in the network have better connections, or more power, with others in the network. Praxair's (.400) reach across the network is rather limited. Table 5.2 shows the Bonacich power for players in Praxair's network.

Table 5.2 Praxair network revenue adjusted Bonacich power derived from dependency of network neighbours

Company	Power	Normalized
Berkshire Hathaway	128.033	8.087
Fuel Systems Solutions	19.810	1.251
General Electric	-6.223	-0.393
ICAHN	31.830	2.011
Metso OYJ	15.391	0.972
Newell Rubbermaid	10.193	0.644
Praxair, Inc.	6.340	0.400
Samsung Electro-Mechanics	7.118	0.450
SKF AB-B Shares	3.086	0.195

Returning to IBM's network, Table 5.3, which considers centrality of the players, weighted by the percentage of its total revenue accounted for by the company listed in the table, provides different results associated with power. Here we see that Samsung clearly dominates as the key player in terms of its central position as a provider of revenue to those in the network, dominating all other players by more than ten-fold. From a network standpoint, IBM should be very aware of the important influence that Samsung could have on its network.

Table 5.3 IBM network Bonacich power derived from network centrality

Company	Centrality	Normalized
Flextronics	122.127	.030
Arrow Electronic	142.796	.035
Celestica	29.298	.007
FedEx	111.940	.027
Hon Hai Precision	341.112	.083
IBM	1082.124	.264
Intel	155.915	.038

Company	Centrality	Normalized
Quanta	57.202	.014
Samsung	42058.023	10.243

Likewise, the power structure in Praxair's network changes when comparing power derived from dependence to power derived from centrality (Table 5.4). General Electric, POSCO and Samsung are much more central in the network than Praxair. They therefore have a great potential influence on the network. This means that Praxair should consider developing strong relationships aligned around its environmental practices with these other players in order to facilitate diffusion of its goals across the network.

Table 5.4 Praxair network revenue adjusted Bonacich power derived from network centrality

Company	Power	Normalized
Berkshire Hathaway	7,736.545	3.341
General Electric	9,676.276	4.178
Huntsman Corp.	1,596.395	0.689
POSCO	10,955.573	4.731
PPG Inds. Inc.	393.773	0.170
Praxair, Inc.	4,756.174	2.054
Samsung Electro-Mechanics	9,082.454	3.922
Samsung Techwin	2,670.688	1.153
Union Pacific	1,636.665	0.707

5.6.2 Environmental sustainability correlation in the networks

This section explores the answer to the first research question: Are the environmental disclosure, activities and performance of a central player (focal firm) in a network related to the environmental disclosure, activities and performance of its key network members?

To answer this question, a multiple regression analysis on network environmental performance data was run, treating the GRI environmental reporting score as the dependent variable. Independent variables tested included revenue derived from the focal firm, the market cap of the supplier, the number of firms in the network with whom the firm had a revenue relationship and the amount of revenue derived from firms within the network. The results were very poorly-fitting models, whether all the variables were loaded or whether they were brought in one at a time. It is difficult to explain why these models do not have any degree of reliability in their current form. While the data was normalized, so market cap data was scaled into four categories rather than left unbounded, approximately two-thirds of the observations fell out of the analysis due to either lack-of-fit or pure error. While these results were disappointing, it does not mean that the network data is not interesting or useful. The next section uses this network data to explore more specifically how members of networks can impact linkages with other network members.

5.6.3 Brokerage relationships

The importance of linkages between a focal firm and indirectly connected resources (actors or sub-groups of actors) is illustrated by the well-known concept of structural holes (Burt, 1992, 2002). These "holes" are bridged by actors that facilitate the exchange of information between the focal firm and indirectly connected actors and sub-groups. By identifying these distant or disconnected actors, a focal firm can develop relationships with the actors to facilitate the flow of environmental goals, practices and processes. Without these actors, the focal firm is restricted to only those with which it has a direct (and often strong) tie. The embeddedness of the focal firm determines the brokering relationships.

5.6.4 Bridging using brokers

Depending on the linkages of the members of the sub-group to other network members, distinct subcultures within the network can form (Wellman, 1983). The challenge for the focal firm in managing environmental initiatives is that if these subcultures do not have access to, or even share, the values of the focal firm, the reach of the focal firm is restricted. Depending on the embeddedness of the focal firm and the strength of ties between the clusters and the focal firm, these subcultures may in fact impede or misdirect the values of the focal firm and instead focus on prioritizing their own potentially conflicting goals (Fernandez and Gould, 1989).

Brokers are actors that simultaneously send and receive resources from other parts of the network in which they are embedded. They form a medium of exchange within the network of the focal firm that helps provide better access for the focal firm to other parts of the network (Burt, 1992; Granovetter, 1973). Fernandez and Gould (1989) called these "brokerage exchanges". Their work classified these exchanges according to the group membership of the actors involved and aligns with the work of Granovetter (1973) and Burt (1992) that shows that information flows within sub-groups are differentiated from information flows between sub-groups of a network. The subgroups are defined by dense, cohesive relationships that promote alignment of values (Belso-Martínez et al., 2015). The embedded focal firm needs to be able to access these indirect clusters to transfer information and resources to which it does not have direct access.

There are specific brokerage roles that provide a bridge for the focal firm to exchange information and resources given the structure of the network and the clustering of sub-groups. These groups have been defined and described in previous literature and exist because of the membership (ties) of the three parties in an exchange (Fernandez and Gould, 1989). The brokerage exchange consists of a triad of members A, B and C. The assumption made is that exchange actor A is the focal firm exchanging information with a targeted actor (or set of actors) C. Actor B is the broker who is the facilitator of this exchange between A and C.

Depending on the membership within the sub-groups or clusters that develop because of the embeddedness of the focal firm within the network, there are five possible configurations of brokerage exchanges (Table 5.5). Group membership can tell us a great deal about the relationships between parties in an exchange, as actors in the same sub-group are characterized by more common connections in localized dense and cohesive relationships. The consultant, representative and liaison roles have the greatest boundary, spanning influences in that they are externally facing, thus feed information out to other groups. Gatekeepers control access to one or more groups, while coordinators are important within groups. Also it is much easier for the focal firm to share its goals and objectives when it is in the same group (A is with C).

Table 5.5 Definitions of brokerage exchange types
Source: Miemcyzk *et al.* (2016); Fernandez *et al.* (1989)

	Coordinator	Consultant	Gatekeeper	Representative	Liaison
Social network definition	All three members are from the same sub-group	The brokering agent (B) is brokering an exchange between two members of the same sub-group in which it is not a member	A is in a different sub-group than B and C, and B is controlling access to the knowledge of its sub-group	A and B are in the same sub-group and B is representing this group to C's sub-group	All three actors are in different sub-groups and B is brokering a relationship between the two other sub-groups of which it is not a part

The brokerage analysis run within UCINet split the IBM network into eight groups (Table 5.5). Many of these influential organizations also are in the top 10% of either Bonacich centrality or dependency measures of power. Benchmark is the only organization broker that does not have power within IBM's very dense network. Working with these brokers is key to getting access to and from the clustered nodes and the focal firm. How these brokers are utilized is important to the diffusion of practices. For example some very powerful players in the IBM network are Microsoft, Hon Hai, Samsung and Intel. Each of these organizations plays a role as a consultant. In this case the broker is an independent party to a within-group exchange of information and resources. This is a case where the focal firm can easily share its policies, codes and practices with other members of its network that are not directly but indirectly connected.

Group #3 might have a few challenges in sharing and implementing the environmental practices of the focal firm. In this case A is separate from C and therefore the broker is acting in the capacity of representative or gatekeeper. These are the most challenging situations that the focal firm can be in when trying to diffuse its environmental objectives. These subgroups may in fact have differing policies, procedures, cultures and interests. Another thing that is interesting to consider is whether or not an organization can access subcultures where there are no influential brokers. Do they need to? Or do they need to understand the connections that are there and see if they can be developed?

Table 5.6 IBM clusters and brokers

Group	Brokers	Role #1	Role #2
Group #1	No influential brokers		
Group #2	No influential brokers		
Group #3	Arrow	Representative	
	Brocade	Gatekeeper	Liaison
	Celestica	Gatekeeper	Liaison
	Jabil	Gatekeeper	
	Benchmark	Gatekeeper	Liaison
	Flextronics	Consultant	Gatekeeper
	Sanmina	Consultant	Gatekeeper
	FedEx	Gatekeeper	Liaison
Group #4	No influential brokers		
Group #5	Microsoft	Consultant	Liaison
	Hon Hai	Consultant	Liaison
Group #6	IBM	Consultant	Liaison
	Quanta	Representative	
Group #7	Samsung	Consultant	Liaison
Group #8	Intel	Consultant	Liaison

Praxair and its brokers paint a very different picture (Table 5.7). This highly distributed network requires many different types of brokers within each of the eight clusters in order to facilitate information exchange. It appears that there are no strong industry clusters here (as is the case with IBM) so members are not as tightly clustered. One thing to consider is looking towards those that are from different industries that are more progressive in environmental practices and have implemented measurement and reporting guidelines (like Samsung). If the ties between Samsung and Praxair are strengthened along environmental sustainability lines, there may be some trickle down effect from the more dense networks with higher standards. Recognition of network members and relationships can help an organization begin to make decisions and potentially influence its own network for the best environmental outcomes.

Table 5.7 Praxair and brokers

Group	Brokers	Role #1	Role #2	Role #3
Group #1	Reynolds	Consultant		
	Samsung	Coordinator	Representative	
	Lorillard	Consultant		
	Genesis	Representative		
	Hershey	Consultant		
	Omnova	Liaison		
	General Electric	Coordinator	Gatekeeper	Representative
	Toll	Consultant		
	Praxair	Coordinator	Representative	
	Ichan	Representative		
	Samsung	Coordinator	Representative	
	ThyssenKrupp	Coordinator	Gatekeeper	Representative
Group #2	Metso	Consultant	Liaison	
	PPG	Consultant	Liaison	
Group #3	Canadian National Railway	Gatekeeper	Liaison	
	SAP	Representative	Liaison	
	Newell	Gatekeeper	Consultant	Liaison
	Posco	Consultant	Liaison	
	Chart	Consultant		

Group	Brokers	Role #1	Role #2	Role #3
Group #4	Altria	Consultant	Liaison	
	SKF	Consultant	Liaison	
Group #5	Berkshire Hathaway	Gatekeeper	Consultant	Liaison
	Amcor	Liaison		
	Union Pacific	Consultant	Liaison	
Group #6	NK	Consultant		
	Eastman	Liaison		
	Huntsman	Consultant	Liaison	
	Fuel Systems	Gatekeeper	Liaison	
Group #7	Ecolab	Consultant		
Group #8	No influential brokers			

Identifying these different broker roles may help focal firms make decisions on how and when to adapt its connections, potentially strengthening ties with some network members, incorporating brokers to bridge structural holes and hence help innovate or "loosen" ties with brokers/sub-groups that are influencing the outcomes.

5.7 Implications and conclusions

There are both practical and theoretical implications in considering network impacts on environmental sustainability adoption and reporting.

5.7.1 Implications for research and theory

We began the research with the following questions: First, are the environmental disclosure, activities and performance of a central player (focal firm) in a network related to the environmental disclosure, activities and performance of its key network members? Second, by understanding the relationships/ties in the network, can supply chain network structure be leveraged by the focal firm to influence the overall environmental performance of the network?

In response to the first research question, we were not able to establish relationship with the available data. However, we believe it is worth investigating this linkage in other ways, perhaps directly, through surveys and interviews. For example, there is some preliminary evidence from interview data that shippers (buyers of transportation services) strongly influence their carriers (suppliers of transportation services) to improve their environmental performance and reporting (Ellram and Golicic, 2015). Does this occur elsewhere and is membership in a voluntary environmental partnership influential in the spread of such behaviours, as it appeared in the aforementioned study?

In response to the second research question, by understanding the relationships/ties in the network, can supply chain network structure be leveraged by the focal firm to influence the overall environmental performance of the network? This research contributes to a further theoretical development and understanding of network theory in the supply chain. Using empirical data from real networks, this study identifies the potential use of brokers to facilitate information and resource exchange. Being able to understand who the powerful brokers are, what part of the network they reach and how a focal firm or other network member might work with them so that they can facilitate information exchange is critical. From a research perspective, this paper also raises the level of awareness of the data available in this rich Bloomberg Professional database as a source of information for future research.

5.7.2 Implications for practice

From a practical standpoint, the results have application for practising managers in supply chain management. First, by understanding their network members and the relationships that these members have with other members in their supply chain, managers can better understand who the key influencers in the network are likely to be and how they can influence, or be influenced by, the behaviour of other network members. Identifying the network and identifying the powerful players in the network is a first step. The focal firm should examine its relationship with these powerful players and recognize the opportunity that engaging such key players in environmentally responsible activities may be an excellent way to influence many other suppliers in their supply chain. The focal firm can also benefit from identifying the brokers and defining the type of role that these brokers can play in helping them on their path to environmental improvements. Identifying others within the network that are attached to highly performing industries or networks may also bring significant improvement opportunities to the network. These connected managers may be gatekeepers or liaisons to other networks that may be a resource to understand how other industries and companies improve their own environmental performance and reporting. Another key insight for managers is that not all networks are created equally or are able to be managed in the same way. Managers must adapt their own approaches based on their network structure and the power that they hold within their network.

5.7.3 Future research opportunities

Utilizing networks to build, facilitate or adapt sustainability programmes and initiatives is key to future success. Sustainability issues have gone beyond being an issue for individual companies and instead have become a network issue that can only be improved with help from many of the members of the network. The ideas in this research should be expanded to go beyond simply environmental practices to embrace corporate social responsibility, including social and financial issues. From a diffusion of innovation standpoint, it will be interesting to see if over time focal firms can get others in the network to align with their environmental and other triple bottom line goals, especially if there are others with greater power (as in more or unique connections) that can help implement change. Identifying the brokers and defining the type of relationship they represent can be an important first step for organizations seeking environmental improvements and can be a rich area of study. Growing emphasis may be placed on making environmental sustainability and other aspects of sustainability an essential supplier selection factor for powerful nodes in the network if focal firms recognize the important role of these players in facilitating supply chain environmental improvement. Companies may find that relationships within the network need to change or be replaced to become more effective.

This research only looked at two tiers of suppliers in the network of IBM and Praxair. Identifying additional network members such as NGOs, government organizations and potentially even customers may create a model with a better explanatory value in linking network characteristics to environmental performance of supply chains. Further, isolating the network to look at key sources of pollution and whether suppliers that contribute to this pollution have more or less closely aligned environmental sustainability performance and reporting could also provide insight into supply chain network configuration and opportunities for improvement.

References

Alonso Almeida, M., Llach, J., & Marimon, F. (2014). A closer look at the "Global Reporting Initiative" sustainability reporting as a tool to implement environmental and social policies: A worldwide sector analysis. *Corporate Social Responsibility and Environmental Management*, 21(6), 318-335.

Argote, L. (1999). *Organizational Learning: Creating, Retaining, and Transferring Knowledge*. New York: Kluwer Academic Publishers.

Bacallan, J.J. (2000). Greening the supply chain. *Business and Environment*, 6(5), 11-12.

Belso-Martínez, J.A., Molina-Morales, F.X., & Martínez-Cháfer, L. (2015). Contributions of brokerage roles to firms' innovation in a confectionery cluster. *Technology Analysis & Strategic Management*, 27(9), 1,012-1,030.

Blacksmith Institute (2012). The World's Top Ten Toxic Pollution Problems 2012. Retrieved from http://www.worstpolluted.org/2012-report.html (20 July 2015)

Bloomberg (2013). Start Putting Knowledge Into Action. Retrieved from http://www.bloomberg.com/professional/ (29 September 2013)

Borgatti, S.P., & Li, X. (2009). On social network analysis in a supply chain context*. *Journal of Supply Chain Management*, 45(2), 5-22.

Brass, D.J., Galaskiewicz, V., Greve, H., & Tsai, W. (2004). Taking stock of networks and organizations: A multilevel perspective. *Academy of Management Journal*, 47(6), 795-817.

Burt, R. (1992). *Structural Holes: The Social Structure of Competition*. Cambridge: Harvard.

Carbon Disclosure Project (2015). Driving Sustainable Economies. Retrieved from https://http://www.cdproject.net/en-US/Pages/HomePage.aspx (September 26, 2015)

Carroll, A.B. (1991). The pyramid of corporate social responsibility: Toward the moral management of organizational stakeholders. *Business Horizons*, 34(4), 39-48.

Eisenhardt, K., & Santos, F. (2000). Knowledge-based view: A new theory of strategy? In A. Pettigrew, H. Thomas, & R. Whittington, *Handbook of Strategy and Management*. London: Sage Publications.

Ellram, L.M., & Golicic, S.L. (2015). Adopting Environmental Transportation Practices. *Transportation Journal*, 54(1), 55-88.

Fernandez, R.M., & Gould, R.V. (1989). Formal approach to brokerage. *Sociological Methodology*, 19, 89-126.

Galaskiewicz, J. (2011). Studying supply chains from a social network perspective. *Journal of Supply Chain Management*, 47(1), 4-8.

Global Reporting Institute (GRI) (2015). What is the GRI? Retrieved from https://http://www.globalreporting.org/information/about-gri/what-is-GRI/Pages/default.aspx (26 September 2015)

Granovetter, M.S. (1973). The strength of weak ties. *American Journal of Sociology*, 78(6), 1,360-1,380.

Gulati, R., & Gargiulo, M. (1999). Where do interorganizational networks come from? *American Journal of Sociology*, 104(5), 1,439-1,493.

Hanneman, R.A., & Riddle, M. (2005). Introduction to Social Network Methods. Riverside, CA: University of California. Retrieved from http://faculty.ucr.edu/~hanneman/nettext/C1_Social_Network_Data.html#toc (11 February 2014)

Madsen, H., & Ulhøi, J. (2001). Integrating environmental and stakeholder management. *Business Strategy and the Environment*, 10(2), 77-88.

Mentzer, J.T., Dewitt, W., Keebler, J.S., Min, S., Nix, N., Smith, C., & Zacharia, Z. (2001). Defining supply chain management. *Journal of Business Logistics*, 22(2), 1-25.

Miemczyk, J., Saunders, L., Tate W.L., & Zsidisin G. (2016), The influence of network exchange brokers on the triple bottom line of sustainable supply networks. Working Paper.

Mollenkopf, D., Stolze, H., Tate, W.L., & Ueltschy, M. (2010). Green, lean, and global supply chains. *International Journal of Physical Distribution & Logistics Management*, 40(1-2), 14-41.

Ritter, T. (1999). The networking company: Antecedents for coping with relationships and networks effectively. *Industrial Marketing Management*, 28, 467-479.

Ritter, T., & Gemünden, H.G. (2003). Interorganizational relationships and networks: An overview. *Journal of Business Research*, 56(9), 691-697.

Scott, J. (2012). *Social Network Analysis*. New York: Sage.

Seuring, S. (2004). Integrated chain management and supply chain management: Comparative analysis and illustrative cases. *Journal of Cleaner Production*, 12(8-10), 1,059-1,071.

Tate, W.L., Dooley, K., & Ellram L. (2011). Transaction cost and institutional drivers of supplier adoption of environmental practices. *Journal of Business Logistics*, 32(1), 6-16.

Tate, W.L., Ellram, L., & Golgeci, I. (2013). Diffusion of environmental business practices: A network approach. *Journal of Purchasing and Supply Management*, 19(4), 264-275.

Tate, W.L., Ellram, L. & Dooley, K. (2009). Corporate social responsibility reports: A thematic analysis related to supply chain management. *Journal of Supply Chain Management*, 46(1), 19-44.

Watts, D.J., & Strogatz, S.H. (1998). Collective dynamics of "small world" networks. *Nature*, 393(6684), 440-442.

Wellman, B. (1983). Network analysis: Some basic principles. *Sociological theory*, 1(1), 155-200.

Lisa M. Ellram, PhD, CPM., CMA, Scor-S is the Rees Distinguished Professor of supply chain management in the department of management at the Farmer School of Business, Miami University in Oxford, Ohio, where she teaches logistics and supply chain management at undergraduate and graduate level.

Her primary areas of research interest include: sustainable purchasing, transportation and supply chain management; services purchasing and supply chain management; offshoring and outsourcing; and supply chain cost management. She has published in numerous top journals spanning a variety of disciplines and including scholarly and managerially relevant research. She is co-author of six books, the most recent entitled, *Logistics Management: Enhancing Competitiveness and Customer Value*, published by MyEducator.com. She currently serves as the Co-Editor in Chief for the *Journal of Supply Chain Management*.

Wendy L. Tate, PhD (Arizona State University, 2006) is an Associate Professor of supply chain management department of marketing and supply chain management at the University of Tennessee. She teaches undergraduate, MBA and PhD students strategic sourcing and manufacturing and service operations and has an interest in the financial impacts of business decisions across the supply chain.

6

Integrating sustainability reporting into global supply chains in Asia and the Pacific

Masato Abe and Michelle Chee[1]

United Nations Economic and Social Commission for Asia and the Pacific (ESCAP), Thailand

This chapter investigates how both governments and businesses in Asia and the Pacific can enhance sustainability within global supply chains (GSCs), in particular through the development and promotion of sustainability (or CSR) reporting. Presently sustainability reporting, whilst gaining popularity among the global business community, has not been fully integrated into GSCs where small and medium-sized enterprises (SMEs) play an important role. This chapter specifically examines how sustainability reporting can contribute to enhance the transparency of GSCs whose governance structure is typically complicated with a large variety of players and which are inherently less transparent. For these purposes, 121 sustainability reporting initiatives at both global and regional levels are examined to develop and propose a sustainable GSC reporting framework in Asia and the Pacific. Before concluding, recommendations are provided for enabling regulatory and policy frameworks in order to implement sustainability reporting within GSCs in cooperation with businesses.

1 The authors appreciate substantive comments made by Lydia Bals, Isabel Buitrago Franco, Wendy Tate, Michael Williamson and anonymous reviewers to this chapter. The opinions expressed in this chapter are those of the authors and do not necessarily reflect the views of the United Nations.

6.1 Introduction

Businesses are beginning to realize the significant impacts their operations make not only within their organization but on their surrounding environment and local communities, affecting a variety of issues such as climate change, pollution, corruption and labour and human rights. Increasing demands from governments, regulators, customers and other stakeholders are encouraging businesses to go beyond the minimum requirements of environmental and social compliance and reporting to be more proactive in making their operations more sustainable including those activities concerning suppliers and distributors. The term describing these efforts is called sustainable development which is most commonly defined as "development that meets the needs of the present without compromising the ability of future generations to meet their own needs" (WCED, 1987, p. 41).

Sustainability reporting has been an important tool for capturing and communicating the environmental and social efforts organizations have undertaken for sustainable development so that their stakeholders can make informed judgments and decisions (Donaldson and Davis, 1991; Eisenhardt, 1989). Sustainability reporting is a natural evolutionary step in the operationalization of sustainability initiatives and, in its essence, represents a managerial effort to measure, monitor and evaluate a company's sustainability performance. It is therefore important that sustainability reports are transparent as they are the vehicle for communication between businesses and their stakeholders. The definition by the International Organization for Standardization (ISO) for transparency is described as "openness about decisions and activities that affect society, the economy and the environment, and willingness to communicate these in a clear, accurate, timely, honest and complete manner" (ISO, 2010). In recent years sustainability reporting has raised considerable interests in both business and academic communities (Abe and Ruanglikhitkul, 2013).

With the exponential increase of global trade over the past decade, about 60% or $20 trillion is attributed to the intermediate production of goods and services (UNCTAD, 2013, p. 122). This reflects the rapid expansion of global supply chains (GSCs), also known as global value chains,[2] comprised of "sequential chains or complex networks ... which may be global, regional or span only two countries" according to the United Nations Conference on Trade and Development (UNCTAD, 2013, p. 122). The development of GSCs has been particularly observed in a variety of industrial sectors in Asia and the Pacific,[3] such as the apparel/garments,

---

2 In many instances both terms are understood to have the same meaning.
3 The Asia–Pacific region comprises 53 members and nine associate members of the United Nations Economic and Social Commission for Asia and the Pacific (ESCAP) plus Taiwan Province of China, which is a non-UN member. ESCAP whose headquarters is located in Bangkok, Thailand, is the regional development arm of the United Nations and serves as the main economic and social development centre for the United Nations in Asia and the Pacific. Its member countries are well diversified including such countries as developed,

automobile, electronics, food and high-tech industries (Forbes, 2015). Presently nearly 50% of world trade and transportation through GSCs are conducted in the region (ESCAP, 2015).

Outsourcing and offshoring, which are the crucial business strategies of GSCs, also represent one of the challenges to sustainability practices. As a result of aggressive outsourcing and offshoring activities, supply chains have been extended around the globe (Christopher, 2011). Unlike a local or national supply chain, a GSC involves dealing with suppliers and customers in different locations and countries and transporting large amounts of supplies across long distances where different regulatory frameworks are enforced. At the same time, the structure of supply chains has become more complex, with more individual production facilities and distribution links involved across borders, which increases the difficulty to monitor and evaluate each GSC partners' sustainability practices. Another factor contributing to the overall challenge of transparency of reporting in GSCs is small and medium-sized enterprises (SMEs), which are inherent in most supply chains that usually lack the knowledge, financial and human capital capacity to report on their sustainability performance. Although large transnational companies typically control GSCs, local businesses in developing countries consisting of a number of SMEs also participate in GSCs and provide goods and services based on their expertise as suppliers, distributors and business service providers (ESCAP, 2007). Consequently, these reasons combined make it more difficult for individual or even lead firms to assess sustainability performance of the entire supply chain.

With the emergence of larger and more complex GSCs, maintaining transparency in sustainability reports is becoming increasingly difficult. In response to this some international and national sustainability reporting frameworks such as the Global Reporting Initiative's G4 Sustainability Reporting Guidelines (GRI, 2013)[4] and China's Shanghai Municipal Local Standards on Corporate Social Responsibility (Shanghai Bureau of Quality and Technical Supervision, 2008) have started incorporating reporting guidelines that aim to address sustainability performance in supply chains, but still with limited coverage and depth.

The research objective of this chapter is to examine how various sustainability reporting frameworks, either applicable internationally or developed specifically for a nation in Asia and the Pacific, enhance the level of transparency throughout GSCs. We begin by describing the development of sustainability reporting and its current landscape, followed by an explanation of why GSCs matter and why they should be covered through sustainability reporting. We then review 121 sustainability reporting frameworks at the global and national levels to determine their typologies and how effective they are in terms of their guidelines to make GSCs more transparent. After analysing the strengths, weaknesses and gaps we will

OECD member, least developed, middle income, landlocked and small islands. Find detailed ESCAP memberships at http://www.unescap.org/about/member-states.

4   Over 90% of the world's largest 250 corporations use the GRI Guidelines and there are thousands of reporting firms in over 90 countries.

finally offer policy recommendations on how these frameworks can be improved overall to enhance transparency throughout supply chains.

6.2 Development of sustainability reporting

Sustainability reporting is a tool for organizations and businesses to communicate to their stakeholders through "the practice of measuring, disclosing, and being accountable for organizational performance while working towards the goal of sustainable development" (GRI, 2006, p. 3). There are numerous names and variations of sustainability reporting frameworks that exist, some of which go by the name of triple bottom line (TBL or 3BL) (Elkington, 1998) reporting, integrated reporting, corporate social responsibility (CSR) reporting and environmental, social and governance (ESG) disclosure along the three environmental, social and economic dimensions. For simplicity, we will use the term sustainability reporting to refer to all these types and variations. The three main dimensions to sustainability reporting frameworks include environmental, social and economic matters that span from climate change and endangerment of species (environmental) to child labour and employment discrimination (social) and value creation in the forms of increased standards of living and growth of employment opportunities (economic).

The roots of sustainability reporting can be traced back to the 1940s when social audit and non-financial reporting practices first arose (Abe and Ruanglikhitkul, 2013). Traditionally, sustainability reporting was presented in brief, narrative form and released along with company financial statements or annual reports, and was not released as separate reports unlike mainstream practice today.[5] Major environmental catastrophes in the Western world in the 1960s and 1970s triggered environmental concern that led to the first mandatory environmental reporting policy of the US Emergency Planning and Community Right-To-Know Act in 1986 (Soderstrom, 2013). The Cadbury Report (Committee on the Financial Aspects of Corporate Governance, 1992) also embraced accountability which improves the effectiveness of corporations as a central enabler of sustainable reporting. Up until today sustainability reporting has evolved towards a more integrated approach incorporating both environmental and social issues with businesses' traditional financial (or economic) disclosure which is typically regulated by the authorities. This type of sustainability reporting is specifically known as TBL or integrated reporting.

A number of sustainability reporting frameworks and initiatives have emerged such as the Guidelines for Multinational Enterprises of the Organisation for

---

5 Annual reports that provide a snapshot in time of the practices and initiatives put in place by an enterprise are a communication tool that may not drive enterprises to improve their sustainability practices.

Economic Co-operation and Development (OECD, 2011) as well as the Sustainability Reporting Guidelines by the Global Reporting Institute (GRI, 2013), which are now two of the most widely adopted sustainability reporting guidelines in the world. With the shift of sustainability reporting towards mainstream practice in developed and developing countries, it seems that sustainability reporting will only become more integrated into other forms of reporting; joining financial reporting, income tax reporting, regulatory reporting and internal reporting (Tschopp and Huefner, 2015).

The majority of sustainability reporting frameworks require disclosures of single or a combination of environmental, social and economic dimension(s) (cf. Freidman, 1970). An example of a mandatory single dimension sustainability reporting requirement for all business entities exists in India (Ministry of Environment and Forests of India, 1986). This can be contrasted with global voluntary initiatives such as the United Nation's Global Compact Communication on Progress programme which covers reporting across two dimensions that are environmental and social (UNGC, 2012). Furthermore, TBL and integrated reporting frameworks combine all three dimensions of environmental, social and economic dimensions in a single form to determine the organization's overall net performance.

In relation to this, coverage of the three dimensions among sustainability reporting frameworks can be separated into four categories as outlined below:

- **Environmental dimension**: includes targets and usage of energy and natural resources, greenhouse gas emissions, biodiversity, effluents and waste management and disposal and recycling. Most sustainability reporting frameworks that only cover the environmental dimension are set by industry regulators or governments who target companies in polluting industries or natural resources, such as the Mandatory GHG Emissions Reporting by Japan (Institute for Industrial Productivity, 2005)

- **Social dimension**: includes human rights and labour subcategories which specifically cover cultural diversity and equal opportunity, employment conditions, occupational health and safety, child labour, anticorruption and bribery among other related aspects. An example of a sustainability reporting framework containing only the social dimension is the Tripartite Declaration of Principles concerning Multinational Enterprises and Social Policy by the International Labour Organization (ILO, 2006)

- **Environmental and social dimensions**: sustainability reporting frameworks that fall under this category contain both environmental and social dimensions. An example of this includes the International Finance Corporation (IFC) Sustainability Framework (IFC, State Securities Commission of Vietnam and Association of Chartered Certified Accountants, 2013), and

- **Environmental, social and economic dimensions**: incorporates the environmental and social performance of a company with its economic performance, offering a holistic assessment of the company's overall net performance in its operations with all three dimensions taken into account. Such sustainability reporting frameworks include International Integrated Reporting Guidelines by the International Integrated Reporting Committee (IIRC, 2013) and the Connected Reporting Framework by the Accounting for Sustainability Project (Prince's Accounting for Sustainability Project, 2009).

Each sustainability reporting framework is associated with its own data collection method, reporting style and format. While some mandatory national laws require companies to provide direct responses to questions along with quantitative data and evidence, other global reporting initiatives offer guidelines for firms to be able to create their own sustainability reports, choosing what information and evidence to include and also exclude. In addition to these, the Dow Jones Sustainability Index (DJSI), a global sustainability index launched in 1999, relies on the top-listed public companies to complete a questionnaire that is used to generate an overall sustainability score and rank (RobecoSAM, 2014). Although the FTSE-4Good Index family launched by the FTSE Group in 2011 competes with DJSI as a global index, their approach to data collection relies on information that is publically available to generate a sustainability score to determine a sustainability ranking (FTSE, 2014).

Regardless of the type of sustainability reporting frameworks, reporting has been typically focused on communicating information only relevant to the reporting firm itself. However, sustainability activities and performance of their supply chains, which comprise of a number and variety of business players, have been largely excluded up until recent times.

6.3 Sustainability needs to expand from individual firms to GSCs

The exponential growth in outsourcing and offshoring over the past decades means that sustainability reporting must expand to include not only the individual company's sustainability efforts and performance but also their GSCs in order to be fully transparent in their entire, often cross-border, operations. The OECD describes GSCs as the intermediary cross-border segment of international production, trade and investments where the different stages of the production process are located across different countries (OECD, 2013). GSCs in Asia and the Pacific are of particular significance due to the region's increasing role in world trade; for example, two thirds of the world's container traffic passes through the region (ISL World Seaborne Container Trade and Port Traffic, 2010). In 2013, nearly one half of GSC-related trades of final products and intermediate goods to the world came from the region (ESCAP, 2015).[6]

The structures of GSCs are broadly comprised of suppliers and customers categorized into different tiers located in different geographical locations or countries. Assuming a simplified GSC with seven chain members, the production begins with raw materials or initial suppliers of goods or services that are categorized into tier-3 suppliers, which provide these goods or services to tier-2 suppliers (see Fig. 6.1). Parties at the tier-2 level are often known as subcontractors, where the products or services from subcontractors flow onto tier-1 suppliers, often known as contractors, who directly provide products or services to the lead firm depicted as the shaded box in Figure 6.1. The final products or services then flow on from the lead firm to its customers (or distributors) that are also categorized into tiers until the product reaches its ultimate end-customers or consumers (tier-3). GSCs also contain pre-manufacturing functions such as planning, development, design and material procurement and extend to post-manufacturing stages like transport, sales application use, waste management, disposal and collection as well as recycling.[7]

Figure 6.1 A simplified global supply chain
Source: authors

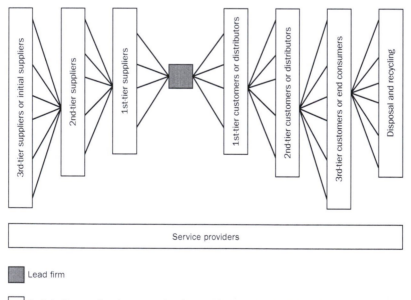

6   However, 90% of those trade flows are concentrated in ten Asia–Pacific countries, namely Australia, China, Japan, India, Indonesia, Malaysia, the Republic of Korea, Singapore, Thailand and Turkey.
7   In this sense, a variety of services providers, such as financial, logistical and professional, are also involved throughout GSCs.

Within the structures of entire GSCs a difference in sustainability reporting behaviour can be distinguished between parties that are involved in business-to-business (B2B) relationships and business-to-consumer (B2C) relationships. B2B relationships are the links between initial, tier-3, 2 and 1 suppliers (parties on the left side of the lead firm in Fig. 3.1) that are shielded from the pressure of reporting from end-customers or consumers. On average, 0–20% of B2B companies reported on sustainability issues compared to 60–80% of B2C companies (Okongwu, Morimoto and Lauras, 2013, p. 842).

Another issue is that an increasing number of SMEs are involved in GSCs as they account for over 99% of total enterprises in most countries of Asia and the Pacific. SMEs[8] are generally suppliers of labour-intensive parts and components or providers of other basic services, usually on a subcontracting basis or at the lower tier (ESCAP, 2007). While larger partners in the supply chain often take advantage of the greater flexibility of SMEs and their adaptability to local economic conditions and an ability to respond to orders for smaller quantities, SMEs are typically a disadvantaged or low-capacity group in the supply chain because of their more modest production facilities, limited financial reserves and smaller workforces (ESCAP, 2009a). SMEs have been identified as less capable of disclosing information compared with their large counterparts while they usually neither conduct sustainability assessment nor produce sustainability reports (ESCAP, 2009b).

As a result of this, it is apparent that there is a lack of information on sustainability issues along entire cross-border supply chains that is important and should be communicated to stakeholders for their fully informed judgement or decision making. A number of GSC players locate and operate at a distance or in different countries under different regulatory frameworks in terms of business' sustainability practices. The limited capacity of smaller players within the supply chain is also an issue which may hinder the widespread implementation of sustainability reporting. Whereas this situation may change as more sustainability reporting frameworks have begun to incorporate clear and practical guidelines to assess and report business's social and environmental performance, commonly practiced sustainability reporting at the global or regional level has yet to be fully developed and SMEs, or lower-tier GSC players, may continuously face obstacles to adopt such sustainability reporting.

---

8   The definition of SMEs varies country by country. Countries in Asia and the Pacific typically define SMEs as commercial entities with less than between 100 and 300 employees while some use the size of investment and also set separate definitions among different segments, such as manufacturing and services (ESCAP, 2012).

6.4 Present sustainability reporting in Asia and the Pacific

For the purpose of analysing sustainability reporting frameworks at present, we identified a non-exhaustive list of 121 sustainability reporting frameworks that applied globally and within Asia and the Pacific through an extensive literature review and online search from May to June 2015 (see Appendix 1). The online search was specifically conducted using the keyword search method for indexing and querying potentially large collections of heterogeneous data (Li *et al.*, 2008). The data collection was also leveraged by the two separate datasets of GRI and the United Nations Environmental Programme (UNEP) on sustainability reporting initiatives (GRI, 2015b; UNEP, 2003). Cross-examinations were conducted among newly-found sustainability reporting initiatives through online search and those listed in the two datasets by reviewing their entries to ensure that they were accurate and up-to-date (Erlandson *et al.*, 1993). If those listed reporting frameworks in the two dataset were not accessible online, they were excluded from the present study. Those frameworks whose English version was not accessible were also excluded from further review. Data coding followed a straightforward content analysis procedure (Charmaz 2000; Yin 1994) based on a few categories and associated classifications, such as geographical coverage (e.g. global or national), applied sectors or segments (e.g. banking or natural resources), sustainability dimensions (i.e. social, environmental and economic), enforcement types (e.g. mandatory or voluntary) and references to supply chains, which were based on the findings of the literature review. The first author acted as an auditor in the coding process (Erlandson *et al.* 1993), verifying both the process (steps followed by the coder or the second author) and the product of data coding.

Among the listed 121 sustainability reporting frameworks, 19 were global frameworks and 102 were national frameworks belonging to 18 Asia–Pacific countries or economies, including three developed countries (i.e. Australia, Japan and New Zealand), 13 developing economies (i.e. China, Hong Kong, India, Indonesia, Malaysia, Pakistan, Philippines, Republic of Korea, Russia Federation, Singapore, Taiwan Province of China, Thailand and Vietnam) and two least-developed countries (i.e. Bangladesh and Myanmar). We found that at least 30% of the Asia–Pacific countries or economies (63 in total) have launched sustainability reporting initiatives so far.

The majority of global frameworks were found to be voluntary (78.9%) and the minority of them mandatory (21.1%). The opposite was found for national frameworks with 56.5% of frameworks being mandatory, 37.0% voluntary and 6.5% categorized as "comply or explain" (i.e. a hybrid between mandatory and voluntary compliance).[9] It is apparent that national initiatives are more likely to be man-

---

9   The "comply or explain" approach allows organizations to omit information but requires for firms to provide a justification on why it was excluded (KPMG, GRI and Unit for Corporate Governance in Africa, 2013).

datory than global counterparts which is understandable as reaching a global or regional agreement on how and when sustainability reporting should occur is a daunting task. See Figure 6.2 for details.

Figure 6.2 Enforcement types of sustainability reporting, by geographical coverage

Source: authors

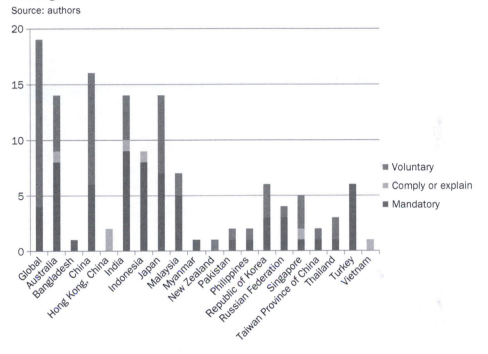

We observe more of the national initiatives and frameworks being updated and aligned with global sustainability reporting initiatives such as the United National Global Compact Principles, ILO's Tripartite Declaration and OECD's Guidelines for Multinational Enterprises (ILO, 2006; OECD, 2011; UNOG, 2012). This harmonization between global and national initiatives is being undertaken to "improve comparability of reports and efficiency of reporting practice, and also enable effective assurance of data" (KPMG, GRI and Unit for Corporate Governance in Africa, 2013, p. 16). Countries in Asia and the Pacific that are following this harmonization trend include China and the Republic of Korea. According to the 2013 Carrots and Sticks report (KPMG, GRI and Unit for Corporate Governance in Africa, 2013), this trend towards harmonization will continue and we should expect to see more national sustainability reporting policies aligned with global reporting frameworks.

Although there have been efforts to harmonize sustainability reporting standards as mentioned above, literature also supports that there are disparities amongst voluntary sustainability reports including inconsistency in reporting time periods, sustainability indicators, reporting formats and metrics (Bowrey, Clements and Cord, 2009; Habek and Wolniak, 2015). In this case, countries with the higher number of sustainability reporting frameworks mandated include India (9), Australia (8), Indonesia (8), Japan (7), China (6), Turkey (6) and Malaysia (5), suggesting that comparability and consistency of their reports may be slightly higher within their own countries (see Fig. 3.2). However, it is not to say that these countries have ideal sustainability reporting frameworks from other perspectives of comprehensiveness, scope and product life cycle (across supply chains), and monitoring and evaluation.

Figure 6.3 below depicts the targeted sectors or segments of each sustainability reporting framework, e.g. types of organization, ownerships, industries, lines of business and sizes. More than half (67) of the sustainability reporting frameworks reviewed are broad in scope and have been developed to apply to all organizations or listed companies. The remaining sustainability reporting frameworks are applicable to banking and finance, public and state-owned enterprises, polluting industries, natural resources, SMEs and specific industries, which typically require specific attention from regulators. Perhaps it is noteworthy that only Japan and the United Nations Industrial Development Organization (UNIDO) have developed SME-focused voluntary sustainability reporting frameworks while some others touch upon SME issues (Carbon Disclosure Project, 2015) (see Appendix 1 again for more details).

Figure 6.3 Targeted sectors or segments of sustainability reporting
Source: authors

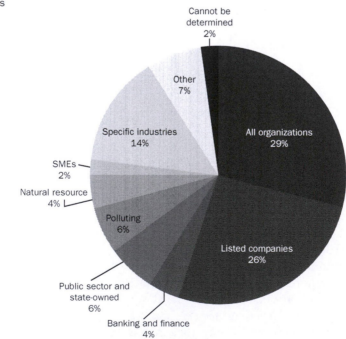

Major sustainability reporting initiatives at the global level include the Global Reporting Initiative (GRI), the United Nations Global Compact (UNGC), OECD Guidelines for Multinational Enterprises, ISO 26000, IIRC's International Integrated Reporting Framework, FTSE4Good and the Dow Jones Sustainability Index (DJSI) (ESCAP, 2009b). All those initiatives more or less cover the "triple bottom line" concept (i.e. economic, social and environmental dimensions) and facilitate sustainability activities through the efficient use of economic capital while simultaneously building and using social and natural capital, although they vary on their focused scopes and areas (e.g. UNGC's strong focus on social and environmental aspects).

Finally, Figure 6.4 presents three sustainability dimensions (i.e. social, environmental and economic) covered by the reviewed 121 sustainability report initiatives in the region. It indicates that an increasing number of sustainability reports now cover both social and environmental aspects while a lesser number of the reports only cover the social dimension. This perhaps indicates that the social dimension has so far received less attention from the reporting initiatives compared with environmental dimension whose majority is mandated. It is also observed that the large number of voluntary reporting frameworks cover both social and environmental dimensions. It is also noted that nearly one fifth of reporting initiatives cover all three dimensions.

Figure 6.4 Dimensions covered in sustainability reporting
Source: authors

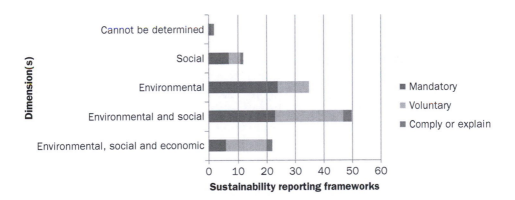

As aforementioned, enhancing transparency through sustainability reporting is a particular challenge in large and complex GSCs, as it becomes increasingly difficult to accurately map, measure and monitor suppliers and customers (and other players like distributors and service providers) in the various tiers. Sustainability indicators and metrics and reporting timeframes need to be standardized and must be consistent with each other in a practical manner among supply chain players in order to maintain comparability for internal and wider public use. The same approach must be taken with reporting scope, i.e. the depth into the supply chain on which sustainability performance is reported. However, SMEs may be hindered in the wider implementation of sustainability reporting if it becomes too complex, long, costly and time consuming as they represent the smaller and disadvantaged players typically at the lower tiers of GSCs, who may not have adequate resources and capacities to work on such costly reporting and may view it as a non-essential task.

6.5 Typologies of sustainability reporting

This section presents the typologies of sustainability reporting, which is important to understand the various ways in which these sustainability reporting frameworks apply at the industrial, local, national and international levels. Based on the reviewed 121 sustainability reporting frameworks, this research identifies four main typologies as outlined below.

6.5.1 International codes, standards and guidelines

Voluntary codes, standards and guidelines at the global level developed by international organizations and non-governmental organizations (NGOs) such as GRI, IIRC, ISO, OECD and United Nations are the first typology. These voluntary codes, standards and guidelines have generally been developed to be utilized by organizations around the world and may incorporate one or more social, environmental and economic dimensions. Examples such as GRI's G4 Sustainability Reporting Guidelines (GRI, 2015a), IIRC's International Integrated Reporting Guidelines (IIRC, 2013) and the UN's Global Compact Communication on Progress (UNOG, 2012) are global voluntary guidelines that incorporate more than one social, environmental or economic dimension. Despite the ISO (2010) releasing the Guidance on Social Responsibility, or ISO 26000:2010, the international organization highlights the purely voluntary nature of the guidelines and states that it is not used for quality system management or for certification, regulatory or contractual use.[10]

6.5.2 Government laws and regulations

The second typology refers to any regulation or law that is enforced by a national or subnational government that mandates sustainability reporting by any type of business in any specified sector or industry. An example of this is The Companies Act of 1956 instated by the Government of India on all enterprises to report on social and environmental sustainability issues (Ministry of Corporate Affairs of India, 2015). Concerns regarding sustainability efforts within public and state-owned

---

10 It can also be said that ISO 26000:2010 aims to set relevant norms for sustainable development for commercial entities.

enterprises are being particularly addressed by countries such as China, India and Indonesia which have enforced mandatory sustainability reporting for public sector enterprises. For countries like China, where the government has a major influence in setting standards for commercial entities to follow, mandatory sustainability reporting is a demonstration of their commitment to addressing social and environmental challenges.

6.5.3 Industry regulations and codes

The third typology is industry regulations and codes. Industries that are known to have particularly negative social and environmental externalities or are considered vital for the function of society are generally regulated and monitored by a public or private industry board (or equivalent) that sets codes of practice and industry standards by which to abide. Examples of these types of industries include banking and finance, mining, oil and gas, textiles and polluting industries. The board or regulator of these industries may require sustainability reporting by the firms (e.g. the Corporate Social Responsibility, Sustainable Development and Non-Financial Reporting Framework of the Reserve Bank of India) (Chakrabarty, 2011).

6.5.4 Stock exchange sustainability regulations, codes and indices

The fourth and final typology is undergoing a shift where an increasing number of stock exchanges (or markets) are requiring listed companies to submit sustainability reports and publish corporate sustainability rankings. This shift has been observed by the stock exchanges of Thailand, Bursa Malaysia, Shanghai Stock Exchange, Australian Securities Exchange and the Securities and Exchange Board of India in Asia and the Pacific among others (Sustainable Stock Exchanges Initiative, 2012). Sustainability indices featured in these exchanges are important for providing information to investors who play an active role in sustainable responsible investment (SRI).[11] Global stock exchange sustainability indices such as the Dow Jones Sustainability Index (DJSI) and the FTSE4Good Index family are used to rank companies in accordance to both their sustainability and financial performance. The goals of the two global indices differ; while DJSI aims to assess the long-term value creation potential of firms, the FTSE4Good aims to measure sustainability performance for companies not only for investors but to also benchmark sustainability performance and allow companies to track their progress and achievements (FTSE, 2014; RobecoSAM, 2014).

---

11 Investors who take an SRI approach seek to gain long-term financial returns on sustainable investments that do not negatively impact on society or the environment (Abe and Ruanglikhitkul, 2013).

6.6 Assessing GSCs by sustainability reporting

Out of the 121 sustainability reporting frameworks identified and reviewed, approximately one third of the frameworks mention suppliers, supply chain or procurement standards. However, only 20 of these (16.5%) actually contain reporting guidelines for supply chains, or value chains, which triggers firms to carry out social and environmental initiatives that address the entire supply chain (or multiple tiers) of the product or service (see Appendix 2).[12] This indicates the lack of general interest or support in the area and the difficult implementation of such guidelines which must cover cross-border linkages of various companies. Several issues are observed and briefed in turn.

First, GRI's G4 Sustainability Reporting Guidelines (GRI, 2013) can be the benchmark for GSC players as the most comprehensive framework among the 20 initiatives to include GSC perspectives. On a voluntary basis, the guidelines require reporting on the supply chain to include changes to size, ownership and governance to manage conflicts and spending on local suppliers. The guidelines also cover environmental aspects in energy consumption outside the organization and the percentage of new suppliers that were screened using environmental criteria. Furthermore, it asks companies to report on significant actual and potential negative environmental impacts in the supply chain and the actions taken to rectify them. Reporting around screening suppliers for social and human rights criteria is also made along with identifying suppliers with significant risks for incidents of forced labour for example. In addition to its comprehensiveness the additional strength of GRI's guidelines is that they have developed an implementation manual that corresponds to the standards and guidelines which helps describe the relevance of each indicator, presents how to compile the information and suggests potential documentation sources. This is viewed to be particularly useful for users that have less experience in sustainability reporting, especially for SMEs that may need further guidance. The strengths of the GRI guidelines also present weaknesses towards transparency that provides disincentives for GSC players to avoid reporting on sustainability performance and activities. High financial and resource implementation costs, particularly for reporting on the cross-border supply chain aspect, the exclusion of supply chain reporting in the core reporting standards and the ambiguity of reporting boundaries for supply chain partners, are weaknesses we have identified. These weaknesses present particularly high barriers for SMEs to be able to report on their supply chains, or prepare information for the lead reporting company. In short, GRI guidelines are still made for large leading companies.

Second, these supply chain guidelines of the existing 20 reporting initiatives severely lack completeness and comprehensiveness in defining reporting coverage

---

12 One of the first sustainability reporting initiatives to incorporate guidelines on supply chain issues was the second edition of OECD's Guidelines for Multinational Enterprises back to 1979 (OECD, 1979). Out of 17 reporting frameworks which cover supply chain issues, nine are at the global level while the remaining ones are national guidelines.

and the required data within supply chains. In particular, the mandatory frameworks that incorporate supply chain reporting requirements (i.e. Dow Jones Sustainability Index (DJSI) and reporting frameworks in India, Myanmar and Turkey) are the least comprehensive as they lack clarity of definitions, scope (i.e. what to report on) and boundaries (i.e. tiers in the supply chain that should be reported on) in reference to supply chain reporting. These mandatory frameworks often serve more as checklists than prescriptive guidelines on reporting. There is clearly a trade-off between the levels of mandated reporting requirements. Businesses may not comply honestly with reporting requirements if they are too stringent and incur high costs to implement; hence, these mandated reporting frameworks are shallow and non-comprehensive. Furthermore, the frameworks are not simple and straightforward to follow, which may inflict high reporting costs and efforts to the reporting firm.

Third, the unique structure of GSC from initial suppliers through multi-tier players to the final customers (see Fig. 6.1) is recognized by nine frameworks (see Appendix 6.2). An advanced example is the EcoAction 21 Guidelines for SMEs in Japan. This initiative applies the broadest scope to sustainability reporting in supply chains from beginning to end of the full product lifecycle compared to the other frameworks and even covers the sustainability performance of end customers. On the downside, it does not offer specific guidance for the reporting of cross-border operations with foreign partners (Ministry of the Environment Government of Japan, 2009). Some other national and global frameworks[13] also suggest reporting firms to provide the data on non-financial performance associated with crucial issues of business partners, such as suppliers and distributors, in order to identify, prevent, mitigate and account for the actual and potential impacts of risks. However, all of them lack clarity and reference to entire GSC participants such as suppliers and distributors across the different tiers, which may undermine the power to assess the sustainability performance of a GSC properly.

Fourth, given that GSCs are made up of a significant number of SMEs, their capacity to report is very much limited due to human resource, time and knowledge constraints (Nulkar, 2014). A crucial knowledge gap exists with SME partners who do not understand the importance, need and methodology of sustainability reporting.[14] Fortunately, some initiatives are found to tackle this issue. The EcoAction 21 Guidelines for SMEs in Japan provides a simple step-by-step guide to enhance SMEs' awareness and knowledge on sustainability reporting which is usually done by the lead or multinational firm (Ministry of the Environment

---

13 Those initiatives include the Charter of Corporate Behaviour by Keidanren (2010) in Japan, the Sustainability Reporting Handbook for Vietnamese Companies in Vietnam (IFC; State Securities Commission of Vietnam; Association of Chartered Certified Accountants, 2013), OECD Guidelines for Multinational Enterprises (OECD, 2011) and IIRC's International Integrated Reporting Framework (IIRC, 2013).

14 For example, the 2015 Carbon Disclosure Project (CDP) Supply Chain Report uncovers a worrying trend that the number of reporting suppliers within GSCs are plateauing and even reversing in some countries (Accenture Strategy, 2015).

Government of Japan, 2009). The OECD Guidelines for Multinational Enterprises also recommends for lead firms to set the expectations and standards for SME partners and to educate and train them on reporting methods and standards (OECD, 2011). However, those initiatives still imply high enough reporting costs for smaller GSC players to be discouraged from reporting.

Fifth, target setting and monitoring and evaluation mechanisms as parts of reporting systems have yet to be included in the majority of existing global and national frameworks. An effective method to lift sustainability within GSCs is to capture and monitor targets and the progress of firms and their supply chains to ensure continuous improvement. By incorporating such reporting methods, internal stakeholders, especially executives that set corporate strategies and the tone at the top of the firm, are held accountable for driving and achieving continuously higher sustainability targets throughout their firms and their supply chains. As advanced examples, the FTSE4Good Index (FTSE, 2014) and Carbon Disclosure Project (CDP) Supply Chain Programme (Carbon Disclosure Project, 2015) consider this an integral part of measuring and benchmarking environmental performance over the long-term.

Lastly, the existing sustainability reporting initiatives have not provided effective tools or methods for entire GSC players to facilitate sustainability reporting across borders. As reviewed, there is a trend that while global initiatives remain voluntary in nature, more nationwide sustainability reports are required by the authorities and regulators. At the same time, more and more firms are dealing with their supply chain partners who operate in different countries under different rules and regulations. Global initiatives lack power to encourage all GSC players to conduct sustainability reporting; national ones naturally only focus within their national boundaries. While sustainability issues have become crucial along GSCs, the existing frameworks have not fully addressed this issue.

6.7 A future towards sustainable GSC reporting

The transparency and visibility of GSCs and their performance in environmental and social dimensions still remain poor in Asia and the Pacific. The ambiguity and inadequacy of the GSC definition, unclear scope and boundaries of sustainability reporting, high reporting costs and lack of mandatory global, or regional, reporting guidelines in this context are incentives for GSC players, particularly SMEs, to avoid reporting on their sustainability performance along GSCs.

This chapter reviewed a number of sustainability reporting frameworks at both global and national levels and revealed a patchy landscape of irregular and immature frameworks from the perspective of GSCs. Regulations and policies across geographical borders vary, or are even non-existent, making compliance with all the various policies extremely difficult for businesses to maintain. More national and subnational policies in Asia and the Pacific need to align their standards and guidelines with (or at least make reference to) global reporting standards and guidelines such as those by GRI and IIRC.

A balance needs to be struck between flexibility and definition on the scope and boundary requirements in sustainability reporting frameworks. The balance should seek to ensure that a sufficient level of transparency on supply chains is apparent without causing aversion for companies to report due to high reporting costs, which are again more likely to discourage SMEs, or lower tier GSC players, to report their sustainability performance along GSCs. The scope for supply chain reporting from concept and production to delivery to the final customers with waste management and recycling is selective at one or a few targeted points along the GSCs for most frameworks. In this respect, reporting instruments should at least allude to the entire product life-cycle of products and services and request reporting of the interlinking relationships among GSC players.

Practical guidance for SMEs like the GRI Implementation Manual (GRI, 2013) should be more readily available whether this is delivered by global initiatives, market regulators or governments. This will enable SMEs and suppliers, who do not face as much scrutiny and pressure from stakeholders, to report as their large multinational customers or partners to better understand the expectations and methods of reporting to meet global and national supply chain reporting standards.

With the shift in national policies and frameworks relying on global initiatives and the vast adoption of global sustainability reporting initiatives like GRI's G4 Sustainability Reporting Guidelines, it seems that international organizations with a large number and variety of networks with stakeholders like GRI have an implied responsibility to address the gaps. This responsibility lies in improving the level of sustainability reporting throughout GSCs in order to enhance transparency and thus allow stakeholders to make more informed decisions towards sustainable development. This is justified by the efforts towards harmonization of reporting standards to increase comparability of reports between firms globally, to therefore provide a more inclusive and transparent overview to stakeholders. In this connection, one challenge we face is that a number of developing countries, at least in Asia and the Pacific, have yet to develop national frameworks on sustainability reporting. As many of them lack resources and knowledge, some types of international cooperation among stakeholders including governments, private sector and international organizations may be required.

Furthermore, unless more governments in the Asia–Pacific region follow suit in providing the tools for SMEs similar to Japan's EcoAction 21 Guidelines (except to include both social and environmental dimensions), the uptake of sustainable practices and reporting will be slow along the supply chain and transparency in first and lower tier value chains will remain murky. SME partners are likely to cooperate with lead firms towards sustainability reporting in order to keep business, so these large customers/multinationals can influence suppliers and even customers to comply by setting expectations and the requirements in business/partnership agreements.

In order to encourage more SMEs to participate in sustainability reporting along GSCs, information and communication technologies (ICTs) could be effectively utilized. As reviewed, issues which often discourage SMEs to report their sustainability performance are high transaction costs and lack of institutional capacities. In this regard, if sustainability reporting initiatives develop an online supporting tool which facilitates SMEs' data collection and report writing with simple and straightforward guidance, more SMEs may wish to conduct the reporting. Furthermore, for established corporations, tools such as online registries and data analytics could be used to review sustainability reports and identify gaps and inconsistencies in the reports that can feedback to various organizations to address them promoting transparency in the information that are communicated to stakeholders.

Finally, a key for success would be that various reporting initiatives at both national and global levels make their detailed reporting requirements by sharing standardized and simplified indicators or criteria. Global and regional cooperation among governments, international organizations and NGOs must be needed in this area. This project may also be easily set up as a comprehensive database by either the private or public sector with a number of sustainability reports.[15] Such online reports on trends allow stakeholders, including governments and industry regulators to use data analytics to react and rectify undesirable trends where other proactive measures have not been effective.

6.8 Conclusion

With efforts by organizations that assist with creating guidelines and standards in facilitating sustainable development through sustainability reporting, stakeholders are able to make informed decisions based on information that has been communicated with transparency. There are still major gaps that need to be addressed in order for sustainability (or CSR) reporting to be sufficiently transparent across GSCs. However, as time progresses and more research is conducted into the reporting outcomes and effects of GSCs, stakeholders need to continue to demand more transparency in the performance and conditions in which GSCs operate. Such efforts and practices must also be replicated in a number of developing countries in Asia and the Pacific. Although the present chapter may not fully cover all sustainability reporting initiatives within the region, it is apparent that developing

---

15 There are presently two main online registers that publish sustainability reports including CorporateRegister.com that maintain over 66,000 reports across over 12,500 companies (CorporateRegister.com, 2015) and the Sustainability Disclosure Database managed by GRI with over 25,000 reports across 7,700 organizations (GRI, 2015b). These two online registers act as portals for stakeholders to easily access sustainability reports and statistics of companies all over the world across multiple industries although their main entries have been made by large/multinational enterprises.

countries in the region lag behind the development and implementation of sustainability reporting. In this connection, country surveys may be useful to collect more information and capture the present status of sustainability reporting practices in those countries.

References

Abe, M., & Ruanglikhitkul, W. (2013). Developments in the concept of corporate social responsibility (CSR), Chapter II. From Corporate Social Responsibility to Corporate Sustainability: *Moving the Agenda Forward in Asia and the Pacific, Studies in Trade and Investment* No. 77. Bangkok: ESCAP.

Accenture Strategy (2015). *Supply Chain Sustainability Revealed: A Country Comparison.* New York: Carbon Disclosure Project.

Bowrey, G., Clements, M., & Cord, B. (2009). *CSR reporting: A process for supply chain legitimation.* 8th Australasian Conference on Social and Environmental Accounting Research.

Carbon Disclosure Project (2015). *CDP's 2015 Supply Chain Climate Change Information Request. Supply Chain Program Guidance.* Retrieved from https://www.cdp.net/CDP%20 Questionaire%20Documents/CDP-supply-chain-information-request-2015.pdf (June 16, 2015).

Chakrabarty, K.C. (2011). KC Chakrabarty: Non-financial reporting: What, Why and How: Indian Perspective. *Bank for International Settlements.* Retrieved from http://www.bis. org/review/r110621e.pdf (July 2, 2015).

Charmaz, K. (2000). Grounded theory: Objectivist and constructivist methods. In Denzin, N.K., & Lincoln, Y.S. (Eds.), *The Handbook of Qualitative Research* (2nd ed.) (pp. 509-535). Thousand Oaks, CA: Sage Publications.

Christopher, M. (2011). *Logistics and Supply Chain Management* (4th ed.). Harlow, UK: Pearson Education.

Committee on the Financial Aspects of Corporate Governance (1992). *Report of the Committee on the Financial Aspects of Corporate Governance.* London: Gee & Co.

CorporateRegister.com (2015). *CorporateRegister.com.* Retrieved from http://www.corporateregister.com (July 14, 2015).

Donaldson, L., & Davis, J.H. (1991). Stewardship theory or agency theory: CEO Governance and shareholder returns. *Australian Journal of Management,* 16(1), 49-64.

Eisenhardt, K.M. (1989). Agency theory: An assessment and review. *The Academy of Management Review,* 14(1), 57-74.

Elkington, J. (1998). Accounting for the triple bottom line, *Measuring Business Excellence,* 2(3), 18-22.

Erlandson, D.A., Harris, E.L., Skipper, B.L., & Allen, S.D. (1993). *Doing Naturalistic Inquiry: A Guide to Methods.* Newbury Park, CA: Sage Publications.

ESCAP (Economic and Social Commission for Asia and the Pacific) (2015). *Global value chains, regional integration and sustainable development: Linkage and policy implications—Note by the secretariat.* Seventy-first session, Bangkok, 25–29 May 2015.

ESCAP (2012). *Policy Guidebook for SME Development in Asia and the Pacific.* New York: United Nations.

ESCAP (2009a). Globalization of Production and the Competitiveness of Small and Medium-sized Enterprises in Asia and the Pacific: Trends and Prospects. *Studies in Trade and Investment No. 65.* New York: United Nations.

ESCAP (2009b). Creating Business and Social Value: The Asian Way to Integrate CSR into Business Strategies. *Studies in Trade and Investment No. 68*. (ST/ESCAP/2565). New York: United Nations.

ESCAP (2007). Globalization of Production and the Competitiveness of Small and Medium-sized Enterprises in Asia and the Pacific: Trends and Prospects. *Studies in Trade and Investment No. 65*. New York: United Nations.

FTSE (ESGFTSE Publications) (2014). *Integrating ESG into investments and stewardship*. Retrieved from http://www.ftse.com/products/downloads/FTSE-ESG-Methodology-and-Usage-Summary-Short.pdf?32 (June 23, 2015).

Forbes (2015). *Global 2000: The World's Biggest Public Company-Forbes*. Retrieved from: www.forbes.com/global2000 (July 9, 2015).

Freidman, M. (1970). The social responsibility of business is to increase its profits. *The New York Times Magazine*.

GRI (Global Reporting Initiative) (2015a). *GRI and Sustainability Reporting*. Retrieved from https://www.globalreporting.org/information/sustainability-reporting/Pages/gri-standards.aspx (July 6, 2015).

GRI (2015b). *Sustainability Disclosure Database*. Retrieved from: http://database.global-reporting.org (July 14, 2015).

GRI (2013). G4 Sustainability Reporting Guidelines. *GRI Empowering Sustainable Decisions*. Retrieved from https://www.globalreporting.org/resourcelibrary/GRIG4-Part1-Reporting-Principles-and-Standard-Disclosures.pdf (May 14, 2015).

GRI (2006). *Sustainability Reporting Guidelines—Global Reporting Initiative*. Retrieved from https://www.globalreporting.org/resourcelibrary/G3-Sustainability-Reporting-Guidelines.pdf (July 7, 2015).

Habek, P., & Wolniak, R. (2015). *Assessing the Quality of Corporate Social Responsibility Reports: The Case of Reporting Practices in Selected European Union member States*. Rotterdam: Springer.

IFC (International Finance Corporation) (2013). State Securities Commission of Vietnam & Association of Chartered Certified Accountants. *Sustainability Reporting Handbook for Vietnamese Companies*. Sustainability at IFC. Retrieved from http://www.ifc.org/wps/wcm/connect/topics_ext_content/ifc_external_corporate_site/ifc+sustainability/learning+and+adapting/knowledge+products/publications/publications_handbook_vietnam-sus (June 16, 2015).

IIRC (International Integrated Reporting Council) (2013). *International Framework. Integrated Reporting*. Retrieved from https://www.globalreporting.org/resourcelibrary/GRIG4-Part1-Reporting-Principles-and-Standard-Disclosures.pdf (June, 14 2015).

ILO (International Labour Office) (2006). *Tripartite Declaration of Principles Concerning Multinational Enterprises and Social Policy*. Geneva: ILO.

Institute for Industrial Productivity (2005). JP-8: Mandatory GHG Emissions Reporting. Retrieved from http://iepd.iipnetwork.org/policy/mandatory-ghg-emissions-reporting (June 13, 2015).

ISL World Seaborne Container Trade and Port Traffic (2010). *World Seaborne Trade and World Port Traffic. ISL Publications and Databases*. Retrieved from http://www.infoline.isl.org/index.php?module=Pagesetter&func=viewpub&tid=6&pid=10 (July 7, 2015).

ISO (International Organization for Standardization) (2010). ISO 26000:2010(en) *Guidance on social responsibility*. Geneva: ISO.

Keidanren (Japan Business Federation) (2010). *Charter of Corporate Behavior & Its Implementation Guidance*. Retrieved from https://www.keidanren.or.jp/english/policy/csr/tebiki6.pdf (June 16, 2015).

KPMG (KPMG Advisory N.V.), GRI (Global Reporting Initiative) & Unit for Corporate Governance in Africa (2013). *Sustainability reporting policies worldwide—today's best practice, tomorrow's trends*.

Li, G., Ooi, B.C., Feng, J., Wang, J., & Zhou, L. (2008). EASE: An effective 3-in-1 keyword search method for unstructured, semi-structured and structured data. In *The Proceedings of the 2008 ACM SIGMOD international conference on management of data* (p. 903-914).

Ministry of Corporate Affairs of India (2015). *Companies Act—Act No. 1 of 1956*. Retrieved from http://www.mca.gov.in/MinistryV2/companiesact.html (July 15, 2015).

Ministry of Environment and Forests of India (1986). *The Environment (Protection) Act, 1986 No. 29 or 1986*. 23 05 1986. Retrieved from http://envfor.nic.in/legis/env/env1.html (June 7, 2015).

Ministry of the Environment Government of Japan (2009). *EcoAction 21 Guidelines 2009*. Retrieved from https://www.keidanren.or.jp/english/policy/csr/tebiki6.pdf (June, 14 2015)

Nulkar, G. (2014). Does environmental sustainability matter to small and medium enterprises? Empirical evidence from India. *International Journal of Environmental Studies*, 2014, 481-489.

OECD (Organisation for Economic Co-operation and Development) (2013). *Interconnected Economies: Benefiting from Global Value Chains*. Paris: OECD Publishing.

OECD (2011). OECD *Guidelines for Multinational Enterprises*, 2011 Edition. Paris: OECD.

OECD (1976). OECD *International Investment and Multinational Enterprises: Review of the 1976 Declaration and Decisions*. Retrieved from http://www.oecd.org/daf/inv/mne/50024869.pdf (July 5, 2015).

Okongwu, U., Morimoto, R., & Lauras, M. (2013). The maturity of supply chain sustainability disclosure from a continuous improvement perspective. *International Journal of Productivity and Performance Management*, 827-855.

Prince's Accounting for Sustainability Project (2009). Connected reporting A practical guide with worked examples. *Accounting for Sustainability*. Retrieved from http://www.accountingforsustainability.org/wp-content/uploads/2011/10/Connected-Reporting.pdf (June 20, 2015).

RobecoSAM AG (2014). *Measuring Intangibles- RobecoSAM's corporate sustainability assessment methodology*. RobecoSAM Corporate Sustainability Assessment. http://www.robecosam.com/images/CSA_methodology_en.pdf (June 23, 2015).

Shanghai Bureau of Quality and Technical Supervision (2008). Shanghai Municipal Local Standards DB31/421-2008 *Corporate Social Responsibility*. Retrieved from http://csrshe.com/info/3764-1.htm (June 7, 2015).

Soderstrom, N. (2013). Sustainability reporting: Past, present, and trends for the future. *Insights Melbourne Business and Economics*. Retrieved from http://www.insights.unimelb.edu.au/vol13/04_Soderstrom.html (July 7, 2015).

Sustainable Stock Exchanges Initiative (2012). *Sustainability Reporting Policies*. Retrieved from http://www.sseinitiative.org/sustainabilityreporting (May 10, 2015).

Tschopp, D., & Huefner, R.J. (2015). Comparing the evolution of CSR reporting to that of financial reporting. *Journal of Business Ethics*, 565-577.

UNCTAD (United Nations Conference on Trade and Development) (2013). *World Investment Report 2013—Global Value Chains: Investment and Trade for Development*. Geneva: United Nations.

UNEP (2003). Sustainability Frameworks Table v2003 (2), *Environmental Programme*. Unpublished database, Nairobi United Nations.

UNGC (United Nations Global Compact) (2012). *Basic Guide Communication on Progress*. Retrieved from https://www.unglobalcompact.org/docs/communication_on_progress/Tools_and_Publications/COP_Basic_Guide.pdf (June 11, 2015).

WCED (World Commission on Environment and Development) (1987). *Our Common Future*. Oxford: Oxford University Press.

Yin, R.K. (1994). *Case Study Research: Design and Methods* (2nd ed). Thousand Oaks, CA: Sage Publications.

Masato Abe is an Economic Affairs Officer in the Business and Development Section, Trade and Investment Division, United Nations Economic and Social Commission for Asia and the Pacific (ESCAP), Bangkok, Thailand. He is also a research fellow at the Faculty of Commerce and Accountancy of Thammasat University, Bangkok and a visiting lecturer of the Graduate School of Asia Pacific Studies, Waseda University, Tokyo, Japan.

Michelle Chee is a researcher in the Business and Development Section, Trade and Investment Division, United Nations Economic and Social Commission for Asia and the Pacific (ESCAP). She is a graduate from the University of Queensland (UQ), Brisbane, Australia in Chemistry and is currently completing a Master of Commerce in Applied Finance at UQ and ESSEC Business School, Cergy-Pontoise, France. She has both public and private sector experience working in the Trade and Investment Division of the Queensland Government in Bangalore, India and in medical device innovation and commercialization for Cook Medical.

Appendix 6.1: Global and Asia–Pacific sustainability reporting frameworks

Source: Compilation by the authors based on various sources.

ID No.	Framework.	Institution	Coverage	Application	Social	Environmental	Economic*	Enforcement
1	RobecoSAM Corporate Sustainability Assessment	Dow Jones Sustainability Index (DJSI)	Global	Listed companies	1	1	1	Mandatory
2	Extractive Industries Transparency Initiative Standard	Extractive Industries Transparency Initiative International Secretariat	Global	Natural resources industry	1	1	0	Mandatory
3	FTSE ESG Ratings	FTSE4Good	Global	Listed companies	1	1	0	Mandatory
4	PRI Reporting Framework	Principles for Responsible Investment	Global	PRI asset owners and investment manager signatories	1	1	0	Mandatory
5	G4 Sustainability Reporting Guidelines	Global Reporting Initiative (GRI)	Global	All enterprises	1	1	1	Voluntary
6	ISO26000:2010	International Organisation for Standardization (ISO)	Global	All enterprises	1	1	1	Voluntary
7	International Integrated Reporting Framework	International Integrated Reporting Committee (IIRC)	Global	All enterprises	1	1	1	Voluntary
8	Conceptual Framework of the Sustainability Accounting Standards Board	Sustainability Accounting Standards Board (SASB)	Global	Listed companies	1	1	1	Voluntary
9	Connected Reporting Framework	Accounting for Sustainability Project	Global	Listed entities and other public interest entities	1	1	1	Voluntary

ID No.	Framework.	Institution	Coverage	Application	Social	Environmental	Economic*	Enforcement
10	Communication on Progress (COP)	United Nations Global Compact (UNGC)	Global	All enterprises	1	1	0	Voluntary
11	Supply Chain Programme–SMEs, Climate Change, and Water	Carbon Disclosure Project	Global	All enterprises	1	1	0	Voluntary
12	IFC Sustainability Framework (Ed. 2012-v2)	International Finance Corporation (IFC), World Bank Group	Global	Banking and finance industry	1	1	0	Voluntary
13	Guidance on Corporate Responsibility Indicators in Annual Reports	United Nations Conference on Trade and Development (UNCTAD)	Global	All enterprises	1	0	1	Voluntary
14	OECD Guidelines for Multinational Enterprises (Ed. 2011-v5)	Organisation for Economic Co-operation and Development (OECD)	Global	Multinational enterprises	1	1	0	Voluntary
15	Enterprise Level Indicators for Resource Productivity and Pollution Intensity	United Nations Industrial Development Organization (UNIDO) and United Nations Environment Programme (UNEP)	Global	Small and medium-sized Enterprises	0	1	1	Voluntary
16	Greenhouse Gas Protocol Corporate Standard	World Resources Institute and the World Business Council for Sustainable Development	Global	Natural resources industry	0	1	0	Voluntary

ID No.	Framework.	Institution	Coverage	Application	Social	Environmental	Economic*	Enforcement
17	United Nations Guiding Principles on Business and Human Rights	United Nations Human Rights Office of the High Commissioner	Global	All enterprises	1	0	0	Voluntary
18	Tripartite Declaration of Principles concerning Multinational Enterprises and Social Policy (Ed. 2014-v4)	International Labour Organization (ILO)	Global	Multinational enterprises	1	0	0	Voluntary
19	ISO 14064-1:2006	International Organization for Standardization (ISO)	Global	Polluting organizations	0	1	0	Voluntary
20	Corporate Governance Principles and Recommendations	Australian Securities Exchange (ASX)	Australia	Listed companies	1	1	1	Comply or Explain
21	NGER Act (National Greenhouse and Energy Reporting)	Australian Government	Australia	All enterprises	0	1	0	Mandatory
22	National Environment Protection (National Pollutant Inventory) Measure	Australian Government	Australia	Polluting organizations	0	1	0	Mandatory
23	ASX Listing Rule 4.10.3	Australian Securities Exchange (ASX)	Australia	Listed companies	0	0	0	Mandatory
24	Financial Services Reform Act	Australian Government	Australia	Banking and finance industry	1	1	0	Mandatory
25	ASIC Section 1013DA Disclosure Guidelines	Australian Securities and Investments Commission	Australia	Listed companies	1	1	0	Mandatory

ID No.	Framework.	Institution	Coverage	Application	Social	Environmental	Economic*	Enforcement
26	Australian Minerals Industry Framework for Sustainable Development	Australian Minerals Industry	Australia	Minerals industry	1	1	1	Voluntary
27	Guidelines for Section 516A reporting - Environment Protection and Biodiversity Conservation Act 1999	Department of Environment, Water, Heritage and the Arts	Australia	Public sector or state-owned enterprises	1	1	1	Voluntary
28	Water Accounting Standard 1 (AWAS 1)	Water Accounting Standards Board	Australia	Water management industry	1	1	1	Voluntary
29	Reconciliation Action Plan	Reconciliation Australia	Australia	All enterprises	1	0	0	Voluntary
30	Triple Bottom Line Reporting—A Guide to Environmental Indicators	Department of Environment, Water, Heritage and the Arts	Australia	All enterprises	0	1	1	Voluntary
31	Environmental Risk Management Guidelines for Banks and Financial Institutions (draft)	Central Bank	Bangladesh	Banking and finance industry	1	1	1	Mandatory
32	Shenzhen Stock Exchange Social Responsibility Guidelines to Listed Companies	Shenzhen Stock Exchange	China	Listed companies: top 100	1	1	1	Mandatory
33	Measures on Open Environmental Information	Environmental Protection Administration (EPA)	China	All enterprises	0	1	0	Mandatory

ID No.	Framework.	Institution	Coverage	Application	Social	Environmental	Economic*	Enforcement
34	Guidelines on Environmental Information Disclosure	Shanghai Stock Exchange	China	Listed companies	0	1	1	Mandatory
35	Green Securities Law	China Securities Regulatory Commission with the Ministry of Environmental Protection	China	Polluting organizations	0	1	0	Mandatory
36	Environmental Information Disclosure Act	State Environmental Protection Administration of China	China	Three types of companies must disclose CSR practices: (1) companies included in the SSE Corporate Governance Index (240), (2) companies listed in both domestic and overseas markets, (3) financial companies.	0	1	Cannot be determined	Mandatory
37	Shanghai Municipal Local Standards on Corporate Social Responsibility	Shanghai Municipal Bureau of Quality and Technical Supervision	China	All enterprises	1	1	0	Voluntary

ID No.	Framework.	Institution	Coverage	Application	Social	Environmental	Economic*	Enforcement
38	Guidelines on Corporate Social Responsibility for Banking Financial Institutions in China	China Banking Association	China	Banking and finance industry	1	1	0	Voluntary
39	Guidelines on Corporate Social Responsibility for Banking Financial Institutions	China Banking Regulatory Commission	China	Banking and finance industry	1	1	0	Voluntary
40	Indicator System for the China CSR Monitoring and Evaluation Platform	State Information Centre	China	All enterprises	1	1	Cannot be determined	Voluntary
41	Sustainability Reporting Guidelines for Apparel and Textile Enterprises	China National Textile and Apparel Council	China	Textile industry	1	1	0	Voluntary
42	CASS CSR Reporting Guide 2.0	Chinese Academy of Social Sciences (CASS)	China	All enterprises	1	1	Cannot be determined	Voluntary
43	Guide on Social Responsibility for Chinese International Contractors	Ministry of Commerce (MOC)	China	Contracting industry	1	1	Cannot be determined	Voluntary
44	Corporate Social Responsibility Compliance by Foreign Invested Enterprises	Ministry of Commerce (MOC)	China	Foreign companies	1	1	Cannot be determined	Voluntary
45	Notice of Improving Listed Companies' Assumption of Social Responsibilities	Shanghai Stock Exchange	China	Listed companies	1	1	Cannot be determined	Voluntary

ID No.	Framework.	Institution	Coverage	Application	Social	Environmental	Economic*	Enforcement
46	Guidelines on Social Responsibility for Industrial Corporations and Federations	11 National industrial federations and associations	China	Specific industries	1	1	Cannot be determined	Voluntary
47	Draft Environmental, Social and Governance Reporting Guide	Hong Kong Stock Exchange	Hong Kong, China	All enterprises	1	1	0	Comply or Explain
48	Board of Directors Diversity Policy	Hong Kong Stock Exchange	Hong Kong, China	Cannot be determined	0	0	0	Comply or Explain
49	Clause 49 of the Equity Listing Agreement (Consultative paper on corporate governance norms)	Securities and Exchange Board of India (SEBI)	India	Listed companies	1	0	0	Comply or Explain
50	Companies Act, 2008	Government of India	India	All enterprises	1	1	1	Mandatory
51	The Environmental (Protection) Act	Ministry of Environment and Forests	India	All enterprises	0	1	0	Mandatory
52	The Companies Bill, 2012	Government of India	India	Profit-making companies	1	1	1	Mandatory
53	The Companies Act of 1956	Government of India	India	All enterprises	1	1	0	Mandatory
54	Companies Act, 2013	Government of India	India	Large companies- min. net worth Rs 500 crore	1	1	0	Mandatory

ID No.	Framework.	Institution	Coverage	Application	Social	Environmental	Economic*	Enforcement
55	Annual Business Responsibility Reporting (ABRR): Clause 55 of the Listing Agreement	Securities and Exchange Board of India (SEBI)	India	Listed companies: top 100	1	1	0	Mandatory
56	DPE Guidelines on Corporate Social Responsibility and Sustainability for Central Public Sector Enterprises	Indian Department of Public Enterprise (DPE)	India	Public sector or state-owned enterprises	1	1	0	Mandatory
57	Charter on Corporate Responsibility for Environmental Protection (CREP)	Ministry of Environment & Forest (MoEF)	India	Large companies	0	1	0	Mandatory
58	Indian Factories Act	Government of India	India	Factories	1	0	0	Mandatory
59	CSR Voluntary Guidelines and Governance Voluntary Guidelines	Government of India	India	All enterprises	1	1	0	Voluntary
60	National Voluntary Guidelines on Social, Environmental, and Economic Responsibilities of Business	Ministry of Corporate Affairs	India	All enterprises	1	1	0	Voluntary
61	Report on activities on society and environment	Government of Indonesia	Indonesia	Listed companies	1	1	Cannot be determined	Comply or Explain
62	Rule No. X.K.6	Bapepam	Indonesia	Listed companies	1	0	Cannot be determined	Mandatory
63	Regulation No.KEP-431/BL/2012	Capital Markets Supervisory Agency	Indonesia	Listed companies	1	1	Cannot be determined	Mandatory

ID No.	Framework.	Institution	Coverage	Application	Social	Environmental	Economic*	Enforcement
64	Regulation No. 24/2012	Ministry of Energy and Mineral Resources	Indonesia	Natural resources industry	1	1	Cannot be determined	Mandatory
65	Art. 66 of law 40/2007	Government of Indonesia	Indonesia	Natural resources industry	1	1	Cannot be determined	Mandatory
66	Regulation No. 47/2012	Government of Indonesia	Indonesia	Natural resources industry	1	1	Cannot be determined	Mandatory
67	State Owned Enterprise Minister Regulation No. KEP-05/MBU/2007	Government of Indonesia	Indonesia	Public sector or state-owned enterprises	1	1	Cannot be determined	Mandatory
68	State Owned Enterprise Minister Regulation No. SE-443/MBU/2003	Government of Indonesia	Indonesia	Public sector or state-owned enterprises	1	0	Cannot be determined	Mandatory
69	Charter of Corporate Behaviour	Keidanren	Japan	All enterprises	1	1	1	Voluntary
70	Principles for Financial Action towards a Sustainable Society	Ministry of the Environment	Japan	All enterprises	1	1	1	Voluntary
71	Law on Recycling of End-of-Life Vehicles (ELV Recycling Law)	Government of Japan	Japan	Automotive sector	0	1	0	Mandatory
72	The Civil Aeronautics Act, 2006	Government of Japan	Japan	Aviation industry	0	1	0	Mandatory
73	Act on Promotion of Global Warming Countermeasures (Act No. 117 of 1998)	Ministry of Environment, Ministry of Economy, Trade and Industry	Japan	Polluting organizations	0	1	0	Mandatory

ID No.	Framework.	Institution	Coverage	Application	Social	Environmental	Economic*	Enforcement
74	The Pollutant Release and Transfer Register Law (PRTR)	Government of Japan	Japan	Specific industries	0	1	0	Mandatory
75	The Railway Enterprise Act, 2006	Government of Japan	Japan	Railway industry	1	1	Cannot be determined	Mandatory
76	JP-8:Mandatory GHG Emissions Reporting	Ministry of Environment, Ministry of Economy, Trade and Industry	Japan	Industrial companies, commercial businesses, universities, freight carriers, etc. who consume more than 1,500 kl (crude oil equivalent) of energy per year or emit more than 3,000 t-CO_2 per year	0	1	Cannot be determined	Mandatory
77	Law Concerning the Promotion of Business Activities with Environmental Consideration by Specified Corporations, etc., by Facilitating Access to Environmental Information, and Other Measures	Government of Japan	Japan	Specified corporations	0	1	0	Mandatory

ID No.	Framework.	Institution	Coverage	Application	Social	Environmental	Economic*	Enforcement
78	Environmental Reporting Guidelines	Ministry of the Environment	Japan	All enterprises	0	1	1	Voluntary
79	Emissions Trading Exchange Preparatory Corporation, Inc. (Joint Venture for emissions trading exchange)	Tokyo Stock Exchange & Tokyo Commodity Exchange	Japan	Cannot be determined	0	1	Cannot be determined	Voluntary
80	JP-2:Japanese Voluntary Emissions Trading Scheme (JVETS)	Ministry of Environment	Japan	Industrial and commercial sectors	0	1	Cannot be determined	Voluntary
81	Principles for Responsible Institutional Investors	Financial Services Authority (FSA)	Japan	Institutional investors	1	1	0	Voluntary
82	EcoAction 21 Guidelines	Japan Ministry of Environment	Japan	Small and medium-sized Enterprises	0	1	0	Voluntary
83	Corporate Governance Blueprint	Securities Commission	Malaysia	Listed companies	1	1	1	Mandatory
84	Corporate Disclosure Guide	Bursa Malaysia	Malaysia	Listed companies	1	1	0	Mandatory
85	CSR Disclosure incorporated into Listing Requirements	Bursa Malaysia	Malaysia	Listed companies	1	1	0	Mandatory
86	CSR in Annual reports	Government of Malaysia	Malaysia	Listed companies	1	1	Cannot be determined	Mandatory
87	Environmental Quality Act	Government of Malaysia	Malaysia	Polluting organizations	0	1	0	Mandatory

ID No.	Framework.	Institution	Coverage	Application	Social	Environmental	Economic*	Enforcement
88	GLCs (Government Linked Companies) Transformation Programme Sejahtera & Silver book on CSR	Putrajaya Committee on GLC High Performance	Malaysia	Public sector or state-owned enterprises	1	1	0	Voluntary
89	Reporting Requirements on Responsible Investment in Burma	Bureau of Democracy Human Rights and Labour	Myanmar	US Oil and Gas investors into Myanmar	1	0	0	Mandatory
90	Framework for Measuring Sustainable Development	Statistics New Zealand	New Zealand	All enterprises	1	1	1	Voluntary
91	Corporate Social Responsibility Voluntary Guidelines	Securities and Exchange Commission(SECP)	Pakistan	All enterprises	1	1	1	Voluntary
92	Companies (CSR) General Order: SRO 983(I)	Securities and Exchange Commission(SECP)	Pakistan	Listed companies	1	1	0	Mandatory
93	Financial Disclosure Checklist	Security Exchange Commission	Philippines	Listed companies	1	1	1	Voluntary
94	Corporate Social Responsibility Act	Government of the Philippines	Philippines	All enterprises	1	1	0	Mandatory
95	Social Contribution Performance Posting System	Financial Supervisory Service	Republic of Korea	Insurance companies	1	0	Cannot be determined	Mandatory
96	Green Posting System	Financial Services Commission	Republic of Korea	Listed companies	0	1	0	Mandatory
97	Framework Act on Low Carbon, Green Growth	Government of the Republic of Korea	Republic of Korea	Polluting organizations	0	1	0	Mandatory

ID No.	Framework.	Institution	Coverage	Application	Social	Environmental	Economic*	Enforcement
98	Environmental Reporting Guidelines	Government of the Republic of Korea	Republic of Korea	All enterprises	0	1	Cannot be determined	Voluntary
99	Environmental Reporting Guidelines	Ministry of Environment	Republic of Korea	Specific industries	0	1	Cannot be determined	Voluntary
100	Sustainability Management(SM) Report Guidelines (BEST)	Ministry of Knowledge Economy	Republic of Korea	All enterprises	1	1	Cannot be determined	Voluntary
101	Federal Law on Environmental Protection No. 7-FZ of January 10, 2002	Government of Russia	Russian Federation	All enterprises	0	1	0	Mandatory
102	Order 11-46/pзn	Russian Federal Financial Markets Service Order	Russian Federation	Listed companies	0	1	0	Mandatory
103	Directive 1710p-P13	Government of Russia	Russian Federation	Public sector or state-owned enterprises	0	1	0	Mandatory
104	Guidance # 03-849/r	Federal Commission on Securities Market	Russian Federation	Listed companies	1	1	0	Voluntary
105	Code on Corporate Governance	Monetary Authority of Singapore (MAS)	Singapore	Listed companies	1	1	1	Comply or Explain
106	Energy Conservation Act	Government of Singapore	Singapore	Polluting organizations	0	1	0	Mandatory
107	Revised Code of Corporate Governance (Draft)	Monetary Authority of Singapore (MAS)	Singapore	All enterprises	1	1	0	Voluntary
108	Guide to Sustainability Reporting	Singapore Exchange	Singapore	Listed companies	1	1	0	Voluntary

ID No.	Framework.	Institution	Coverage	Application	Social	Environmental	Economic*	Enforcement
109	Singapore Packaging Agreement	National Environment Agency	Singapore	All enterprises	0	1	0	Voluntary
110	CSR Best Practice Principles for TWSE/GTSM Listed Companies	Financial Supervisory Commission, R.O.C Securities and Futures Bureau	Taiwan Province of China	Listed companies	1	1	1	Voluntary
111	CSR Performance Disclosure	Financial Markets Regulator	Taiwan Province of China	Public and listed companies	1	1	Cannot be determined	Mandatory
112	Principles of Good Corporate Governance for Listed Companies	Stock Exchange of Thailand	Thailand	Listed companies	1	1	0	Mandatory
113	Guidance Document 'Approach to Social Responsibility Implementation for Corporations'	Stock Exchange of Thailand's Corporate Social Responsibility Institute (CSRI)	Thailand	Listed companies	1	1	Cannot be determined	Voluntary
114	Six CSR & sustainability directions in 2012: Reinforcing your CSR	Corporate Social Responsibility Institute of Stock Exchange of Thailand and Thaipat Institute	Thailand	Listed companies	1	1	Cannot be determined	Voluntary
115	Labour Law No. 4857	Government of Turkey	Turkey	All enterprises	1	0	0	Mandatory
116	Occupational Health and Safety Law No. 6331	Government of Turkey	Turkey	All enterprises	1	0	0	Mandatory

ID No.	Framework.	Institution	Coverage	Application	Social	Environmental	Economic*	Enforcement
117	Communique on 'Corporate Governance Principles'	Capital Markets Board of Turkey	Turkey	Listed companies	1	1	0	Mandatory
118	Environment Law No. 2872	Government of Turkey	Turkey	All enterprises	0	1	0	Mandatory
119	Protection of Consumer Law No. 4077	Government of Turkey	Turkey	All enterprises	0	1	0	Mandatory
120	Greenhouse Gas Regulation	Turkish Ministry of Environment and Urbanism	Turkey	Heavy industries	0	1	0	Mandatory
121	Sustainability Reporting Handbook for Vietnamese Companies	International Finance Corporation (IFC) Advisory Services in East Asia and the Pacific in collaboration with State Securities Commission of Vietnam	Vietnam	Listed companies	1	1	0	Comply or Explain

* The economic dimension of sustainability concerns the organization's impacts on the economic conditions of its stakeholders and on economic systems as defined per GRI G4 Guidelines.

Appendix 6.2: Sustainability reporting frameworks that reference GSCs

Sources: Compilation by the authors based on various sources.

ID No.	Framework	Institution	Coverage	Application	Social	Environmental	Economic	Enforcement	Considers whole or part GSC
1	RobecoSAM Corporate Sustainability Assessment	Dow Jones Sustainability Index (DJSI)	Global	Listed companies	1	1	1	Mandatory	Part
3	FTSE ESG Ratings	FTSE4Good	Global	Listed companies	1	1	0	Mandatory	Cannot be determined
5	G4 Sustainability Reporting Guidelines	Global Reporting Initiative (GRI)	Global	All enterprises	1	1	1	Voluntary	Whole
7	International Integrated Reporting Framework	International Integrated Reporting Committee (IIRC)	Global	All enterprises	1	1	1	Voluntary	Part
9	Connected Reporting Framework	Accounting for Sustainability Project	Global	Listed entities and other public interest entities	1	1	1	Voluntary	Whole
10	Communication on Progress (COP)	United Nations Global Compact (UNGC)	Global	All enterprises	1	1	0	Voluntary	Part
11	Supply Chain Programme–SMEs, Climate Change, and Water	Carbon Disclosure Project	Global	All enterprises	1	1	0	Voluntary	Part

ID No.	Framework	Institution	Coverage	Application	Social	Environmental	Economic	Enforcement	Considers whole or part GSC
12	IFC Sustainability Framework (Ed 2012-v2)	International Finance Corporation (IFC), World Bank Group	Global	Banking and finance industry	1	1	0	Voluntary	Part
13	Guidance on Corporate Responsibility Indicators in Annual Reports	United Nations Conference on Trade and Development (UNCTAD)	Global	All enterprises	1	0	1	Voluntary	Whole
14	OECD Guidelines for Multinational Enterprises (Ed. 2011-v5)	Organisation for Economic Co-operation and Development (OECD)	Global	Multinational enterprises	1	1	0	Voluntary	Whole
16	Greenhouse Gas Protocol Corporate Standard	World Resources Institute and the World Business Council for Sustainable Development	Global	Natural resources industry	0	1	0	Voluntary	Part
37	Shanghai Municipal Local Standards on Corporate Social Responsibility	Shanghai Municipal Bureau of Quality and Technical Supervision	China	All enterprises	1	1	0	Voluntary	Whole
55	Annual Business Responsibility Reporting (ABRR): Clause 55 of the Listing Agreement	Securities and Exchange Board of India (SEBI)	India	Listed companies: top 100	1	1	0	Mandatory	Whole

ID No.	Framework	Institution	Coverage	Application	Social	Environmental	Economic	Enforcement	Considers whole or part GSC
60	National Voluntary Guidelines on Social, Environmental, and Economic Responsibilities of Business	Ministry of Corporate Affairs	India	All enterprises	1	1	0	Voluntary	Whole
69	Charter of Corporate Behaviour	Keidanren	Japan	All enterprises	1	1	1	Voluntary	Whole
82	EcoAction 21 Guidelines	Japan Ministry of Environment	Japan	Small and medium-sized Enterprises	0	1	0	Voluntary	Part
89	Reporting Requirements on Responsible Investment in Burma	Bureau of Democracy Human Rights and Labour	Myanmar	US oil and gas investors into Myanmar	1	0	0	Mandatory	Part
110	CSR Best Practice Principles for TWSE/GTSM Listed Companies	Financial Supervisory Commission, R.O.C Securities and Futures Bureau	Taiwan Province of China	Listed companies	1	1	1	Voluntary	Part

ID No.	Framework	Institution	Coverage	Application	Social	Environmental	Economic	Enforcement	Considers whole or part GSC
117	Communique on 'Corporate Governance Principles'	Capital Markets Board of Turkey	Turkey	Listed companies	1	1	0	Mandatory	Part
121	Sustainability Reporting Handbook for Vietnamese Companies	International Finance Corporation (IFC) Advisory Services in East Asia and the Pacific in collaboration with State Securities Commission of Vietnam	Vietnam	Listed companies	1	1	0	Comply or explain	Whole

Methodology

7

The sustainability blind spot

Identifying and managing climate risk in global supply chains

Nik C. Steinberg
Four Twenty Seven Climate Solutions

Managing risk and sustainability in global supply chains has never been as challenging as it is today, especially in the face of climate change. During the last few years, extreme weather and resource constraints have created an uneasy environment in the C-suites of the world's largest multinational corporations. Global supply chains are experiencing more frequent and costly disruptions due to increasingly powerful climate-induced events, yet many companies do not have the appropriate means to measure and manage climate risks. A limited purview of suppliers and a limited spectrum of risks can leave people, products and assets exposed. Equipped with the right tools, businesses are uniquely positioned to support local risk reduction efforts through parallel efforts to reduce climate risks in their own supply chains. This chapter will present the case for why climate risk reduction in the supply chain and business-led community risk reduction are complementary endeavours, and present a method for identifying risk and prioritizing supplier and community engagement opportunities.

7.1 Introduction

Environmental and social impact from global production and consumption are inextricably tied to, and exacerbated by, changes in the natural environment (Dauvergne and Lister, 2012). In 2011, California-based Intel lost US$1 billion in revenue as a result of flooding in Thailand (driven by the strongest monsoon in 50 years). Locally, over 800 people were killed and 350,000 manufacturing employees were laid off (Garside, 2012). Notably, the damage was in large part due to too much precipitation in a short timeframe, one of the most fundamental effects of global warming due to greater evaporation from the oceans, leading in turn to more intense rainfall events. Similarly, elevated storm surge and energy content in the north-eastern United States following Hurricane Irene in 2011 and Hurricane Sandy in 2012, led to widespread black-outs lasting days and even weeks in some areas, with millions without power and transportation systems crippled, disrupting global trade flows and the regional economy.

The recent push for lean supply chains and just-in-time deliveries has concentrated goods and built-up inventories in some of the most climate-vulnerable regions of the world. A majority of the world's manufacturing occurs near river deltas or low lying coastal regions that are particularly sensitive to floods. Growing water stress, stemming from rising demands due to higher incomes, growing populations and prolonged periods of intense drought, is also driving companies to rethink water use in the manufacturing process (Levinson *et al,*. 2008). Still today, many companies do not actively monitor and manage climate risks, including the conditions that may lead to more extreme events and resource shortages. And rarely do companies know the full origin of their global supply chains—into the farms and factories where the initial ripples of climate change impacts begin.

The focus on climate change in the context of supply chains is relatively new and few tools exist for managers to make climate-informed decisions. Fortunately, there is a familiar framework to help supply chain managers better manage and understand the impacts of climate change. Sustainable supply chain management (SSCM)—the concept of minimizing ecological impact throughout the supply chain while meeting global demands. The SSCM field has evolved rather disproportionately with a bias towards theory development over practical applications and a thematic preference for environmental dimensions over social ones (Ashby *et al.*, 2012). Climate change impacts on supply chains will continue to threaten the solidarity of many communities around the world, disrupting the food, medicine, energy and products that support economies (GAO, 2015). The tendency to emphasize one part of the supply chain and one process in isolation has also fragmented an otherwise holistic framework intended to address economic, environmental and social dimensions (Burgess *et al.*, 2006; Rao and Holt, 2005).

In the SSCM field, no coherent steps have been taken to incorporate the challenges and opportunities that arise from climate change, including the multitude of threats to triple bottom line (TBL) sustainability. To date, the sustainability, financial and development fields have developed strong links between supply chains and climate change including, but not limited to:

- Commodity risk (Gledhill *et al.*, 2013)

- The impact on small-scale producers (Thorpe and Fennel, 2013)

- Emission reduction and energy efficiency (CDP, 2014; Halldórsson *et al.*, 2008) and

- Economic performance (Simchi-Levi *et al.*, 2013).

A natural by-product of operations research and environmentally focused frameworks (e.g. Green Supply Chain Management (GSCM) and Environmental Supply Chain Management (ESCM), SSCM is challenged with consolidating the challenges and theoretical frameworks of yesterday with the social and ecological challenges of tomorrow.

There remains a tangible need to develop a clearer understanding of climate change impacts in relation to SSCM practices. Inaction on the matter is largely attributable to particularly limited information about climate risks in relation to supply chains, inherent uncertainties about future outcomes and a lack of practical guidance on the matter (EA, 2013; GAO, 2015).

SSCM has, however, continued to popularize the use of important environmental performance metrics and methods, taking into account the inputs and outputs of various environmental aspects (Pimenta and Ball, 2015). One practical linkage of the SSCM framework and climate change is the utility of life-cycle assessment and environmental footprint methods to address complex industrial ecology questions for managers. Such methods have thus far produced useful quantitative sustainability indicators (Hendrickson *et al.*, 2006) and will continue to play a pivotal role in advancing the understanding and management of resource use and logistics in increasingly unstable environments. While this focus on production efficiency and impact minimization is critical to achieving a proactive sustainability approach, it merely addresses yesterday's ecological challenges.

As of late, climate models are achieving higher resolution and generating verifiably accurate forecasts (Allen *et al.*, 2013). The use of climate information is also slowly shifting to business-relevant impacts. Second-order variables such as Cooling Degree Days[1] and Water-Limited Crop productivity[2] (Lim *et al.*, 2009) are helping managers make better design and sourcing decisions under the prospect of rising temperatures and prolonged droughts stemming from climate change. Yet there are real barriers to addressing the direct and indirect impacts of climate change in a supply chain, especially in a way that results in meaningful change at both the business and community level.

---

1 Cooling degree days are the number of degrees that a day's average temperature is above 65° Fahrenheit and energy demand (and costs) for cooling can rise linearly in buildings.
2 Water-Limited Crop productivity is a metric used to gauge yield potential where water is a limiting factor in crop production.

Businesses plan for the short-term; making decisions based on events and processes occurring over seconds, days and years, as opposed to the decadal trends commonly provided in even the most sophisticated climate models. Likewise, businesses tend to grow and evolve within the bounds of scaling laws, competing for space, resources and customers at spatial scales of about one kilometre or less (Batty, 2008). In contrast, climate processes, which are physical and chemical in nature, have only been reasonably resolved and downscaled to about four kilometres, a resolution that is not readily and freely available in most climate change projections (Fernandez, 2014). Such spatial and temporal disparities may inhibit a business from mapping economic and climate processes together. Even when such incongruities are resolved, climate data, largely inaccessible in its original format, and divergent extrapolation methods can make the standardization of data difficult. Given the technical nature of mapping production and climate processes on the same grid, current operational and risk management systems may not be well equipped to measure or manage future risks stemming from climate change.

Thanks to emerging pressures placed upon corporations to provide more traceable and sustainable products, some firms are beginning to blend sustainability and risk-reduction efforts through the lens of climate change (e.g. Mars, Coca-Cola, EMC and Puma). There are multiple reasons why a company may try to reduce the exposure of their supply chain. Internally, considerations may include:

- Physical risks of climate change that may inflict damage to infrastructure or other assets

- Price risks due to raw material shortages and commodity price fluctuations, and

- Product risks due to market shifts and preferences caused by climate change.

For major brands with high external exposure, the risk of negative perception can place pressure on companies to account for:

- Ratings risk determined by third-party organizations (e.g. CDP) dedicated to reporting risk exposure

- Regulatory risk enforced by government; and to a lesser extent, and

- Reputation risk based on public and investor perception of a supply chains' contribution to climate change or its dependence on cheap labour, conflict minerals, or limited shared resources.

Figure 7.1 Typology of potential impacts in global supply chains, from end use to raw material extraction

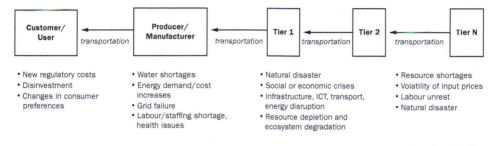

- New regulatory costs
- Disinvestment
- Changes in consumer preferences

- Water shortages
- Energy demand/cost increases
- Grid failure
- Labour/staffing shortage, health issues

- Natural disaster
- Social or economic crises
- Infrastructure, ICT, transport, energy disruption
- Resource depletion and ecosystem degradation

- Resource shortages
- Volatility of input prices
- Labour unrest
- Natural disaster

Taken together, these internal and external concerns have driven some global companies to employ climate-specific tools to assess these risks into the future (C2ES, 2013). For these companies, the supply chain is an important milestone in their journey to become more resilient to climate change.

This chapter presents the benefits and outcomes of modelling climate impacts on the supply chain and a method for identifying climate risk in the supply chain. By developing greater insight into risks driven by climate change, businesses may be better equipped to protect bottom-lines and the communities upon which they depend. These efforts first require a full view of the supply chain, a process referred to as supply chain mapping, which can help unveil suppliers and producers to points of raw material extraction (where some of the largest impacts from climate change first manifest). Following supply chain mapping, production processes can then be modelled to quantify environmental impact and resource consumption requirements within the local operating area. Next, spatial overlays of climate change forecasts can help inform where, and to what extent, climate change poses a material risk to the company and may also negatively affect surrounding communities.

If supply chains are ever to serve as a conduit for climate risk reduction in supply chains and communities, then firms must embrace a new order of SSCM. To address this novel challenge, firms can incorporate a variety of data-driven tools to better understand the relationship between climate risk and supply chain risk. The following approaches and methods are presented not as a prescriptive sequence of actions, but a roadmap for firms seeking more sustainable and resilient supply chains. These actions are discussed in three parts:

- Supply chain mapping,

- Connecting production data to environmental impacts, and

- Utilizing climate change models to prioritize engagement efforts.

Taken together, such methods can generate the combination of data needed to reach beyond existing sustainability efforts and address long-term, unmeasured risks inextricably tied to TBL performance.

7.2 Mapping the invisible

Supply and supplier visibility is the great enabler. Supply chain visibility gives companies a competitive advantage by providing data on the status of materials and assets in a supply chain (Hanebeck and Tracey, 2003). However, the scale and complexity of global supply chains today can make upstream visibility difficult. In 2015 only 14% of the 385 global manufacturing senior executives surveyed reported to have visibility beyond their tier-1 suppliers (Global Manufacturing Outlook, 2015). Limited visibility across tiers means that the vast majority of potential disruptions, typically occurring upstream (tier-2 to tier-N suppliers), are invisible to managers. This blind spot increases risk and, in turn, increases the probability of disruption when risks go unmanaged.

The problem is not merely one of poor management. The magnitude of short-term weather impacts can be volatile and often unpredictable, and today's supply chains are covering a wider swathe of the globe. Risk and uncertainty lead to a lack of confidence that, ultimately, is due to a lack of visibility both vertically and horizontally (Christopher and Lee, 2001; Brandon-Jones *et al.*, 2014). As a result, some supply chain managers compensate with inventory build-ups, adding additional and costly nodes to an already complex supply chain.

Achieving full visibility into a supply chain requires much more than just tracking shipments from point A to B. Geographical supply chain mapping is an inherently difficult process without the right tools. Traditional methods to network mapping rely upon surveys and questionnaires distributed to tier-1 suppliers, which are aimed at gaining information about additional (direct and indirect) suppliers until the network map connects retailers to upstream suppliers. This technique, however, can be cumbersome and time-consuming. The average supply chain may involve thousands of suppliers and each tier depends on many indirect suppliers. Following an exhaustive inventory of thousands of surveys and questionnaires, the map of suppliers and producers may or may not include points of raw material extraction; an increasingly important source of disruption risks related to extreme weather, resource shortages, commodity price spikes and labour unrest (O'Shea *et al.*, 2013).

As an alternative, companies can follow the trade flow of their products using a number of widely and freely available online modules (e.g. The Atlas of Economic Complexity, 2013; UN Comtrade Database, 2014). These databases incorporate a country's export mix and its intermediary role in global supply chains (i.e. back-end manufacturing, assembly, packaging and distribution). For example, the typical semi-conductor manufacturing value chain in 2013 may have involved the following: manufacturers in Taiwan or South Korea, software suppliers in northern India, suppliers responsible for testing and assembly functions in Malaysia and, based on proximity to tech manufacturers and active shipping industry, at least one distributor in Singapore (The Atlas of Economic Complexity, 2013). Taken together, this network represented the most probable, albeit not exact, chain of suppliers and producers that contributed to the manufacturing and distribution of semiconductors to the world marketplace in 2013.

Yet location data holds little inherent value without context. For example, the leading country-level index of climate vulnerability and readiness, the Notre Dame Global Adaptation Index (ND-GAIN), incorporates logistic performance indicators developed by the World Bank to help planners, donors and businesses consider trade- and transport-related risks in the context of climate change for any given country. There are a number of other social, economic and ecological indicators in the index, such as food and energy security or the integrity of communication technology, that can all help inform the magnitude and likelihood of a potential disruption within a country. Thus, with the right location data, supply chain managers can overlay a wealth of contextual information, via mapping, about any given node in the supply chain. It can also help managers evaluate the quality of roads, reliability of the local energy grid, or the overall ease of doing business. Turning local data into local knowledge requires mapping data and a rich subtext about the local infrastructure, people, politics and climate.

The benefits of businesses utilizing modelled trade flow data, rather than questionnaires, to map a complex global supply chain is not only savings in time and cost but the ability to match the full geographic spectrum of possible suppliers to locally relevant risk reduction and sustainability considerations. Deep visibility into a company's supply network can also give direction to the company's environmental management efforts, linking production with a particular place where suppliers may be overly concentrated and dependent on weak core infrastructure such as roads and utilities. Moreover, the interplay between resource extraction and looming resource constraints (e.g. water requirements and local water supply) can be identified early and avoided before shifting climatic and population conditions lead to local conflict or a costly disruption.

7.3 Connecting production data to environmental impacts

Companies increasingly need to know about the supply chain risks related to climate change (O'Shea *et al.*, 2013). First-degree climate change impacts such as extreme weather events often cascade into second-degree impacts such as resource shortages, infrastructure failure or social unrest, having significant implications for costs and overall company value. While climate change poses its own inherent risks, institutional drivers are equally important. A company's own production processes can outweigh other physical climate drivers. In 2014, water authorities in northern India ordered the closure of a large Coca-Cola bottling plant after local groundwater levels dropped to a level that prevented the irrigation of local crops and inhibited the delivery of drinking water for surrounding residents (AFP, 2014).

Water withdrawal requirements at a Coca-Cola facility exceeded groundwater recharge rates (and water needs of local farmers), creating a situation in which both the supply chain and local community were negatively affected.

Had a company official investigated the local water regime and climate, including satellite observations and field data of regional groundwater fluctuations dating back to the 1960s (Rodell, Velicogna and Famiglietti, 2009), such outcomes may have been avoided altogether. Even if such groundwater supply estimates were initially overlooked, a basic water footprint analysis—accounting for the volume of water required in the local watershed—would have spelled out near-term water shortages. The amount of water required for a 0.5 litre of Coke includes approximately three litres for processing at the bottling plant and another 28 litres for growing ingredients and seven litres for packaging, according to 2010 estimates of Coca-Cola's global production.[3] In 2013, the bottling plant was able to produce 600 polyethylene terephthalate (PET) bottles every minute (AFP 2014), processing at least 108,000 litres of groundwater every hour of operation at the plant and as much as 1.1 million litres of groundwater to grow ingredients in nearby farms. With growing consumer classes around the world, the competition for water for subsistence-based agriculture and water for the agricultural and production supply chains is driving major ecological pressures.

"Footprinting" was a method first championed in the early 1980s and later used in life-cycle-assessments (LCA) in order to better understand the magnitude of environmental impacts associated with the creation, processing, delivery and use of products (Galli *et al.*, 2012; Butchart *et al.*, 2010). Today, LCA is the primary methodology for quantifying environmental impacts and identifying "hot spots" in the supply chain by pinpointing the most impactful, and thereby resource-dependent activities (Acquaye *et al.*, 2011). Footprinting enables the quantification of resource consumption (and emission of greenhouse gases and toxins) between and among industries for a particular commodity, which allows managers to measure the degree of environmental pressure, resource depletion and resource dependency associated with a particular process.

Resource constraints are often the first signal of ecological stress and consuming natural resources as production inputs can induce local ecological crisis and costly business disruptions when coupled with concurrent drivers. The world's second largest beer maker, SABMiller, commissioned a report with the World Wildlife Fund (WWF) in 2009 to investigate its water footprint in South Africa, a country rife with physical and social water scarcity (Tapela, 2012). The report found that beers such as Castle lager and Carling Black Label required approximately 155 litres of water for every litre of beer, with farms in South Africa accounting for 90% of the total water use. Following the assessment, which determined the specific volume and

---

3   The Nature Conservancy, with the support of the Water Footprint Network, conducted a Product Water Footprint Assessment for Coca-Cola in 2010 and found that while a significant amount of blue water (i.e. surface and groundwater) is required in Coca-Cola's bottling process, the supply chain accounted for more than 98% of total water usage.

efficiency of SABMiller's water use in South Africa, Anna Swaithes, Head of Water and Food Security Policy at SABMiller, said the following:

> We fully understand that, while reducing our own water use is essential, it is only part of the solution. We—and all businesses—must urgently look beyond our own operations. After all, we depend on the same water as local communities, farmers, and the other businesses that fuel local economies. We must work with these stakeholders to secure our shared water resources—so that communities have uninterrupted access to safe water, farmers can productively grow food and earn their livelihood, and our breweries can continue to brew great beer.

The food and beverage sector benefits from a relatively short supply chain with few tiers existing between the raw materials and the final manufacturing process. Not all sectors (e.g. apparel, high-tech/electronics, automotive, food, biotechnology/pharmaceuticals, forest- and paper-based) can readily match a group of suppliers to a product footprint due to the breadth and depth of the supplier network; hence the need for many firms to elevate the connection between supply chain mapping and footprinting.

Footprinting relies on input-output (IO) analysis to capture the cumulative contributions of upstream services for the production of a particular product. This can be done using hybrid IO-LCA models, an approach based on the work of Wassily Leontief (1906–1999). Using matrix algebra, Leontief was able to compare the amount of output from one industry required to produce one dollar of output from a related industry. For example, the demand for cotton fabric from the clothing manufacturing sector results in a demand for dye from the ink dying sector (first-tier). That demand results in a demand for electricity from the electricity generation sector (second-tier) to operate the ink dye manufacturing facilities. Additional supplier requirements are calculated with further multiplication of the direct requirements by the final output.

Connecting production data, including the multiple sectors involved in the production of a single product, to environmental impact data via IO analysis can be computed using a number of free and readily available online modules: Global Environmental Management Institute Tool, Carnegie Mellon Green Design Institute and OpenLCA to name but a few. These models typically utilize archives of historical pollution and consumption rates for specific industries allowing them to capture "cradle-to-gate" environmental impact data, meaning they can quantify a breadth of resource inputs (e.g. embodied water, energy, land and wood) from extraction all the way to the production floor. What makes these models so useful is their ability to disentangle complex production networks and estimate the environmental requirements associated with millions of transactions in the supply chain.

There are, however, limitations to models such as hybrid IO-LCAs that aggregate for environmental impact. For longer and more fragmented supply chains, where each link acts independently, supplier data tends to get aggregated at the industry level and may overlook best-practices and efficiencies carried out by individual suppliers. Also, data is often derived from industry averages, which may under or over represent the impacts of a specific supply chain (O'Rourke, 2014). This is especially true when imports are treated as products created within defined economic boundaries (Hendrickson *et al.*, 2006). Production-level metrics across the life-cycle, including up- and down-stream of facilities may also not generate the same precision as site-level metrics.

Still, for common resource shortages tied to internal production processes, these methods are sufficient for using production data to understand the firm's connection to local resource scarcity by rapidly assessing thousands of products in a company's supply chain. Connecting environmental impact data to production processes is not only an important consideration for determining the suitability of a site or a supplier but it is also an important indicator of future supply chain disruptions.

7.4 Utilizing climate change models to identify hidden exposures

Unveiling important characteristics of place and product can, together, enable real-time monitoring deep in the supply chain. While these methods may lead to better monitoring and day-to-day management, they alone will not change business models or forge long-term stakeholder engagement programmes. There is a critical need to turn location and product data into meaningful information about a future beset by climate change.

The weight of climate change upon social and economic dimensions of the supply chain will increasingly demand more attention. It amplifies or alters existing risks and creates new, often unpredictable risks. Limiting global warming to the two °C threshold set by the UN Framework Convention on Climate Change (UNF-CCC) could be exceeded by the end of the century in the absence of aggressive mitigation in the first half of the century. Predictive models focused on the impacts of climate change in the 2020s suggest droughts will become longer and markedly more severe, especially across Asia (Forster *et al.*, 2012). Foreseen impacts related to just a two °C increase in global warming by the end of the century suggest significant amplification of risks for the most exposed nodes of a supply chain. Above the two °C threshold of global warming, sea level rise threatens many major cities, significant water shortages affect crop production and drinking water availability in developing countries and more species face extinction, with 10% of species believed to be at risk for every one °C of warming (Thomas *et al.*, 2004). A two °C future also indicates more frequent and intense extreme weather, as well as a growing risk of abrupt and major irreversible changes in the climate system. To make more prudent decisions about these risks and better understand the severity of impact on supply chains and the communities they depend upon, climate change models can offer a glimpse into the future.

The most recent and advanced models from the Fifth Assessment of the Intergovernmental Panel on Climate Change (IPCC) generate outlooks to the end of the century and beyond. Although there is no way to know exactly how accurate these models depict discrete events, they represent the best source of information available for understanding future climate conditions that may lead to more extreme events. In fact, simulations conducted in the 1990s of warming observed in the last decade have proven remarkably accurate (Allen *et al.*, 2013).

One method of minimizing inherent model uncertainties is through an ensemble of models that balance biases and sensitivities (Flato *et al.*, 2013). Models can be further refined through a process called downscaling, or the systematic approach to simulating climates at a higher spatial resolution, incorporating local topography (e.g. coastlines and mountain ranges) and small-scale processes (e.g. convective precipitation) (Feser *et al.*, 2011; Feser and Barcikowska, 2012). In light of the typical business horizon (zero to five years), it has been suggested that decadal models better represent some aspects of internal climate variability, which can weigh heavily upon local climates in the short-term (Meehl *et al.*, 2010; Mochizuki *et al.*, 2012).

After selecting the appropriate models and timeframe, it may be necessary to establish thresholds and calculate the magnitude of an event that has triggered past disruptions. This can provide some sort of baseline for future events that are of a potentially dangerous magnitude. Examples may include a prolonged drought that elevated grain prices, or a heat wave that increased energy costs. Understanding the signature of past events (e.g. timing, magnitude and impact) can further refine the type of future qualifying events. After the relevant thresholds have been established for a particular location and activity, the climate models can be further refined to estimate the frequency and severity of similar and more intense events. This data can then be applied to each node in the supply chain across relevant time horizons. Long-term forecasts (i.e. 5–50 years in the business context) can be supplemented with forecasts that capture, though do not distinguish, short-term anomalies in the local climate (e.g. inter-annual and inter-seasonal oscillations).

Next, probability estimates can be generated for multiple locations within the same timeframe, enabling the comparison and suitability of sites and suppliers based on their respective climate risk profiles. As described earlier, local climate data does not necessarily equate to local knowledge and other climate risk considerations should be taken into account. Examples include demographic shifts, land use change and dependence on fragile infrastructure and ecosystems. Each of these variables may have a nonlinear response to changes in the climate, reinforcing the importance of a holistic approach to risk analysis when using climate change models.

Risk indexing is a systematic approach to identifying and classifying risk units delineated in a number of statistical units, ranges and scales, essential to avoid problems inherent when mixing measurements of variable units and types. For example, the climate risk profile of a supplier may include multiple measurements regarding the prevailing physical, social, environmental and financial risks to a specific climate hazard. A manufacturer in Thailand or the US Gulf Coast may consider the forecasted severity of future rainfall events, along with the residences of employees, the integrity of storm water infrastructure and the value-at risk to various flood levels. Some data extrapolation may be required to build relationships between changes first-degree impacts (temperature and precipitation) identified through climate models with second-degree impacts that induce disruptions and cost increases in the supply chain. These causal and semi-causal relationships could be based on historical disruptions (e.g. 100-year flood results in a 10-day facility closure) or linear cost relationships (e.g. 5% rise in CDD results in 3% rise in cooling demand).

Take, for example, a cluster of manufacturers in a supply chain that have been mapped to the same climate zone in Asia.[4] Climate change projections suggest an intensification of drought in this region in the next 10–15 years while the company-specific IO-LCA models suggest above average water consumption relative to expected regional water availability. Now consider another case downstream in the supply chain, involving a warehouse in Central Europe that requires significant cooling. Climate change projections suggest significant warming by 2020 and near-linear increases (holding technology constant) in energy consumption to meet building cooling requirements.

In the first example, variability in precipitation stemming from climate change would affect the continuity and/or cost to a concentrated group of manufacturers with elevated dependence on water. In the Central Europe facility, temperature increases stemming from climate change would increase the energy expenditures required for cooling. All across the supply chain, multiple climate change risks can negatively affect the cost, quality and timing of goods based on the location and efficiency of key suppliers.

When climate models and their local impacts are coupled with supply chain maps, managers are better prepared to reconfigure their supply chains. Managers can pinpoint reliance on sole suppliers and concentrated inventories. As evidenced by the 2011 Thailand floods, a high degree of supplier concentration can freeze the delivery of entire product lines following an extreme weather event. Having multiple locations with similar climate risk profiles only increases the risk of disruption. A conditional probability analysis can help ensure that a disruption at one location does not result in a disruption at another. This can be done by developing redundancies that are geographically and climatically diverse with distinct exposure types. Climate risk metrics not only help determine adequate insurance coverage and logistics preparedness but they can also help indicate where sustainability and engagement efforts are most needed. Where suppliers otherwise performed

---

4 The Köppen Climate Classification system, which is made of 31 unique climate zones, evaluates monthly precipitation and temperature observations from global datasets to determine a region's climate zone.

adequately in regard to community rights, environment or governance, they may falter in preparedness to looming climate change impacts.

The weight of climate change upon the TBL of supply chains requires better insight into climate futures. The scope of what matters to companies is expanding and companies are now expected to manage and mitigate risks within the communities upon which they depend. This is why the traceability of products and the critical nodes connecting them to consumers is so important for defining boundaries and identifying hotspots. Footprinting exercises can subsequently give companies a better understanding of where requirements will outpace availability—and the disruptions and stakeholder conflicts that may follow.

Figure 7.2 Modular steps to assessing character and level of climate-related risks in global supply chains

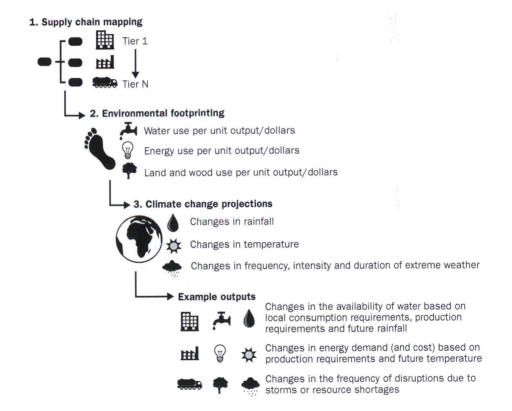

Addressing the full spectrum of potential consequences that stem from climate change will require a re-conceptualization of how managers connect and mange supply chains, with particular attention to changing resource regimes, increasingly vulnerable social groups and new weather patterns. Anticipating and responding to such changes will still require managers to utilize sustainability performance metrics, but it will also require a wider temporal and spatial purview for the suitability of suppliers and supplier locations, and the health of communities within which they operate. While substantial work is still needed to integrate climate change models into the SSCM framework, these tools and methods represent a practical step towards addressing this dynamic set of new challenges.

References

Acquaye, A.A., Wiedmann, T., Feng, K., Crawford, R.H., Barrett, J., Kuylenstierna, J., Duffy, A.P., Lenny Koh, S.C., & McQueen-Mason, S., (2011). Identification of "carbon hot-spots" and quantification of GHG intensities in the biodiesel supply chain using hybrid LCA and structural path analysis. *Environmental Science Technology*, 45(6), 2,471-2,478.

AFP (Agence France Presse) (2012). *Indian officials order Coca-Cola plant to close for using too much water.* Retrieved from http://www.rt.com/news/indian-officials-demolish-coke-plant-171 (June 18, 2015)

Allen, M.R., Mitchell, J.F., Stott, B., & Peter A. (2013). Test of a decadal climate forecast. *Nature Geoscience*, 6, 243-244.

Ashby, A., Leat, M., & Hudson-Smith., M. (2012). Making connections: A review of supply chain management and sustainability literature. *Supply Chain Management: An International Journal*, 17(5), 497-516.

Batty M. (2008). The size, scale, and shape of cities. *Science*, 319(5864), 769-771.

Brandon-Jones, E., Squire, B., & Rossenberg, Y.G.T. (2014). The impact of supply base complexity on disruptions and performance: The moderating effects of slack and visibility. *International Journal of Production Research*, (ahead-of-print). doi: 10.1080/00207543.2014.986296.

Burgess, K., Singh, P.J., & Koroglu R. (2006). Supply chain management: A structured literature review and implications for future research. *International Journal of Operations & Production Management*, 26, 703-729.

CDP (Carbon Disclosure Product) (2014) Collaborative Action on Climate Risk. *Supply Chain Report 2013–2104.* Retrieved from http://www.cdp.net (February 16, 2015).

Christopher, M., & Lee, H.L. (2001). *Supply Chain Confidence—The Key to Effective Supply Chains through Improved Visibility and Reliability.* Cranfield and Stanford: Vastera Corporation.

C2ES (Center for Climate and Energy Solutions) (2013). *Weathering the Storm: Building Business Resilience to Climate Change.* Retrieved from: http://www.c2es.org (July 20, 2015).

Dauvergne, P., & Lister, P. (2012). Big brand sustainability: Governance prospects and environmental limits. *Global Environmental Change*, 22(1) (February), 36-45.

EA (UK Environment Agency) (2013). *Assessing and managing climate change risks in supply chains.* Retrieved from http://publications.environmentagency.gov.uk

Fernandez S., Allen M., & Walker K. (2014). Perspective: The climate-population-infrastructure modelling and simulation fertile area for new research. *Journal of Climatology & Weather Forecasting*, 2, 116.

Feser, F., & Barcikowska, M. (2012). The influence of spectral nudging on typhoon formation in regional climate models. *Environmental Research Letters*, 7, 014024.

Feser, F., Rockel, B., Von Storch, H., Winterfeldt, J., & Zahn, M. (2011). Regional climate models add value to global model data: A review and selected examples. *Bulletin of the American Meteorological Society*, 92, 1181-1192.

Flato, G., Marotzke, J.,Abiodun, B., Braconnot, P., Chou, S.C., Collins, W., Cox, P., Driouech, F., Emori, S., Eyring, V., Forest, C., Gleckler, P., Guilyardi, E., Jakob, C., Kattsov, V., Reason, C., & Rummukainen, M. (2013). Evaluation of climate models. In T.F. Stocker, D. Qin, G.-K. Plattner, M. Tignor, S.K. Allen, J. Boschung, A. Nauels, Y. Xia, V. Bex, P.M. Midgley (Eds.), Climate Change 2013: *The Physical Science Basis. Contribution of Working Group I to the Fifth Assessment Report of the Intergovernmental Panel on Climate Change*. Cambridge, UK and New York, NY: Cambridge University Press.

Forster, P., Jackson, L., Lorenz, S., Simelton, E., Fraser, E., & Bahadur, K. (2012). *Food security: Near future projections of the impact of drought in Asia*. The Centre for Low Carbon Futures.

GAO (US Government Accountability Office) (2015). *Federal supply chains: Opportunities to improve the management of climate-related risks*. GAO-16-32, a report to the Honorable Matthew Cartwright, House of Representatives. Retrieved from http://gao.com

Garside J. (2012). Thailand flooding costs Lloyd's of London $2.2bn. *The Guardian*. Retrieved from http://www.theguardian.com/business/2012/feb/14/lloyds-thailand-flooding-2bn-dollars

Gledhill R, Hamza-Goodacre D, & Ping Low L. (2013). Business-not-as-usual: Tackling the impacts of climate change on supply risk. *Resilience: A Journal of Strategy and Risk*. Retrieved from http://www.pwc.com/resilience

Hanebeck, H. L. & Tracey, B (2003). The Role of Location in Supply Chain Management: How Mobile Communication Enables Supply Chain Best Practice and Allows Companies to Move to the Next Level. *International Journal of Mobile Communications*. 1(1/2), p148-166.

Halldórsson A., & Kovács, G. (2010). The sustainable agenda and energy efficiency: Logistics solutions and supply chains in times of climate change. *International Journal of Physical Distribution & Logistics Management*, 40(1/2), 5-13.

Hendrickson, C.T., Lave, L.B., & Matthews, H.S. (2006). *Environmental Life Cycle Assessment of Goods and Services: An Input-Output Approach*. Resources for the Future Press.

Levinson, M., Lee, E., Chung, J., Huttner, M., Danely, C., McKnight, C., & Langlois, A. (2008). *Watching water: A guide to evaluating corporate risks in a thirsty world*. New York, NY: JPMorgan.

Lim, W.H., & Roderick, M.L. (2009). *An Atlas of the Global Water Cycle Based on the IPCC AR4 Climate Models*. Canberra, Australia: ANU ePress.

Meehl, G.A., Hu, A., & Tebaldi, C. (2010). Decadal prediction in the Pacific region. *Journal of Climatology*, 23, 2959.2973.

Meehl, G.A., Stocker, T.F., Collins, W.D., Friedlingstein, P., Gaye, A.T., Gregory, J.M., Kitoh, A., Knutti, R., Murphy, J.M., Noda, A., Raper, S.C.B., Watterson, I.G., Weaver, A.J., & Zhao, Z.-C. (2007). Global climate projections. In S. Solomon, D. Qin, M. Manning, Z. Chen, M. Marquis, K.B. Averyt, M. Tignor, H.L. Miller (Eds.), *Climate Change 2007: The Physical Science Basis*. Contribution of Working Group I to the Fourth Assessment Report of the Intergovernmental Panel on Climate Change. Cambridge, UK and New York, NY: Cambridge University Press.

Mochizuki, T., Chikamoto, T., Kimoto, M., Ishii, M., Tatebe, H., Komuro, Y., Sakamoto, T., Watanabe, M., & Mori, M. (2012). Decadal prediction using a recent series of MIROC global climate models. *Journal of Meteorological Society of Japan*. 90A, 373-383.

O'Rourke, D. (2014). The science of sustainable supply chains. *Science*. 344, 6188, 1124-1127.

O'Shea T., Golden J.S., & Olander L. (2013). Sustainability and earth resources: Life cycle assessment modelling. *Business Strategy and the Environment*, 22(7), 429-441.

Pimenta, H., & Ball, P. (2015). Analysis of environmental sustainability practices across upstream supply chain management. *Procedia CIRP*. 26, 2015, 677-682.

Rao, P., & Holt D. (2005). Do green supply chains lead to competitiveness and economic performance? *International Journal of Operations & Production Management*, 25, 898-916.

Rodell M., Velicogna I., & Famiglietti, J.S. (2009). Satellite-based estimates of groundwater depletion in India. *Nature*, 460, 999-1002.

Simchi-Levi, D., Kyratzoglou, I.M., & Vassiliadis, C.G. (2013). *Supply Chain and Risk Management*, MIT Forum for Supply Chain Innovation and PWC.

Tapela, B.N. (2012). *Social Water Scarcity and Water Use, African Centre for Water Research* (ISBN 978-1-4312-0178-5). Retrieved from http://www.plaas.org.za/bibliography/socialwater-scarcity-wrc

Thomas, C.D., Cameron, A., Green, R.E., Bakkenes, M., Beaumont, L.J., Collingham, Y.C., Erasmus, B.F.N., Siqueira, M.F.D., Grainger, A., & Hannah, L. (2004). Extinction risk from climate change. *Nature*, 427(6970), 145-148. doi:10.1038/nature02121.

Thorpe, J., & Fennel, S. (2013). Climate Change Risks and Supply chain Responsibility. *Oxfam Discussion Papers*. Retrieved from http://oxfam.org

World Wildlife Fund-UK and SAB Miller (2009). *Water Footprinting: Identifying and Addressing Water Risk in the Value-Chain*. Retrieved from http://wwf.panda.org/?171861/Water-Footprinting (June 18, 2015)

Nik C. Steinberg is a water and climate risk specialist and the Director of Research at Four Twenty Seven Climate Solutions. He works with a range of industry sectors including Fortune 100 manufacturing, health care, utility and food and beverage, identifying climate hotspots in their value chain and addressing social-ecological challenges. He holds a Master's degree in Natural Resources and Sustainable Development from American University, Washington, DC.

8

Evaluating supply chain networks by incorporating the triple dimensions of sustainability paradigm

Anthony Halog and Nga H. Nguyen
University of Queensland, Australia

Considering that supply chain network operations have become increasingly competitive and globalized, a critical challenge for any group of organizations is to develop an integrated set of performance metrics that can be used to evaluate the sustainability of different supply chain designs. However, the interface of environmental, economic and social aspects in supply chain management is not yet well-covered in the current literature. In this chapter, we attempt to develop mathematical programming-based efficiency metrics, which are called "sustainable network operational efficiency" (SNOE), in order to assess supply chain performance and evaluate possible design configurations of a global supply chain. The SNOE metrics could also be used to detect the factors of unsustainability in a supply chain network. This chapter may be of interest to organizations that are planning to design new supply chain networks or evaluate its existing networks with an aim to allocate its resources efficiently and improve its overall supply chain efficiency.

8.1 Introduction

There is no doubt that businesses in general, and supply chains in particular, have become increasingly globalized (Gereffi and Lee, 2012; Baldwin, 2012). Besides a number of benefits, globalization brings about some challenges to the supply chains. First, there has been a shift from less value added operations to more value added ones in developed countries and an opposite shift in developing countries. Business enterprises in dynamic markets have been outsourcing their extractive and basic manufacturing-related activities to developing countries (Doh, 2005; Marvin, 2011). As a result, the natural capital consumption per unit of economic capital in developed countries has been reduced (Ukidwe and Bakshi, 2005). At the same time, the absorption of the outsourced activities in developing countries has led to the creation of economic capital at the expense of a disproportionately large amount of natural capital consumed (Copeland and Taylor, 2004; Dinda, 2004). Another challenge of globalized supply chains is increasing emissions and wastes globally. Free trade may shift pollution-intensive manufacturing processes from countries with strict environmental regulations to those with less restrictive ones (Nagurney and Nagurney, 2010). However, the pressures from legal requirements and customers are forcing the whole supply chain process, including suppliers, manufacturers, and distributors (Hill, 1997), to shift towards sustainability. Poor environmental performance at any stage of the supply chain will damage the reputation of a firm and therefore threaten its survival (Nagurney and Nagurney, 2010). Finally, there are a number of social and cultural challenges to address within global supply chains. These include the need to adapt to different ways of working, cultural norms of social behaviour, attitudes to authority, language issues (Krishna *et al.*, 2006) and other process-related aspects of operations that affect human safety, welfare and community development (Klassen and Vereecke, 2012).

The challenges of globalization require the development of a sustainable supply chain network which considers not only economic but also ecological and social factors. Nevertheless, there are constraints behind the concept of sustainable supply chains. These constraints may arise from the limited resources, labour and economic capital, or the limited capacity of the biosphere to accommodate emissions and wastes from human activities (Whiteman *et al.*, 2013). For example, in Canada's oil sands industry, greenhouse gas (GHG) is considered as one of the constraints on the extensive development of bitumen resources for synthetic crude oil production (Halog and Chan, 2006, 2007). Therefore, the assessment of sustainable supply chain networks should be performed holistically besides optimizing individual participants' value. The competition among supply chain networks may help to ensure that organizations in the latter stages of a global supply chain, particularly those operating in developed countries, can assume some of the responsibility for the social and environmental impacts due to the changes of basic infrastructure industries in developing countries. The creation of these fully integrated and efficient supply chain networks appears to be an essential step for the successful implementation of sustainable development at a global scale.

This chapter aims to develop analytical efficiency metrics, which can be used to continuously evaluate supply chain configurations over time. In eco-efficiency studies, for example, metrics have been formulated to assess some of the Japanese economic sectors and to indicate the direction for improving the environmental and economic performance (Halog *et al.*, 2004). In this research we attempted to formulate sustainable network operational efficiency (SNOE) metrics which can be applied to assess and design supply chains for any goods. This work is valuable because it contributes to the conceptual development of performance metrics that allows efficient supply chains' participation into sustainable development. It can also assist in restructuring an existing network to increase, or even sustain, the value for suppliers, manufacturers, customers and other stakeholders in the long-term while acknowledging the long-term environmental and social consequences in a global extent.

This chapter is organized as follows: first, in the next two sections, we describe supply chain networks and discuss how to possibly restructure them. Second, examples of eco-efficiency metrics are reviewed, followed by the formulation of sustainable network operations efficiency (SNOE) metrics and models. Finally, the last two sections provide managerial implications, limitations, and conclusions as well as directions for future research.

8.2 Supply chain networks and performance measures

A supply chain is a network of actors including suppliers, manufacturers, distributors and retailers that are collectively concerned with the conversion of raw materials into goods that can be delivered to customers (Herrmann *et al.*, 2003). Supply chain management (SCM) is therefore a means of understanding and improving the effectiveness and efficiency of network business processes undertaken by participating firms (actors/agents) to progress goods and services from initial procurement and use of inputs in primary production through delivery to end users (Gattorna and Walters, 1996; Harland, 1996).

Although environmental impacts, as well as the social impacts of supply chain operations, are not yet accounted in the current definition of a supply chain, the interest of integrating societal and ecological concerns into supply chain management has grown continuously (Srivastava, 2007). Greening of supply chains and sustainable supply chain management have been evolving as an active area of research (Walton *et al.*, 1998; Kho *et al.*, 2001; Sarkis, 2003; Zhu and Cote, 2004; Sheu *et al.*, 2005; Carter and Rogers, 2008; Crum *et al.*, 2011; Sarkis *et al.*, 2011). Seuring and Müller (2008, p. 1,700) defined sustainable supply chain management as "the management of material, information and capital flows as well as cooperation among companies along the supply chain while taking goals from all three dimensions of sustainable development, i.e. economic, environmental and social, into account which are derived from customer and stakeholder requirements". Research indicates that greening the supply chain is an important strategy for both business and sustainable development goals. A good discussion of various systems and requirements that can aid the development of green supply chains can be found in Sarkis *et al.*, (1995, 2011).

There have been several studies on how to design supply chains and evaluate supply chain efficiency (Ross *et al.*, 1998; Talluri *et al.*, 1999; Ross and Drogen, 2004; Camerinelli and Cantu, 2006; Chen *et al.*, 2006; Liang *et al.*, 2006; Wong and Wong, 2007). These studies used various generic performance measures. However, only a few have included sustainable supply chain management metrics. For example, Ukidwe and Bakshi (2005) developed a thermodynamic-based supply chain analytical approach, which included the contribution of ecological goods, ecosystems services, human resources, and impact emissions in an economic input-output model. Clift and Wright (2000) developed a metric which considered both economic value added (EVA) and environmental emissions using the overall business impact assessment approach.

In many related supply chain metrics studies there is no discussion on sustainability indicators (Gunasekaran and Kobu, 2007). Hassini *et al.* (2012) also noted that no study has comprehensively addressed the three dimensions of sustainability (i.e. economy, society and environment). This chapter argues that in addition to calculating performance measures such as cycle time, delivery time, inventory, cost performance, resource utilization, total supply chain cost, service level, inventory, cash-to-cash cycle or reliability (Beamon, 1998; Ross *et al.*, 1998; Sarkis, 2003; Ross and Drogen, 2004; Chen *et al.*, 2006; Liang *et al.*, 2006; Wong and Wong, 2007), it is essential to develop metrics that integrate economic, environmental and social parameters in order to sustain the value in globally competitive networks.

8.3 Restructuring supply chain networks

Restructuring a supply chain network over time is essential for businesses to retain their competitive edge (Ross *et al.*, 1998; Sarkis, 2003). Ross *et al.* (1999) proposed a general methodology on how to restructure an existing supply chain network. Though the method was applied to outbound logistics supply chain network, it can be used to design many supply chains. Talluri *et al.* (1999) also proposed a framework on how to design efficient value chain networks. They introduced a two-stage decision model in the selection of partners in the formation of value chain networks. Stage one involves a filtering procedure which identifies efficient participants at each stage of the value chain networks. This allows inefficient participants to be screened out and eliminated. Stage two utilizes an integer goal programming model which is used for selecting an optimal combination of potential participants in the formation of efficient value chain networks. Though these two studies have provided us with useful frameworks for developing supply chain networks, we need to include sustainability performance measures (i.e. environmentally and socially-related metrics) as well as consider the participation of relevant stakeholders who may play important roles for the development of sustainable supply chains that are operating globally.

Restructuring may involve attempts to manage network behaviour by designing it so as to change the scope of the activities performed by each participant and the nature of the relationships between them when necessary. This may involve parts of the operation being merged, which does not mean that the ownership of any part of the operation need to be changed but responsibilities may be reallocated for carrying out activities. In converting supply chains to sustainable value chains, activities—including global operations within a chain—should be designed to increase its economic value added but, at the same time, environmental impacts are decreased and social benefits for all network participants are increased.

Streamlining a supply chain that has fewer direct suppliers and much shorter lead times is another way of reconfiguring a network. In order to sustain network value, companies may limit the number of participants at each stage to those who practice corporate social responsibility (CSR) or at least implement environmental management systems (EMS) (e.g. ISO 14001, EMAS, GEMI). There is a belief in value investment that superior environmental performance is an indicator of superior overall management. Superior environmental performance leads to reduced risk and therefore improved financial performance (Thompson, 2002, pp. 49-51; Sarkis, 2003). This can be the reason why some corporations wishing to improve their overall environmental and societal performance have now proactively required suppliers to have an effective EMS. Greater collaboration among the members (actors/agents) of a supply chain can foster the development of improved environmental systems through both technological innovation and better resource management, which can reduce the overall environmental impact across one or more segments of the supply chain (Klassen and Vachon, 2003).

Another strategy to restructure a network, which is widely adopted in Western countries, which aim to increase their long-term profitability by reducing costs (e.g. labour and raw materials) and avoid stricter environmental regulations in their home countries (Tate *et al.*, 2009) is global outsourcing. This is directly related to the "make or buy decision" when individual components or activities are being considered. Though economic and customer-oriented benefits have been the main drivers of designing efficient supply chains, it is necessary to consider the environmental and social impacts of globally outsourced operations. Besides the tangible and intangible success factors for inter-firm relationships, the overall value of a supply chain network should take into account environmental, economic and social performance measures. This requires organizations to design or configure global and sustainable supply chains.

In short, restructuring supply chain networks to make them more efficient and sustainable is an important strategy that progressive corporations have been performing to organize their economic relationships effectively. For these firms, the challenge of adjusting to globalization trends is really about how to redesign their organizational relationships with other participants of the supply chain and devise new operational systems within that chain.

8.4 Designing sustainable supply chains

In previous sections we have discussed the importance of sustainable supply chain management metrics and how to restructure existing supply chain networks. This section discusses two sample ways for sustainability measurements, which are Overall Business Impact Assessment and Data Envelopment Analysis, and suggests formulating sustainable network operations efficiency metrics and models.

8.4.1 Eco-efficiency and data envelopment analyses

Eco-efficiency has been proposed as one of the main tools to promote a transformation from unsustainable development to one of sustainable development (Yu *et al.*, 2013). It is based on the concept of creating more goods and services while using fewer resources and creating less waste and pollution (Yu *et al.*, 2013).

One of the few eco-efficiency metrics that attempted to integrate both environmental and economic performance was developed by Unilever (Taylor and Postlethwaite, 1996), which is known as overall business impact assessment (OBIA). OBIA is an approach to normalization, which generates a set of eco-metrics that relate environmental impacts to economic values. Applying the OBIA approach to the case of supply chains, the normalized parameter measuring the performance of a chain *j* in environmental impact category *i* is defined as:

Equation 8.1

$$
\Theta_{i,j} = \frac{\textit{Impact in category i / Value of chain j}}{\textit{Total anthropogenic contribution to impact category i / Total global network activities}}
$$

In the Equation 8.1, the environmental impacts of a chain are evaluated over the whole life cycle and the value is taken as the total profit from the overall chain configuration. This measure can be used to assess the eco-efficiency of supply chain networks and to determine which impact categories in each chain should be targeted for environmental improvement. However, this approach did not account explicitly for the resource consumptions as well as relevant social variables. Clift and Wright (2000) used the OBIA approach to assess the supply chain of mobile telephones and found that the greatest environmental damage was associated with primary resource industries. The ratio of environmental impact to economic value added (EVA) decreases along the supply chain.

Another approach which is called data envelopment analysis (DEA) has been applied for assessing the eco-efficiency performance of industrial economic sectors in Japan (Halog *et al.*, 2004). DEA is an empirical procedure described by Charnes *et al.* (1978) for estimating the relative efficiency of any decision-making units (e.g. suppliers, manufacturers and supply chains). It has been proven to be a powerful tool for assessing eco-efficiency performance for several reasons. First, DEA is a systems approach, which means that it accounts for the relationship between all inputs and outputs simultaneously (Aramyan *et al.*, 2006). Second, DEA generates detailed information about efficient decision-making units within a sample and tells which of them are important as benchmarks (Fraser and Cordina, 1999). Third, DEA does not require parametric specification of a functional form to construct the frontier (Fraser and Cordina, 1999). Thus, there is no need to impose restrictions on the functional forms that very often cause distorted measures (Fraser and Cordina, 1999). Fourth, DEA enables the identification of potential improvement for inefficient units and indicates the sources and the level of inefficiency for each of its inputs and outputs. In addition, Callens and Tyteca (1999) reported that DEA models have:

- A clear and obvious standardization, since all units are ranked according to a scale with the convention that the value of unity represents the best performance

- An important flexibility, since various versions of DEA models can be formulated stressing important factors and

- Robustness of the (non-) linear programming methods used to compute indicators.

With respect to eco-efficiency, the advantage of DEA models over the OBIA approach is that the causes of inefficiency can be identified and the extent of reducing resource consumptions and emission, increasing the economic value added, or improving social benefits (e.g. increased employment) can be relatively quantified. The eco-efficiency of service sectors is relatively efficient while the primary resource industries are relatively inefficient (Halog *et al.*, 2004). In addition to economic and environmental variables, DEA-based efficiency models are developed herein to integrate and account for social and environmental factors. These metrics will be used to assess supply chain designs in view of sustainable development, which is described in the next section.

8.4.2 Sustainable network operational efficiency

To conceptualize and develop sustainability metrics for supply chains, it is essential to define a sustainable supply chain. Section 8.2 defined sustainable supply chain management. However, it appears impossible to answer the question of "what is a sustainable supply chain?" in absolute terms because it depends on many uncontrollable factors. We aptly rephrase this question as "in what way would a given supply chain be more or less sustainable than another?"

In order to compare the sustainability of different supply chain designs, we attempt to formulate sustainable network operational efficiency (SNOE) metrics and models. SNOE refers to the overall efficiency of all business operations included in a supply chain network. Such efficiency can be improved by reducing or increasing a chain's complexity, reducing the cost of doing business with other activities in the chain and increasing societal benefits as well as reducing environmental emissions and resource consumptions.

Table 8.1 below provides a set of possible factors for which information would be required in the framework of sustainability analysis. This list is not meant to be exhaustive and is provided here as an example. It can be seen in Table 8.1 that some factors reflect sustainability goals for the supply chain while others (i.e. socio-economic and ecological factors) mainly reflect sustainability goals for the society. It is also apparent that some of the items cover more than one category of aspects. For example, the use of natural resources clearly has economic benefits, ecological impacts but also social impacts, related to resource availability for future generations. Some items may have contradictory influences depending on the aspects being considered. For example, employment would tend to be minimized from a business point of view but should rather be maximized from a social perspective. Also, the intervention of certain factors might evolve with the level of scientific knowledge, which will influence the way in which they should be accounted for in the elaboration of metrics. As an example, one may think of the chlorofluorocarbons (CFCs), which was once considered useful, inert auxiliary in various industries, but is now identified as one of the major pollutants contributing to the ozone layer depletion.

Table 8.1 Sample list of information required in the development of SNOE metrics at the supply chain level

	Short-term	Long-term
Economic aspects	Value-added, output production, turnover, resources used as inputs (including reused, remanufactured and recycled products and energy)	Profitability, competitiveness, market shares, product durability, research and development efforts
Environmental aspects	Natural resources, solid wastes, air and water emissions, transportation modes and distances	Global warming impacts: global warming, biodiversity, acid deposition, landscape, ultimate waste disposal, product recycling ability
Social aspects	Employment, salaries, labour intensiveness or productivity, accidents, risk, noise, odour	Welfare, education, availability of (non-renewable), resources (including energy), size (SME vs. big), personnel rotation rate

Data on the factors listed in Table 8.1 can be used in two possible ways. First, we could use past observations on the values of these factors. The metrics would then be a static/snapshot indicator that would help us to identify efficient and less efficient supply chains among a given set. Second, we could use projected values that would reflect a set of possible alternatives. In this case, the metrics would be a prospective indicator (in a form of future trends or forecasts). In both cases, we have to assume that we have observations on the factors for a set of (existing or possible) supply chain configurations. Indeed, to be operational, the metrics should evaluate supply chains that are really comparable, in the sense that they produce similar products or services that are designed to fulfill analogous purposes, similar to conducting environmental life cycle assessment.

Table 8.2 shows the notations used to represent the model variables in Table 8.1. For each of the three aspects (i.e. economic, social and environmental), we consider factors whose value should be minimized (all other things being equal) and those whose value should be maximized, in order to reach eco-efficiency, or more generally, from the perspective of sustainability. For example, consumption of natural resources should be minimized from economic as well as ecological standpoints, while durability is a factor which tends to be maximized in a sustainability framework. P $(p=1,..., P)$ refers to participants/actors of a supply chain network.

Table 8.2 Notations used in formulating SNOE models for assessing supply chains

	Variables to maximize	Variables to minimize
Economic aspects	$EC_{max,np}$, n=1,...,N1	$EC_{min,np}$, n=1,..., N2
Social aspects	$SC_{max,np}$, n=1,..., N3	$SC_{min,np}$, n=1,..., N4
Environmental aspects	$EV_{max,np}$, n=1,..., N5	$EV_{min,np}$, n=1,...,N6

Note: n = model inputs; p = network participants

Given a set of possible supply chain configurations with a number of participants that use a set of production inputs (e.g. material and energy resources, labour and economic capital) to produce a set of desirable outputs (e.g. value added, output production) and a set of undesirable outputs (e.g. emissions and wastes), three DEA models are formulated here to calculate the sustainable operational efficiency (ε) of a supply chain indexed "t" and outlined below. However, we can combine different variables (as shown in Table 8.2) to formulate new DEA models, suitable for the analysis we are interested to perform. The three below are just a few of the models that can be formulated to support sustainability analysis of supply chains.

Model t: input–output productive efficiency framework

From a productive efficiency perspective, input-output analysis quantifies inter-organizational relationships and offers a means of evaluating the impacts across firms. Similar thinking can be applied for the analysis of social impacts of business operations (e.g. direct and indirect employment) within a network.

Figure 8.1 Multi-input and multi-output system

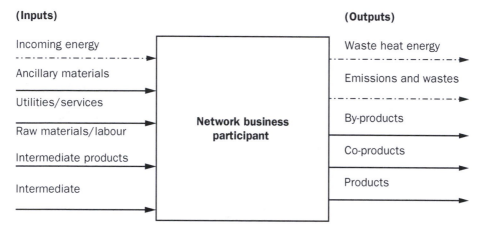

In this model, we considered a composite metric defined as a ratio between a weighted sum of quantities that are considered desirable, and a weighted sum of quantities that are viewed as inputs and whose intervention has to be minimized. The idea of the theory of productive efficiency had been extended to the consideration of environmental factors, in which the wastes were taken as undesirable outputs (Tyteca, 1996, 1997; Belegri-Rompoli and Tsolas, 2003; Halog *et al.*, 2004). In the basic standpoint of productive efficiency, we want to compare a set of possible supply chain design configurations with respect to defined sustainability performance criteria such as shown in Table 8.1.

In this model, where we have more than one output and one input, one supply chain network (indexed "t") is compared to the whole set of supply or value chain configurations. In this way, we offer the possibility of incorporating various different kinds of quantities, with different measurement units (i.e. physical, economic, social, technical, etc.) and meanings (i.e. stocks, flows, impacts, transformations, etc.) that have to be aggregated to reflect their distance to efficiency, without requiring any assumption on the weights used in the aggregation. The weights are the solution of the mathematical model as shown below and will be computed in such a way that the distance to the efficiency frontier is minimized. The general formulation for the input-output productive efficiency model is shown in Equation 8.2.

Index k designates a supply chain (consists of selected participants, p) in the set of K possible supply chain networks for analysis. The selection of a few efficient partners at each stage of supply chain can be done *a priori* through the use of filtering approach proposed by Talluri *et al.* (1999). The constraints in this model define the feasible set, i.e. the set of combinations of the factors taken into account that are feasible in the present state of technology. The frontier of that set is constituted by supply chains that exhibit the best practice in terms of sustainability.

The objective function in Equation 8.2 indicates the efficiency of supply chain "t" which is to be maximized, given that the efficiency of all supply chains is set to be smaller than or equal to unity by the constraints. The efficiency of supply chain "t" is either equal to or smaller than unity, in which cases it is considered "efficient" or "inefficient" respectively. The meaning of efficient and inefficient in this context might be taken as "sustainable" and "unsustainable", under the assumption that Model t appropriately reflects sustainability. It should be cautioned, however, that a supply chain network that would be declared "efficient" because its index value is unity is not necessarily sustainable. This could appear to be efficient because it is better than all other chains on a single factor. Thus, it is possible to refer to supply chains that are unsustainable because they are inefficient, but being efficient by no means implies sustainable, the former being only a necessary condition for the latter.

Equation 8.2

$$Max \in_t = \frac{\displaystyle\sum_{p=1}^{P}\sum_{n=1}^{N1} a_{np} EC^t_{max,np} + \sum_{p=1}^{P}\sum_{n=1}^{N3} c_{np} SC^t_{max,np} + \sum_{p=1}^{P}\sum_{n=1}^{N5} e_{np} EV^t_{max,np}}{\displaystyle\sum_{p=1}^{P}\sum_{n=1}^{N2} b_{np} EC^t_{min,np} + \sum_{p=1}^{P}\sum_{n=1}^{N4} d_{np} SC^t_{min,np} + \sum_{p=1}^{P}\sum_{n=1}^{N6} f_{np} EV^t_{min,np}}$$

s.t.

$$\frac{\displaystyle\sum_{p=1}^{P}\sum_{n=1}^{N1} a_{np} EC^k_{max,np} + \sum_{p=1}^{P}\sum_{n=1}^{N3} c_{np} SC^k_{max,np} + \sum_{p=1}^{P}\sum_{n=1}^{N5} e_{np} EV^k_{max,np}}{\displaystyle\sum_{p=1}^{P}\sum_{n=1}^{N2} b_{np} EC^k_{min,np} + \sum_{p=1}^{P}\sum_{n=1}^{N4} d_{np} SC^k_{min,np} + \sum_{p=1}^{P}\sum_{n=1}^{N6} f_{np} EV^k_{min,np}} \leq 1 \qquad ,k = 1,\ldots,K$$

$a_{np}, c_{np}, e_{np}, b_{np}, d_{np}, f_{np} \geq 0,$ $\qquad a_{np}, c_{np}, e_{np}, b_{np}, d_{np}, f_{np}$ are intensity variables

Equation 8.2 assumes constant returns to scale. In the context of supply chain networks, this assumption is inappropriate since not all networks are operating at optimal scale. For example, imperfect information flows, imperfect competition and constraints on resources may cause a chain not to be operating at optimal scale. However, a variable return to scale can be assumed by simply introducing a constraint that the sum of the weights assigned to the inputs and outputs is equal to unity (Banker *et al.*, 1984).

Based on this model, supply chains are deemed efficient if they are lying on the frontier of the production technology set. Otherwise, they are inefficient and should be redesigned by reducing the level of resources consumed and undesirable outputs emitted by participants, or increasing the EVA of each operation. The environmental impact category of a supply chain for which its efficiency value is disproportionately large, indicates where and how the high environmental emissions arise and thus shows which operations of the network should be subjected to improvement to achieve optimal (sustainable) configuration.

Nevertheless, in extreme cases when the possibility of having zero weights (i.e. all the weights concentrated on one unique output or input) arises, Callens and Tyteca (1999) suggested a method that allows one to incorporate experts' judgments. With relation to the methods used in DEA, such judgments can take the form of intervals within which the relative weights given to some factors should be included. For example, considering the economic inputs such as in Equation 8.2, possible weight can take the form of Equation 8.3.

Equation 8.3

$$\alpha_{np}^{k} \leq \frac{b_{np} EC_{\min,np}^{k}}{\sum\limits_{p=1}^{P} \sum\limits_{n=1}^{N2} b_{np} EC_{\min,np}^{k}} \leq \beta_{np}^{k}$$

This equation states that, for a supply chain k, the weight given to model input "n" of participant p with respect to the whole set of model inputs for all participants be comprised between α_{np}^{k} and β_{np}^{k}. This implies that zero weights, as well as the possibility of giving the totality of the weight to the sole input n, can be avoided. Other combinations and standpoints can be reflected as well. For example, if for some strategic inter-organizational reasons, the relative weight of an undesirable output (e.g. greenhouse gas) is associated with the use of a given resource (e.g. coal) this can be reflected by a constraint on the ratio between appropriate quantities as in Equation 8.3.

Model one: environmental and social factors oriented model

Model one puts stress on environmental and social factors as the main variables (the numerator) for evaluating supply chains over time. Equation 8.2 only mimics the productive efficiency framework of DEA. In a further and more realistic step, we might consider three categories of factors, i.e. the production inputs, the desirable outputs and the undesirable outputs. In this model, there are various ways in which the problem can be viewed and we first consider one in which we try to minimize negative environmental and social impacts that are opposed to the necessity of producing economic outputs using adequate quantities of inputs (which is a necessary condition for a whole supply chain to compete successfully). This formulation is shown in Equation 8.4.

In Equation 8.4, the sign restrictions on the variables indicate that all (economic, social and environmental) factors are considered strongly disposable. This means that we can decrease output production down to nil at no cost and we can substitute inputs among themselves, or decrease emissions, provided additional levels of appropriate inputs are used. This assumption is sometimes being relaxed, especially in the case of emissions. These are considered weakly disposable. This means that beyond a given threshold, a given emission can be reduced only at the cost of a reduction of the desirable output or some other variables. One additional set of constraints could be added to the model, stating that the denominators should be positive, in order to ensure that the conditions for a supply chain's survival are met. Figure 8.2 illustrates the simplified case where we have one environmental impact category (e.g. global warming) and one social impact (e.g. accident records), the reduction would correspond to improved sustainability. One can add a third axis to incorporate economic dimension of sustainability. With Model one, because both impacts must be reduced, a move towards south-west (as shown in Fig. 8.2) will yield an improvement, which is feasible until the point reaches the sustainability frontier. If we consider, without loss of generality, that the reduction in both impacts is proportional, this will lead us to point S1, where impacts have been reduced by a factor θ. The latter can be taken as the sustainability (eco-efficiency) metric value. This corresponds to the inverse of the value of ε_t obtained after solving model one in Equation 8.4.

Equation 8.4

$$
Min\ \varepsilon_t = \frac{\displaystyle\sum_{p=1}^{P}\sum_{n=1}^{N4} d_{np} SC^t_{min,np} - \sum_{p=1}^{P}\sum_{n=1}^{N3} c_{np} SC^t_{max,np} + \sum_{p=1}^{P}\sum_{n=1}^{N6} f_{np} EV^t_{min,np} - \sum_{p=1}^{P}\sum_{n=1}^{N5} e_{np} EV^t_{max,np}}{\displaystyle\sum_{p=1}^{P}\sum_{n=1}^{N1} a_{np} EC^t_{max,np} - \sum_{p=1}^{P}\sum_{n=1}^{N2} b_{np} EC^t_{min,np}}
$$

s.t.

$$
\frac{\displaystyle\sum_{p=1}^{P}\sum_{n=1}^{N4} d_{np} SC^k_{min,np} - \sum_{p=1}^{P}\sum_{n=1}^{N3} c_{np} SC^k_{max,np} + \sum_{p=1}^{P}\sum_{n=1}^{N6} f_{np} EV^k_{min,np} - \sum_{p=1}^{P}\sum_{n=1}^{N5} e_{np} EV^k_{max,np}}{\displaystyle\sum_{n=1}^{P}\sum_{n=1}^{N1} a_{np} EC^k_{max,np} - \sum_{p=1}^{P}\sum_{n=1}^{N2} b_{np} EC^k_{min,np}} \geq 1 \qquad , k = 1,\ldots, K
$$

$$a_{np}, c_{np}, e_{np}, b_{np}, d_{np}, f_{np} \geq 0$$

Figure 8.2 Production set and efficiency frontier (one environmental impact and one social impact)

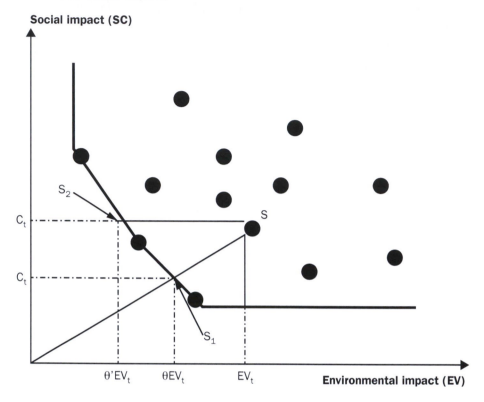

Model two: environmental factors oriented model

This model emphasizes the minimization of environmental impacts (numerator of the model) of the whole supply chain. This is shown in Equation 8. Though the treatment of undesirable outputs depends on the level of aggregation, the environmental impact categories are used as model variables. The sign conventions at the denominator of the objective function and the constraints are based on the fact that we now consider the social factors as making part of the inputs. In this model, a reduction has been sought only in the direction of environmental impacts and the point reached from point S is point S2 (as shown in Fig. 8.2), resulting in a SNOE metric value θ'.

The above three models served as conceptual models that one can formulate. However, similar models can be formulated with either economic or social variables as the main performance factors (numerator of the model) in assessing the sustainability of supply chain networks. Though it would be good if we had one unique indicator, the methodology outlined here allows us the flexibility, using the available information, to specify as many metrics as required by the specific application considered. The choice among the metrics depends upon strategic, managerial or political decisions that are important for all network participants. Additionally, models can also be developed to assist partners' selection at each stage of the supply chain. Talluri *et al.* (1999) showed that we can presume here that only efficient participants are included to develop efficient (sustainable) supply chain networks. This implies that a filtering procedure can be applied first to identify possible efficient participants at each stage of the value chain networks. This allows inefficient participants to be screened out and eliminated, such as network participants (e.g. suppliers) in developed and developing countries that do not have environmental management systems (EMS) in place, or not pursuing cleaner production practices can be screened out.

Equation 8.5

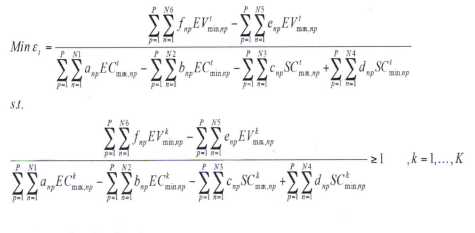

$$Min\, \varepsilon_t = \frac{\displaystyle\sum_{p=1}^{P}\sum_{n=1}^{N6} f_{np}EV_{\min,np}^{t} - \sum_{p=1}^{P}\sum_{n=1}^{N5} e_{np}EV_{\max,np}^{t}}{\displaystyle\sum_{p=1}^{P}\sum_{n=1}^{N1} a_{np}EC_{\max,np}^{t} - \sum_{p=1}^{P}\sum_{n=1}^{N2} b_{np}EC_{\min,np}^{t} - \sum_{p=1}^{P}\sum_{n=1}^{N3} c_{np}SC_{\max,np}^{t} + \sum_{p=1}^{P}\sum_{n=1}^{N4} d_{np}SC_{\min,np}^{t}}$$

s.t.

$$\frac{\displaystyle\sum_{p=1}^{P}\sum_{n=1}^{N6} f_{np}EV_{\min,np}^{k} - \sum_{p=1}^{P}\sum_{n=1}^{N5} e_{np}EV_{\max,np}^{k}}{\displaystyle\sum_{p=1}^{P}\sum_{n=1}^{N1} a_{np}EC_{\max,np}^{k} - \sum_{p=1}^{P}\sum_{n=1}^{N2} b_{np}EC_{\min,np}^{k} - \sum_{p=1}^{P}\sum_{n=1}^{N3} c_{np}SC_{\max,np}^{k} + \sum_{p=1}^{P}\sum_{n=1}^{N4} d_{np}SC_{\min,np}^{k}} \geq 1 \quad , k = 1,\dots,K$$

$$a_{np}, c_{np}, e_{np}, b_{np}, d_{np}, f_{np} \geq 0$$

8.5 Discussion and limitations

DEA models have been successfully applied in a number of cases (for example Ramanathan, 2006; Halog *et al.*, 2004; Belegri-Rompoli and Tsolas, 2003; Tyteca, 1997). Results from these studies show the feasibility of the proposed metrics and models. However, they are still subject to several limitations. The following paragraphs present these weaknesses and discuss possible solutions to improve them.

First, as it is necessary to take into account as many variables for sustainability metrics as possible (Gramlich, 1990), the application of DEA models might result in the extreme situation where all supply chains in a given set are considered efficient. Therefore, there must be some kind of trade-off between the number and the representability of the characteristics accounted for, which can be solved by some preliminary investigation of data (using principal component analysis or regression analysis for example) to remove redundant explanatory variables. As a rule of thumb, Reiner and Hofmann (2006) proposed that the number of decision-making units (DMU) is greater than or equal to the number of model variables as shown in Equation 8.6. In some publications a factor of two instead of four is considered appropriate (Dyson *et al.*, 2001; Homburg, 2001).

Equation 8.6

$$Number\ of\ DMUs \geq 4 \times \left[\sum input\ variables + \sum output\ variables \right]$$

The problem might also be partially solved if, instead of trying to develop one unique aggregate SNOE metric (such as in Model one above), we define two or three partial indicators that stress different aspects of the sustainability of supply chains. For example, we could consider three metrics: one is centred on environmental factors (such as in Model two above), another focuses on social performance measures (as commented under Model two) and another stresses economic variables. In this way we could obtain an accurate description of sustainability performance of the supply chain being considered while simultaneously provide the participants of the supply chain a possibility of meaningful trade-off to improve their social and environmental performance at an organizational level.

One possible weakness of DEA methods may be the way in which the intensity factors are determined, which is not straightforward from the perspective of managers and decision-makers. To overcome this difficulty, we should emphasize the importance of using graphical representations of the interaction between variables such as the one shown in Figure 8.1. This could help illuminate and illustrate the way in which trade-offs are being made and the possible directions towards improvement. The flexibility of the DEA methods with the use of available software packages easily allows expert judgments and managerial perceptions to be incorporated into the models, thereby improving their acceptability. In fact, mathematical programming problems can be solved using algorithms (e.g. GAMS, GAUSS). Modern spreadsheet solvers (e.g. Excel Solver) can also handle increasingly large problems. There are also some commercially available software packages such as Frontier Analyst, Warwick, and On Front, which can be installed easily on managers' desktops.

The fact that no priori weights are required for factors is often considered an advantage over other methods. However, this can have significant drawbacks. For example, the existence of supply chains that will be declared "efficient by default" because they are best on only one aspect, even though they might be much worse in all other aspects. As mentioned, this can be solved through the use of weight-limiting techniques (e.g. Equation 8.3). However, these SNOE models are useful as they can help recognize which chains, or operations within a chain, are less efficient and provide explanatory factors, which may be helpful in identifying the causes of unsustainability.

Another limitation is that the frontier obtained from observations on existing supply chains merely reflects best practice. Indeed, DEA-based models can only yield results that reflect what has been incorporated into the data, i.e. if past observations are being used, the results obtained will be based on how the decisions had been made in the recent past. From a sustainable development perspective, there may be important trade-offs to be made with regard to production inputs (e.g. the future use of (non-)renewable resources), social implications of global outsourcing and production. Such trade-offs can be reflected in Equation 8.4. Thereby the present or past decisions can be gauged with respect to trade-offs that appropriately translate the choices we need to formulate for the future.

In fact, a few comments can be made about the actual use of sustainability metrics. Not only could they be exploited to compare supply chain networks from a sustainability perspective but, more importantly from an international trade standpoint, these metrics could serve to evaluate supply chains operating across developed and developing countries, which is aligned with the current emphasis of the United Nations Sustainable Development Goals (UNSDG). These countries can significantly differ in the way they take social and environmental goals into account for economic development. This work may result in the formulation of inter-organizational strategies and multilateral trade policies since the causes of unsustainability can be detected from the indicators.

8.6 Conclusions and directions for research

As competition among supply chain networks intensifies, effectively restructuring supply chains or designing sustainable supply chain networks becomes an important global and inter-organizational strategy. The metrics that we formulated would provide corporate and public organizations with tools to identify and adopt strategies (e.g. regulations and incentives) which can ensure sustainable development. Metrics can be used to compare similar existing units (products, technologies, partners, supply chains, sectors and countries) in terms of their performance to some specified targets (economic, environmental, social, etc.). The utility of these metrics is to identify "laggers" (those behind expectations relative to the efficiency frontier) among the units considered (within a chain or among supply chains) as well as the causes of lagging, and to adopt relevant supply chain management strategies. These metrics indicate the extent to which reduction of environmental impacts as well as an increase in economic added value and social benefits may be possible.

The SNOE metric serves as a surrogate indicator for the sustainable value of a whole supply chain. This approach may also allow players in a supply chain to assess the overall competitiveness of the chain while enabling individual players to focus improvement efforts at an organizational level. This might provide a way of distinguishing between economic activities within a network which are and are not capable of sustainable development. To cope with the multidimensionality of sustainable development, it is important not to base decisions on one unique aggregate metric when assessing supply chains. Instead, it is suggested herein to develop two or three partial SNOE metrics that stress different aspects of assessing supply chains in view of sustainability.

Additionally, this study might show how organizations in the later stages of a supply chain can assume some of the responsibilities for the environmental and social impacts of primary resource industries. This study has a greater implication for why corporate social responsibility (CSR) is increasingly evident nowadays in the management of corporations. There is a recent tendency for companies in Western countries to position themselves in the latter stages of the supply chain. This further shows that, in the present climate of international trade, economies that remain dependent on primary resource industries will suffer environmental damage without adequate economic benefits. Thus, when designing a supply chain network of any product, a global and sustainable development strategy should be adopted as an overall guiding principle. Besides securing economic benefits, environmental and social impacts should be considered in assessing and eventually optimizing the whole supply chain network. It is thus vital to encourage suppliers, particularly those that supply materials from overseas, to implement at least environmental management systems while profiting as a result of economic development. Design of efficient (sustainable) global supply chain networks appears to be essential if sustainable development is to be brought about.

The models developed herein can be modified to take into account participants' interactions in a game theory context, where the relationship between the seller and buyer is treated first as one of a leader-follower type and second as a cooperative type. In the leader-follower structure, the leader will be evaluated first and then the follower is evaluated using information related to the leader's efficiency. In a cooperative structure (such as in the case of industrial ecology), the joint efficiency can be modelled on maximizing the average of the participants' efficiency scores (where all supply chain members are evaluated simultaneously).

Finally, the proposed SNOE metrics can be applied in evaluating the efficiency of a closed-loop supply chain system to reduce the fragility (in terms of resource supply risks) within the system as well as its exposure to competitive global supply chains. This methodology could be further applied in designing value chains for commercializing novel green energy products and technologies. The results of these applications will be reported and published elsewhere later.

References

Aramyan, L., Ondersteijn, C., Oude Lansink, A., Van Kooten, O., & Wijnands, J. (2006). Analyzing greenhouse firm performance across different marketing channels. *Agribusiness*, 22(2), 267-280.

Baldwin, R.E. (2012). *Global supply chains: Why they emerged, why they matter, and where they are going*. Retrieved from: http://papers.ssrn.com/sol3/papers.cfm?abstract_id=2153484

Banker, R., Charnes, A., & Cooper, W. (1984). Some models for estimating technical scale inefficiencies in data envelopment analysis. *Management Science*, 30(9), 1078-1092.

Beamon, B.M. (1998). Supply chain design and analysis: Models and methods. *International Journal of Production Economics*, 55(3), 281-294.

Belegri-Rompoli, A., & Tsolas, I. (2003). Environmental performance measurement at sectoral level: Electricity, gas and water. *Proceedings of the 8th International Conference on Environmental Science and Technology*, Lemmos Island, Greece, 77-83.

Callens, I., & Tyteca, D. (1999). Towards indicators of sustainable development for firms: A productive efficiency perspective. *Ecological Economics*, 28, 41-53.

Camarinelli, E., & Cantu, A. (2006). Measuring the value of the supply chain: A framework. *Supply Chain Practice*, 8(2), 40-59.

Carter, C.R. & Rogers, D.S. (2008). A framework of sustainable supply chain management: Moving toward new theory. *International Journal of Physical Distribution & Logistics Management*, 38, 360-387.

Chen, Y., Liang, L., & Yang, F. (2006). A DEA game model approach to supply chain efficiency. *Annals of Operations Research*, 145, 5-13.

Christopher, M. (1992). *Logistics and Supply Chain Management*, London: Pitman.

Clift, R. (2003). Metrics for supply chain sustainability. *Clean Technology Environmental Policy*, 5, 240-247.

Clift, R., & Wright, L. (2000). Relationships between environmental impacts and added value along the supply chain. *Technological Forecasting and Social Change*, 65, 281-295.

Copeland, B.R., & Taylor, M.S. (2004). Trade, growth, and the environment. *Journal of Economic Literature*, XLII, 7.

Crum, M., Poist, R., Carter, C.R., & Liane, E. (2011). Sustainable supply chain management: Evolution and future directions. *International Journal of Physical Distribution & Logistics Management*, 41, 46-62.

Dinda, S. (2004). Environmental Kuznets curve hypothesis: A survey. *Ecological Economics*, 49, 431.

Doh, J.P. (2005). Offshore outsourcing: Implications for international business and strategic management theory and practice. *Journal of Management Studies*, 42, 695-704.

Dyson, R.G., Allen, R., Camanho, A.S., Podinovski, V.V., Sarrico, C.S., & Shale, E.A. (2001). Pitfalls and protocols in DEA. *European Journal of Operational Research*, 132(2), 245-259.

Fraser, I., & Cordina, D. (1999). An application of data envelopment analysis to irrigated dairy farms in Northern Victoria, Australia. *Agricultural Systems*, 59, 267-282.

Gattorna, J., & Walters, D (1996). *Managing the Supply Chain: A Strategic Perspective*. Basingstoke: Macmillan Press.

Gereffi, G., & Lee, J. (2012). Why the world suddenly cares about global supply chains. *Journal of Supply Chain Management*, 48, 24-32.

Gramlich, E.M. (1990). *A Guide to Benefit-Cost Analysis*. Englewood Cliffs, NJ: Prentice Hall.

Gunasekaran, A., & Kobu, B. (2007). Performance measures and metrics in logistics and supply chain management: A review of recent literature (1995–2004) for research and applications. *International Journal of Production Research*, 45, 2819-2840.

Halog, A., & Chan, A. (2007). Developing a dynamic systems model for sustainable develop-ment of the Canadian oil sands industry. *International Journal of Environmental Technology and Management* (Special Issue on "Contribution of Management Science to Sustainable Development) (forthcoming/in press).

Halog, A., & Chan, A. (2006). Toward sustainable production in the Canadian oil sands indus-try. *Proceedings of the 13th CIRP International Conference on Life Cycle Engineering*, Leu-ven, Belgium, May 31-June 2, 2006, 131-136.

Halog, A., Sagisaka, M. Tahara, K., Yamaguchi, K., & Inaba, A. (2004). Sectoral eco-efficiency by input-output and data envelopment analysis. *Proceedings of the 6th International Conference on EcoBalance*, Tsukuba, Japan, 727-730.

Halog, A. (2004). An approach to selection of sustainable product improvement alternatives with data uncertainty. *Journal of Sustainable Product Design*, 4 (1-4), 3-19.

Harland, C. (1996). Supply chain management: Relationships, chains and networks. *British Journal of Management*, 7 (special issue), S63-S80.

Hassini, E., Surti, C., & Searcy, C. (2012). A literature review and a case study of sustainable supply chains with a focus on metrics. *International Journal of Production Economics*, 140, 69-82.

Herrmann, J., Lin, E., & Pundoor, G. (2003). Supply chain simulation modeling using the supply chain operations reference model. *Proceedings of DETC'03 ASME 2003 Design Engineering Technical Conferences and Computers and Information in Engineering Con-ference*, Chicago, IL, USA.

Hill, K. (1997). Supply-chain dynamics, environmental issues, and manufacturing firms. *Environment and Planning A*, 29, 1257-1274.

Homburg, C. (2001). Using data envelopment analysis to benchmark activities. *International Journal of Production Economics*, 73(1), 51-58.

Kho, H., Spedding, T., Bainbridge, I., & Taplin, D. (2001). Creating a green supply chain. *Greener Management International*, 35, 71-88.

Klassen, R.D., & Vachon, S. (2003). Collaboration and evaluation in the supply chain: The impact on plant-level environmental investment. *Production and Operations Manage-ment*, 12(3), 336-352.

Klassen, R.D., & Vereecke, A. (2012). Social issues in supply chains: Capabilities link responsi-bility, risk (opportunity), and performance. *International Journal of Production Econom-ics*, 140, 103-115.

Krishna, S., Sahay, S., & Walsham, G. (2006). *Managing Cross-Cultural Issues in Global Soft-ware Outsourcing*. Berlin, Heidelberg: Springer.

Lambert, D.M. (2008). *Supply Chain Management: Processes, Partnerships, Performance*, Sup-ply Chain Management Inst.

Liang, L., Yang, F., Cook, W., & Zhu, J. (2006). DEA models for supply chain efficiency evalua-tion. *Annals of Operations Research*, 145, 35-49.

Marvin, K.T. (2011). *Global Trends in Outsourcing and their Impact*. Worcester: Worcester Polytechnic Institute.

Nagurney, A., & Nagurney, L.S. (2010). Sustainable supply chain network design: A multicrite-ria perspective. *International Journal of Sustainable Engineering*, 3, 189-197.

Ramanathan, R. (2006). A multi-factor efficiency perspective to the relationships among world GDP, energy consumption and carbon dioxide emissions. *Technological and Fore-casting Change*, 73, 483-494.

Reiner, G., & Hofmann, P. (2006). Efficiency analysis of supply chain processes. *International Journal of Production Research*, 44(23), 5065-5087.

Ross, A., & Drogen, C. (2004). An analysis of operations efficiency in large-scale distribution systems. *Journal of Operations Management*, 21, 673-688.

Ross, A., Venkataramanan, M.A., & Ernstberger, K. (1998). Reconfiguring the supply network using current performance data. *Decision Sciences*, 29(3), 707-728.

Sarkis, J. (2003). A strategic decision framework for green supply chain management. *Journal of Cleaner Production*, 11, 397-409.

Sarkis, J. (1995). Supply chain management and environmentally conscious design and manufacturing. *International Journal of Environmentally Conscious Design and Manufacturing*, 4(2), 43-52.

Sarkis, J., Zhu, Q., & Lai, K.H. (2011). An organizational theoretic review of green supply chain management literature. *International Journal of Production Economics*, 130, 1-15.

Seuring, S., & Muller, M. (2008). From a literature review to a conceptual framework for sustainable supply chain management. *Journal of Cleaner Production*, 16, 1699-1710.

Sheu, J.B., Chou, Y.H., & Hu, C.C. (2005). An integrated logistics operational model for green supply chain management. *Transportation Research Part E*, 41, 287-313.

Srivastava, S. (2007). Green supply chain management: A state-of-the-art literature review. *International Journal of Management Reviews*, 9(1), 53-80.

Talluri, S. (2000). A benchmarking method for business process reengineering and improvement. *International Journal of Flexible Manufacturing Systems*, 12(4), 291-304.

Talluri, S., Baker, R.C., & Sarkis, J. (1999). A framework for designing efficient value chain networks. *International Journal of Production Economics*, 62, 133-144.

Tate, W.L., Ellram, L.M., Bals, L. & Hartmann, E. (2009). Offshore outsourcing of services: An evolutionary perspective. *International Journal of Production Economics*, 120, 512-524.

Taylor, A.P., & Postlethwaite, D. (1996). *Overall business impact assessment (OBIA), 4th LCA Case Studies Symposium*. Brussels: Society for Environmental Toxicology and Chemistry, 181-187.

Thompson, D. (2002). *Tools for Environmental Management: A Practical Introduction and Guide.* Calgary: University of Calgary Press.

Tyteca, D. (1997). Linear programming models for the measurement of environmental performance of firms—concepts and empirical results. *Journal of Productivity Analysis*, 8(2), 183-197.

Tyteca, D. (1996). On the measurement of the environmental performance of firms: A literature review and a productive efficiency perspective. *Journal of Environmental Management*, 46, 281-308.

Ukidwe, N., & Bakshi, B. (2005). Flow of natural versus economic capital in industrial supply networks and its implications to sustainability. *Environmental Science and Technology*, 39, 9759-9769.

Walton, S., Handfield, R., & Melnyk, S. (1998). The green supply chain: Integrating suppliers into environmental management. *International Journal of Purchasing and Materials Management*, 34(2), 2-11.

Whiteman, G., Walker, B., & Perego, P. 2013. Planetary boundaries: Ecological foundations for corporate sustainability. *Journal of Management Studies*, 50, 307-336.

Wong, W.P., & Wong, K.Y. (2007). Supply chain performance measurement system using DEA modeling. *Industrial Management & Data Systems*, 107(3), 363-381.

Yu, Y., Chen, D., Zhu, B., & Hu, S. (2013). Eco-efficiency trends in China, 1978–2010: Decoupling environmental pressure from economic growth. *Ecological Indicators*, 24, 177-184.

Zhu, Q., & Cote, R. (2004). Integrating green supply chain management into an embryonic eco-industrial development: A case study of the Guitang group. *Journal of Cleaner Production*, 13, 1025-1035.

Anthony Halog is a Lecturer in Industrial Environmental Management and a Research Group Leader for Industrial Ecology and Circular Economy at the University of Queensland, Australia. He was an Assistant Professor in Operations Management at Brock University, Canada and an Assistant Professor in Industrial Ecology at the University of Maine, USA. His research focuses on the industrial applications of life-cycle assessment, circular economy, sustainable operations management and greening supply chains.

Nga Nguyen has a Master's degree in environmental management and is a PhD candidate at the University of Queensland. She has been building expertise in different areas such as environmental management, water and sanitation, trade and SME development. Her research interests are environmental adaptation, sustainable operations management, corporate social responsibility and green growth.

9

The valorization of social sustainability

Using quality seals to drive continuous improvement in global supply chain management

Claire Moxham
University of Liverpool Management School, UK

Katri Kauppi
Aalto University, Finland

Ascribing a value to goods that have been produced or traded in a manner deemed to be socially sustainable is a relatively recent phenomenon. Whilst socially sustainable supply chain practices are laudable, the valorization of social sustainability is heavily dependent on the quality of the information that is available to stakeholders. With this in mind, this chapter examines quality seals: standards, certifications, codes of conduct and labelling that are used as proxies for socially sustainable supply chain management. The findings highlight pluralism and opacity as regards purpose, measurement and verification. The chapter raises questions about the ability of existing quality seals to support the progression of sustainability practices across global supply chains when the focus seems to be rooted in compliance rather than continuous improvement.

9.1 Introduction

The requirement for sustainable practices across global supply chains is largely uncontested (Pagell and Wu, 2009). Studies explore interfaces between the three elements of the triple bottom line (TBL), with economic and environmental aspects receiving relatively more research attention than those related to the social dimension of sustainable supply chain management (Huq *et al.*, 2014; Karjalainen and Moxham, 2013; Miemczyk *et al.*, 2012). To contribute to discourse regarding the currently under-researched social sustainability considerations of the TBL, this chapter focuses on quality seals: an overarching term for standards, certifications, codes of conduct and labelling that act as proxy measures for sustainable practices. Specifically, the chapter examines the value assigned to goods that are produced or traded in a socially sustainable manner, explores the mechanisms that are used to assure socially sustainable supply chain management, considers how social sustainability can be evidenced in global supply chains and questions the role that quality seals play in the continuous improvement of sustainable supply chain management. To do this, the chapter is structured around three key research questions:

- What factors have contributed to the proliferation of quality seals as proxies for the social sustainability credentials of global supply chains?

- What are the key differences among quality seals that assure social sustainability?

- How are quality seals used to improve the social dimension of the triple bottom line?

9.2 Social sustainability and the triple bottom line

Consider the classical economic argument made by Milton Friedman in the 1960s that management's only responsibility is profit maximization and that, rather than business, it is the free market, government or legislation that are the levers for addressing social problems (Carroll and Shabana, 2010). Such an argument may have resonated in the period of post-World War II economic expansion alongside the mantra of "the business of business is business" (Stuart, 2011). Yet today, against a backdrop of scarce natural resources, global warming and unsustainable global consumption patterns, this argument no longer holds true. Consequently, there is now a widely held view that the responsibility for acting in ways that can be considered as sustainable rests with business, society and individuals. The notion that business can abdicate its responsibilities regarding sustainable practices has been viewed as outmoded by some for decades (Davis, 1973). To this end, the concept of the TBL in which businesses report on their economic, environmental and social performance has emerged (Elkington, 1998).

Despite the three distinct pillars of the TBL there is an important focus on the interconnectedness between people, planet and profit (Stenzel, 2012). Some hold the view that the growing corporate focus on the TBL is driven less by sustainability and more by a desire for price premiums, increased access to new markets and/ or a positive public image (Gulbrandsen, 2006). Indeed, when examining the business case for engaging in the TBL, Kurucz *et al.* (2008) propose the following four arguments:

- Reducing cost and risk

- Strengthening legitimacy and reputation

- Building competitive advantage and

- Creating win–win situations through synergistic value creation.

Whether the rationale for reporting against the TBL is motivated by money or morals, the onus on businesses to consider the economic, social and environmental impacts of their decisions is far from unfavourable from a sustainability standpoint (Stenzel, 2012).

Whilst recognizing the interconnectedness of the TBL, we focus this chapter predominantly on its social dimension. The reasons for this are essentially twofold:

- As the majority of research on this topic has concentrated on economic sustainability with a growing focus on environmental sustainability we see a knowledge-gap as regards social sustainability, and

- As the social dimension of the TBL can be considered as rather nebulous we would like to augment existing studies by developing a greater understanding of how this important aspect is measured.

By focusing on quality seals, we will examine how social sustainability is operationalized in global supply chains. We are particularly interested in the valorization of social sustainability: the assigning of a value to the social sustainability attributes of a product. Research shows how supply chain management practices play an important part in the sustainability of an organization (Tate *et al.*, 2010). By examining global supply chains through a social sustainability lens we can deepen our understanding of current practice.

9.3 The valorization of social sustainability

There is growing demand for information about the conditions under which goods have been produced or traded. Muradian and Pelupessy (2005) view this trend as largely driven by wealthy consumers, yet there is also evidence to suggest a number of stakeholders, including non-governmental organizations (NGOs), industry associations and environmental organizations, have been instrumental in calling for change towards a new model of governance based on sustainability (Gulbrandsen, 2006; Raynolds *et al.*, 2007). Conceivably as a consequence of more and better information on supply chain practices, the economic value of goods differentiated by the demonstration of their sustainable credentials has increased (Horne, 2009; Renard, 2005). For example, studies have shown how sustainably produced coffee earns higher margins than "regular" versions of the same product (Giovannucci and Ponte, 2005). The shift in the market recognition of socially sustainable products has not happened by chance; it has been a collective process championed by supply chain actors and associated interested parties. Once socially sustainable production is widely accepted as an attractive product attribute it subsequently acquires market value. Consequently, in order to assure the socially sustainable credentials of a product, information must be imparted to the consumer. Hence the valorization of social sustainability is contingent on proof and guarantees (Renard, 2005).

Providing this assurance of socially sustainable practices remains a particular challenge for global supply chains. Measures of social sustainability place emphasis on ethics, social justice and fairness: concepts that can be ambiguous and contentious (Reinecke *et al.*, 2012). Furthermore, because the focus is on the conditions under which the goods are produced or traded, it is impossible to verify these conditions by examining the final product (Raynolds *et al.*, 2007). As has often been quoted when considering process sustainability, "nothing distinguishes physically a fair trade banana from a conventional one" (Becchetti and Huybrechts, 2008, p. 734). Because of this, socially sustainable products can be considered as "credence goods" as they possess attributes that consumers cannot evaluate themselves, even after they have consumed the product (Balineau and Dufeu, 2010). Consumers therefore rely on the information that is imparted to them about the product and its associated production or trading practices. It subsequently follows that the valorization of social sustainability rests on consumer confidence that this information is true (Ballet and Carimentrand, 2010). Should consumer confidence in the authenticity of social sustainability erode, its ability to continue to attract a differentiated price premium would diminish. It is therefore important that information pertaining to social sustainability is accurate and legitimate (Renard, 2005).

9.4 Quality seals as a proxy for socially sustainable supply chains

The focus on process rather than product attributes for credence goods leads to information asymmetries between producer and consumer (Daviron and

Vagneron, 2011). As mentioned, because customers cannot identify the social sustainability characteristics of a product by its look, taste, feel or smell they rely on information from producers (Van Amstel *et al.*, 2008). There is no standard mechanism for imparting such information; however, a proliferation of quality seals as a proxy for socially sustainable supply chain management has recently emerged. Quality seals are designed to set quality, social and/or environmental performance criteria and impart such information to interested stakeholders, thus reducing information asymmetries (Raynolds *et al.*, 2007). In short, quality seals are a mechanism for codifying information related to the trading practices of a particular (often global) supply chain with the expected outcome of increased consumer confidence (Muradian and Pelupessy, 2005). Such quality seals take a variety of forms including standards, certifications, codes of conduct and labelling.

The administration of social sustainability quality seals differs and can be classified as mandatory, voluntary and private (Giovannucci and Ponte, 2005; Horne, 2009). Those that are mandatory are set by governments as a form of regulation, those that are voluntary are usually a collective agreement across supply chains monitored by a third party and those that are private are constructed and regulated by corporations (Giovannucci and Ponte, 2005). It is possible that consumers are unaware of the different forms that quality seals may take and this complexity is further compounded by the variety of quality seals currently available that all claim to assure the social sustainability of a particular product. Studies document multiple variants of sustainability-focused quality seals (Hartlieb and Jones, 2009; Raynolds *et al.*, 2007; Reinecke *et al.*, 2012). Many of these studies focus predominantly on environmental performance and there is a particular interest in the coffee industry. To complement these existing studies, we examine quality seals that focus predominantly on social sustainability across a variety of product ranges. We aim to establish the variants on offer and the key facets of each one.

From a literature and online search we identified 12 quality seals focused predominantly on social sustainability. This was not an easy task, as it quickly became apparent that the majority of sustainability quality seals look at environmental performance (e.g. Organic Trust, Forest Stewardship Council, Marine Stewardship Council). As our interest is social sustainability we excluded quality seals with a stronger focus on environmental or economic sustainability. It is important to note, however, that each element of the TBL is far from mutually exclusive and of course many dependencies are present (Boiral and Gendron, 2011). The key facets of each of the social sustainability quality seals are included as Table 9.1. It is evident from this comparison that some quality seals focus on particular products (i.e. Rainforest Alliance or GoodWeave) whereas others are overarching seals that can be applied to a wide range of industrial sectors (i.e. Ethical Trading Initiative or ISO 26000).

Table 9.1 Key facets of social sustainability quality seals

Source: compiled from Muradian and Pelupessy 2005; Hartlieb and Jones 2009; Raynolds *et al.* 2007; Giovannucci and Ponte 2005; websites of quality seals

Quality seal	Administration	Overarching performance criteria	Product range	Verification mechanism	Covers cost of verification
Fairtrade	Voluntary	Price premium to promote long-term development in producer communities, labour practices	Food, beverage, flowers, cosmetics, sports equipment	FLO-Cert (approved independent certifier dedicated to Fairtrade)	Producer
Rainforest Alliance	Voluntary	Labour practices	Flowers, plants, food, beverage	RA-Cert (Rainforest Alliance auditing division)	Producer
Utz Kapeh	Voluntary	Labour practices	Cocoa, coffee, tea	Utz-Kapeh approved third party certifier	Producer
GoodWeave	Voluntary	Labour practices	Rugs	Random factory inspections by GoodWeave	Producer
Fair Flowers Fair Plants	Voluntary	Labour practices	Flowers, plants	Mystery shoppers or third party audits	Producer
African Cashew Alliance	Voluntary	Labour practices	Cashews	Overseen by approved industry experts	Producer
Ethical Sourcing Certification	Voluntary	Labour practices	Food	Approved audits	Producer
Ethical Trading Initiative	Voluntary	Labour practices	Any supply chain	Submission of ethical trade strategy or annual report	Individual supply chain actors
Global Reporting Initiative	Voluntary	Labour practices	Any organization	Submission of sustainability report	N/A

Quality seal	Administration	Overarching performance criteria	Product range	Verification mechanism	Covers cost of verification
International Organization for Standardization (ISO) 26000	Voluntary	Labour practices	Any organization	ISO audit	Individual supply chain actors
Starbucks Shared Planet	Private	Community development	Cocoa, coffee, tea, manufactured items	Internal monitoring	Difficult to ascertain from information available
H&M Conscious	Private	Community development	Textiles	Internal monitoring	Difficult to ascertain from information available

As per previous work on environmentally sustainable quality seals (often referred to as "eco-labels"), we found striking similarities between the 12 quality seals that we examined. Primarily, that the majority were voluntary (it was only Starbucks Shared Planet and H&M Conscious that operated privately), used third party verification mechanisms and had very similar overarching social sustainability performance criteria. Almost all focused on labour practices (e.g. absence of child labour, absence of forced labour, collective bargaining, fair remuneration, absence of abuse, harassment or inequity, health and safety and transparency in trading practices). Half of the quality seals passed the cost of verification on to the producer, with the remainder either not incurring a cost of membership (e.g. the Global Reporting Initiative) or requiring individual actors from any part of the supply chain to pay fees. From the information available it was very difficult to ascertain how the cost of verification for the private quality seals was assigned. So in the case of both Starbucks Shared Planet and H&M Conscious we were unable to come to a definitive conclusion as to whether the corporations or other actors in the supply chain covered the cost of administering the social sustainability verification procedures required.

In examining the governance of these quality seals further, there is evidence to suggest unease around the claims of independence asserted by some of those studied. For example, Raynolds *et al.* (2007) report that the NGO base surrounding Utz Kapeh has been created retrospectively and believe this to be driven by a desire to legitimize a system focused on dominant distributors. In the same study, Rainforest Alliance is criticized for excluding small farmers, workers and consumers from its coordinating body, which raises questions about its level of stakeholder engagement when developing its social sustainability criteria (Raynolds *et al.*, 2007). For the private quality seals, criticism of H&M Conscious is centered on its business model of planned obsolescence (often referred to as "fast fashion"), which seems at odds with its claims of sustainability (White 2015). For Starbucks, critics have questioned the lack of external monitoring of Shared Planet, describing it as "Fair-trade-lite" (Boughton, 2008).

In parallel with these questions about the true independence of social sustainability quality seals and their congruence with private sector business models, questions have also been raised about the need for such proliferation. The multiplicity of quality seals has been criticized for poor coordination, duplication of activity, increased costs and consumer confusion (Fransen, 2011). There may be a clear rationale for these parallel, and most likely competing, quality seals, however, this is difficult to glean from the information provided by the majority of the quality seals that were examined. Recent research finds that the proliferation of quality seals is partly driven by those stakeholders with an interest in maintaining their own particular "brand" of social sustainability (Reinecke *et al.*, 2012). The plurality may also be due to the slightly differing objectives or ideologies of particular quality seals. For example, Fairtrade offers a guaranteed price premium whereas Utz Kapeh does not. Whether consumers understand these differences when making their product choice is the subject of continued debate (Getz and Shreck, 2006). Horne (2009) argues that quality seals may make little impact, as purchasing decisions are often predicated on practice norms rather than the information contained on product labels. Furthermore, in light of the need for accurate and legitimate information it is striking how current research suggests that the information provided to consumers is perceived as opaque (Meise *et al.*, 2014).

9.5 Improving social sustainability in global supply chains

By examining the quality seals highlighted in Table 9.1, it is interesting to note the emphasis on compliance to key performance criteria. Much of the information to potential producers or other supply chain actors focused on adherence to standards and engagement in a monitoring process. With a couple of notable exceptions, most of the quality seals seemed to be concerned with retrospective accountability rather than future performance improvement. Producers are supplied with a list of key performance indicators and must demonstrate how they meet or surpass these criteria. Verification is generally carried out through self-assessment reports and audit visits. When reading the information available on the websites of each of the quality seals, for many there is a real onus on the short-term cycle of verification (often between one and three years) yet limited information is available about the development of the relationship over the medium- and long-term.

As none of the quality seals that we looked at were mandatory, for all of the quality seals in Table 9.1 supply chains must opt into the verification process. It is worth considering the ease with which supply chains can either opt out or switch to an alternative social sustainability assurance mechanism. In many of the examples in

Table 9.1 the producer covers all of the costs related to verification. It may conceivably be the case that it is complex and costly to switch, as supply chain governance and operational practices have been tailored to a particular social sustainability "brand". Because of the slightly different focus of the quality seals, there could also be instances whereby supply chains are operating two or more in parallel. We have yet to find clear confirmation of the parallel use of distinctively social sustainability focused quality seals. Nevertheless, there is evidence of this practice in the coffee industry where quality seals which focused on the environment (e.g. Soil Association or Organic) are used in parallel with Fairtrade or Rainforest Alliance (Getz and Shreck, 2006; Raynolds *et al.*, 2007).

Important questions are being raised about the ability of existing quality seals to actually improve social sustainability performance. For example, it is argued that whilst private quality seals may be viewed as an acceptance by corporations of the importance of social sustainability, such approaches are almost universally perceived by the sustainability community as a threat because the majority of private quality seals are diluted versions of existing standards (Giovannucci and Ponte, 2005). Criticism has been levied at certain multinational coffee shops for implementing a "bait and switch" approach to social sustainability whereby the retailer offers a very limited range of socially sustainable coffee that is not always available, thus requiring customers to opt for an alternative product (Fridell, 2009). Jaffee (2012, p. 110) notes how "pressure from corporate participants to lower the standards bar should be expected" and reframes criticism in this regard towards the ability of quality seals to withstand such pressure. Private standards may be perceived by some as weak proxies for social sustainability, however there is limited evidence to suggest that the majority of consumers share this view despite scholars raising concerns about the erosion of more rigorous, internationally accepted quality measures (Daviron and Vagneron, 2011).

Furthermore, in the setting of social sustainability performance criteria, criticism regarding the exclusion of developing country suppliers has been raised (Giovannucci and Ponte, 2005). Exclusion is often due to governance protocols, including the composition of the board (Utting, 2015). If those that are aiming to adhere to particular standards or codes of conduct are not involved in their establishment, this may be a real barrier to uptake. Moreover, whilst the adoption of quality seals is seen by some as providing the opportunity for producers to add value and improve their products (Jaffee, 2010), this view is not shared by all. As the widespread uptake of socially sustainable products has yet to be realized, the efficacy of quality seals is being called into question (Horne, 2009). For example, aggregated sales of certified sustainable coffee represent less than 1% of total global coffee sales (Muradian and Pelupessy, 2005). This is a thought-provoking statistic given the multiplicity of sustainability quality seals currently in operation.

9.6 Implications for triple bottom line sustainability and directions for further research

To conclude our exploration of social sustainability quality seals, it is important to recap on the key research questions that frame the chapter and to offer propositions and interesting avenues for further research. The research questions are addressed thus:

- What factors have contributed to the proliferation of quality seals as proxies for the social sustainability credentials of global supply chains?

The recognition and acceptance of social sustainability as a desirable supply chain attribute appears to be the key driver for the multiple quality seals that have recently emerged. Using quality seals as proxies provides proof and guarantees to stakeholders, thus supporting the achievement of price differentials for goods that are produced and traded in a socially sustainable manner. We therefore propose:

> **Proposition 1**: *The valorization of social sustainability supports higher economic returns and is contingent on the information provided to stakeholders.*

- What are the key differences among quality seals that assure social sustainability?

Despite the growing number of social sustainability-focused quality seals, our analysis points to more similarities than differences between those that were examined. Whilst each may have a particular focus or ideology (e.g. operating in one particular industrial sector or the eradication of child labour), the key performance criteria used are almost identical. Such similarities may make it difficult to discern one quality seal from another, thus leading to an undifferentiated crowded market. In comparing social sustainability quality seals with those focused on the environment, we find a much more differentiated market. Whilst there are a number of environmental sustainability quality seals available, there is less overlap in focus. In the case of coffee, for example, quality seals tend to focus on one particular primary attribute, for example, price premiums, organic agricultural methods, bird-friendly or shade-friendly characteristics (Raynolds *et al.*, 2007). We have acknowledged earlier in the chapter that such environmental quality seals may operate in parallel (e.g. organic and price premium), often due to their distinct focus. It may be the case that social sustainability quality seals are at an early stage of development, hence their proliferation and the use of similar performance criteria. As the market for social sustainability quality seals matures, we may see a more differentiated focus and the possible merging of existing quality seals. In supporting the development of quality seals that assure social sustainability we thus propose:

> **Proposition 2**: *Using similar social sustainability key performance criteria makes it difficult for stakeholders to differentiate between quality seals and leads to increased competition for membership.*

- How are quality seals used to improve the social dimension of the triple bottom line?

The compliance focus of many of the quality seals examined may be a real barrier to improving the social dimension of the TBL. Our findings suggest that many of the social sustainability quality seals that we looked at pay much attention to retrospective auditing and we posit that this may be to the detriment of forward-looking continuous improvement. In the spirit of the quality improvement Deming cycle of plan–do–check–act (Dale, 2003), those quality seals that focus only on "check" may miss out on the learning to be gained from completing the cycle. We propose that developing action plans and engaging in the continuous improvement cycle will have a more positive impact on the social dimension of TBL than maintaining a focus on compliance only. We therefore posit:

> **Proposition 3**: *Quality seals with a predominantly retrospective compliance focus have a lesser impact on the triple bottom line than those with a forward-looking continuous improvement approach.*

In offering further directions for future research, we believe the proliferation of sustainability-focused quality seals that span global supply chains to be an interesting avenue to explore. While we have discussed the potentially negative aspects of plurality in this chapter, research has also identified advantages. For example, the multiplicity of quality seals related to the TBL may promote greater awareness of the different arguments used to substantiate the claims made (De Boer, 2003). This awareness may form part of a sustainable consumption strategy as it has been pointed out that quality seals alone do not address issues of consumption as they are limited to imparting information about the supply chain (Horne, 2009). Empirical research examining consumer views of sustainable quality seals could be used to examine whether a gap exists between perceptions and expectations and whether the multiplicity of quality seals is actually seen as advantageous when making a purchasing choice.

In discussing concepts of the TBL, sustainability and supply chains, there can be a tendency to focus on the status quo and to retrospectively attempt to justify the decisions made (we see this for example through life cycle analysis and social return on investment). The emergence and growth in the number and availability of quality seals is an interesting case in point. The purpose of quality seals is to impart information to substantiate sustainability claims to a broad and varied audience. In moving the sustainability challenge forward it may now be time to shift our focus away from our predisposition for accountability towards new ways of configuring supply chains so that quality seals are no longer necessary because sustainable practices are taken as a given. For example, supply chain disintermediation may improve quality by reducing the number of supply chain actors and engendering trust and partnerships: the ideals of the Fairtrade trading relationship. In addition, rather than retrospectively assessing whether a product conforms to sustainability norms, a dedicated focus on the relationship between supply chains and consumption may have a tangible positive impact on all aspects of the TBL. Decoupling supply chain management from consumption has real potential for inertia as the drivers for innovation and change will be predominantly market-based rather than sustainability-focused. For example, improving the sustainability of supply chain practices will only go so far towards improving the TBL if existing consumption patterns go unchecked. Further research on new ways of managing supply chains for sustainable production and consumption is important and timely. To conclude our thoughts in this chapter, we would like to draw on Horne's (2009, p. 181) often overlooked point that in considering sustainability "in some circumstances the most (environmentally) sustainable option is no purchase at all, and in this case there is nowhere to place the label".

References

Balineau, G., & Dufeu, I. (2010). Are fair trade goods credence goods? A new proposal, with French illustrations. *Journal of Business Ethics*, 92(2), 331-345.

Ballet, J., & Carimentrand, A. (2010). Fair trade and the depersonalization of ethics. *Journal of Business Ethics*, 92(2), 317-330.

Becchetti, L., & Huybrechts, B. (2008). The dynamics of fair trade as a mixed-form market. *Journal of Business Ethics*, 81(4), 733-750.

Boiral, O., & Gendron, Y. (2011). Sustainable development and certification practices: Lessons learned and prospects. *Business Strategy and the Environment*, 20(5), 331-347.

Boughton, I. (2008). Starbucks launch of ethical espresso draws criticism. *The Caterer.* Retrieved from https://www.thecaterer.com/articles/323561/starbucks-launch-of-ethical-espresso-draws-criticism (24 September 2008)

Carroll, A., & Shabana, K. (2010). The business case for corporate social responsibility: A review of concepts, research and practice. *International Journal of Management Reviews*, 12(1), 85-105.

Dale, B.G. (2003). *Managing Quality.* Oxford, UK: Blackwell Publishing.

Daviron, B. & Vagneron, I. (2011). From commoditisation to de-commoditation ... and back again: Discussing the role of sustainability standards for agricultural products. *Development Policy Review*, 29(1), 91-113.

Davis, K. (1973). The case for and against business assumption of social responsibilities. *Academy of Management Journal*, 16(2), 312-322.

De Boer, J. (2003). Sustainability labelling schemes: The logic of their claims and their functions for stakeholders. *Business Strategy and the Environment*, 12(4), 254-264.

Elkington, J. (1998). *Cannibals with Forks: The Triple Bottom Line of 21st Century Business.* Gabriola Island, BC: New Society Publishers.

Fransen, L.W. (2011). Why do private governance organizations not converge? A political-institutional analysis of transnational labour standards regulation. *Governance*, 24(2), 359-387.

Fridell, G. (2009). The co-operative and the corporation: Competing visions of the future of fair trade. *Journal of Business Ethics*, 86(1), 81-95.

Getz, C., & Shreck, A. (2006). What organic and Fair Trade labels do not tell us: Towards a place-based understanding of certification. *International Journal of Consumer Studies*, 30(5), 490-501.

Giovannucci, D., & Ponte, S. (2005). Standards as a new form of social contract? Sustainability initiatives in the coffee industry. *Food Policy*, 30(3), 284-301.

Gulbrandsen, L. (2006). Creating markets for eco-labelling: Are customers insignificant. *International Journal of Consumer Studies*, 30(5), 477-489.

Hartlieb, S., & Jones, B. (2009). Humanising business through ethical labelling: Progress and paradoxes in the UK. *Journal of Business Ethics*, 88(3), 583-600.

Horne, R. (2009). Limits to labels: The role of eco-labels in the assessment of product sustainability and routes to sustainable consumption. *International Journal of Consumer Studies*, 33(2), 175-182.

Huq, F., Stevenson, M., & Zorzini, M. (2014). Social sustainability in developing country suppliers. *International Journal of Operations and Production Management*, 34(5), 610-638.

Jaffee, D. (2012). Weak coffee: Certification and co-optation in the Fair Trade movement. *Social Problems*, 59(1), 94-116.

Jaffee, D. (2010). Fair Trade standards, corporate participation, and social movement responses in the United States. *Journal of Business Ethics*, 92(2), 217-240.

Karjalainen, K., & Moxham, C. (2013). Focus on Fairtrade: Propositions for integrating Fairtrade and SCM research. *Journal of Business Ethics*, 116(2), 267-282.

Kurucz, E., Colbert, B., & Wheeler, D. (2008). The business case for corporate social responsibility. In A. Crane, A. McWilliams, D. Matten, J. Moon & D. Siegal (Eds.), *The Oxford Handbook of Corporate Social Responsibility* (pp. 83-112). Oxford, UK: University.

Meise, J., Rudolph, T., Kenning, P., & Phillips, D. (2014). Feed them facts: Value perceptions and consumer use of sustainability-related product information. *Journal of Retailing and Consumer Services*, 21(4), 510-519.

Miemczyk, J., Johnsen, T.E., & Macquet, M. (2012). Sustainable purchasing and supply management: A structured literature review of definitions and measures at the dyad, chain and network levels. *Supply Chain Management: An International Journal*, 17(5), 478-496.

Muradian, R., & Pelupessy, W. (2005). Governing the coffee chain: The role of voluntary regulatory systems. *World Development*, 33(12), 2,029-2,044.

Pagell, M., & Wu, Z. (2009). Building a more complete theory of sustainable supply chain management using case studies of ten exemplars. *Journal of Supply Chain Management*, 45(2), 37-56.

Raynolds, L., Murray, D., & Heller, A. (2007). Regulating sustainability in the coffee sector: A comparative analysis of third-party environmental and social certification initiatives. *Agriculture and Human Values*, 24(2), 147-163.

Reinecke, J., Manning, S., & von Hagen, O. (2012). The emergence of a standards market: Multiplicity of sustainability standards in the global coffee industry. *Organization Studies*, 33(5-6), 791-814.

Renard, M.-C. (2005). Quality certification, regulation and power in fair trade. *Journal of Rural Studies*, 21(4), 419-431.

Stenzel, P. (2012). The pursuit of equilibrium as the eagle meets the condor: Supporting sustainable development through fair trade. *American Business Law Journal*, 49(3), 557-642.

Stuart, M. (2011). *The good, the bad and the indifferent: Marketing and the triple bottom line*. *Social Business*, 1(2), 173-187.

Tate, W., Ellram, L., & Kirchoff, J. (2010). Corporate social responsibility reports: A thematic analysis related to supply chain management. *Journal of Supply Chain Management*, 46(1), 19-44.

Utting, P. (2015). Corporate accountability, fair trade and multi-stakeholder regulation. In L. Raynolds & E. Bennett (Eds.), *Handbook of Research on Fair Trade* (pp. 61-79). Cheltenham, UK: Edward Elgar Publishing Ltd.

Van Amstel, M., Driessen, P., & Glasbergen, P. (2008). Eco-labelling and information asymmetry: A comparison of five eco-labels in the Netherlands. *Journal of Cleaner Production*, 16(3), 263-276.

White , S. (2015). H&M's "conscious" collection? Don't buy into the hype. *Huffington Post*. Retrieved from http://www.huffingtonpost.com/shannon-whitehead/hms-conscious-collection-_b_7107964.html (22 April 2015)

Claire Moxham is Senior Lecturer in Operations Management at the University of Liverpool Management School, UK. Claire's research interests are broadly in the area of performance improvement, particularly in the context of public and non-profit organizations. She became particularly interested in socially sustainable supply chains when working as a volunteer in Ethiopia from 2001–2003.

Katri Kauppi is Assistant Professor in Logistics and Supply Chain Management at Aalto University, Finland. She has previously worked at several UK universities. Katri's research focuses on purchasing and supply chain management, particularly on purchasing behaviour and global sourcing. She has previously published under her maiden name Karjalainen.

Education

10

The role of business schools in developing leaders for triple bottom line sustainability

Tim London

Graduate School of Business, University of Cape Town, South Africa

The creation and impact of triple bottom line (TBL) practices and thinking is a fundamentally challenging proposition. While there is much agreement that these approaches are necessary, there is a need to build the capacity to make these concepts into practical realities. Business schools are a particularly effective leverage point for enabling sustainability to become a more widespread and more impactful proposition. They have two fundamentally powerful aspects to them: the large numbers of students attending a wide variety of programmes and their capacity for creating events that will attract discussion of these issues. It is essential, in both of these areas, that while unique components of different sustainability concepts are built, the focus is on putting these ideas into a wider "business" context. This will help to connect these practices together, ensuring that TBL and related approaches become part and parcel of good business practice and not just a niche "nice to have".

10.1 Introduction

Sustainability in general, and triple bottom line (TBL) processes and measurement specifically, have become much talked about in the business sphere and, to some degree, the wider public (Hubbard, 2009; Pava, 2007; Slaper and Hall, 2011; Smith and Sharicz, 2011), with much of this driven by the work of John Elkington. TBL accounting practices, effective global supply chain management, environmental/social/economic inputs and outcomes and business model innovation all play significant roles in sustainable business (Lamberton, 2005; Manuj and Mentzer, 2008). While interrelated in many ways, each of these concepts is also made up of unique skills, outlooks and processes. While no single intervention or approach will completely address all of these components, a key leverage point for embedding these concepts in practice lies with business schools. Business schools have several avenues for making a profound impact on these issues, including a range of programmes (award and non-award bearing), executive education connections, conferences and seminars, and other advocacy.

The impact of business schools across these inputs on the world of business cannot be underestimated. Given the sheer volume of the workforce who will have been impacted by business schools in some way, it is essential that this force be brought to bear on issues such as TBL sustainability practices. Many will enter the workforce with undergraduate business degrees in hand; many more will earn graduate/post-graduate degrees and awards, receive executive education training, or attend seminars and conferences that are designed by business school faculties. Business degrees and awards are being earned at an incredible rate: in the United States, in 2012–13 alone, almost 190,000 students graduated with a Master's degree in Business (NCES, 2015, Table 323.10). The top 18 business schools in the UK (out of approximately 150) have enrolled over 1,500 students per year on their MBA programmes since at least 2005 (Bradshaw and Ortmans, 2013). Beyond the programmatic side, business school faculties are producing research that has impacts in journals, books and trade publications as well as the popular media, where they are often asked to speak about news stories. With this impact on the skills and viewpoints of a large part of the business community, combined with the power to influence public perception of business issues, it is imperative that business schools are leveraged to ensure that TBL sustainability practices actually become common and effective.

Many companies trumpet their advances and commitment in these areas on their websites and in publicity materials. There is the potential danger, however, of companies not actually being able to implement such measures with the efficiency and/or effectiveness required to make TBL more than a slogan. Leaving the development of these new processes to chance, thinking that revisions to existing related practices and systems will be implemented perfectly, or simply pasting a new "TBL" sticker on existing practices, will ensure that this level of sustainability remains an add-on or "nice to have" (Lamberton, 2005; Perrini and Tencati, 2006;

Smith and Sharicz, 2011). Similarly, for entrepreneurs and new businesses, a commitment to TBL sustainability requires more than an awareness of these issues, it demands nuanced appreciation for what these processes mean, both for the company as well as the wider community (Carter and Rogers, 2008).

Sustainability practices are about drawing critical connections between the individual business situations of companies/organizations, based on wider community, social and ecological grounds (Carter and Rogers, 2008; Hamann, 2007; Slaper and Hall, 2011). This requires a more comprehensive view of "business", moving beyond simply developing accounting, economics, marketing and other isolated skills (Lamberton, 2005). These are certainly necessary pieces, but TBL requires that they be brought together in significantly different and challenging ways; this bridging and connecting of multiple facets is the leadership component to making sustainability ideals into effective practice (Jamali, 2006). How do choices throughout the organization impact on the TBL dimensions and processes? What external pressures will support our efforts, challenge our goals, or cause us to move in new directions? Looking for these types of signals requires a keen eye to what is happening both internally and externally, across many different levels of an organization.

Crucially, it must be noted here that this chapter is about leaders in their truest sense: these are people who make things happen with other people and help make sense of internal and external challenges (Pye, 2005). This means that the focus here is not simply on the most senior members in an organizational hierarchy. For TBL approaches to be fully implemented to their maximum capacity they need to be pushed and supported by leaders throughout an organization. Similarly, it must be recognized that development of sustainability approaches and practices cannot simply focus on those in, or currently aspiring to, leadership roles but must also develop the pipeline for the future. Today's accountant may become the CFO down the line; an analyst may open his or her own firm in the future. Business schools have the opportunity to interact with people across all levels and situations, so their impact on leadership can be both immediate (MBAs or executive education offerings targeted at C-level leaders) or based on a longer timeline (equipping those in technical areas with the skills and perspectives that will serve TBL thinking as they move into different leadership roles). There are three key ways in which business schools can be most potent in the drive to build capacity and impact of leaders for TBL sustainability: TBL specific training, incorporation of TBL concepts into the fabric of programmes, and advocacy beyond those already committed to these viewpoints.

10.2 Teaching triple bottom line sustainability

While this chapter argues for a more in-depth use and integration of TBL thinking and practices into the norms of business, there are also key aspects of TBL sustainability that require explicit development. The skills that need to be addressed in this are important, but the first imperative is to facilitate and engage with the thinking underpinning why TBL is necessary. Without this change in viewpoints and critical dialogue, the danger is that any further learning about TBL practices will either be unclear or lacking in application (Strand, 2011). Therefore, the first step in teaching about TBL needs to be a fundamental engagement with the question of "what is the purpose of the organization?" whether that be a for-profit company or a non-profit organization (Slaper and Hall, 2011). For those working in, or looking to start, companies, the traditional bottom line is always going to be an enormous factor for them—so how they see this meshing with other pressures and goals is essential (Carter and Rogers, 2008; Lamberton, 2005; Strand, 2011). This will drive not only the behaviours and structures they implement, but also their viewpoints of what they do, and should do, going forward.

Given this need to think through implications that come from incorporating TBL sustainability, the second major issue to address in teaching/training is more "big picture", as well. Stepping back to look at the purpose of the organization including, but also beyond, profit requires careful analysis of just what structures need to be in place, what culture the organization will need to have and what people are best suited to work within, and drive, those particular dynamics (Pirson, 2012; Zahra *et al.*, 2009). Leaders of entrepreneurial ventures face the same challenges, though in these cases it is less about changing these aspects and more about what to create if their new venture is to make TBL sustainability a reality (Zahra *et al.*, 2009). Once these first two stages have been interrogated thoroughly (and it must be a rigorous "interrogation" to identify what taking a TBL stance will mean for their whole organization), the next stage is to get into training for specific skills that must be in place to make a TBL approach one that has real impact beyond a mere reporting activity (Perrini and Tencati, 2006). This is the process of taking some of the thinking and concepts currently located in "social entrepreneurship", and moving them into standard business practices (Pirson, 2012; Seelos and Mair, 2005; Zahra *et al.*, 2009).

It is at the point of specific skills and approaches that it makes sense to cease addressing TBL concepts on their own and begin integration into other, "traditional", business activities and skills. While arguments could be made that TBL practices have their own unique nuances, the reality is that those nuances will be branches from established practices (discussed below) and are better understood in that context (Jamali, 2006; Lamberton, 2005). It is also important to note the dangers of keeping TBL entirely distinct from the rest of a business curriculum. By treating it as a "special subject", it gives the appearance that TBL and related sustainability approaches and practices are extras to what happens in "real" business (Pirson, 2012; Seelos and Mair, 2005). While there is value in creating TBL experts (and, to be clear, there is a need for experts in this area), there is significant value that is lost if they are kept on the margins of wider discussions on business, with sustainability becoming a niche venue (Pirson, 2012). For a more significant impact on the practices of organizations after training, TBL approaches must then be incorporated ubiquitously into business school curricula (Strand, 2011).

10.3 Weaving triple bottom line thinking into the fabric of programmes

While the unique perspectives that come from TBL thinking must be learned, it must also be recognized that these aspects cannot make an impact unless they are woven into a much larger picture of "business" (Strand, 2011). This requires taking the TBL-specific training discussed above and meshing it with wider principles and practices that are taught in business school programmes. While the most obvious connections would be to courses such as accounting, finance, ethics and operations management, to be truly effective, TBL thinking needs to extend across a range of other, perhaps less obvious, subject areas as well (Lamberton, 2005). Since the focus here is on thinking about business differently, these issues will be important to the curricula in such courses as strategy, leadership, entrepreneurship and other courses that are often (unfortunately somewhat dismissively) referred to as "soft skills". Failure to include TBL thinking in these areas will relegate the concept to a functional add-on, rather than a fundamental focus and driver of the full business. It would also ignore the fact that many students may enter their programmes with preconceived negative or dismissive opinions regarding concepts that do not fit neatly into popular tropes of business being all about maximizing profit or that the financial bottom line is the only indicator that really matters (Giacalone and Promislo, 2013).

This means that the full spread of standard business school curricula should reflect a shared vision for the same underpinnings as TBL concepts. Such an approach reflects not only how embedded these practices will need to be across a range of issues but also the leadership required to create an environment where all the parts align around TBL sustainability goals. Lining these areas up leads to much greater impact of all facets; the negative implications that stem from not orienting these aspects together is impotent implementation at best and fractured agendas at worst. While the full range of content areas should be aligned, a few of these (beyond the obvious candidates mentioned already) present particularly potent opportunities for leaders to develop their abilities to embed TBL processes in business practices.

10.3.1 Strategic thinking

Courses on strategic thinking will study the business environment, governmental inputs, markets, competitors and internal resources (Porter, 2008). For any organization, whether for profit or not, understanding where your organization stands in the midst of these variables is essential (Foran *et al.*, 2005). Analysis of these external and internal factors must include examining how organizational strategies speak to societal issues. This brings the benefits and potential pitfalls of utilizing corporate social responsibility initiatives and building shared value fully into planning and evaluation of strategy (Porter and Kramer, 2006, 2011; Pirson, 2012). Understanding these challenges and opportunities provides clarity on current threats and opportunities, as well as seeing where the edge of the curve is moving forward. It could be argued that TBL thinking is no longer ahead of the curve but it is also true that it has not been adopted with much vigour, nor with real intent or coordination, in a significant number of arenas (Porter and Kramer, 2006). This means that sustainability issues and risks remain opportunities for benefit or potential threats if organizations are seen as being left behind (Manuj and Mentzer, 2008; Porter and Kramer, 2006).

This is a key "opportunity/threat" that can be addressed in an overall strategy course. Analysing TBL concepts in this way makes it clear that this is part of a sound business strategy and not simply a marketing exercise or niche market to explore (Porter and Kramer, 2006, 2011). Depending on the audience involved, this can address foundational changes in strategy (those in the energy field, for example) or more nuanced adaptations (hospitality and service industries) (Smith and Sharicz, 2011; Porter and Kramer, 2011). By not keeping TBL concepts on their own, it becomes clear that, as resources get tight and consumers become more demanding for evidence of these types of practices, the issues of sustainability are not going to be optional in the future (Perrini and Tencati, 2006). This will also serve to drive related conversations for intrapreneurship and other business model innovations, as many traditional practices will be clearly seen to be inadequate in the future, requiring further strategic evaluation.

10.3.2 Leadership

While there are multiple ways people can be prepared for leadership, many of them not requiring extensive formal education, business schools certainly have a large part to play in shaping both the conception of "business" as well as how it is practiced for leaders at all levels of organizations. Leadership here refers to the management side of a leader's role as well as more transformational and visionary aspects. Both of these components are necessary for individuals as well as for organizations as a whole, as each component is more effective when combined with the other. This speaks to the need for TBL concepts to be spread not just across individual programmes or concentrations, but to permeate all levels of business schools' trainings. Doing so enables leadership at all levels of an organization, from small teams to those at C-level, to speak the same language around TBL principles and ensure a coherent approach throughout the organization's practices and decisions (Jamali, 2006; Perrini and Tencati, 2006; Smith and Sharicz, 2011).

The transformational side of leadership for driving sustainability approaches is hugely important both for creating change in existing organizations to make them more in tune with TBL concepts as well as for leaders who will be called upon to create organizations that can incorporate TBL from the start (including both intra-preneurial and entrepreneurial ventures) (Jamali, 2006; Smith and Sharicz, 2011). Beyond setting the vision and strategy for a company and/or its various divisions and individual workers, transformational leaders will need to empower individuals to achieve TBL objectives. They must also ensure that the structures and culture of the organization are conducive to making these objectives valuable and achievable (Foran *et al.*, 2005; Seelos and Mair, 2005). Most leadership courses in business schools already incorporate work on vision setting and engaging with people, structure and cultures in an organization. This means that work on TBL-focused activities can easily be incorporated, with these broader ideals more explicitly linked into what it means for leaders in terms of developing an organization that is built around sustainability practices (Perrini and Tencati, 2006; Smith and Sharicz, 2011).

The management aspect of the equation is no less important, as this gets into the day-to-day practices that must happen if TBL is to move from concept to reality for an organization. This means that the incentive schemes (such as promotions and pay), interactions between colleagues, and performance feedback are all tied into TBL sustainability ideas (Perrini and Tencati, 2006). One of the most important ways this can be done is defining KPIs that reflect wider thinking than just financial outcomes (Foran *et al.*, 2005; Hubbard, 2009). This requires more thought and engagement with the strategic plans of the organization as well as with how progress in these plans is actually going to be assessed (Hubbard, 2009; Pava, 2007; Smith and Sharicz, 2011). Crucially, leaders looking to grow the focus on TBL need to understand how to develop KPIs that are geared towards both outcomes and processes, as well as to develop ways of measuring these factors in meaningful ways (Hamann, 2007; Hubbard, 2009). Again, these broad concepts are already being addressed in leadership programmes in business schools, so the key element here is ensuring that there is engagement with these ideas beyond the traditional financial outcomes and what that change in approach might mean for leaders.

10.3.3 Human resources

Several of the structural and cultural issues discussed are inherently driven and supported by related human resource practices. Human resources (HR) courses already stress issues of how and who to hire; this naturally fits into the discussion around which people are committed to approaching their work with a vested interest in TBL thinking. It also needs to contribute to the analysis of what happens with these people once they are brought on board with a company. How people are inducted, the training with which they are provided, the incentive schemes in place, and the retention/promotion policies are all crucial HR functions that will directly impact not only who is in the company but how they are encouraged to act and see the world and organization in light of TBL sustainability goals (Jamali, 2006).

Again, there is no need to build in an entirely different section around these issues, as these are all fundamental matters of HR. What is required is for TBL thinking to be one of the factors raised in these wider analyses. The goal here is to highlight that people are the actual force behind the policies and ideas, so they need to be directly connected to the TBL sustainability concepts in as many ways as possible. A key part of HR courses is about developing an understanding of how processes impact people and vice versa; an organization that has aspirations of implementing sustainability practices will need to ensure that their HR systems are well equipped to bring in people who believe in sustainability and then invests in aligning the structures and culture of the organization to those same ideals (Jamali, 2006).

10.4 Driving the triple bottom line discussion

While business schools already hold conferences, seminars and panel sessions around sustainability issues, there is a fundamental flaw to just about all of them: they wind up collecting only the voices of those already on board with these concepts. To be clear, this is not an indictment of the current efforts, which remain important for their ability to nurture, sustain and evolve the discussions of sustainability. Rather, the point here is that more efforts need to be made to connect the conversations with individuals and groups who would not attend such sessions, including those in the wider public, business and/or governmental agencies. This is a daunting task, as any event planner would tell you: how do you organize events for people who are not particularly interested in the theme of those events? Just as with the need to incorporate TBL thinking into a full range of taught courses, so too must these types of conferences and seminars explicitly connect TBL issues with a larger context if this type of thinking is to be made more meaningful to a wider range of people.

This is not a bait-and-switch process, rather it is about deepening the discussions of topics in the business school curricula to include TBL thinking. Getting the balance right between context, TBL approaches and other related concepts is incredibly difficult but it is necessary if the sustainability discussion is to widen into new areas and groups. Failure to do so will keep it in a more activist status which, while better than being ignored, locates it on the outskirts of many important and fundamentally interconnected discussions. To get these types of interrelated conferences and seminars moving, faculties from business schools need to plan for how the topic can be clearly meshed with existing major events. For example, creating a TBL sustainability theme for major annual conferences in areas such as organizational behaviour, business ethics, or business leadership would go a long way towards inculcating the sustainability dimensions into these wider debates, making it clear that they are part and parcel of these bigger issues. Again, while conferences specifically on sustainability or TBL are wonderful opportunities to share new insights, they will only attract other enthusiasts; by branching out into interdisciplinary discourses, this specific expertise can be used to enrich other areas, deepening and widening the understanding of multiple areas of study.

10.5 Conclusion

Business schools have an enormous reach in terms of both the number of students they serve as well as the multiple stages in which they interact with future and current business leaders (undergraduate, graduate and executive education programmes). This access to a wide range of students, through a variety of courses, means that business schools can fundamentally impact on the perceptions of "business as usual". Similarly, there is potential to create the next pipeline of leaders, both with advanced programmes for leaders (such as MBAs) and also via courses for those who may become leaders in the future. Further, their ability to leverage the expertise of their faculty along with international connections can make them powerful advocates for expanding and enhancing the debate of TBL issues, and also improving the chances of these approaches taking hold in individual organizations and the wider thinking around business (Strand, 2011). The key here is that this promotion of TBL processes and sustainability more generally does not become a niche endeavour and that real effort is put into going beyond encouraging debate about these issues and moves into a wider discussion on what these ideas mean for "business as usual" (Pirson, 2012).

The key distinction here is between the "teaching to the converted" model and that of encouraging more people, in more areas, to get on board with these initiatives. While teaching more courses on TBL accounting or global supply chain management is helpful in cultivating greater aptitude, the majority of people who will be taking these courses are already in tune with these ideals. To make these sustainability concepts truly impactful, a greater emphasis must be made by business schools to integrate these concepts into the full range of business disciplines, rather than keep them isolated as a speciality. This means courses from technical areas (finance, accounting, operations management or marketing, for example) as well as those devoted to conceptual thinking and planning (strategy, leadership, negotiations and other "soft skill" areas) must all be imbued with TBL thinking if there is to be a real impact on students and, through them, the business world (Porter and Kramer, 2011). Business schools must also leverage their resources and networks more effectively to broaden the discussions around these issues. Forums and conferences on the topic will always be well attended but increasing attention must be paid to those who are not attending these events, as they are the ones who will need convincing if the impact of TBL thinking and sustainability is to spread across a greater audience and impact on organizational practices more powerfully.

References

Bradshaw, D., & Ortmans, L. (2013, January 21). *International students shun UK MBAs. FT.com.* Retrieved from: http://www.ft.com/intl/cms/s/2/86b43890-5671-11e2-aaaa-00144feab49a.html#axzz3hnugCr00.

Carter, C.R., & Rogers, D.S. (2008). A framework of sustainable supply chain management: Moving toward new theory. *International Journal of Physical Distribution & Logistics Management*, 38. doi: 10.1108/09600030810882816

Foran, B., Lenzen, M., Dey, C., & Bilek, M. (2005). Integrating sustainable chain management with triple bottom line accounting. *Ecological Economics*, 52(2), 143-157. doi: 10.1016/j.ecolecon.2004.06.024

Giacalone, R.A., & Promislo, M.D. (2013). Broken when entering: The stigmatization of goodness and business ethics education. *Academy of Management Learning & Education*, 12(1), 86-101.

Hamann, R. (2007). Is corporate citizenship making a difference? *The Journal of Corporate Citizenship*, 44, 15-29.

Hubbard, G. (2009). Measuring organizational performance: Beyond the triple bottom line. *Business Strategy and the Environment*, 18, 177-191. doi: 10.1002/Bse.564

Jamali, D. (2006). Insights into triple bottom line integration from a learning organization perspective. *Business Process Management Journal*, 12(6), 809-821. doi: 10.1108/14637150610710945

Lamberton, G. (2005). Sustainability accounting: A brief history and conceptual framework. *Accounting Forum*, 29(1), 7-26. doi: 10.1016/j.accfor.2004.11.001

Manuj, I., & Mentzer, J.T. (2008). Global supply chain risk management strategies. *International Journal of Physical Distribution & Logistics Management*, 38(3), 192-223. doi: 10.1108/09600030810866986

National Center for Education Statistics (NCES) (2015). Table 323.10, *Master's degrees conferred by postsecondary institutions, by field of study: Selected years, 1970–71 through 2012-13*. Retrieved from https://nces.ed.gov/programs/digest/d14/tables/dt14_323.10.asp?current=yes (August 2015).

Pava, M.L. (2007). A response to "Getting to the Bottom of 'Triple Bottom Line'". *Business Ethics Quarterly*, 17(1), 105-110.

Perrini, F., & Tencati, A. (2006). Sustainability and stakeholder management: The need for new corporate performance evaluation and reporting systems. *Business Strategy and the Environment*, 15, 296-308.

Pirson, M. (2012). Social entrepreneurs as the paragons of shared value creation? A critical perspective. *Social Enterprise Journal*, 8(1), 31-48.

Porter, M.E. (2008). The five competitive forces that shape strategy. *Harvard Business Review*, (January), 78-94.

Porter, M.E., & Kramer, M.R. (2011). Creating shared value. *Harvard Business Review*, 89(1/2), 62-77.

Porter, M.E., & Kramer, M.R. (2006). Strategy and society. The link between competitive advantage and corporate social responsibility. *Harvard Business Review*, 84(12), 78-92.

Pye, A. (2005). Leadership and organizing: Sensemaking in action. *Leadership*, 1(1), 31-49.

Seelos, C., & Mair, J. (2005). Social entrepreneurship: Creating new business models to serve the poor. *Business Horizons*, 48(3), 241-246.

Slaper, T.F., & Hall, T.J. (2011). The Triple Bottom Line: What is it and how does it work? *Indiana Business Review*, Spring, 4-8. Retrieved from http://www.ibrc.indiana.edu/ibr/2011/spring/article2.html

Smith, P., & Sharicz, C. (2011). The shift needed for sustainability. *The Learning Organization*, 18(1), 73-86. doi: 10.1108/09696471111096019

Strand, R. (2011). Toward sustainable sustainability learning: Lessons from a U.S. MBA study abroad program in Scandinavia. *Journal of Strategic Innovation and Sustainability*, 7(2), 41-63.

Zahra, S.A., Gedajlovic, E., Neubaum, D.O., & Shulman, J.M. (2009). A typology of social entrepreneurs: Motives, search processes and ethical challenges. *Journal of Business Venturing*, 24(5), 519-532.

Tim London is a Senior Lecturer at the Allan Gray Centre for Values Based Leadership within the Graduate School of Business at the University of Cape Town. Much of his work is focused on rethinking the concepts of organizations, leaders and leadership. He has lived and worked in many countries (USA, Egypt, Saipan, Northern Ireland, England and South Africa) which, in combination with his diverse academic training, has developed an international and interdisciplinary approach to the challenges of organizations and leaders. He currently holds EdD, LLM, MA, PGCHET and BA degrees and is due to be awarded his MBA (Entrepreneurship) in 2016.

Part III
Cases:
how to do it

11

Sustainable supply chain in a social enterprise

Gloria Camacho
Tecnológico de Monterrey, Mexico

Mario Vázquez-Maguirre
Universidad de Monterrey, Mexico

Firms need to move towards sustainability and supply chains offer an opportunity to achieve it. However, in this context, few academics have explored sustainability from a triple bottom line (TBL) approach, which includes the integration of the economic, social and environmental dimensions of sustainability (Carter and Rogers, 2008; Seuring and Müller, 2008). Building on stakeholder orientation and TBL approach, we develop a framework which focuses on the introduction of sustainability into supply chains. To test our framework, we study a social enterprise that focuses on community well-being through value creation and sustainability. Our contribution is to extend supply chain literature by studying supply chains within a social enterprise in order to understand how this kind of company integrates sustainability in its supply chain from a TBL approach.

11.1 Introduction

Firms have been pressured by their different stakeholders to take responsibility for their environmental and social impacts (Hall and Matos, 2010; Carter and Easton, 2011). Therefore, firms need to move towards sustainability and their supply chains offers an opportunity to achieve this. For example, from a stakeholder-oriented approach, supply chains have moved towards sustainability through the integration of economic, environmental and social issues (Kleindorfer *et al.*, 2005; Pagell and Wu, 2009; Liu *et al.*, 2012).

Even though business to business (B2B) firms implement social and environmental activities through their supply chain and use their social sustainability initiatives to build relationships with other organizations along their value chain (Mariadoss *et al.*, 2011), there is a tendency to focus only on the environmental issues of sustainability in the context of a supply chain (Sarkis, 2001; Walker *et al.*, 2008; Wu and Pagell, 2011). Few academics have explored sustainability from a triple bottom line (TBL) approach, which includes the integration of the three dimensions of sustainability (Carter and Rogers, 2008; Seuring and Müller, 2008).

Building on a stakeholder orientation and the TBL approach, we develop a framework that focuses on how sustainability is introduced into the supply chain in order to contribute to TBL sustainability. To test our framework, we study an indigenous social enterprise that focuses on the community's well-being through value creation, profit generation, sustainability and the strengthening of its supply chain through local suppliers and the generation of new local ventures. This entity, which is located in southern Mexico, is nationally recognized for its value-creation mechanisms in the social and environmental dimensions. Value creation implies that the benefits of engaging in a new venture exceed its costs, positively influencing the stakeholders involved (Peredo and Chrisman, 2006; Porter and Kramer, 2006; Weerawardena and Mort, 2006; Porter and Kramer, 2011). Also, when value creation simultaneously generates economic, social and environmental benefits, the concept of sustainability is introduced (Elkington, 1994).

Social enterprises pursue sustainable solutions to problems of neglected positive externalities (Santos, 2012). These entities focus on the creation of social value, which involves the fulfilment of basic, long-standing needs to those members of the society who are in deprivation (Certo and Miller, 2008). Social enterprises try to solve social problems with business solutions that respect community rights and the sustainable use of natural resources (Thompson and Doherty, 2006; Giovannini, 2012), while increasing stakeholders' abilities to contribute to the solution of their problems in order to achieve greater welfare (Santos, 2012). The main challenge is the lack of governance mechanisms and structures that could drive the implementation of equitable tasks in order to promote the community's well-being (Perez, 2013). In addition, the study of social organizations located in less developed parts of the world can offer insights on how to change and do things in a sustainable manner (Pagell and Shevchenko, 2014). The study of this social enterprise is important within the supply chain context because this case can offer in-depth insights into how the supply chain of a social business contributes to TBL sustainability. According to Pagell and Shevchenko (2014), if we want to contribute to the creation of truly sustainable supply chains, we need to study supply chain business models in which profits are necessary but secondary to environmental and social impacts, such as this case.

Our aim is to contribute to the supply chain literature by studying the supply chain within a social enterprise in order to understand how this kind of firm integrates sustainability in its supply chain from a TBL perspective.

This chapter is structured as follows: first, we develop our conceptual framework and our propositions. Second, we analyze the Ixtlán Group case, which illustrates how to integrate sustainability in a social enterprise's supply chain. Finally, we present a final discussion and the conclusions section.

11.2 Conceptual framework

From a supply chain approach, the supply chain is a network made up of nodes and links. Nodes are represented by agents, such as firms, who have control over resources and make decisions to maximize their own operational gain. Links can be transactions related to information, materials, products (e.g. physical supply chain) and/or financial exchange (e.g. support supply chain) between agents (Carter *et al.*, 2015).

11.2.1 Stakeholder orientation

The ability of stakeholders to influence firms' decision-making and how firms balance stakeholders' demands are the focus of stakeholder theory (Mainardes *et al.*, 2011). A stakeholder is understood as "any group or individual who can affect or is affected by the achievement of the organization's objectives" (Freeman, 1984, p. 46, as cited in Laplume *et al.*, 2008, p. 1,160). Stakeholder orientation is understood as the extent to which a firm understands and addresses stakeholder interests (Crittenden *et al.*, 2011, p. 78)

In order to do ethical and sustainable business with transparency and accountability within the supply chain it is important to understand and satisfy internal and external stakeholders' demands (Kleindorfer *et al.*, 2005).

> **Proposition 1.** *The more the focal firm addresses stakeholders demands related to sustainability, the more likely it is for the supply chain members to move towards sustainability*

11.2.2 TBL approach

TBL involves "the simultaneous pursuit of economic prosperity, environmental quality, and social equity" (Elkington, 1997, p. 397). For the purpose of this chapter, the definition of the three dimensions of TBL are shown in Table 11.1

Table 11.1 Understanding the three sustainability dimensions

Source: Elaborated by authors with information from Bansal, 2005; Lee and Rhee, 2007; Wood, 1991.

Dimension	Definition
Environmental	It is related to environmental-friendly practices and activities within different areas where environmental issues are considered; such as production processes, environmental management, supply chain, product recovery and communication with stakeholders (Lee and Rhee, 2007)
Social	Is related to the embedding of social issues (such as improving working conditions related to health and safety, diversity and child labour avoidance) to develop positive relationships with stakeholders (Wood, 1991)
Economic	It is related to creating value for the different stakeholders of a firm (e.g. offering products with minimum negative environmental and social impacts; improving the quality of life of workers through training, education and competitive salaries; and creating welfare for community) (Bansal, 2005)

Scholars have analyzed TBL dimensions separately. Walker and Jones (2012) suggested that a supply chain can integrate the economic dimension of sustainability by buying from local suppliers to support local economic development; the environmental dimension by minimizing its negative environmental impacts; and the social dimension by including decent working conditions. Kleindorfer *et al.* (2005) suggest that firms include environmental and health and safety concerns into their supply chain, specifically in activities such as research and design, quality, logistics and transportation, marketing, distribution and warehousing. Sarkis (2001) suggests closing the supply chain loop through product recovery and renewed consumption of end-life materials in the production process. Firms should ask their suppliers to engage in environmental initiatives, to ensure safe and humane working conditions for its employees and also to participate in product recovery (Carter and Jennings, 2004, as cited in Carter and Rogers, 2008). In addition, Pagell and Wu (2009) emphasize the development and implementation of measurement and reward systems to guide sustainability behaviour, investments in human capital and the creation of reverse chains.

> **Proposition 2a.** *The greater the number of environmentally-friendly activities developed by the focal firm, the more likely it is for its supply chain to move towards environmental sustainability.*

Proposition 2b. *The greater the improvement in working conditions and community welfare creation by the focal firm, the more likely it is for its supply to move towards social sustainability.*

Proposition 2c. *The greater the pursuit of value creation for the stakeholders of the focal firm, the more likely it is for the supply chain to move towards economic sustainability.*

11.3 The Ixtlán Group case

11.3.1 Background

The social enterprise Ixtlán Group is located in the community of Ixtlán, in the southern state of Oaxaca, Mexico. The community is approximately 400 km southeast of Mexico City and 550 km northwest from the border with Guatemala. Indigenous communities occupy 14.3% of the surface of the country (Freshwateraction, 2012) and are mainly organized under communal property. The governance in most indigenous communities in Mexico, including Ixtlán, is determined by a system called *usos y costumbres*. Governance is based on democratic principles and accountability. The highest authorities are the assembly of *comuneros*[1] and the assembly of citizens, which are renewed every three years. The assembly of *comuneros*, under the elected leadership of the president and adjunct authorities composing the Comisariado de Bienes Comunales (CBC, Committee of Communal Resources), manages communal forests and other natural resources owned by the community, including Ixtlán Group.

Forest-related activities are the main source of income for the community but these are relatively new activities as inhabitants used to live in a subsistence economy based on agriculture and farming. Timber exploitation in Ixtlán started in the 1940s when a concession was granted to a foreign firm. The only benefit that the community obtained from this concession was the creation of employment under poor conditions but no other payment was given to the community for the exploitation of its natural resources (Rainforest Alliance, 2001).

In 1968, 14 communities created a separate organization to increase the workers' bargaining power on this issue and also to boycott the firm's operations and seek to regain control of their own natural resources. In 1974, the government finally agreed and created a new local organization to exploit the forest. Four neighbouring communities formed this new entity: Ixtlán, Capulálpam, La Trinidad and Santiago Xiacuí. The new enterprise was called Ixcasit and had around 60 workers.

---

1 *Comuneros* are usually the first dwellers of a community; they hold common land property of the community and its resources.

These four communities began to learn about sustainability strategies, as well as how to manage their forests and logging operations. They split up in 1988; thus, the Unidad Comunal Forestal Agropecuaria y de Servicios (UCFAS) was established in 1988 (Ixtlán Group's first enterprise) as an attempt to provide employment for the community. UCFAS remained the sole entity in charge of an increasing variety of industries and business opportunities that the organization exploited until 2007, when the comuneros decided to split the enterprise into smaller entities seeking better management and closer accountability. Nowadays, Ixtlán Group has expanded to eight enterprises and over 200 employees (Table 11.2).

Table 11.2 Ixtlán Group business units and its role within supply chain

Source: Elaborated by the authors

	Business unit (node)	Main activity
Physical supply chain	Technical Forest Services (TFS)	Sustainable forest management
	UNFOSTI	Timber exploitation
	UCFAS	Sawmill and furniture factory
	TIP Muebles	Furniture trade and furniture stores
Support supply chains	Tienda Comunitaria Ixtleca	Building materials and hardware store
	Gasolinera Comunidad Agraria	Gas station
	Ecoturixtlán SPR de RI	Eco-tourism park
	SOFOM Ixtlán	Productive micro-lending

As the organization started growing, the need for a strong supply chain became the primary concern since there were no reliable suppliers in the region. In addition, furniture and wood traders used their bargaining power and monopolistic approach to keep most of the value, leaving the community with only a small gain that was not enough to boost its social and economic welfare. Table 11.1 illustrates the composition of Ixtlán Group's supply chain. Ixtlán Group's physical supply chain includes four enterprises that help bring the product from the forest to the final customer. TFS provides sustainable management for their resources by implementing plans that regenerate the forest at the same rate that it is exploited; it has a greenhouse with over half a million pine trees grown each year. UNFOSTI executes the plan, extracting the wood from the forest to the sawmill. Then, UCFAS' sawmills, furniture factory and over 100 employees turn the wood into fine furniture. Finally, TIP Muebles, a company created in partnership with two other indigenous communities, trades with major departmental chains and also owns half a dozen stores.

Ixtlán Group´s support supply chain also includes four fully-owned enterprises and multiple external entities. Tienda Comunitaria Ixtleca was created to provide building materials and hardware to the community and also to the other entities of the group. Gasolinera Comunidad Agraria supplies gas and energy-related services and SOFOM Ixtlán provides financial resources to both the community and the group. Ecoturixtlán SPR de RI has the necessary infrastructure to hold meetings and conferences. Since Ixtlán Group is a democratic entity, where most of their managers are elected and many decisions are taken by majority vote, Ecoturixtlan is a place for gathering, decision-making and accountability. The support supply chain is complemented by external entities such as banks, service providers and local entrepreneurs that strengthen the group's operations.

11.3.2 Stakeholder orientation and the sustainability of the supply chain

The purpose of creating a social enterprise was, and still is, the creation of employment and welfare for the community, in order to stop the immigration of its inhabitants to the United States. Therefore, the orientation of the entity has been primarily to benefit Ixtlán, which includes local workers, suppliers, government and the preservation of the natural ecosystem. In the local indigenous cosmovision, man and nature are one entity and any harm men inflict on nature threatens the very existence of humankind. The result of this belief is a constant search for developing sustainable operations. For instance, most of the waste generated by the sawmill is reused by the community as fertilizer to grow crops, as energy to cook their meals or as material to build fences or walls. As a consequence of this philosophy, Ixtlán Group is certified by the Forest Stewardship Council for its sustainable operations and the WWF also named the ecotourism facility as the best managed and environmentally friendly in the region. Table 11.3 lists the impacts generated by Ixtlán Group, classified according to their economic, social and environmental dimensions.

Table 11.3 Impacts from a TBL approach generated by Ixtlán Group

Source: Elaborated by the authors

Economic	Social	Environmental
· Emergency interest-free loans · Greater amount of money flowing in the community · Access to products and services · Employee's profit sharing · Local and regional growth · Higher purchasing power by the inhabitants · Job stability	· Social benefits for employees · Gender equality · Training and promotion opportunities · Building of public infrastructure · Job creation · Decline in emigration · Women empowerment · Preservation of local values	· Plague combat · Forestation of grasslands and reforestation · Protection of ecosystems, water and endemic fauna · Creation of environment protection culture · Waste management · Wildfire combat

Since Ixtlán Group is vertically integrated, every step of the supply chain is managed with the same principles (stakeholder orientation, sustainable operations, democracy and accountability). Hence, a virtuous cycle is generated where people in the community have stable jobs, access to credit and social benefits. They have lately started creating new ventures that foster local and regional development. Women have been able to take special advantage of these benefits, given the prevalent gender-biased culture in the communities. One third of the households are led by women and most of them work at Ixtlán Group under the same conditions as men. This is an uncommon situation in male-dominated cultures such as this.

Ixtlán Group has also the implicit policy of buying all inputs from local suppliers, if available. One of the people in charge of purchasing inputs in Ecoturixtlan comments "I was telling the new manager that we usually buy all the provisions from small local business ... so the money stays in the community and triggers further development". Ixtlán Group has become the main client of many local businesses allowing them to survive. As the economy grew in size, local business diversified and consolidated, building a stronger local economy.

11.4 Discussion

The Ixtlán Group case illustrates how to integrate sustainability within a supply chain from a TBL perspective.

When analyzing this case, we corroborated that Proposition 1 holds true, since the community of Ixtlán wanted to control the exploitation of its natural resources as well as the creation of employment for its inhabitants. Thus, by considering their demands, Ixtlán Group was capable of delivering prosperity to its main stakeholders, such as its employees and the community, while gaining the necessary legitimacy to continue expanding its operations. At the same time, it has built a supply chain in which the group integrates the notions of sustainability that have always been present in the indigenous community of Ixtlán.

Proposition 2a, which states that the integration of environmentally friendly activities by the focal firm promotes environmental sustainability in its supply chain was also validated. Ixtlán Group develops several activities to protect its surrounding ecosystems. In addition, this group promotes an environmentally friendly culture among its employees but also within the community. Thus, considering that Ixtlán Group is vertically integrated, every member of its supply chain is managed with the same environmental purpose.

Proposition 2b was also substantiated, since the organization recognizes the intrinsic value of its stakeholders and invests heavily in safety and better working conditions for its employees. This perspective spreads to every member of Ixtlán Group supply chain.

Proposition 2c is also supported. Ixtlán Group has created value for its different stakeholders, such as employees and the local community. For example, the employees have better working conditions, which translates into job stability for Ixtlán inhabitants. In addition, Ixtlán Group has become the main client of many local businesses, which strengthens the local economy. As a result of its vertical integration, each member of its supply chain focuses on value creation for its stakeholders.

Ixtlán Group's case has proven that it is possible to balance the environmental, social and economic benefits in a supply chain. This case is an example which shows that economic and social prosperity do not necessarily carry an environmental cost. On the contrary, the organization plans to produce more pine trees and forest grasslands and now it has the economic resources to better address wildfires, plagues and the illegal hunting and timber trade.

11.5 Conclusion

Given the pressures that stakeholders (e.g. community and government) exert over firms to be responsible for the environmental and social impact of their operations (Carter and Easton, 2011), supply chains have moved towards sustainability through the integration of economic, environmental and social issues from a stakeholder orientation perspective (Pagell and Wu, 2009; Liu *et al.*, 2012).

In this case, a sustainable supply chain also contributes to a more efficient use of resources, that ultimately takes pressure off the forests and nearby rivers. Even more, Ixtlán Group is adding more value to its operations, obtaining a higher profit margin per cubic metre of wood extracted from its forest. Ixtlán has become one of the most prosperous communities in the region, attracting foreign labour and trade and creating new educational institutions and public facilities. In 1988, when the Ixtlán Group was created, the community was one of the most marginalized in the country. This social enterprise has had a primary role in the transformation, setting an example of how building a sustainable supply chain can boost local development. The conclusions reached in this chapter may also apply to managers and non-social businesses, as this case shows how an organization's sustainable supply chain also contributes to a more efficient use of resources while gaining legitimacy through the generation of positive externalities.

References

Bansal, P. (2005). Evolving sustainability: A longitudinal study of corporate sustainable development. *Strategic Management Journal*, 26, 197-218.

Carter, C.R., & Easton, L. (2011). A framework of sustainable supply chain management: Moving toward new theory. *International Journal of Physical Distribution & Logistics Management*, 41(1), 46-62.

Carter, C.R., & Rogers, D.S. (2008). A framework of sustainable supply chain management: Moving toward new theory. *International Journal of Physical Distribution & Logistics Management*, 38(5), 360-387.

Carter, C.R., Roger, D.S., & Choi, T.Y. (2015). Toward the theory of the supply chain. *Journal of Supply Chain Management*, 51(2), 1-25.

Certo, S.T., & Miller, T. (2008). Social entrepreneurship: key issues and concepts. *Business Horizons*, 51(4), 267-271.

Crittenden, V.L., Crittenden, W.F., Ferrell, L.K., Ferrell, O.C., & Pinney, C.C. (2011). Market-oriented sustainability: A conceptual framework and propositions. *Journal of the Academy of Marketing Science*, 39, 71-85.

Elkington, J. (1997). *Cannibals with Forks: The Triple Bottom Line of 21st Century Business.* Oxford, UK: Capstone Publishing.

Elkington, J. (1994). Toward the sustainable corporation: Win–win–win business strategies for sustainable development. *California Management Review*, 36(2), 90-100.

Freshwateraction (2012). *Freshwateraction.* Retrieved from http://www.freshwateraction. net/sites/freshwateraction.net/files/comunidades_indigenas_illsley.pdf

Giovannini, M. (2012). Social enterprises for development as buen vivir. *Journal of Enterprising Communities: People and Places in the Global Economy*, 6(3), 284-299.

Hall, J., & Matos, S. (2010). Incorporating impoverished communities in sustainable supply chains. *International Journal of Physical Distribution & Logistics Management*, 40(1/2), 124-147.

Kleindorfer, P.R., Singhal, K., & Van Wassenhove, L.N. (2005). Sustainable operations management. *Production and Operations Management*, 14(4), 482-492.

Laplume, A.O., Sonpar, K., & Litz, R.A. (2008). Stakeholder theory: Reviewing a theory that moves us. *Journal of Management*, 34 (6), 1,152-1,189.

Lee, S.Y., & Rhee, S. (2007). The change in corporate environmental strategies: A longitudinal empirical study. *Management Decision*, 45(2), 196-216.

Liu, S., Kasturirartne, D., & Moizer, J. (2012). A hub-and-spoke model for multidimensional integration of green marketing and sustainable supply chain management. *Industrial Marketing Management*, 41(4), 581-588.

Mainarders, E.W., Alves, H., & Raposo, M. (2011). Stakeholder theory: issues to resolve. *Management Decision*, 49(2), 226-252.

Mariadoss, B.J., Tansujah, P.S., & Mouri, N. (2011). Marketing capabilities and innovation-based strategies for environmental sustainability: an exploratory investigation of B2B firms. *Industrial Marketing Management*, 40, 1305-1318.

Pagell, M., & Shevchenko, A. (2014). Why research in sustainable supply chain management should have no future. *Journal of Supply Chain Management*, 50(1), 45-55.

Pagell, M., & Wu, Z. (2009). Building a more complete theory of sustainable supply chain management using case studies of ten exemplars. *Journal of Supply Chain Management*, 45(2), 37-56.

Peredo, A.M., & Chrisman, J.J. (2006). Toward a theory of community-based enterprise, *Academy of Management Review*, 31(2), 309-328.

Perez, J.C. (2013). Social enterprise in the development agenda: Opening a new road map or just a new vehicle to travel the same route? *Social Enterprise Journal*, 9(3), 247-268.

Porter, M.E., & Kramer, M.R. (2011). Creating shared value. *Harvard Business Review*, 89 (1/2), 62-77.

Porter, M.E., & Kramer, M.R. (2006). Strategy and society: The link between competitive advantage and corporate social responsibility. *Harvard Business Review*, 84(12), 78-92.

Rainforest Alliance (2001). *Resumen público de certificación de comunidad Ixtlán de Juárez*. Retrieved from http://www.rainforest-alliance.org/forestry/documents/comunidad-ixtlan.pdf

Santos, F.M. (2012). A positive theory of social entrepreneurship. *Journal of Business Ethics*, 11(3), 335-351.

Sarkis, J. (2001). Manufacturing's role in corporate environmental sustainability. *International Journal of Operations & Production Management*, 21(5/6), 666-686.

Seuring, S., & Müller, M. (2008). From a literature review to a conceptual framework for sustainable supply chain. *Journal of Cleaner Production*, 16, 1,699-1,710.

Thompson, J., & Doherty, B. (2006). The diverse world of social enterprise a collection of social enterprise stories. *International Journal of Social Economics*, 33(5/6), 361-375.

Walker, H., & Jones, N. (2012). Sustainable supply chain management across the UK private sector. *Supply Chain Management: An International Journal*, 17/1, 15-28.

Walker, H., Di Sisto, L., & McBain, D. (2008). Drivers and barriers to environmental supply chain management practices: Lessons from the public and private sectors. *Journal of Purchasing & Supply Management*, 14, 69-85.

Weerawardena, J., & Mort, G.S. (2006). Investigating social entrepreneurship: A multidimensional model. *Journal of World Business*, 41, 21-35.

Wood, D. (1991). Corporate social performance revisited. *The Academy of Management Review*, 16(4), 691-718.

Wu, Z., & Pagell, M. (2011). Balancing priorities: Decision-making in sustainable supply chain management. *Journal of Operations Management*, 29, 557-590.

Gloria Camacho has a PhD in Management Sciences at EGADE Business School, Tecnológico de Monterrey. She is a Professor of Marketing in the Marketing and International Business Department at Tecnológico de Monterrey, Mexico. Her main research areas are sustainable marketing, corporate sustainability, corporate social responsibility and humanistic management. She has research and publishing experience working as an assistant researcher at EGADE Business School.

Mario Vázquez Maguirre is PhD (Business) at EGADE Business School, Tecnológico de Monterrey and MSc (Economics and Public Policy) at EGAP, Tecnológico de Monterrey. He is currently a professor of entrepreneurship and corporate social responsibility at Universidad de Monterrey (UDEM). His primary research lines include social entrepreneurship, social enterprises and social development, humanistic management and sustainability. He has research and publishing experience working as an assistant researcher at EGADE Business School and Harvard Kennedy School. He has also worked in corporations such as BBVA and UPS Capital.

12

Sustainable procurement in social enterprises

Comparative case studies from India and Scotland

Sreevas Sahasranamam[1]
Indian Institute of Management Kozhikode

Christopher Ball
Stirling Management School, UK

In this chapter we compare the case studies of two social enterprises, one from the context of a developing country in India and another from the context of a developed country in Scotland. Through these case studies we illustrate how social enterprises integrate triple bottom line (TBL) aspects into their procurement or help other organizations in achieving sustainability in their procurement. These case studies highlight the importance of the social sustainability dimension, which has received relatively less scholarly attention in comparison to the environmental and economic sustainability dimensions.

1   Sreevas Sahasranamam would like to thank Strategic Management Society (SMS) Strategic Research Foundation (SRF) grant for supporting his thesis, of which the case study forms a part.

12.1 Introduction

In today's global world, public and private sector organizations face increased pressure from NGOs and civilian society to ensure that their operations are sustainable. The recent Living Wage Campaign in the United Kingdom, championed by Poverty Alliance, is directed at ensuring social and human sustainability. Similarly, organizations like Fair Trade and Action Aid are involved in campaigns to educate the public on sustainable procurement practices. These are just some examples of the increased stakeholder pressure that organizations are facing to improve the sustainability of their supply chains. In the academic literature on sustainable supply chains, discussions have been dominated by environmental issues (Carter and Rogers, 2008; Hall and Matos, 2010; Touboulic and Walker, 2015; Winter and Knemeyer, 2013). In some cases, the terms sustainability and environment are interchangeably used (Carter and Easton, 2011). However, the triple bottom line (TBL) conceptualization of sustainability calls for the reconciliation of social, environmental and economic sustainability (Carter and Rogers, 2008; Elkington, 1998). Specifically, there is an increasing call for future research to examine sustainable procurement in a more holistic manner by moving from a focus on environmental outcomes to incorporating social and economic dimensions as well (Miemczyk *et al*. 2012; Walker and Phillips, 2008; Winter and Knemeyer, 2013). In an attempt to respond to this call, in this chapter we take the cases of two social enterprises, one from the context of a developing country in India and another from the context of a developed country in Scotland, studying how these social enterprises have achieved TBL sustainability in their own procurement or have helped other organizations achieve these TBL outcomes in their procurement. We analyze the two case studies using the sustainable procurement framework developed by Walker *et al*. (2012).

Sustainable supply chain management (SSCM) focuses on multiple aspects like sustainable procurement, sustainable packaging and sustainable transportation (Abbasi and Nilsson, 2012). The focus of this chapter is on sustainable procurement. Sustainable procurement is defined as "procurement that is consistent with sustainable development, such as ensuring a strong, healthy and just society, living within environmental limits, and promoting good governance" (Walker and Brammer, 2009, p. 128). The Walker *et al*. (2012) framework of sustainable procurement details how social, environmental and economic sustainability can be achieved at multiple levels, namely individual, organization, buyer–supplier dyad, supply chain and market. Social sustainability in procurement could be achieved through activities such as supplier training in sustainability, avoiding child labour and developing CSR purchasing policies. Environmental sustainability in procurement could be achieved by activities such as carbon trading practices, reducing CO_2 emissions and recycling strategies. Economic sustainability in procurement could be achieved through reduction in fuel consumption, innovation in management of the supply chain network and by sourcing from disadvantaged or minority-owned suppliers (Walker *et al.*, 2012).

The majority of research on sustainable procurement is concentrated within particular countries like the UK (Hall and Purchase, 2006), Sweden (Faith-Ell *et al.*, 2006), USA (Coggburn, 2004) and Germany (Gunther and Scheibe, 2006) and there is limited research on sustainable procurement that is comparative across countries (Brammer and Walker, 2011). These scholars also point out that there has been little research studying the direct achievement of social and environmental ends through procurement. This is another research gap to which this study intends to make a contribution.

As stated earlier in this chapter, we use case studies of two social enterprises operating in different institutional environments, namely India and Scotland. The contrasting contexts offer us a means to better explore the inter-relationships among social, economic and environmental parameters in sustainable procurement. We study the following research question: how do social enterprise organizations help the achievement of TBL sustainable outcomes in procurement either:

- Through their own procurement activities or

- Through helping corporations to fulfil TBL outcomes in their procurement?

These two cases also offer us the possibility of comparing private sector and public sector procurement. In the remaining part of the chapter, first, we give a background to the country's context of India and Scotland. Second, we elaborate upon the data collection methodology. Then, we briefly describe the two social enterprises and discuss how they have incorporated TBL sustainability in their own procurement or have helped corporations achieve TBL sustainability in their supply chain.

12.2 Background on the country context

12.2.1 India

India is one of the fastest growing developing economies in the world with a growth rate of 7.4% in 2014. According to current statistics, India's GDP has crossed the $2trillion mark (World Bank, 2014). Despite the high growth rate, India remains in the World Bank's "lower middle income" category of countries (Raghavan, 2015) and faces multiple development challenges, with 33% of the Indian population living below the international poverty line of US$1.25 per day (Purchasing Power Parity basis) (World Bank, 2010). Moreover, the number of under-weight children in India is double that of sub-Saharan Africa (IANS, 2012). In such a context it is imperative to have an innovative model of value creation in the form of social enterprise that will overcome these constraints and provide services to the poor.

The region where EcoAd operates, Pune, fares poorly in the poverty index and on pollution. According to Pune Municipal Corporation data, 40% of the population in the city lives in multidimensional poverty, suffering residential, occupational and social vulnerabilities (Centre for Communication and Development Studies, 2014). The environmental pollution levels in Pune are among the highest in the country (Numbeo, 2015; Rao, 2014) and it is among the top ten largest plastic waste-producing cities in India (Press Trust of India, 2014). Though there is a ban by the government on the use of plastic bags, their use is still widespread owing to advantages such as lower price, better chemical resistance and greater durability (Rashid, 2014). EcoAd, the social enterprise that is illustrated in this chapter, aims to tackle the environmental problems posed by plastic bags while tackling the social exclusion of rural women through an economically sustainable business model. The condition of women in India, especially rural women, has been at the centre of global attention. For instance, women in some parts of rural India are not allowed to go out of their house to seek work and the region where EcoAd operates is one of these areas.

12.2.2 Scotland

In recent decades, Scotland has experienced problems with unemployment caused by industrial decline and the re-orientation of the economy during the 20th century (Robertson 2014) and Lochgelly, the town in which recycling social enterprise Recycle Fife is located, is classified as belonging to the top 15% of most deprived areas in Scotland (Scottish Government, 2012). Economic inequality is an endemic and enduring problem in Scotland—indeed, researchers at the University of Stirling have recently highlighted that inequality has grown between 1997 and 2013, with the poorest seeing a drop in their real income during this period (Bell and Eiser, 2015). This highlights the ever-increasing need for social enterprise to address these terrible problems of poverty and inequality. Martin and Thompson (2010) argue that social enterprise is a way of "local capacity building" and a response to "social disadvantage" (p. 9). Recycle Fife fulfils these aims through providing job opportunities to local unemployed and disadvantaged people by undertaking recycling work for the public and private sectors.

In recent years, Scottish public services have undergone market-orientated reforms and part of this involved contracting public services out to the private and civil society sectors (Mackie, 2005). The financial crisis and subsequent fiscal contraction has placed great pressure on public services to reduce costs and has led to the growth of social enterprise involvement in the delivery of public services, as part of David Cameron's "Big Society" vision (Evans, 2011; Danson and Whittam, 2011; Kelly, 2007). It is suggested that an increased role for social enterprises in the delivery of public services offers a way of reducing the cost of those services whilst respecting social and environmental outcomes.

12.3 Data collection

To develop the case studies, we relied on both primary and secondary sources. We interviewed the founding team members of both social enterprises to understand their business models and sustainability practices. We also relied on publicly-available secondary data sources, such as company websites, management interviews and newspaper publications. The two case studies are described in the next section, followed by cross-case analysis comparing them.

The choice of these two cases was based on the following criteria. First, both social enterprises are focussed on the mission of reducing environmental pollution. Second, we chose social enterprises from two different countries so that country level differences could be highlighted. Third, both of these social enterprises have gained significant media attention and have managed to attract investors' interest. This is indicative of some level of early success and, hence, could offer learning for aspiring social entrepreneurs.

12.4. Case studies

12.4.1 EcoAd

EcoAd, a for-profit social enterprise, was started by Rohit Nayak, Sudhir Deshpande and Satyaprakash Arora in 2009. Rohit was inspired to take action when he saw large parts of the land littered with plastic bags during a train journey. This encouraged him to come up with a business idea for promoting the use of newspaper bags. However, the problem was that newspaper bags were not popular owing to their higher cost. To work around this, EcoAd developed a business model that overcame this problem. They sold the space on the external side of the newspaper bags for advertisements from local businesses. The main client/advertisers of the newspaper bags produced by EcoAd are pharmacies, grocery stores and retail stores in Pune. These bags are produced by over 200 rural women who are organized in the form of self-help groups. These newspaper bags come in different dimensions for different purposes such as boutique, grocery, home-delivery, laundry, pharmacy, shoe-box and stationery (EcoAd, 2015). They have varying weight-carrying capacities in the range of two kg to six kg. For the different varieties of bags, different amounts of newspaper sheets are used. EcoAd now sells over 50,000 newspaper bags on a monthly basis.

Taking note of the social impact and livelihood empowerment that EcoAd was creating, big corporations have partnered with EcoAd as part of their CSR initiative to provide financial support. Through this partnership, the corporations gained intangible benefits in the form of goodwill in the community. EcoAd uses CSR funding from corporations to provide training for the rural women and also to procure kits needed for producing the newspaper bags.

There are three materials needed for making the newspaper bags: newspapers, cardboard and jute strings. The old newspapers are collected from the villages. Cardboard is used for attaching the jute strings to the newspaper bag. The procurement of cardboard is from the excess materials produced as waste in the printing press. The procurement of jute is from local grocery shops at retail rates. The procurement of these materials is either done by the coordinator of the company in possession of the CSR funds or by the local self-help group leader.

The business model of EcoAd offers newspaper bags at a lower rate to its clients, covering the remaining costs through selling advertising space on the bags to local businesses. For those shops which can afford to buy bags at the retail rate and not add the burden onto the end customer, EcoAd sells the bags at retail rate itself.[2]

The rural women with whom EcoAd chooses to work are those who do not have any other full-time employment options but are part of some self-help group activity. Many of these women used to receive low wages at irregular intervals since the demand for their produce was not stable. EcoAd has tried to rectify this problem by providing market linkage for newspaper bags, thereby ensuring a steady source of revenue. EcoAd also ensures fair wages for the women and this has improved their standard of living. Now these women are able to earn around 3,500–4,000 INR (around US$50–60) per month. In the regions where EcoAd operates, women face social exclusion and are not allowed to leave their houses for work. By providing a steady source of revenue from working at home, EcoAd empowers these women and manages to raise their self-esteem and dignity. The founders of EcoAd recollect multiple instances of the satisfaction they got from seeing smiles on the women's faces. In addition to working with rural women, EcoAd is now partnering with Parivartan Trust, an NGO which works with mentally-ill people. With support from this NGO, the EcoAd team has provided training in a mental hospital for such people and is now doing a pilot order with them.

In addition to the non-employed criteria for choosing the rural women, the other parameters considered while choosing them include the capability of the group to deliver orders and the cost of transportation from their location to EcoAd's centre. EcoAd's team also ensures that there is no conflict within the groups, as that reduces their productivity. The parameters used by retail stores/pharmacies for procuring the newspaper bags are cost competitiveness, dimensions of the bag, weight-carrying capacity and the number of days within which delivery can be provided after placing an order.

2 See website for retail rates http://www.ecoad.in/shop/?add-to-cart=1424.

12.4.2 Recycle Fife

Recycle Fife was founded in 2003 in Lochgelly, Fife, by local residents Frankie Hodge and Jackie Dunsmuir. The idea for the social enterprise evolved out of citizen activism. Recycle Fife was proposed as an alternative to Fife Council's plans for a landfill site. The social enterprise would recycle the waste that the council would have otherwise have landfilled in the local area. As stated in the previous section, its social goal is to provide employment to disadvantaged people in the local community whilst its environmental mission is to recycle waste that would have otherwise been landfilled, thus helping to conserve natural resources and enhance the local environment. Recycle Fife is a provider of waste services to both private companies and public sector organizations in Scotland, so, ultimately, it contributes to social and environmental sustainability in the supply chain of these organizations. Through purchasing waste services from Recycle Fife, private companies and public sector organizations have an opportunity to improve their corporate social responsibility due to the positive social outcomes of Recycle Fife's activities. Scottish public sector organizations are encouraged to reconcile economic, social and environmental outcomes in their procurement of services, provided this offers value for money to the taxpayer (Scottish Government, 2008). Public contracts, such as the provision of waste services for a town, should include sustainability criteria; "value for money" should not be defined by the price of the contract alone but should be balanced with social and environmental sustainability criteria (Scottish Procurement Directorate, 2009).

At Recycle Fife's inception, the local authority, Fife Council, was the main client, with the social enterprise starting its life servicing a council contract to recycle cans and bottles. In Scotland, councils have the ultimate responsibility for collecting and managing waste that is generated by households, so the council was, naturally, the main commercial relationship for Recycle Fife at the beginning. Contracting with Recycle Fife enabled Fife Council to divert waste from landfill and, therefore, substantially reduce its landfill tax bill as per the European Landfill Directive and the Scottish Government's Zero Waste policy. It can be said that the council achieved economic and environmental outcomes by purchasing services from Recycle Fife.

Less tangible social outcomes were also created thanks to the awarding of the contract to Recycle Fife. In creating employment opportunities for disadvantaged local people, Recycle Fife is helping to address the terrible problem of unemployment and its related ills in the community. It is suggested that the problem of unemployment is entrenched in the community, with the presence of third or fourth generation unemployment resulting from structural changes in the economy, namely the decline of traditional industries such as mining. It is therefore necessary to change the culture and mindset in order to address this social exclusion. It is proposed that the activities of social enterprises, such as Recycle Fife, present substantial opportunities to generate social value. Indeed, Recycle Fife has demonstrated that for every pound invested in the organization, there is over £5 social return on investment in terms of improved social outcomes locally. These wider social benefits offer public sector organizations powerful reasons to integrate social enterprise organizations into their supply chains when contracting out services.

While Recycle Fife has had a close trading relationship with the public sector, a feeling was expressed that the local authority does not fully integrate social value into its procurement process and that there is a need for greater understanding of social enterprise and its potential wider impacts on local communities on the part of public sector organizations. Recycle Fife alluded to a lack of consideration of community benefit when awarding contracts and believed that cost issues continued to dominate purchasing decisions within local authorities. Failing to integrate this community benefit aspect in procurement could be detrimental to the efforts made by social enterprises to contribute to local economic and social renewal. There were calls for a local businesses clause which would enable such considerations about the implications of purchasing decisions on the local economy to be taken into account and, ultimately, act as a vehicle for supporting community social enterprises and integrating social outcomes into supply chains. Local authorities were perceived as not fully understanding the concept of social enterprise, especially the ways in which they differ from charities and the nature of the social value they seek to generate.

12.5 Cross case analysis

We use the sustainable procurement framework developed by Walker *et al.* (2012) for analysing the case studies of EcoAd and Recycle Fife. The framework developed by Walker *et al.* (2012) consists of several levels of focus in analysing the social, economic and environmental dimensions of sustainable procurement along with illustrative examples. A cross-case analysis table analysing the two cases along the different dimensions is provided in Table 12.1.

In the case of EcoAd, social sustainability was achieved at the individual, organizational and supply chain level. At the individual level, the eco-label of EcoAd was able to influence end-users to adopt environmentally friendly newspaper bags in place of plastic bags. At the organizational level, EcoAd gets support from CSR funds for providing training to rural women. At the supply chain level, EcoAd employs rural women and people with mental illness and pays them wages at market rates. Environmental sustainability was achieved at the individual and supply chain level. At the individual level, environmental sustainability was achieved by raising consumer awareness on the harmful effects of plastic bags and encouraging the buying of newspaper bags. At the supply chain level, EcoAd's activities were able to reduce the pollution which plastic bags created. EcoAd exhibits economic sustainability at the market or society level by supporting rural women and people with mental illness who are disadvantaged sections of society in India.

In the case of Recycle Fife, sustainability is embedded at the organizational level. Its recycling activities fulfil environmental sustainability and its employment of disadvantaged groups tackles social exclusion and poverty, thereby enhancing social sustainability. Individuals who have been unemployed for a substantial period of time can renew their skills within Recycle Fife and improve their well-being through work. Success in embedding sustainability into the wider supply chain is dependent on the commitment of public sector organizations to integrating social sustainability outcomes into their procurement processes. On an organizational level, Recycle Fife engages in efforts to promote awareness of waste through educational interventions, such as creating a computer game about recycling aimed at school children. This is part of Recycle Fife's wider activities to bring about environmental change through raising awareness among future generations. External forces, such as the EU Landfill Directive, have ensured that environmental outcomes, namely waste minimization, must be respected in the procurement process. However, social sustainability appears to be the poor relation in public sector procurement processes and this disadvantages social enterprises competing for public contracts.

Table 12.1 Cross-case analysis of EcoAd and Recycle Fife

Parameter	EcoAd	Recycle Fife
Social problem being tackled	Environmental pollution caused by plastic bags, rural poverty and social exclusion of women.	Environmental pollution caused by landfill waste, unemployment and social exclusion of disadvantaged people.
Stakeholders considered in the supply chain	Rural women/people with mental illness, companies providing CSR investment, local companies providing ads, village head, EcoAd team, retail stores.	The local community, Recycle Fife's trainees, the local taxpayer, public sector organizations.
Social sustainability	Eco-label of EcoAd influencing user adoption of environmentally friendly bags.	Disadvantaged individuals improve their economic and mental well-being through employment.
	Providing training and employment to rural women and people with mental illness thereby reducing social exclusion and economic inequality.	Recycle Fife specializes in employing disadvantaged people (i.e. those with disabilities and the long-term unemployed).
	Uses CSR fund of corporations to provide training to rural women.	Competes for public contracts partly on the basis of the positive social outcomes of its activities, as shown by SROI.
Environmental sustainability	Raising awareness of the harmful effects of plastic bags due to their non-biodegradable properties.	Raising awareness of recycling through, for example, school visits and the creation of a computer game for school children about recycling.

Parameter	EcoAd	Recycle Fife
	Reduce the pollution which plastic bags create, thereby reducing CO_2 emissions.	Through its recycling activities, it diverts waste that would otherwise have been landfilled, contributing to resource conservation and reduced CO_2 emissions.
		European Landfill Directive requires waste minimization across the supply chain.
Economic sustainability	Providing a steady source of income for marginalized sections of the society.	Using income generated from waste management activities and welfare-to-work contracts to create training and employment opportunities for disadvantaged people.
Country context influence	33% of the population fall below the international poverty line of US$1.2/day, with a majority of them concentrated in rural areas. Patriarchal society not allowing women in rural areas to go out of home in pursuit of jobs.	Industrial decline has led to high levels of structural unemployment which has affected certain communities particularly severely.

12.6 Conclusion

In this chapter, by examining the case studies of EcoAd and Recycle Fife, we high-light the sustainable procurement practices of these social enterprises. Integrating environmental, social and economic goals into EcoAd's procurement is complex, as these goals are conflicting. To reconcile these goals, EcoAd has developed an innovative business model around advertising opportunities and partnering with corporations, the latter interested in supporting EcoAd because of its creation of social value which is consistent with their CSR activities. Likewise, Recycle Fife has emphasized its potential to create social and environmental value to overcome dis-advantages that it may face as a social enterprise in competing for public contracts. In essence, Recycle Fife and EcoAd have designed business models enabling the integration of the TBL outcomes.

Corporations and public sector bodies can improve their sustainability perfor-mance by integrating social enterprise into their supply chains. Importantly, this helps with a rather tricky social aspect of the supply chain. Purchasing from a social enterprise aimed at radical social change is, arguably, a more powerful strategy than simply auditing suppliers to ensure that they are paying fair wages and respecting labour laws. Purchasing from EcoAd contributes to the economic development of "Base of the Pyramid" communities, the needs of which have thus far been over-looked (Hart, 2010) whereas buying services from Recycle Fife leads to local social and economic renewal in a community affected by long-term industrial decline. Social enterprise is a proactive response to the wicked issues of inequality, poverty and social exclusion.

Stakeholder needs are rather complex in both cases. For EcoAd, there is a need for close cooperation with the local community to allow the rural women to engage in economic activity and this is based on trust. Equally, at the purchaser end of the supply chain, corporations are interested in the impact of their support on the social cause and the extent to which this bolsters their CSR performance. As for Recycle Fife, given the social value it generates, the welfare of the community is affected by local authority purchasing decisions. Whilst local authorities appear to understand the environmental dimension of the supply chain, the Recycle Fife case demonstrates a greater need to appreciate more complex social outcomes in public sector procurement. Purchasing from a social enterprise may imply wider social benefits which should be factored into procurement decisions. Integrating social enterprise into supply chains could be a promising strategy for the public sector to improve its social sustainability outcomes. However, there is a need for greater awareness of social entrepreneurship and for a framework for the wider inclusion of less tangible, less measurable, social outcomes into purchasing processes.

Given the relative paucity of research in management literature focussing on such human or social sustainability aspects (Pfeffer, 2010), these case studies provide an insight into how more holistic sustainable procurement practices can be designed which take these broader sustainability dimensions into account. A future stream of research exploring social sustainability in sustainable procurement could be developed by studying other examples of the integration of social enterprises into the supply chain and other social enterprise business models. There is also need for researchers to expand on theories relating to social sustainability aspects of supply chain management, as this is underdeveloped compared to the economic and environmental dimensions.

References

Abbasi, M., & Nilsson, F. (2012). Themes and challenges in making supply chains environmentally sustainable. *Supply Chain Management: An International Journal*, 17(5), 517-530.

Bell, D, & Eiser, D. (2015). *Scotland's widening inequality highlighted by Stirling economists*. Retrieved from http://www.stir.ac.uk/news/2015/06/widening-inequality-in-scotland-highlighted-by-stirling-economists

Brammer, S., & Walker, H. (2011). Sustainable procurement practice in the public sector: An international comparative study. *International Journal of Operations and Production Management*, 31(4), 452-476.

Carter, C.R., & Easton, P.L. (2011). Sustainable supply chain management: evolution and future directions. *International Journal of Physical Distribution & Logistics Management*, 41(1), 46-62.

Carter, C.R., & Rogers, D.S. (2008). A framework of sustainable supply chain management: Moving toward new theory. *International Journal of Physical Distribution & Logistics Management*, 38(5), 360-387.

Centre for Communication and Development Studies. (2014). *Multidimensional poverty in Pune*. Retrieved from http://infochangeindia.org/agenda/urban-poverty/multidimensional-poverty-in-pune.html (July 5, 2015)

Coggburn, J.D. (2004). Achieving managerial values through green procurement? *Public Performance & Management Review*, 28(2), 236-258.

Danson, M., & Whittam, G. (2011). Scotland's civic society v. England's big society? Diverging roles of the VCS in public service delivery. *Social Policy & Society*, 10(3), 353-363

EcoAd (2015). *Shop*. Retrieved from http://www.ecoad.in/shop/?add-to-cart=1424 (17 October 2015)

Elkington, J. (1998). *Cannibals with Forks: The Triple Bottom Line of 21st Century Business*. Mankota, MN: Capstone.

Evans, K. (2011). Big society in the UK: A policy review. *Children & Society*, 25(2), 164-171.

Faith-Ell, C., Balfors, B., & Folkeson, L. (2006). The application of environmental requirements in Swedish road maintenance contracts. *Journal of Cleaner Production*, 14(2), 163-171.

Gunther, E., & Scheibe, L. (2006). The hurdle analysis: A self-evaluation tool for municipalities to identify, analyse and overcome hurdles to green procurement. *Corporate Social Responsibility and Environmental Management*, 13, 61-77.

Hall, J., & Matos, S. (2010). Incorporating impoverished communities in sustainable supply chains. *International Journal of Physical Distribution & Logistics Management*, 40(1), 124-147.

Hall, M., & Purchase, D. (2006). Building or bodging? Attitudes to sustainability in UK public sector housing construction development. *Sustainable Development*, 14(3), 205-218.

Hart, S.L. (2010). *Capitalism at the Crossroads* (3rd ed.). Upper Saddle River, NJ: Pearson Education.

IANS. (2012). *India has twice the number of underweight children than sub-Saharan Africa*. Retrieved from http://www.dnaindia.com/india/report-india-has-twice-the-number-of-underweight-children-than-sub-saharan-africa-1635844 (5 July 2015)

Kelly, J. (2007). Reforming public services in the UK: Bringing in the third sector. *Public Administration*, 85(4), 1,003-1,022.

Mackie, R. (2005). *The New Public Management of Scotland: Local Government and the National Health Service*. Edinburgh: W. Green.

Martin, F., & Thompson, M. (2010). *Social Enterprise: Developing Sustainable Business* (1st ed.). Basingstoke: Palgrave Macmillan.

Miemczyk, J., Johnsen, T.E., & Macquet, M. (2012). Sustainable purchasing and supply management: A structured literature review of definitions and measures at the dyad, chain and network levels. *Supply Chain Management: An International Journal*, 17(5), 478-496.

Numbeo (2015). *Pollution in Pune, India*. Retrieved from http://www.numbeo.com/pollution/city_result.jsp?country=India&city=Pune (5 July 2015)

Pfeffer, J. (2010). Building sustainable organizations: The human factor. *Academy of Management Perspectives*, 24(1), 34-45.

Press Trust of India. (2014). *Delhi among top 10 largest plastic waste producing cities in India*. Retrieved from http://www.ndtv.com/delhi-news/delhi-among-top-10-largest-plastic-waste-producing-cities-in-india-593315 (5 July 2015)

Raghavan, T.S. (2015). *India is now a $2-trillion economy*. Retrieved from http://www.thehindu.com/business/Economy/india-is-now-a-2trillion-economy-says-world-bank-data/article7380442.ece (5 July 2015)

Rao, R. (2014). *Beware! The pollution "time bomb" is ticking in Pune*. Retrieved from http://www.dnaindia.com/pune/speak-up-beware-the-pollution-time-bomb-is-ticking-in-pune-1970946 (5 July 2015)

Rashid, A. (2014). *Few care for ban on plastic bag*s. Retrieved from http://indianexpress.com/article/cities/pune/few-care-for-ban-on-plastic-bags (5 July 2015)

Robertson, D. (2014). *Regeneration and Poverty in Scotland: Evidence and Policy Review*. Sheffield: Sheffield Hallam University, Centre for Regional Economic and Social Research.

Scottish Government (2012). *Scottish index of multiple deprivatio*n. Retrieved from http://www.sns.gov.uk/Simd/Simd.aspx

Scottish Government (2008). *Scottish Procurement Policy Handbook*. Edinburgh: Crown Copyright.

Scottish Procurement Directorate (2009). *Sustainable Procurement Action Plan for Scotlan*d. Edinburgh: Scottish Government.

Touboulic, A., & Walker, H. (2015). Theories in sustainable supply chain management: A structured literature review. *International Journal of Physical Distribution & Logistics Management*, 45(1), 16-42.

Walker, H., & Brammer, S. (2009). Sustainable procurement in the United Kingdom public sector. *Supply Chain Management*, 14(2), 128-137.

Walker, H., Miemczyk, J., Johnsen, T., & Spencer, R. (2012). Sustainable procurement: Past, present and future. *Journal of Purchasing and Supply Management*, 18(4), 201-206

Walker, H., & Phillips, W. (2008). Sustainable procurement: Emerging issues. *International Journal of Procurement Management*, 2(1), 41-61.

Winter, M., & Knemeyer, A.M. (2013). Exploring the integration of sustainability and supply chain management: Current state and opportunities for future inquiry. International *Journal of Physical Distribution & Logistics Management*, 43(1), 18-38.

World Bank (2014). *India—Country at a glance*. Retrieved from http://www.worldbank.org/en/country/india (27 October 2015)

World Bank. (2010). *India-Global Poverty Estimates*. Retrieved from http://povertydata.worldbank.org/poverty/country/IND (10 July 2013)

Sreevas Sahasranamam is a doctoral student in strategic management area at the Indian Institute of Management Kozhikode. His dissertation is focussed on understanding the effect of institutional context on social entrepreneurship. His research interests also include corporate social responsibility and innovation of emerging market firms. He is a recipient of the Strategic Management Society's (SMS) Strategic Research Foundation Dissertation Fellow Programme for the period 2015–16.

Christopher Ball is completing his ESRC-funded PhD at Stirling Management School in Scotland. His research concerns energy policy and environmental entrepreneurship in France, Germany and the UK. He is also interested in social entrepreneurship and public management and teaches on a variety of undergraduate and post-graduate courses.

13

Sustainable supply chain management and the role of trust at the base of the pyramid (BoP)

An exploratory case study[1, 2]

Sigfried Eisenmeier

Zeppelin University, Germany

The present work analyzes the role of trust in sustainable supply chains at the base of the pyramid (BoP). It follows the BoP 2.0 approach which argues that poverty can be alleviated by integrating actors at the base of the global income pyramid, as producers and suppliers, into global supply chains. There are three reasons why in-depth research about the role of trust in supply chains at the BoP is needed:

- **First, in-depth knowledge about the role of trust at the BoP is missing in sustainable supply chain management (SSCM) and BoP literature**
- **Second, there is an empirical relevance of trust at the BoP, and**

1   This research project was partly funded by a German retail chain. Additional financial support was received in form of small research scholarships from Zeppelin University. The presented thoughts and findings are those of the author alone.
2   Special thanks go to Tim Weiss, Herwart Groll, Johannes Da-Fieno, Dimitri Eisenmeier and the reviewers of this chapter.

- **Third, the institutional context at the BoP is different to the one at the top of the pyramid.**

Common institutions, such as contracts, might play a different role at different levels of the pyramid and trust, as a crucial part of every economic transaction, needs to be understood. This study is based on a specific BoP project conducted in Peru. The data analysed consisted of 27 in-depth interviews with different actors at the BoP. The work concludes that there is low mutual inter-personal trust between farmers and suppliers at the BoP, which consequently leads to a low level of association and organization. The implications for trade relations between a company and the BoP are discussed. The work also mentions different explanations for the low level of interpersonal trust and several mechanisms of gaining the farmers' trust are presented.

13.1 Introduction

Sustainable supply chain management (SSCM) has become an established field of study in recent years and its relevance is widely accepted in academia and in business practice. Integrating triple bottom line (TBL) sustainability (Elkington, 1997) into global supply chains is a necessary step to solving current global issues and to realize the sustainable development goals called for by the Millennium Development Goals (Griggs *et al.*, 2013; United Nations, 2008). The TBL approach defines three pillars of sustainability: the economic, environmental and social pillar. Nevertheless, SSCM literature has mainly focused on economic and ecologic sustainability and this has led to limited research on the social dimension of sustainability (Seuring and Müller, 2008). The research at hand focuses on the social sustainability of global supply chains that include the BoP (Prahalad and Hart, 2002).

A crucial feature to build socially sustainable supply chains is trust, as it is a relevant part of social and economic interactions (Zaheer *et al.*, 1998; Zucker, 1986). But there is a lack of research about the role of trust in global supply chains that include suppliers from the BoP. The present research examines the role of trust between the different actors in a supply chain that includes the BoP. Two literature streams are combined: the SSCM literature and the BoP literature.

The idea of the BoP approach is to connect the bottom of the global income pyramid, the poorest four billion people of the world (Prahalad and Hart, 2002; Prahalad, 2010), with non-local markets. Multinational corporations (MNCs) in particular could combine additional profit with poverty alleviation by selling innovative products to the BoP and using new distribution channels. Thus, the BoP is seen as a market and people from the BoP are considered mainly as consumers. This approach has been criticized (Chatterjee, 2014) and a second dimension in the BoP debate is now receiving more attention: the BoP 2.0 approach. This approach considers people at the BoP not as consumers but rather as producers, entrepreneurs, co-inventors and suppliers (Hahn, 2009; London and Hart, 2010; Simanis and Hart, 2008). Integrating producers from the BoP into global supply chains might eradicate poverty at the BoP while allowing MNCs to gain competitive advantages and improve their financial performance.

This work focuses on the role of trust regarding sustainable supply chains that include the BoP. There are three main reasons why this research is needed:

- First, BoP and SSCM scholars know that trust is a relevant issue but detailed literature about the role of trust in sustainable supply chains at the BoP is missing in the current debate

- Second, there is empirical evidence that trust at the BoP is a fundamental issue that affects building sustainable supply chains

- Third, the institutional context at the BoP is different from the institutional context at the "Top of the Pyramid" (ToP).

Common mechanisms to manage economic transactions, such as contracts, play a different role at the BoP as regulative institutions differ (Scott, 2001). Consequently, it is important to understand the role of trust at the BoP as that trust is a crucial part of every economic transaction, especially when the institutional context differs.

This research is based on a BoP project in the Peruvian Sierra. A German supermarket chain wants to commercialize fruit purees made of Peruvian tropical fruits. These fruit purees should be produced locally at the place where the fruits are ripening in order to achieve maximum fruit quality: thus, value creation would stay in Peru. Consequently, small local farmers, fruit producers and local fruit processors at the BoP would be integrated into a global supply chain. Additionally, environmentally friendly production strategies in agriculture are supported.

An exploratory and qualitative approach is chosen in order to gain detailed understanding of social realities at the BoP. The collected data consists of 27 in-depth interviews with small farmers, merchandisers, entrepreneurs and governmental agents. Participant observation and self-reflexive observation, in the form of continuous memo writing, provides further data (Charmaz, 2013).

The results of the study indicate that there is a lack of interpersonal trust between small farmers and suppliers at the BoP. This causes little organization and association among the local farmers which consequently affects the collaboration with companies. The reasons for the lack of interpersonal trust are complex and include historical, political, social, cultural and economic aspects. Companies can gain farmers' trust by fair prices, direct payment, local investment and formal contracts but because the institutional context at the BoP is different from the one at the ToP, companies need to apply different strategies. The results of this research have important implications for companies, governments, and public agents.

This paper is structured as follows: first, key terms are defined and the BoP concept is presented. Second, it is explained in detail why it is important to focus on the role of trust in sustainable supply chains at the BoP. The third part explains the chosen method and comments on the process of data collection and data analysis. The fourth part presents the results which are discussed in the fifth part. Finally, a short conclusion is given that includes limitations and future research possibilities.

13.2 Theoretical framework and key terms

This first part defines key terms and presents the concept of the BoP. The next part explains why research about the role of trust in sustainable supply chains at the BoP is needed.

13.2.1 Sustainable supply chain management and TBL sustainability

The present paper adopts the definition of sustainability by the WCED (1987). Sustainable development is understood as a "development that meets the needs of the present without compromising the ability of future generations to meet their own needs" (WCED, 1987, p. 43). A way to operationalize this broad understanding of sustainability is to rely on the TBL approach (Elkington, 1999; Seuring and Müller, 2008).

Following Seuring and Müller (2008), sustainable supply chain management is defined as "the management of material, information and capital flows as well as cooperation among companies along the supply chain while taking goals from all three dimensions of sustainable development, i.e., economic, environmental and social, into account" (Seuring and Müller, 2008, p. 1,700).

This definition shows a clear inclusion of the TBL (Elkington, 1999). These three dimensions of sustainable development are interrelated and might affect one another. The present research focuses on the social dimension of sustainable supply chains and relates it to the BoP.

13.2.2 The BoP concept

Prahalad and Hart (2002) argue that the BoP concept enables MNCs to alleviate poverty while making additional profit at the same time. This can happen by applying innovative business strategies, novel product designs and different ways of distribution in order to enter new markets at the BoP and to detect growth possibilities. The literature about the BoP is steadily growing and various aspects have been analysed (Kolk *et al.*, 2014). Nevertheless, more research about the broader social and political environment at the BoP is needed (London *et al.*, 2014). Chatterjee states that "there is little examination of what life is like at the BOP" (2014, p. 896) as the BoP proposition contains a "decontextualized, ahistorical and apolitical" (Chatterjee, 2014, p. 900) view of the BoP. There is a lack of in-depth knowledge relating to this point in current literature. The present research follows this call and analyses the context of a BoP project in Peru, focusing on the role of trust.

Part of the BoP debate is led by a growing number of scholars who criticize and enhance the BoP approach (Agnihotri, 2012; Chatterjee, 2014; Hahn, 2009; Karnani, 2009, 2007a, 2007b; Landrum, 2007). This stream of criticism led to an important advancement: the BoP 2.0 concept. Although Prahalad argues that he recognizes the poor at the BoP as "resilient and creative entrepreneurs and value-conscious consumers" (2010, p. 25), most of the BoP literature and BoP initiatives consider the BoP only as a market and people at the BoP as consumers and not as entrepreneurs (Kolk *et al.*, 2014, pp. 16ff). This is changed in the BoP 2.0 approach.

Following this BoP 2.0 concept, Simanis and Hart (2008) argue that MNCs should focus more on seeing the BoP as business partners and co-inventors instead of merely consumers. Further authors argue in a similar direction claiming a realignment of the BoP approach: the BoP should no longer be seen as a market or consumers but as producers, entrepreneurs and suppliers (Altman *et al.*, 2009; Hahn, 2009; Karnani, 2007b; London *et al.*, 2010). It is about "fortune-creating with the BoP" instead of "fortune-finding" at the BoP (London and Hart, 2010). "[V]entures serving the BoP can achieve economic self-sufficiency and scalability by combining revenues for serving BoP consumers and producers with resources and 'smart subsidies' from the development community and government agencies" (London and Hart, 2010, p. 11). Integrating those at the BoP as producers into global supply chains might lead to competitive advantages for companies while helping to alleviate poverty by generating income for those actors at the BoP. The present project follows the BoP 2.0 approach.

13.2.3 Why we need to understand the role of trust in sustainable supply chains at the BoP

Trust is a relevant feature of every economic and social transaction (Knack and Keefer, 1997; Yu *et al.*, 2015; Zaheer *et al.*, 1998; Zucker, 1986). Panayides and Lun (2009) write "The importance of trust in the context of facilitating social and business interactions is recognized and evidenced" (Panayides and Venus Lun, 2009, p. 35) and Capaldo and Giannoccaro (2015) stress the beneficial effect of trust on performance in supply chains.

As a consequence, trust is also relevant to make supply chains more sustainable. A company that fails to build trusting relationships with its suppliers will have difficulties to implement the environmental and social dimension of sustainability in its supply chain. Handfield and Bechtel (2002) demand trusting relationships with suppliers in order to improve supply chain responsiveness. Sharfman *et al.* (2009) point out that, if there is a higher degree of trust between firms and their suppliers, companies are more likely to realize cooperative supply-chain environmental management.

Nevertheless, the relationship of trust and sustainable supply chains has not been applied extensively to the BoP context. Why is it particularly relevant to investigate about the role of trust at the BoP? This section provides three arguments:

> 1. Lack of in-depth knowledge about the role of trust at the BoP and its implications for SSCM in current literature
>
> 2. Empirical relevance of trust at the BoP, and
>
> 3. Importance of informal mechanisms at the BoP as the institutional context differs.

1. Several scholars point out the importance of trust when talking about projects at the BoP. Gardetti (2006) examines barriers to BoP projects and identifies that a lack of trust could be a constraint to its success. Simanis and Hart (2008) state that trust building is crucial when companies enter the BoP community as an "outsider" (Simanis and Hart, 2008, p. 12). In their BoP protocol, the authors even suggest precise actions such as community homestays where corporate representatives live at least one week in the community in order to build trust and rapport (Simanis and Hart, 2008, p. 20). This would lead to "'locally embedded' business founded on trust and shared commitment between the corporation and the community" (Simanis and Hart, 2008, p. 41). However, the present research suggests that a one week community homestay of corporate members will not give a serious insight to the complexity of trust at the BoP. BoP scholars know that trust somehow matters but so far the role of trust at the BoP has not been examined in a more detailed way. An extensive answer to the question "[h]ow can we build trust in the informal economy?" (Gardetti, 2006, p. 75) is still missing. Moreover, the connection to SSCM is not sufficiently analysed in literature.

2. The issue of trust also appeared during the first stay in Peru. In a one week visit in June 2014, the strong scepticism and distrust of local producers and farmers regarding the cooperation with Peruvian and/or foreign companies was identified. Even agricultural support programmes from the Peruvian government did not initially succeed because of local farmers' distrust. Thus, empirical data of the author's pre-tests shows that trust is an essential issue at the BoP.

3. Further literature demonstrates the importance of trust at the BoP. BoP environments differ from those that MNCs might be accustomed to. Silvestre (2015) states the following proposition referring to emerging economies "As the inadequate infrastructure, corruption, pressing social issues and informality increase, the degree of trust decreases, and consequently institutions

become weaker" (Silvestre, 2015, p. 165). This leads to additional challenges for sustainable supply chains that operate in the context of emerging economies.

As a result, corporations need to apply different strategies at the BoP as the ones they would at the ToP. Rivera-Santos and Rufin (2010) wrote "For an outsider, building legitimacy and trust, [...] is both a necessity and a challenge [...], as the strength of ties within communities is paralleled by deep-rooted divisions, mistrust, and potential conflicts between communities." (Rivera-Santos and Rufín, 2010, p. 128). Additionally, Rivera-Santos and Rufin (2010) argue that the institutional environment of the BoP is different: formal institutions such as enforcement of laws, property rights, contract enforceability and state regulations are less important at the BoP. Instead, informal institutions such as norms and traditional ties play a more important role. On account of this, Rivera-Santos and Rufín (2010) on the one hand argue that trust building at the BoP is crucial and on the other hand they assume that interactions at the BoP rather rely on informal institutions than on formal institutions. But how do these two facts relate to one another? What is the role of trust when, for example, economic exchange relies rather on informal than on formal institutions? Can trust substitute the role of formal institutions such as contracts? Does the low priority of formal institutions cause more or less interpersonal trust?

Kistruck et al. (2012)[3] point out the institutional difference between the BoP and the ToP. Formal institutions play a minor role at the BoP which leads to higher monitoring costs for companies that operate supply chains at the BoP. Large local organizations are therefore "uncomfortable with engaging directly with BoP producers and consumers" (Kistruck et al., 2012, p. 56). Trust could be a mechanism to overcome the issue of monitoring.

Rivera-Santos et al. (2012) apply a more differentiated perspective on institutions when they analyze partnerships in subsistence markets. Rivera-Santos et al. (2012) refer to Scott (2001) who distinguishes between regulative, normative and cognitive institutions. Rivera-Santos et al. (2012) argue that in subsistence markets, or at the BoP, regulative institutions are less important compared to normative and cognitive institutions. Regulative institutions might not completely protect property rights or enforce contracts less effectively at the BoP (De Soto, 2000).[4] This has strong implications for companies, as regulative institutions matter less than normative and cognitive institutions; business transactions are rather governed by informal mechanisms than by formal mechanisms (Rivera-Santos et al., 2012, p. 1,722). Whereas formal mechanisms are built on for example contracts, monitoring and sanctioning, informal mechanisms are rather built on traditional ties, "such

---

3   See also Kistruck et al., 2013.
4   My own empirical data shows that property rights and contract enforceability are not provided by legal authorities in the case of the analyzed context.

as non-specialized kinship, age-group, religious, or other intra-group ties" (Rivera-Santos *et al.* 2012, p. 1,722), reciprocity and trust (Ostrom, 2003).

Thus, institutions at the BoP differ from those at the ToP and therefore business transactions need to be governed differently. In a context where formal institutions are important, contracts might be an adequate mechanism to manage supply chains. At the BoP, where informal institutions are more important, different mechanisms need to be applied and the role of trust needs to be considered.

13.2.4 Understanding of trust

Trust is a complex phenomenon that is widely researched among different disciplines and applied to different units of analysis. In order to keep this work manageable, this chapter does not provide a detailed review of the trust literature but instead concentrates on important aspects of trust that are relevant to the research question.

Zucker (1986) writes "Trust has been acknowledged in economics and organization theory as the most efficient mechanism for governing transactions" (Zucker, 1986, p. 5). Rousseau *et al.* (1998) analyze similarities between understandings of trust in different disciplines (e.g. economics, psychology and sociology). They identify two aspects that are part of the majority of trust definitions "confident expectations and a willingness to be vulnerable" (Rousseau *et al.*, 1998, p. 394). Sitkin and Roth (1993) state that research on trust could be organized into four categories:

- Trust as an individual attribute
- Trust as a behaviour
- Trust as a situational feature, and
- Trust as an institutional arrangement.

This categorization is needed in further analysis to understand different dimensions of trust in supply chains at the BoP.

A different approach as to how to structure the trust literature is given by Bigley and Pearce (1998). They argue that trust research should always be applied to a specific research problem. They identified three main categories:

- Interactions among unfamiliar actors
- Interactions among familiar actors, and
- Organization of economic transactions (Bigley and Pearce, 1998, p. 409).

This research fits best into the final category.

Despite the large amount of literature, so far there is no universally accepted concept of trust. One definition of trust that has been cited frequently is formulated by Mayer *et al.* (1995). Trust is defined as "the willingness of a party to be vulnerable to the actions of another party based on the expectation that the other will perform a particular action important to the trustor, irrespective of the ability to monitor or control that other party" (Mayer *et al.*, 1995, p. 712). The willingness to be vulnerable can be understood in terms of risk taking. Consequently, to trust in someone or in something also means to take a risk for something (Mayer *et al.*, 1995). The present paper adopts this definition. Trust is assumed as a steady state and feedback issues are not considered at this point of research.

13.3 Methods and research setting

As there is little in-depth literature about the role of trust in supply chains at the BoP so far, qualitative research methods and an exploratory approach are applied. The idea is to get a better understanding of "life-worlds" (Flick *et al.*, 2004, p. 3) and social realities by focusing on a specific case and its context. This research follows the definition by Yin who defines case studies as "an empirical inquiry that investigates a contemporary phenomenon in depth and within its real-life context." (Yin, 2009, p. 18). There are various claims against case studies (Gerring, 2007, pp. 68ff; Gummesson, 2000, pp. 84ff; Yin, 2009, pp. 15ff), especially when generalizations are made on the base of one single case. Nonetheless, it is not necessarily the objective of this exploratory case study to formulate general statements. The point is rather to end up with a better understanding of the role of trust in global supply chains that include the BoP which might be retested afterwards in different contexts.

13.3.1 Research context

Data was collected around Tarma in Peru. Tarma is the provincial capital of Junin with 55,000 inhabitants it is located at an altitude of 3,050 m in the Peruvian Central Andes. In Peru, 23.9% of the population lives in poverty (poverty headcount ratio at national poverty line, 2013).[5] Applying a $1.25 per day poverty line, 2.9% of population (2012) lives in poverty and the GINI Index for Peru is 45.7 in 2011 (World Bank, 2015). Thus, income is unequally distributed. In the Peruvian Sierra, 34.7% of the population lives in poverty and in the rural Sierra even 52.9% (national poverty line).[6] The main income source in the rural Sierra is agriculture. The present work adopts a multi-dimensional understanding of poverty following Kolk *et al.* (2014, pp. 24-25) and the World Development Report 2000/01 (Grootaert *et al.*, 2000, pp. 15ff): poverty is not only understood in economic terms but also includes further criteria such as lack of education, insufficient health systems, social exclusion and lack of capabilities (Ansari *et al.*, 2012).

---

5   See   http://data.worldbank.org/indicator/SI.POV.NAHC/countries/PE?display=graph (accessed: 20 December 2014).
6   See INEI (n.d.), accessed 2 February 2015.

A German commercial enterprise (sales: one billion €/year, employees: >5,000) wants to commercialize fruit purees made of tropical fruits. These fruit purees should be processed locally at the place where fruits are grown in order to achieve maximum fruit quality. Fresh tropical fruits that are normally offered in Germany, for example, have been harvested before they were completely ripened, as they must be transported over long distances. This causes a loss of quality which needs to be avoided. The idea is to process fruits locally at the moment when they are completely ripened. Thus, value creation would stay in Peru. Consequently, small local farmers and fruit processors at the BoP would be integrated into the global value chain of a foreign company. Meanwhile, organic material that is not needed for these purees, such as pips and parings, stay in Peru and re-enters the local organic circle, in form of compost for example, instead of ending up as waste as would be the case when these fruit purees are produced in Germany. This is an important aspect that relates to the ecologic sustainability of the supply chain (closed-loop supply chain).

According to an interview with a company representative, there are three main TBL-related reasons why the company is embarking on this project:

- To produce fruit purees with highly qualitative tropical fruits in order to increase sales (economic dimension)

- To support sustainable production and industrialization of agricultural products (ecologic dimension), and

- To support local development and job creation by integrating local producers into global supply chains (social dimension).

13.3.2 Data sources and analysis

The data collection process included two stages. Initial knowledge of the context in Peru was acquired during a one week stay in June 2014 and a subsequent two month stay in October and November 2014 was used to collect extensive data. This involved in-depth interviews, group discussions and participant observation. In advance, an interview protocol was developed and reviewed. Interviews were discovery-oriented and open-ended. Self-reflexive observation in form of continuous memo-writing (Charmaz, 2013, pp. 162ff) provided additional data.[7] 27 interviews were conducted; three of them were group discussions. The interviews were audio taped, all except four cases where the informants did not give their permission or the situation was not suitable for recording. The total amount of recorded interview time is 944 minutes. 26 interviews were conducted in Spanish and one in German. The quotations in this work are translated by the author. Subsequently, data was systemically analysed and structured, especially on the base of written memos which critically summarized and reflected the research process. The entire process

7   The researcher's place of origin is Germany.

was accompanied by continuous exchange with other scholars. Table 13.1 provides an overview of the interview partners.

Table 13.1 Interview partners

Actors	Number of interviews
Small farmers	12
Medium-sized farmers	4
Local start-up (group discussion)	1
Land manager	1
Merchandiser	1
Governmental agents	4
Local employees	2
Representative and members of a cooperative (group discussion)	1
Representative of foreign company	1
Total	27

13.4 Results

The following chapter first describes empirically how the role of trust might affect global supply chains that include the BoP. Afterwards, some reasons for local distrust are mentioned. Finally, different mechanisms of gaining the farmer's trust are presented.

13.4.1 Role of trust

The collected data shows that it is important to distinguish between two cases:

- Trust of the local farmers in a (foreign) company, and
- Trust among the farmers themselves which then impacts the relation with the company.

Figure 13.1 Trust between farmers and company

Figure 13.2 Trust between farmers

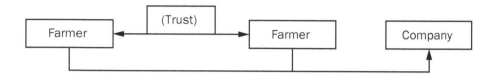

It turned out that farmers were generally open-minded and wanted to build trade relations with companies. One farmer stated "It would be important that there is a company which says: 'we will buy your products.'" Some, but not all, of the interview participants argued that they would rather trust in a foreign company than in a Peruvian company because foreign companies have a higher reputation.

Data shows that farmers (small and medium-sized) would trust in a company, if certain conditions were fulfilled (see Section 13.4.3). Once a company gains the trust of the producers, farmers are believed to be loyal. A government agent, who has experience in working with the target group, argues "When they [the farmers] really catch confidence, they are not going to leave the company anymore." But if a company is not able to build trusting relationships with the farmers there is a higher probability that farmers will not comply with the agreements that were made. A continuous risk of non-compliance consequently leads to higher transaction costs for the company as monitoring strategies need to be applied. If there is a lack of trust between the different actors, trade relations and supply chains will be socially unsustainable.

However, it is not only the trust between farmers and the company that matters. A crucial point is the trust among the farmers themselves, among community members at the BoP. Several interview partners said that farmers or community members in general do not trust one another. A peasant told me: "The community often doesn't trust in anyone. They don't trust in anyone. […] I don't know why that is the case or things went wrong [in the past]—I don't know it but they don't trust in anyone. Often they don't even trust themselves, I guess." One interview partner, a small farmer, was asked who or what he trusts and he answered: "I don't trust in anybody. There is no trust. There is no trust in anybody […] I don't trust."

A further governmental agent who promotes and supervises public agricultural support programmes for farmers was interviewed. He spends a lot of time working with low-income peasant communities and he says:

> Both, at the coast and in the mountains, there is much individualism pre-
> cisely because of the experiences, right? The experiences they have made.
> After the cooperative system [and] the agricultural enterprises that were
> built [...] there was mismanagement by many leaders, [...] and this cre-
> ated a total distrust between them [the farmers]. So, nobody wanted to
> talk about organization. And in some areas it is still like that: they do not
> want to know anything about organization.

So, the argument is that bad experiences in the past caused a lack of trust in agricultural organizations. At the same time, the low level of mutual trust leads to a low level of organization. It was observable that there is only very little associa-tion among the farmers. The previously cited government agent says "But even among themselves they do not trust one another and that is why they do not want to associate". The knowledge of these circumstances is important as they have strong implications for companies that want to establish supply chains with those farmers. Transaction costs for a company will be much higher if the company has to deal with multiple suppliers and trade partners compared to one association of producers.

In a nutshell, trust is crucial in building supply chains with farmers at the BoP. Not considering this factor will lead to an isolation of the company. If farmers do not trust in the company they will not comply with agreements. On the other hand, if companies gain the farmer's trust, farmers will be loyal.

Beside the company–farmer relationship, trust especially matters between the farmers themselves. There seems to be little trust between the farmers which conse-quently leads to non-cooperative behaviour that deteriorates market transactions. Farmers do not want to organize themselves nor to associate with one another. Everyone coordinates his own production independently. Consequently, the role of trust in farmer–farmer relationships has strong implications for companies and the social sustainability of supply chains. A company which is used to work with 20 farmers who are organized into one producer co-operative will not be able to coordinate with 20 independent farmers using the same amount of resources.[8] Transaction costs will be much higher in the latter case. Low trust within peasant communities at the BoP and a resulting low level of cooperation demands differ-ent strategies in order to integrate farmers from the BoP into global supply chains.

13.4.2 Different explanations for the lack of trust at the BoP

Explaining the lack of interpersonal trust between farmers is complex. Several explanations were given by interview partners. Subsequently, some of them are mentioned without going into too much detail.

---

8   For example, the Cooperativa Agraria Cafetalera La Florida in Peru unites several small-
    scale coffee farmers (see e.g. Ruben and Fort, 2012). Foreign companies only have to gov-
    ern transaction with this single cooperative instead of multiple small suppliers.

One dimension that needs to be considered to understand the low level of trust between the farmers is historical. In the 1960s and 1970s, Juan Velasco Alvarado realized the Peruvian agrarian reform. "Haciendas" (large land estates) were distributed to the employees of those haciendas and to the peasant communities. Agricultural production was organized in cooperative systems and Agrarian Production Cooperatives were formed (Kay, 1982; Mosley, 1985). Most of these cooperatives broke down because of mismanagement and deception. In the end, farmers stayed with their own piece of land and a retained a distrust regarding everything that was related to organization in general.

Later, in the '80s, the armed conflict between the left-oriented guerrilla group "sendero luminoso" (Shining Path) and the Peruvian government took place. The region studied in this research was intensively affected by this conflict. Participants told me that it was not possible to trust in anyone at this time. A local government agent argues:

> Mistrust is already very old. There have been many problems. [...] The strongest problem was terrorism, right? [...] So, why mistrust? People did not know where to turn to get support. It was frustrating. I worked here in this area in this time. And you were going down the street and you saw dead people all over the street. And you could not get close to see who it was. You had to keep walking straight. So, those have been hard times, right? [...] Terrorism was very tough in this area. [...] So, that is where this tremendous mistrust comes from.

Another answer to the question of why farmers do not trust one another is the fact that there is a lot of deception and betrayal among the farmers and community members. This aspect comes up several times throughout the data. But why does so much cheating exist? One explanation is that there is widespread egoism and a "culture of envy". One farmer says "The Peruvian is an enemy of the same Peruvian. [...] They don't let you work right? So, [...] there is envy [and] resentment. Sometimes one progresses and they put a lot of obstacles in your way, a lot of pretexts so that you cannot progress".

Another answer was given in a different group discussion with medium-sized fruit producers. They argued that people start to defraud because of the necessity to do so because of their poverty. If people are poor, they have to utilize every opportunity they can find to get some additional income even if that means engaging in illegitimate or illegal activities. "I think it is because there is a necessity, right? The situation is so hard that if you can take advantage of someone, you do it. I think that is why [people cheat on others]. [...] It is because of the necessity".

An additional rationale for cheating resulting in low mutual trust was that the state or the government does not enforce property and contract rights. In most cases these are not ensured by the state. It can be seen that regulative institutions (Scott, 2001) play a different role here than the one to which companies are accustomed.

13.4.3 Mediating variables: how to gain the farmers' trust?

Farmers and interview partners mentioned different aspects that should be fulfilled in order to create trust in a company. The following six variables were generated out of the answers that were given by interview partners and provide several ideas how companies could gain the trust of the small farmers at the BoP.

- **Price and payment**. One crucial argument for farmers to trust a company is the price for the traded commodity. The price has to be good and fair. Therefore, prices should be fixed and independent from fluctuations in the market. This gives the farmers more security and enables them to plan. Payments need to be direct and without delay. Farmers have had many bad experiences with local merchandisers who received the farmer's products, promised payment in several weeks and never showed up again. At the beginning of a new cooperation, farmers only trust if payments are made directly.

- **Local investment by the company**. Farmers want the company to invest locally. Additionally, farmers would prefer payment in advance or loans given by the company. This money would be used for buying seeds and fertilizers for the next season. Seeds and fertilizers are the major expense items for small farmers. Local investment shows that the company is interested in long-term relationships and not only in quick, profitable business dealings. Financial support by the company also serves as a trust building mechanism.

- **Contracts**. Farmers and interview partners argued that formal contracts and documentation might enhance the farmers' trust in a company. This is an interesting issue as it is not common to use formal, written contracts for economic transactions in this region. There is a high rate of informal agreements being made. The role of contracts is discussed more in detail in Section 13.5.

- **Support, knowledge and know-how**. Farmers continuously request support by experts or by companies. On the one hand, this can include technology transfer and technical assistance. On the other hand, farmers are open-minded towards knowledge and know-how transfers. Training and workshops with local farmers might result in higher trust. Farmers are also open-minded towards new ideas concerning the choice of crops.

- **Open communication**. Trust is also produced by direct interaction between the company and the farmers without relying on intermediaries. One strategy might be to invite farmers for short internships in the company. This could result in higher trust because the farmers would better understand the activities of the company. In general, a company's communication strategy should be open and honest so that farmers can understand and anticipate the company's intentions.

- **A local presence**. Finally, trust can be produced if the company has a local presence. Local buildings and offices, machinery, visible technology and a corporate identity leads to increased trust by the farmers.

13.5 Discussion

The Results section 13.4 shows that trust is an important and complex factor that needs to be considered when we want to build sustainable supply chains with the BoP. Figure 13.3 summarizes the current results. Beyond that, various questions arise when looking at how different actors react to the situation of low local trust. For example: which strategies should be applied by (foreign) companies in order to successfully integrate suppliers from the BoP into their global supply chains? And what could be the role of contracts given the fact that on the one hand data shows that they are demanded but on the other hand it is unclear whether farmers would adhere to the requirements of formal contracts. Companies have to make sure that they build trusting relations with the small farmers but it will be very hard for a company to change the low level of mutual trust by farmers since the reasons for this are very complex (see Section 13.4.2).

Figure 13.3 Conceptual framework

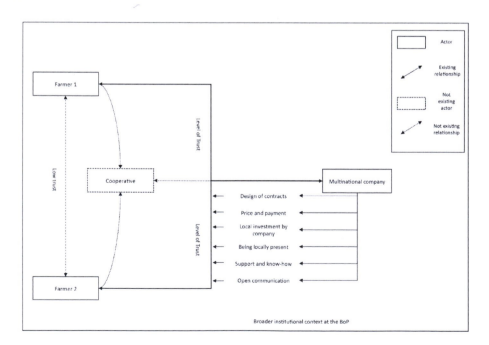

Section 13.4.3 points out some possibilities for a company as to how to gain the trust of small farmers at the BoP. The first variable (price and payment) is not necessary new. To get the first transaction to happen in a low-trust environment and without previous interaction between the trading partners, market mechanisms, such as price and payment, become relevant. Because of that, local investments by the company (second and sixth variable) enhance farmers' trust in the company. This aspect is an important supplement to existing literature. Also, the importance of knowledge transfers as a trust-building measurement is a new and valuable insight.

Further mediating variables were contracts. Data shows that farmers ask for formal, written contracts in order to trust a company but, at the same time, empirical data shows that it is not common to have formal contracts.[9] What does this mean? Is there actually a lot of interpersonal trust so that formal contracts are not needed? Or is there no trust in formal contracts as the institutional context differs (see Section 13.2.2) and it is questionable if contracts would be maintained? Data shows that the first case does not apply. As a result, it might rather be the second one. Nonetheless, participants answered that formal contracts would enhance their trust in companies.

Poppo and Zenger (2002) review the argument that trust replaces contracts.[10] However, they conclude that contracts and relational governance (understood in terms of trust) are complements rather than substitutes, given that the institutional context means relying on contracts. Thus, trust as an individual attribute is low in this region and the reasons for low interpersonal trust are complex. But if interpersonal trust is low, it can be substituted by institutional trust. Referring to various scholars, Sitkin and Roth (1993) write: "when the interpersonal roots of trust are no longer available [...], trust will take the form of institutional arrangements" (Sitkin and Roth, 1993, p. 369). Beckman *et al.* (2005) argue that trust can be created by both people and institutions. However, the data of this research shows that interpersonal trust is not substituted by institutional trust as the institutional context at the BoP does not seem to provide this trust.

"Trust is not either present or absent, but can be produced", writes Zucker (1986, p. 10) and considers the institutional context as a "formal mechanism of trust production" (1986, p. 12). Several informal mechanisms of trust production that rely on shared, local understandings of "how things are usually done" exist. Besides, contracts can be an additional trust production mechanism (Zucker, 1986, p. 20). Contracts are needed because the company does not form part of the local community. For transactions inside the community, formal mechanisms are not necessary as the transaction can be easily monitored and sanctioned by the community itself.

---

9   I interviewed a land manager who is responsible for 1,200 hectares of land and who has various employees. This interview partner has never signed a written contract and this is not an exception.

10 For more literature on the relationship of trust and formal institutions see Ahlerup *et al.* 2009.

The incentive to cheat is therefore low. But as soon as the transaction takes place with an external actor (foreign company), formal mechanisms (such as contracts) are needed as informal mechanisms do not work in this situation. In the present case, the foreign company does not form part of the community and hence is not familiar with the shared norms of the community. As a result, formal mechanisms are needed. That would explain why farmers mentioned the aspect of contracts.

Thus, we can conclude that managing supply chains at the BoP is essentially different to managing supply chains at the ToP. Trust is a relevant issue due to the fact that interpersonal trust of suppliers at the BoP is low which negatively affects the level of organization among the suppliers. In turn this affects negatively the company's transaction costs (see also Fafchamps and Minten, 2002). In addition, low interpersonal trust is not replaced by institutional trust as this institutional context does not seem to be provided at the BoP. Consequently, it is crucial for companies to consider mediating variables (Section 13.4.3) that can create trust between the suppliers and the company.

Summing up, Sections 13.4 and 13.5 show that trust in sustainable supply chains at the BoP is a crucial issue that has strong implications for a company's strategies.

13.6 Conclusion, limitations and future research

The present work provides important research into the role of trust at the BoP and its implication for sustainable supply chain management. It shows that trust is a relevant issue and points out how it affects different actors in a supply chain at the BoP. The BoP and SSCM literature is enhanced by providing in-depth knowledge about how trust matters and considering the BoP as producers and not as consumers. This work follows recent calls for more research about BoP 2.0 projects and the role of trust in sustainable supply chains at the BoP. It shows that there is a lack of trust at the BoP and explanations for this lack of trust are mentioned. Furthermore, valuable information about how companies could gain the farmers' trust is provided and the role of contracts and institutional trust is discussed.

The implications of this research are manifold. Section 13.4.3 showed that local investment by corporations facilitates the building of trust at the BoP. So, MNCs should invest in trust-building measures in order to build sustainable global supply chains with the BoP. The corporations' particular contribution to poverty reduction consists of integrating the BoP into global supply chains and connecting it to global markets. By doing so, MCNs also satisfy their own economic interests. SSCM initiatives at the BoP can be facilitated by complementary trust-building actions of third-party actors such as governments, NGOs and donors. These actions have to consider both trust between corporation and farmer and among the farmers themselves.

The strongest limitation to this work is that it focuses on a single case. Consequently, generalizations have to be handled carefully. Similar research should be done in different contexts in order to gain more knowledge about the role of trust in supply chains that include the BoP from a comparative perspective. Afterwards, hypotheses could be tested quantitatively on a larger sample. A further limitation is the amount of collected data: future research should include longer stays in the communities in order to collect more data.

There are many future research possibilities. One important finding of this work is that there is little trust among farmers and consequently little organization. This complicates collaboration with companies. Future research should focus on the question of how local forms of organization at the BoP can be facilitated. Moreover, it is probable that trust exists at the BoP as trust is part of every social interaction but it is not clear in which form. Future research should find out how local trust-building mechanisms operate, who are the key players of this process and which forms of local organization are implemented. A third area for future research could be to analyze the affect of culture on trust in supply chains (Ueltschy *et al.*, 2007).

References

Agnihotri, A. (2012). Revisiting the debate over the bottom of the pyramid market. *Journal of Macromarketing*, 32(4), 417-423.

Ahlerup, P., Olsson, O., & Yanagizawa, D. (2009). Social capital vs institutions in the growth process. *European Journal of Political Economy*, 25(1), 1-14. doi: 10.1016/j.ejpoleco.2008.09.008.

Altman, D.G., Lyndon, R., & Peg, R. (2009). Expanding opportunity at the base of the pyramid. *People & Strategy*, 32(2), 46-51.

Ansari, S., Kamal, M., & Tricia G. (2012). Impact at the 'bottom of the pyramid': The role of social capital in capability development and community empowerment. *Journal of Management, Studies*, 49(4), 813-42.

Beckmann, M., Mackenbrock, T., Pies, I., & Sardison, M. (2005). Vertrauen, Institutionen und mentale Modelle. In M. Held, G., Kubon-Gilke & R. Sturn (Eds.), *Reputation und Vertrauen* (pp. 59-83). Marburg: Metropolis-Verlag.

Bigley, G.A., & Pearce, J.L. (1998). Straining for shared meaning in organization science: Problems of trust and distrust. *Academy of Management Review*, 23(3), 405.

Capaldo, A., & Giannoccaro, I. (2015). How does trust affect performance in the supply chain? The moderating role of interdependence. *International Journal of Production Economics*, 166 (August), 36-49. doi: 10.1016/j.ijpe.2015.04.008.

Charmaz, K. (2013). *Constructing Grounded Theory* (2nd ed.). Thousand Oaks, CA: Sage Publications.

Chatterjee, S. (2014). Engaging with an emergent metanarrative: A critical exploration of the BOP proposition, *Organization*, 21(6), 888-906.

De Soto, H. (2000). *The Mystery of Capital: Why Capitalism Triumphs in the West and Fails Everywhere Else*. New York : Basic Books.

Elkington, J. (1997). *Cannibals with Forks: The Triple Bottom Line of 21st Century Business*. Oxford: Capstone.

Fafchamps, M., & Minten, B. (2002). Returns to social network capital among traders. *Oxford Economic Papers*, 54(2), 173-206. doi: 10.1093/oep/54.2.173.

Flick, U., Von Kardorff, E., & Steinke, I. (Eds.) (2004). *A Companion to Qualitative Research*. London; Thousand Oaks; CA: Sage Publications.

Gardetti, M.A. (2006). A base-of-the-pyramid approach in Argentina. *Greener Management International*, 51 (Summer), 65-77.

Gerring, J. (2007). *Case Study Research: Principles and Practices*. New York: Cambridge University Press.

Griggs, D., Stafford-Smith, M., Gaffney, O., Rockström, J., Öhman, M.C., Shyamsundar, P., Steffen, W., Glaser, G., Kanie, N., & Noble, I. (2013). Policy: Sustainable development goals for people and planet. *Nature*, 495(7441), 305-307. doi:10.1038/495305a.

Grootaert, C., Kwakwa, V., Kanbur, R., Gupta, M.D., Lustig, N., & Malmberg Calvo, C. (2000). World Development Report 2000/2001: Attacking Poverty. 22684. *The World Bank*. Retrieved from http://documents.banquemondiale.org/curated/fr/2000/09/17408018/world-development-report-20002001-attacking-poverty

Gummesson, E. (2000). *Qualitative Methods in Management Research* (2nd ed). Thousand Oaks, CA: Sage.

Hahn, R. (2009). The ethical rational of business for the poor: Integrating the concepts bottom of the pyramid, sustainable development, and corporate citizenship. *Journal of Business Ethics*, 84(3), 313-324.

Handfield, R.B., & Bechtel, C. (2002). The role of trust and relationship structure in improving supply chain responsiveness. Industrial Marketing Management, *Cycle Time and Industrial Marketing*, 31(4), 367-382. doi:10.1016/S0019-8501(01)00169-9.

INEI (2015). *PERU Instituto Nacional de Estadística E Informática INEI*. Retrieved from http://www.inei.gob.pe/estadisticas/indice-tematico/sociales (3 February 2015)

Karnani, A. (2009). Romanticising the poor harms the poor. *Journal of International Development*, 21(1), 76-86. doi:10.1002/jid.1491.

Karnani, A. (2007a). Doing well by doing good. Case study: "Fair & Lovely" whitening cream. *Strategic Management Journal*, 28(13), 1,351-1,357.

Karnani, A. (2007b). The mirage of marketing to the bottom of the pyramid: How the private sector can help alleviate poverty. *California Management Review*, 49(4), 90-111.

Kay, C. (1982). Achievements and contradictions of the Peruvian agrarian reform. *Journal of Development Studies*, 18(2), 141.

Kistruck, G.M., Beamish, P.W., Qureshi, I., & Sutter, C.J. (2013). Social intermediation in base-of-the-pyramid markets. *Journal of Management Studies*, 50(1), 31-66.

Kistruck, G., Sutter, C., Lount, R., & Smith, B. (2012). Mitigating principal-agent problems in base-of-the-pyramid markets: An identity spillover perspective. *Academy of Management Journal*, 56(3), 659-682.

Knack, S., & Keefer, P. (1997). Does social capital have an economic payoff? A cross-country investigation. *Quarterly Journal of Economics*, 112(4), 1,251.

Kolk, A., Rivera-Santos, M. & Rufín, C. (2014). Reviewing a decade of research on the 'base/bottom of the pyramid' (BOP) concept. *Business & Society*, 53(3), 338-77.

Landrum, N.E. (2007). Advancing the "base of the pyramid" debate. *Strategic Management Review*, 1(1), 1-12.

London, T., Anupindi, R., & Sheth, S. (2010). Creating mutual value: Lessons learned from ventures serving base of the pyramid producers. *Journal of Business Research*, 63(6), 582-594.

London, T., Sateen, S., & Hart, S. (2014). *A Roadmap for the Base of the Pyramid Domain: Re-Energizing for the next Decade*. Ann Arbor, MI: William Davidson Institute at the University of Michigan.

London, T., & Hart, S.L. (2010). *Next Generation Business Strategies for the Base of the Pyramid: New Approaches for Building Mutual Value*. Upper Saddle River, NJ: FT Press.

Mayer, R.C., Davis, J.H., & Schoorman, F.D. (1995). An integrative model of organizational trust. *Academy of Management Review*, 20(3), 709-34. doi: 10.5465/AMR.1995.9508080335.

Mosley, P. (1985). Achievements and contradictions of the Peruvian agrarian reform: A Regional Perspective. *Journal of Development Studies*, 21(3), 440-448.

Ostrom, E. (2003). Toward a behavioral theory linking trust, reciprocity, and reputation. *Trust and Reciprocity: Interdisciplinary Lessons from Experimental Research*, 6, 19-79.

Panayides, P.M., & Venus Lun, J.H. (2009). The impact of trust on innovativeness and supply chain performance. *International Journal of Production Economics, Transport Logistics and Physical Distribution Interlocking of Information Systems for International Supply and Demand Chains Management* ICPR19, 122 (1), 35-46. doi:10.1016/j.ijpe.2008.12.025.

Poppo, L., & Zenger, T. (2002). Do formal contracts and relational governance function as substitutes or complements? *Strategic Management Journal*, 23 (8), 707-725. doi:10.1002/smj.249.

Prahalad, C.K. (2010). *The Fortune at the Bottom of the Pyramid: Eradicating Poverty through Profits* (revised and updated 5th anniversary ed.). Upper Saddle River, NJ: Wharton School Pub.

Prahalad, C.K., & Hart, S.L. (2002). The fortune at the bottom of the pyramid. *Strategy+Business*, 26, 1-14.

Rivera-Santos, M., & Rufín, C. (2010). Global village vs. small town: Understanding networks at the base of the pyramid. *International Business Review*, 19(2), 126-39.

Rivera-Santos, M., Rufín, C., & Kolk, A. (2012). Bridging the institutional divide: Partnerships in subsistence markets. *Journal of Business Research*, 65 (December), 1,721-1,727. doi: 10.1016/j.jbusres.2012.02.013.

Rousseau, D.M., Sitkin, S.B., Burt, R.S., & Camerer, C. (1998). Not so different after all: A cross-discipline view of trust. *Academy of Management Review*, 23(3), 393-404. doi:10.5465/AMR.1998.926617.

Ruben, R., & Fort, R. (2012). The impact of fair trade certification for coffee farmers in Peru. *World Development*, 40(3), 570-582. doi: 10.1016/j.worlddev.2011.07.030.

Scott, W.R. (2001). *Institutions and Organizations*. Thousand Oaks, CA: Sage.

Seuring, S., & Müller, M. (2008). From a literature review to a conceptual framework for sustainable supply chain management. *Journal of Cleaner Production, Sustainability and Supply Chain Management*, 16(15), 1,699-1,710. doi:10.1016/j.jclepro.2008.04.020.

Sharfman, M.P., Shaft, T.M., & Anex, R.P. (2009). The road to cooperative supply-chain environmental management: Trust and uncertainty among pro-active firms. *Business Strategy and the Environment*, 18(1), 1-13. doi:10.1002/bse.580.

Silvestre, B.S. (2015). Sustainable supply chain management in emerging economies: Environmental turbulence, institutional voids and sustainability trajectories. *International Journal of Production Economics*, 167 (September), 156-69. doi: 10.1016/j.ijpe.2015.05.025.

Simanis, E., & Hart, S.L. (2008). *The Base of the Pyramid Protocol: Toward Next Generation BoP Strategy*. Ithaca, NY: Cornell University.

Sitkin, S.B., & Roth, N.L. (1993). Explaining the limited effectiveness of legalistic "remedies" for trust/distrust. *Organization Science*, 4(3), 367-92. doi: 10.1287/orsc.4.3.367.

Ueltschy, L.C., Ueltschy, M.L., & Fachinelli, A.C. (2007). The impact of culture on the generation of trust in global supply chain relationships. *Marketing Management Journal*, 17(1), 15-26.

United Nations (2008). The Millennium Development Goals Report 2008. *United Nations Publications*. Retrieved from http://www.un.org/millenniumgoals/2008highlevel/pdf/newsroom/mdg%20reports/MDG_Report_2008_ENGLISH.pdf

WCED (World Commission on Environment and Development) (1987). *Our Common Future*. Oxford: Oxford University Press.

World Bank (2015). *Poverty & Equity Peru*. Retrieved from http://databank.worldbank.org/data/Views/Reports/ReportWidgetCustom.aspx?Report_Name=Country_Char3_June04&Id=103a719c84&wd=430&ht=380&tb=y&dd=n&pr=n&export=y&xlbl=y&ylbl=y&legend=y&isportal=y&inf=n&exptypes=Excel&country=PER

Yin, R.K. (2009). Case Study Research: Design and Methods (4th ed.). *Applied Social Research Methods*, v. 5. Los Angeles, CA: Sage.

Yu, S., Beugelsdijk, S., & De Haan, J. (2015). *Trade, trust and the rule of law. European Journal of Political Economy*, 37 (March), 102-115. doi: 10.1016/j.ejpoleco.2014.11.003.

Zaheer, A., McEvily, B., & Perrone, V. (1998). Does trust matter? Exploring the effects of inter-organizational and interpersonal trust on performance. *Organization Science*, 9(2), 141-159.

Zucker, L.G. (1986). Production of trust: Institutional sources of economic structure, 1,840-1,920. *Organizational Behavior*, 8, 53-111.

Sigfried Eisenmeier studied Sociology, Politics and Economics at the Zeppelin University in Friedrichshafen (Germany), at the Universidad de los Andes in Bogotá and at the University of California, Berkeley. He focuses on topics related to development studies, Latin American studies, public policy and political economy. Sigfried Eisenmeier is interested in finding ways to enable bottom-up approaches that improve the life realities of small farmers (self-organization, collective action, co-operatives, BoP, sustainable global supply chains). He mainly focuses on Latin America and travels frequently to this region as he is involved in a wide range of projects. Sigfried Eisenmeier is a scholar of the German National Academic Foundation.

14

Addressing the triple bottom line

Lowering construction emissions through the implementation of collaborative supply chains

Emily Jervis
University of Wolverhampton, UK

Joanne Meehan, Claire Moxham
University of Liverpool Management School, UK

Rising CO_2 emissions have encouraged the construction industry to make environmental changes to their operations management practices in order to reduce emissions impacts (Ahi and Searcy, 2015). Responsible for approximately half of global greenhouse gas emissions, the industry has made steps towards implementing CO_2 measurement systems. These systems however are not perceived to be capable of addressing the triple bottom line (TBL) in construction (Kucukvar and Tatari, 2013; Asif *et al.*, 2007). Emphasis on mathematical solutions to the emissions problem has encouraged a disregard of the social and economic implications of environmental sustainability. The aim of this chapter is to understand how a movement away from technological solutions to environmental problems, towards an integrated supply chain approach could provide insight into how TBL can be applied to construction; the product of which could provide environmental, social and economic benefits for the industry.

14.1 Introduction

With rising concerns over the climatic effects of increasing anthropogenic CO_2 emissions, many industries are moving towards making positive environmental changes to their supply chain management practices (Ahi and Searcy, 2015). The construction industry is no exception; responsible for approximately 50% of global greenhouse gas emissions, the environmental effects from construction practices are extreme (Ramesh *et al.*, 2010). In recent times the industry has made steps towards implementing life-cycle analysis (LCA) measurement systems to combat the emissions problem. These systems alone are not perceived to be capable of addressing the triple bottom line (TBL)—an approach that assesses business performance using environmental, social and economic impacts (Elkington, 1997). The primary reason for this can be attributed to the emphasis that current LCA systems place on the mathematical calculation of CO_2 emissions, which disregard the social and economic implications of sustainability through scientific focus (Heijungs *et al.*, 2009).

The main principle of sustainability is the integration of the relationships between ecological, social and financial systems (Tam, 2008; Shen *et al.*, 2010). The construction industry, like many others, requires collaborative supply chain practices to deliver the TBL. In the construction industry in particular, buildings must improve the environment and advance society while simultaneously gaining economic competitive advantage (Shen *et al.*, 2010). The TBL approach in construction requires the implementation of economic, social and environmental improvements in performance in an attempt to operationalize sustainability (Ahi and Searcy, 2015; Elkington, 1997). The construction industry has traditionally focused its business efforts on time, cost and quality in an effort to remain highly financially competitive through design build contracts (Xia *et al.*, 2013; Abanda *et al.*, 2013; Monghasemi *et al.*, 2015). With the movement towards addressing environmental impact, the underlying social effect of emissions reduction has come to the fore as forward-thinking clients demand more socially responsible buildings. The importance of the social implications of construction can no longer be overlooked, particularly as we spend up to 90% of our lives in buildings (Evans and McCoy, 1998). Buildings are considered to be social and cultural products and so, therefore, the acknowledgement of the environment and social impacts of construction are essential for the modern world (King, 2003).

The aim of this chapter is to provide insight into how the TBL approach can be applied to construction by addressing CO_2 lifecycle analysis through the consideration of supply chain impacts. The chapter moves away from the predominant academic and industry focus on technological solutions towards integrated carbon calculation methods. Instead it assesses how low-carbon decision making could be implemented quickly, and at low cost, in the wake of calculation software failure. An integrated approach to sustainability could theoretically address the environmental and societal impacts of the industry while maintaining the focus on the key components of construction—capital cost, quality and time (Abanda *et al.*, 2013; Femenias *et al.*, 2009). Increased integration incorporates social and environmental considerations into decision making via supply chain networks, sharing responsibility for CO_2 emissions and sustainability. Our focus on integrated supply chain approaches will aid the understanding of technological failures of LCA. We posit how a more holistic approach to LCA, incorporating both technology and integrative supply chain collaboration, could provide an inexpensive solution for low-carbon decision making and social responsibility in construction—addressing the TBL. We develop our discussion by drawing on empirical data collected from an expert focus group held in 2014, thus providing a contemporary analysis of key issues. The results included in this chapter provide a contribution to both supply chain integration and emissions analysis in construction; evaluating how integrative methods in the industry could provide more positive solutions to LCA by addressing economic and environmental impacts. Previous studies have assessed the supply chain and carbon emissions as singular problems (Briscoe and Dainty, 2005). In contrast, this chapter develops an understanding of the potential benefits of merging integrative supply chain methods with CO_2 emissions analysis achieved via the use of empirical data in an effort to answer the following research question.

> *How can collaborative supply chains aid low-carbon decision-making processes and address the triple bottom line in construction?*

14.2 LCA software failures and the importance of supply chain collaboration

One of the key shortcomings of current measurement software is that it is generally focused on the firm using it with a disregard of external supply chain inputs (Koh, *et al.*, 2013). One reason for this may be the myopic view adopted by construction projects, whereby the perception is that only those directly involved in the on-site project have any control over emissions calculations (Vrijhoef and Koskela, 2000). Emissions are generally assessed retrospectively and only if there is client demand (Poudelet *et al.*, 2012). Expanding the responsibility for CO_2 calculation across the construction supply chain, rather than concentrating solely on the firm carrying out the assessment could have significant and positive implications for carbon calculation and social sustainability.

The production of buildings which emit less carbon dioxide can have a positive effect on society by reducing respiratory health risks and climate change impacts (Evans and McCoy, 1998). In addition, the reduction in materials consumption via low-carbon selection would not only preserve materials for future generations but, additionally, protect the environment which would theoretically undergo reduced raw material extraction processes and environmental degradation (Shen *et al.*,

2010). The attainment of the TBL approach in the construction industry has been difficult, most likely due to the focus on cost to the detriment of environmental and social aspects of construction practice (Femenias *et al.*, 2009). The development of LCA technologies which require a capital cost outlay have not encouraged positive environmental change. They are often acknowledged as an unnecessary and additional cost, avoided to retain healthy profit margins (Yang and Chen, 2015). Furthermore, the retrospective analysis strategy is said to lead to ineffective and inaccurate measurement systems which disregard supply chain impacts; crucial for accurate emissions measurement data sharing and TBL (Poudelet *et al.*, 2012; Cheng *et al.*, 2001). The lack of understanding surrounding supply chain impacts has also been linked to the problematic linear nature of the chain which fragments key supply chain actors into singular entities, making the dissemination of environmental and social data problematic (Korneleus and Wamelink, 1998; Cheng, *et al.* 2001).

14.3 Building Information Modelling

As the evidence suggests, achieving sustainability through widespread engagement and collaboration enables organizations to gain support for sustainable practices throughout the entire supply chain, shaping a firm's stance on sustainability (Persson and Orlander, 2004). Communication flow has been found to be beneficial for encouraging sustainable practices (Jefferey, 2009). With this knowledge, the most recent and government-endorsed technology termed as Building Information Modelling (BIM) has been driven by its application as a collaborative tool. The key element is that it is not just a technology but also a process (Hardin, 2011; Azhar, *et al.*, 2009). Collaborative working is at the heart of the implementation of the BIM software system and its adoption has soared in both the UK and the USA. BIM is defined as:

A process that involves creating and using an intelligent 3D model to inform and communicate project decisions. Design, visualization, simulation, and collaboration enabled by Autodesk BIM solutions provide greater clarity for all stakeholders across the project lifecycle (Autodesk, 2013, paragraph 2).

BIM is seen by some as a revolutionary development which could have a significantly positive impact on the construction industry (Azhar *et al.*, 2009). The process element of the technology could also facilitate a collaboration platform in order for communication on issues such as social responsibility to take place (Hardin, 2011). The BIM "process" enables the management of data, potentially having far-reaching implications throughout the supply chain by assisting communication flows throughout the project and eradicating the need for retrospective environmental and social assessments. The main problem however is that despite acknowledgment and praise of BIM's collaboration element, the technology aspect regarding statistics and 3D drawing processes remains the most interesting aspect for those who use it (Azhar *et al.*, 2009; Hardin, 2011). Collaborative supply chain processes are essential for successful projects, therefore applying it to carbon calculation could increase success in sustainability (London and Singh, 2013). In addition, the benefit of a facilitated collaborative platform could encourage the multidisciplinary approach required in construction for environmental issues, thus easing the transition of a move towards implementing the TBL approach (Kiker *et al.*, 2005). BIM could aid multidisciplinary decision making by formulating a platform for stakeholders to manage data and make decisions in their specialisms within the project (Azhar *et al.*, 2009). The key challenge with the use of BIM appears to be encouraging users to focus on collaboration as well as technology.

The emphasis on software tools and increasing emissions levels has provided the impetus to initiate the move towards lifecycle assessment as a more rounded concept. There is a need to incorporate and utilise both technology and collaboration in decision-making processes to implement the TBL. The sheer number of practices encompassed in supply chain management is testament to this need (Burgess *et al.*, 2006). The lack of current progress towards the implementation of TBL suggests that technology alone will not solve this problem. The basis for using collaboration and communicative networks alongside technology for increased CO_2 emissions accuracy works on the assumption of increasing corporate social responsibility throughout the supply chain (Heiskanen, 2002; Lofgren *et al.*, 2011). Understanding the sustainability impacts of a supply chain must begin with collaboration. Enabling collaboration through technology allows multidisciplinary information sharing, useful for environmental decision making due to the differing range of expertise required in the process (Kiker *et al.*, 2005).

14.4 The construction supply chain

Construction practitioners are beginning to question traditional assumptions of their business practices, particularly in light of LCA software failures and the movement towards supply chain thinking in combating environmental problems (Gimenez and Tachizawa, 2012; Chen and Paulraj, 2004; Carter and Rogers, 2008). The emerging critical challenge for the construction industry is twofold; to understand how lifecycle data can be managed collaboratively throughout construction supply chains, aiding the low-carbon decision-making process and reducing social impacts, whilst simultaneously focusing on cost, quality and time (Florez *et al.*, 2013; Kurul *et al.*, 2012). Collaboration for sustainability requires the integration of supply chain actors and an assessment of the benefits of collaborative decision-making processes. Higher levels of communication are required in almost every aspect of construction and are particularly relevant and applicable to environmental issues. The multidisciplinary nature of environmental decision making requires information sharing (Kiker *et al.*, 2005). Sharing information is generally problematic in construction as the supply chain is linear in nature and so, therefore, discussions between actors at opposite ends of the chain do not readily occur. When addressing carbon outputs, the supply chain must be assessed in order to achieve accurate calculations and understand economic and social benefits (Janda, 2011). Currently, the nature of construction projects (design build and short term), coupled with supply chain structures, are inhibiting the development of sustained social networks (Cheng *et al.*, 2001; Korneleus and Wamelink, 1998; Xia *et al.*, 2013) which could be critical for supply chain-based LCA.

It is argued by Cheng *et al.* (2001) that the linear configuration of the supply chain (see Fig. 4.1) has inhibited the development of relationships. The formation of collaborative networks could theoretically aid the implementation of TBL via information sharing, a key component for implementing novel practice through education (Janda, 2011). The structure of the construction supply chain separates supply chain actors and divides each task into individual components (Kornelius and Wamelink, 1998). Each supply chain actor therefore performs as an individual thus creating personal objectives that often exclude multi-actor considerations. In essence, each decision is made for the benefit of the individual rather than the collective (Cheng *et al.*, 2001). The linear model also discourages coordination and communication (Cheng *et al.*, 2001). The supply chain structure may offer a rationale as to why environmental assessments in construction are carried out retrospectively; collecting data from the commencement of the project is often seen as too difficult as data is often unobtainable due to supply chain structures and limited collaboration (Poudelet *et al.*, 2012).

Figure 14.1 Typical construction supply chain
Source: authors

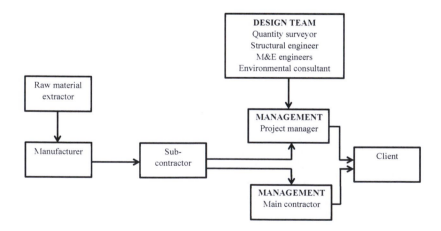

The literature surrounding emissions analysis, technology failures and the construction supply chain points towards shortcomings in collaboration as a significant barrier to the implementation of sustainability practices and the TBL. The focus on technology, a disregard of human interaction, linear supply chain processes and a lack of collaboration have all inhibited the development of a low-carbon construction approach. Therefore to develop an understanding of how integrated supply chain approaches could aid the implementation of the TBL empirical data was collected.

14.5 Methodology and data collection

To address the research question, empirical data was collected from a focus group with construction industry experts in 2014. The lack of scholarly evidence on supply chain collaboration to reduce CO_2 emissions and assess social and economic applications in construction necessitated the use of an inductive approach to data collection. Focus groups were therefore a useful method to explore the prospects for implementing the TBL approach. The focus group took the format of a round table discussion panel with a sample of five construction industry experts, who were environmental consultants, building surveyors, and LCA experts. Participants were chosen as experts in their respective fields and invited to the focus group via email, following university ethical approval guidelines. Twenty participants were invited, nine agreed to attend with five taking part on the day. The participation figure is close to academic recommendations which state six to twelve participants as the optimum number (Del-Rio Roberts, 2011).

Questions were asked by the authors of this chapter and the discussion was recorded. The recording was transcribed verbatim to facilitate data analysis. A number of thematic concepts were developed from an extensive review of the relevant literature prior to data collection, as shown in Table 14.1. The transcripts of the data were analyzed against these themes. The data was coded in line with key words from the academic literature using categories which encompassed TBL concepts such as "cost" "behavioural change", "supply chain", "collaboration", "social impact" and "BIM." Data from the focus group was used to assess whether the perceived CO_2 collaboration benefits elusive in the scholarly literature could help the construction industry to achieve the TBL; increasing profits, whilst simultaneously focusing on environmental and social costs.

Table 14.1 Summary of key literature themes

Overarching theme	TBL concept Ec. Env. Soc	Thematic concepts	Key references
BIM	Ec. Env.	Technology, collaboration, communication processes information exchange, design, multidisciplinary facilitation	Hardin, 2011 Azhar, *et al.*, 2009
Supply chain engagement and integration	Ec, Env, Soc	Inter-firm collaboration, green supply chains, data sharing, relationships, influence, networks, communication	Beamon, 1998 Cheng, *et al.*, 2001 Love, *et al.*, 2004
Collaboration	Env. Soc.	Influence, communication, relationships, integration, information sharing, team work, participation,	Dainty *et al.*, 2001 Briscoe and Dainty, 2005 Persson and Orlander, 2004
Behavioural change	Env. Soc.	New work strategies, changing thought processes	Male and Stocks, 1991 Janda, 2011
The client	Ec.	Power roles, key decision maker, traditional structures, finance, influence	Ahmed and Kangari, 1995 Ryd, 2014
Cost	Ec.	Cost minimization, supply chain selection, key decision making factor, cost quality, time	Sheu et al., 2005 Rodriguez-Melo and Mansouri, 2011
Social impacts	Soc.	Health, sustainable development, culture, triple bottom line, societal benefits	Evans and McCoy, 1998 Shen *et al.*, 2010 King, 2003 Tam, 2008 Tseng *et al.*, 2009

14.6 Results

Themes for the focus group were formulated via the assessment of TBL concepts and the relevant LCA literature. Table 14.1 highlights how these themes were derived from the literature. The establishment of themes prior to data collection taking place guided the research and confirmed an important gap in the literature. It established the need for further assessment in the reduction of the environmental and social impacts of buildings through an increase in collaborative working. The lack of integrated working strategies in the construction industry has arguably inhibited the development of emissions analysis and the TBL approach, supported by the data extracted from the focus group as shown in Table 14.2.

Table 14.2 Focus group data extraction

Overarching theme	Participant supporting quotes
BIM	"I think that's going to be the huge driver [of sustainability]...looking at the wider picture" "The driver for lifecycle going forward" "They are using it effectively in collaborative work" "BIM is going to revolutionize the industry" "The focus around BIM, amongst BIM users, is around the technology and the software" "We still continue to focus on technology and I think as an industry we need to focus on collaborative working"
Supply chain engagement	"You've got to look back...to the manufacturers in terms of what information they are providing" "If you get primary data from your supply chain, you can go in and change it" "It's having flexibility and reliability" [of information through collaboration] "The RIBA plan of work...encourages the designers to engage with stakeholders"
Collaboration	"We don't know the everything and anything...so it's that level of information which you have available [through collaboration]" "We are just not talking to each other" "We still continue to focus on technology and I think as an industry we need to focus on collaborative working" "Collaborative working is key" "Working together...the business isn't used to doing that...used to working in its own little silo and trying to break that down is quite difficult"
Behavioural change	"I think it's very much a behavioural change" "So I think there's more behavioural training at that level of the industry" "The case that I mentioned in the States, have a fascinating tenant agreement, so you might pay a slight premium for renting a property ... but then all your water, all your energy, is free, up to a certain point. If you go over that point you really get clobbered. So that sort of forcing behavioural change within the users as well" "Legislation will take it so far, because then it is behaviour"
Client power	"It's very much ... enlightening the client...the better understanding you have as a client, in terms of sustainability, and ...promoting that, then it effectively ...goes down the chain" "It depends what the drivers are in terms of you know whether it be cost or sustainability" "The [company] said we want one, there you go, they want one, they can have one" "They're not having anything super risky market because the market want what the market want" "We just get the green guide out and say do you really think you want to get that from there, this is the green guide ... no, no, you want that black, looks awful, but that's what they wanted, and they're paying the bill"

Overarching theme	Participant supporting quotes
Cost	"It depends what the drivers are in terms of you know whether it be cost or sustainability"
	"Obviously looking at the cost side, purely the costs, you know, discount and everything else, then that's a different obviously issue"
	"Yes, well I think in terms of … it's an interesting thing because I mean to say CO_2 and to say cost savings you know although it can be you know the same thing in essence, you know, it depends who you are speaking to"
	"Everybody's just looking for the cheapest option"
	"Lifecycle analysis has a capital cost depreciation going all the way down, you know, like I.T., it's out of date in five years"
	"There's a perception that green costs more"
	"We still have them but they've been hijacked by getting the lowest cost, rather than getting fit for purpose"
	"We saved about 20% cost. So it influenced the client to always want to be green and do the right thing"
Social impact	"In America people are getting better rental per foot square on greener buildings that are naturally ventilated, they all come off a district heating system"
	"Talking about sustainability in its wider sense, you know, it's the planet, it's the people"
	"A few projects within [company] for schools, six schools I think as well, they had a lot of questions on the working environment for the children"

The findings from the focus group were in line with the perceived gaps in the literature surrounding emissions analysis and its application to the TBL approach. The empirical analysis showed that between industry experts there is a clear understanding of the need for a more holistic approach to LCA. An approach that is capable of disseminating an understanding of social and economic values across the supply chain (Kuckuvar and Tatari, 2013). Interestingly, despite a clear understanding and acceptance of the potential for integrated supply chain approaches to increase social and environmental responsibility, technology underpinned the focus group discussion with continued reference to Building Information Modelling (BIM). The technological focus is highlighted by the frequency of themes as shown in Figure 14.2.

Figure 14.2 Frequency of themes (extracted from the empirical focus group findings)

Source: authors

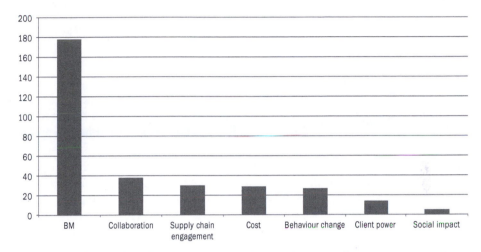

Figure 14.2 shows that despite key technology failures and an awareness of the importance of collaboration, the participants remained focussed on a technological solution to environmental concerns in the industry as emphasis was placed on BIM. BIM's importance provided a requirement for the inclusion of technology in future sustainability applications in the industry, as this appeared to be an area with which the industry was familiar and comfortable. BIM accounted for approximately 45% of the discussion in the focus group; collaboration and supply chain engagement, cost, behaviour change and client power followed. The final but small proportion of the discussion was taken up by social impacts thus indicating a lack of attention on this in construction supply chains. These findings suggest that any future applications for the implementation of the TBL may require some technological input simply to gain acceptance in the construction industry. In the case of BIM, its ability to behave as a collaborative platform may be its most beneficial application to sustainability. Whilst maintaining the technological solution preference in the industry, it also provides a solution for increased collaboration.

A further important sustainability driver is the emphasis on the client and the power that they hold (see Table 14.2). The importance of the client is particularly influential in the development of a collaborative approach to sustainability in the construction industry. The client is the central character in the supply chain and remains the cornerstone of stakeholder relationships which could influence a TBL approach to construction (Ryd, 2014; Gatignon and Robertson 1985).

14.7 Reflecting on collaboration

This chapter proposes a networked supply chain approach to increase collaboration and implement TBL (Cheng *et al.*, 2001). Increased communication flow could proliferate multidirectional supply chain influence, increasing the client's ability to make more informed low-carbon decisions through increased information (Albanese, 1994). As the findings show, often the client was guided by cost and all decisions were centred on finance (Yang and Chen, 2015). Evidence suggests however that some clients from certain construction sectors are more inclined to act responsibly towards society and the environment. Public buildings in the UK, for example, are subject to EU procurement regulations, which include the Social Value Act (2012). The Act ensures that those who commission public services consider the social and environmental costs of their practices as well as the economic impacts (Cabinet Office, 2012). The Social Value Act provides an indication that some UK construction companies are addressing the TBL and remaining competitive, although the pressures to do so are being driven by external regulation (Hart, 1995; Rodriguez-Melo and Mansouri, 2011; Florez *et al.*, 2013). The Social Value Act however only requires consideration of impact rather than a full TBL approach. The limited references to the social impact of construction highlighted that it is not a high construction priority, but one which could be implemented via sustainability—potentially through the increase of collaborative networks.

14.7.1 Construction collaboration and CO_2

The research has shown that the most beneficial enabler for implementing the TBL in the construction industry is the application of collaborative supply chain networks through influence and technology. To answer the research question of how collaborative supply chains can aid low-carbon decision-making processes and implement the TBL, the focus must remain on collaborative approaches. Creating symbiotic relationships via integrated construction supply chains could increase the success of the implementation of the TBL (Stock *et al.*, 2010). The TBL requires high levels of interacting forces (Ahi and Searcy, 2015; Yakovleva *et al.*, 2012). The linear supply chain in construction has inhibited the process by which TBL is most successful by reducing interaction, supported by the supply chain evidence in Table 14.2. The management of organizational supply chains has evolved into the study of material and information flows, within and between companies, expanding the number of activities addressed using supply chain considerations. This is highly applicable to the TBL approach which requires the acknowledgement of several factors for its successful implementation (Cooper *et al.*, 1997).

Supply chain study is beneficial to the adoption of sustainability in the construction industry as it is based on multi-organizational and multidisciplinary decision making (Kiker *et al.*, 2005). The evolution of the supply chain could aid the development of sustainable practice in the construction industry via the TBL approach, which could be achieved through the incorporation of information flows and influ-ential inter-organizational relationships (Stock *et al.*, 2010; Wong *et al.*, 2012; Trent, 2004). An integrated approach could not only aid the low-carbon decision-making process and increase social responsibility through information exchange but also resolve conflict and increase efficiency leading to economic gains (Cheng *et al.*, 2001; Love *et al.*, 2004). With collaboration between construction supply chain actors seen as minimal at best, occurring primarily at the design stage (Basbagill *et al.*, 2013), the chain has remained fragmented making multidisciplinary deci-sion making problematic. A reason for this is that TBL focus requires a holistic and interdisciplinary approach to social, economic and environmental issues via sup-ply chains (Ahi and Searcy, 2015).

The implementation of a TBL approach in construction would not be without difficulty. Studies have shown an array of problems that inhibit progress towards sustainability in a supply chain context including the desire to reduce costs and management of risk (Green and Morton, 1996; Walker *et al.*, 2008). In construction, capital cost and risk management are key drivers and are arguably the two concepts that inhibit the development of innovative strategy (Martins and Terblanche, 2003; Abderisak and Lindahl, 2015). Additionally, the client has the power to influence the entire project, taking the central position in the chain held in place by the hier-archical supply chain structure (Rosinski *et al.*, 2014; Dirix *et al.*, 2013). Any imple-mentation of new strategies would need to be implemented by the key innovator and decision maker (Ryd, 2014). The two final inhibitors are collaboration (Klassen and Vachon, 2003) and supply chain integration (Vachon and Klassen, 2006). The lack of both components in current global construction systems has inhibited the development of environmentally and socially-sustainable practices, due to frag-mented components and individual supply chain goals (Ahi and Searcy, 2015).

14.8 Towards a solution

Based on the literature and empirical findings in this chapter, the argument is that greater social, economic and environmental benefits could be achieved via col-laborative supply chains that implement the TBL approach. The dissemination of information between supply chain actors and increasing collaboration, integration and communication flow could provide the means to educate and inform mem-bers of the chain about low-carbon options and socially-responsible actions. A strategy such as this could increase the reach of influential relationships (Dubois and Gadde, 2002). It is these relationships that can aid the spread of the TBL approach through collaborative supply chain networks (Coelho and Novaes, 2008; Singh *et al.*, 2011). The implementation of collaborative networks would theoreti-cally provide a low-cost solution to the emissions problem as it would eliminate the need for consistently implementing new data systems. The ability to change working practices could be much more beneficial than a technological approach as the ability to change behaviour has greater impacts (McKenzie-Mohr, 2011). Perhaps the key technology applicable to this research was the implementation of BIM, a global model built for a global construction system set to revolutionise the industry (Azhar *et al.*, 2011). With BIM uptake increasing in the USA, China and the UK, alongside its backing from global governments (HM Government, 2012; Shapiro, 2014), the process element of BIM could be beneficial to the collaborative approach for identifying social, environmental and economic benefits in construction. It has the potential to provide a facilitated platform using the construction supply chain and highlighting its importance as a collaborative entity in achieving the TBL (Love *et al.*, 1999).

14.9 Conclusion

This chapter has addressed how collaborative supply chains could act as an enabler for low-carbon decision-making strategies and the implementation of the TBL in the construction industry. It has addressed failures of technological LCA and the benefits of a collaborative supply chain approach. The extant literature highlighted a paucity of research in supply chain integration directly related to construction emissions analysis. Although our study is limited to UK construction participants and was carried out on a small scale, it is able to provide a preliminary analysis of supply chain contributions to the TBL in the construction industry. Evidence from the focus group findings provides support for the need for an integrated approach to lowering emissions, increasing sustainability and reducing the social impact of buildings while maintaining a focus on finance. The potential solution was found to be a holistic approach to TBL concepts, encompassing behavioural, supply chain and technological approaches. A solution such as this could be implemented to ease the transition to socially and environmentally-driven construction. A leaning towards maintaining traditional technological methods with the implementation of collaborative processes could be the most successful way to achieve acceptance of the TBL approach in global construction industries.

References

Abanda, F.H., Tah, J.H.M., & Cheung, F.K.T. (2013). Mathematical modelling of embodied energy, greenhouse gases, waste, time–cost parameters of building projects: A review. *Building and Environment, 59*(0), 23-37.

Abderisak, A., & Lindahl, G. (2015). Take a chance on me? Construction client's perspectives on risk management. *Procedia Economics and Finance, 21*, 548-554.

Ahi, P., & Searcy, C. (2015). Assessing sustainability in the supply chain: A triple bottom line approach. *Applied Mathematical Modelling*, 39(10), 2882-2896.

Ahmed, S.M. & Kangari, R. (1995). Analysis of client-satisfaction factors in construction industry. *Journal of Management in Engineering*, 11(2), 36-44.

Albanese, R. (1994). Team-building process: Key to better project results. *Journal of Management in Engineering*, 10(6), 36-44.

Asif, M., Muneer, T., & Kelly, R. (2007). Life cycle assessment: A case study of a dwelling home in Scotland. *Building and Environment*, 42(3), 1391-1394.

AutoDesk (2013). *Building Information Modelling*. [Online] Available at http://www.autodesk.com/solutions/building-information-modeling/overview. [Accessed 10/07/15]

Azhar, S., Brown, J., & Farooqui., R. (2009). BIM-based Sustainability Analysis: An Evaluation of Building Performance Analysis Software. *Proceedings of the 45th ASC Annual Conference.*

Basbagill, J., Flager, F., Lepech, M., & Fischer. M. (2013). Application of life-cycle assessment to early stage building design for reduced embodied environmental impacts. *Building and Environment*, 60, 81-92.

Beamon, B.M. (1998). Supply chain design and analysis: Models and methods. International *Journal of Production Economics*, 55(3), 281-294.

Briscoe, G. & Dainty. A., (2005). Construction supply chain integration: an elusive goal? *Supply Chain Management: An International Journal*, 10(4), 319-326.

Burgess, K., Singh, P., & Koroglu, R. (2006). Supply chain management: A structured literature review and implications for future research. *International Journal of Operations and Production Management*, 26(7), 703-729.

Cabinet Office (2012) Social Value Act. *TSO publishing London* [online document] Available at http://www.legislation.gov.uk/ukpga/2012/3/pdfs/ukpga_20120003_en.pdf [Accessed 01.07.15]

Carter, C.R., & Rogers, D.S. (2008). A framework of sustainable supply chain management: Moving toward new theory. *International Journal of Physical Distribution & Logistics Management*, 38(5), 360-387.

Chen, I.J., & Paulraj, A. (2004). Towards a theory of supply chain management: The constructs and measurements. *Journal of Operations Management*, 22(2), 119-150.

Cheng, E.W.L., Li, H., Love, P.E.D., & Irani, Z. (2001). An e business model to support supply chain activities in construction. *Logistics Information Management*, 14(1/2): 68-78.

Coelho, C.S. & Novaes, C.S. (2008). *Construction for Information Modelling (BIM) and Collaborative Environments for Project Management in Construction*. National Workshop Design Process Management in Building Construction.

Cooper, M.C., Lambert, D.M., & Pagh, J.D. (1997). Supply chain management: More than a new name for logistics. *The International Journal of Logistics Management*, 8(1), 1-14.

Dainty, A.R.J., Millett, S.J., & Briscoe., G.H., (2001). New perspectives on construction supply chain integration. *Supply Chain Management: An International Journal*, 6(4), 163-173.

Del Rio-Roberts, M. (2011). How I learned to conduct focus groups. *Qualitative Report*, 16(1), 312-315.

Dirix, J., Peeters, W., Eyckmans, J., Jones, P.T., & Sterckx, S. (2013). Strengthening bottom-up and top-down climate governance. *Climate Policy*, 13(3), 363-383.

Dubois, A. & Gadde, L.E. (2002). The construction industry as a loosely coupled system: Implications for productivity and innovation. *Construction Management & Economics*, 20(7), 621-631.

Elkington, J. (1997). *Cannibals with Forks: The Triple Bottom Line of the 21st Century*. Oxford: Capstone.

Evans, G.W. & McCoy, J. M. (1998). When buildings don't work: The role of architecture in human health. *Journal of Environmental Psychology*, 18(1), 85-94.

Femenias, P., Kadefors, A., & Edén, M. (2009). The demonstration project as a tool for client driven innovation: Exploring the possibilities from a Swedish perspective. In *Proceeding from the international conference Changing Roles; New Roles, New Challenges*. Noordwijk an Zee, The Netherlands, 5-9 October 2009 (pp. 199-210).

Florez, L., Castro, D., & Irizarry, J., (2013). Measuring sustainability perceptions of construction materials. *Construction Innovation: Information, Process, Management*, 13(2), 217-234.

Gatignon, H., & Robertson, T.S. (1985). A propositional inventory for new diffusion research. *Journal of Consumer Research*, 11 4), 849-867.

Gimenez, C., & Tachizawa, E.M. (2012). Extending sustainability to suppliers: A systematic literature review. *Supply Chain Management: An International Journal*, 17(5), 531-543.

Green, K., Morton, B., & New, S. (1996). Purchasing and environmental management: Interactions, policies and opportunities. *Business Strategy and the Environment*, 5(3), 188-197.

Hardin, B. (2011). *BIM and Construction Management: Proven Tools, Methods, and Workflows*. John Wiley & Sons.

Hart, S.L. (1995). A natural-resource-based view of the firm. *Academy of Management Review*, 20(4), 986-1014.

Heijungs, R., Huppes, G., & Guinée, J. (2009). *A scientific framework for LCA. Deliverable (D15) of work package*, 2. CALCAS project. [online] Available at: http://www.leidenuniv.nl/cml/ssp/publications/calcas_report_d15.pdf [Accessed 05.07.15]

Heiskanen, E. (2002). The institutional logic of life cycle thinking. *Journal of Cleaner Production*, 10(5), 427-437.

HM Government. (2012) Department of Business Innovation and Skills, Industrial strategy: government and industry in partnership. *Building Information Modelling*. [Online Article] [Available at] http://uk.practicallaw.com/0-522-8823?source=relatedcontent [Accessed 04.07.15]

Janda, K.B. (2011). Buildings don't use energy: people do. Architectural Science Review 54(1), 15-22.

Jeffery, N. (2009). *Stakeholder engagement: A road map to meaningful engagement*. [Online article] available at http://www.som.cranfield.ac.uk/som/dinamic-content/media/CR%20Stakeholder.pdf [accessed 1.07.15]

Kiker, G.A., Bridges, T.S., Varghese, A., Seager, T.P. & Linkov, I. (2005). Application of multicriteria decision analysis in environmental decision making. *Integrated Environmental Assessment and Management*,1(2), 95-108.

King, A.D. (Ed.). (2003). *Buildings and Society: Essays on the Social Development of the Built Environment*. London: Routledge.

Klassen, R.D., & Vachon, S. (2003). Collaboration and evaluation in the supply chain: The impact on plant level environmental investment. *Production and Operations Management*, 12(3), 336-352.

Koh, S.C.L., Genovese, A., Acquaye, A. & Barratt, P. (2013). Decarbonising product supply chains: design and development of an integrated evidence-based decision support system—the supply chain environmental analysis tool (SCEnAT). *International Journal of Production Research*, 51(7), 2092-2109

Kornelius. L., & Wamelink, J.W.F., (1998), The virtual corporation: Learning from construction, *Supply Chain Management: An International Journal*, 3(4), 193-202.

Kucukvar, M., & Tatari, O. (2013). Towards a triple bottom-line sustainability assessment of the US construction industry. *The International Journal of Life Cycle Assessment*, 18(5), 958-972.

Kurul, E., Tah, J. H., &Cheung, F. (2012). Does the UK built environment sector have the institutional capacity to deliver sustainable development? *Architectural Engineering and Design Management*. 8(1), 42-54.

London, K. & V. Singh (2013). Integrated construction supply chain design and delivery solutions. *Architectural Engineering & Design Management*, 9(3), 135-157.

Love, P.E., Irani, Z., & Edwards, D.J. (2004). A seamless supply chain management model for construction. *Supply Chain Management: An International Journal*, 9(1), 43-56.

Love, P.E., Li, H., & Mandal, P. (1999). Rework: A symptom of a dysfunctional supply-chain. *European Journal of Purchasing & Supply Management*, 5(1), 1-11.

Male, S. & Stocks, R., (1991). *Competitive Advantage in Construction*. Oxford: Butterworth Heinemann.

Martins, E. C. and Terblanche. F., (2003). Building organisational culture that stimulates creativity and innovation. *European Journal of Innovation Management*, 6(1), 64-74.

McKenzie Mohr, D. (2000). New ways to promote pro environmental behaviour: promoting sustainable behaviour: an introduction to community based social marketing. *Journal of Social Issues*, 56(3), 543-554.

Monghasemi, S., Nikoo, M.R., Fasaee, M.A.K., & Adamowski, J. (2015). A novel multi criteria decision making model for optimizing time–cost–quality trade-off problems in construction projects. *Expert Systems with Applications*, 42(6), 3,089-3,104.

Persson, U. & Olander, S., (2004). Methods to estimate stakeholder views of sustainability for construction projects. *Proceedings from the 21st International Conference Passive and low energy architecture, Built environment and environmental buildings*.

Poudelet, V., Chayer, J.A., Margni, M., Pellerin, R., & Samson, R (2012). A process-based approach to operationalize life cycle assessment through the development of an eco-design decision-support system. *Journal of Cleaner Production*, 33(0), 192-201.

Ramesh, T., Prakash, R., & Shukla, K.K., (2010). *Life cycle energy analysis of buildings: An overview. Energy and Buildings*, 42(10), 1,592-1,600.

Rodriguez Melo, A. & S.A. Mansouri (2011). Stakeholder engagement: Defining strategic advantage for sustainable construction. *Business Strategy and the Environment*, 20(8), 539-552.

Rosinski, J., Klich, J., Filipkowska, A., & Pettinger, R. (2014). Top-down and bottom-up approach to competence management implementation: A case of two central banks. *Tourism & Management Studies*, 10(Special), 26-34.

Ryd, N. (2014). Facilitating construction briefing–from the client's perspective. *Nordic Journal of Surveying and Real Estate Research*, 1(1), 86-100.

Shapiro, G. (2014). Setting a standard: The United States is behind in embracing national BIM guidelines. Here's a look at the industry leaders who are trying to effect change and why architects should care. *Architect*. 103(4), 80 [online serial] Accessed 13.07.15.

Shen, L.Y., Tam, V.W., Tam, L., & Ji, Y.B. (2010). Project feasibility study: The key to successful implementation of sustainable and socially responsible construction management practice. *Journal of Cleaner Production*, 18(3), 254-259.

Sheu, J.B., Chou, Y.H., & Hu, C.C. (2005). An integrated logistics operational model for green-supply chain management. *Transportation Research Part E: Logistics and Transportation Review*. 41(4), 287-313.

Singh, B., Strømman, A H., & Hertwich, E.G. (2011). Comparative impact assessment of CCS portfolio: Life cycle perspective. *Energy Procedia*, 4, 2486-2493.

Stock, J.R., Boyer, S.L., & Harmon, T. (2010). Research opportunities in supply chain management. *Journal of the Academy of Marketing Science*, 38(1), 32-41.

Tam, W.Y.V. (2008). Economic comparison of concrete recycling: A case study approach. *Resources. Conservation and Recycling*, 52. 821-828.

Trent, R.J. (2004). What everyone needs to know about SCM. *Supply Chain Management Review*, 8(2), 52-59.

Tseng, M.L. Yuan-Hsu, L., Chiu A.S.F. (2009). Fuzzy AHP based study of cleaner production implementation in Taiwan PWB manufacturer. *Journal of Cleaner Production*, 17, 1249-56.

Vachon, S., & Klassen, R.D. (2006). Extending green practices across the supply chain: The impact of upstream and downstream integration. *International Journal of Operations & Production Management*, 26(7), 795-821.

Vrijhoef, R. and Koskela, L. (2000). The four roles of supply chain management in construction. *European Journal of Purchasing & Supply Management*, 6(3), 169-178.

Walker, H., Di Sisto, L., & McBain, D. (2008). Drivers and barriers to environmental supply chain management practices: Lessons from the public and private sectors. *Journal of Purchasing and Supply Management*, 14(1), 69-85.

Wong, C.W.Y., Lai, K., Shang, K.C., Lu, C.S., & Leung, T.K.P. (2012). Green operations and the moderating role of environmental management capability of suppliers on manufacturing firm performance. *International Journal of Production Economics*, 140(1), 283-294.

Xia, B., Molenaar, K., Chan, A., Skitmore, M., & Zuo, J. (2013). Determining optimal proportion of design in design-build request for proposals. *Journal of Construction Engineering and Management*, 139(6), 620-627.

Yakovleva, N., Sarkis, J., & Sloan, T. (2012). Sustainable benchmarking of supply chains: The case of the food industry. *International Journal of Production Research*, 50(5), 1,297-1,317.

Yang, J.B. and C.C. Chen (2015). Causes of budget changes in building construction projects: An empirical study in Taiwan. *Engineering Economist*, 60(1), 1-21.

Emily Jervis is a Lecturer in Environmental Technology based at the University of Wolverhampton School of Architecture and the Built Environment. Emily's key research interests are in the application of supply chain based approaches to low-carbon decision making in the construction industry.

Claire Moxham is Senior Lecturer in Operations Management at the University of Liverpool Management School. Claire's research interests are broadly in the area of performance improvement, particularly in the context of public and non-profit organizations.

Joanne Meehan is a Senior Lecturer in Strategic Purchasing at the University of Liverpool Management School. Jo's research interests cover power and value in buyer–seller relationships, sustainability in social housing networks and public procurement collaboration. Her background in industry includes 11 years in purchasing management for a blue-chip multinational organization.

15

Value chain connectedness as a framework for sustainability governance

Mark Heuer

Sigmund Weis School of Business at Susquehanna University, USA

Rapid advances in communications technology, coupled with high-profile natural disasters and garment factory accidents in developing countries, have focused attention on value chain governance, as well as the environmental, social and economic performance of lead firms in value chains. Three heuristic models of value chain connectedness discussed in this chapter differentiate governance based on interdependence, trust and power. These models illustrate how global economic transactions in value chains can influence the social and environmental well-being of stakeholders in a uniquely pervasive manner, not dissimilar to the impact of nation-states prior to the ascendance of neo-liberalism. By focusing on the ready made garment (RMG) industry, where several high-profile factory accidents have occurred, this chapter illustrates the implications of value chain governance, particularly involving relationships between developed country lead firms and suppliers in developing countries. The three models provide practical guidance on how managing governance in value chains through different types of connectedness can influence social, environmental and economic results.

15.1 Introduction and background

The March 2011 tsunami in Japan, followed by massive flooding in Thailand, laid bare the vulnerability of global supply chains. Indeed, The Wall Street Journal described 2011 as the "Year of the Oops", partially due to the massive disintegration of tightly managed supply chains that global companies spent years constructing but which took natural disasters mere days to break apart (Mattioli, 2012, p. B5). Moreover, for several months following these disasters, industries as disparate as automobiles and computers struggled with supply shortages. More recent natural disasters, such as the devastation Hurricane Sandy dealt to New York City, the global financial centre, underscore the interconnected nature of global value chains from environmental, social and economic perspectives.

Global value chains connect organizations through various combinations and interrelationships in order to transact business across disparate geographies. In this respect, connectedness in global value chains refers to the interactions among the participants in the value chain and can be explained based on types of trust, power and interdependence. Overall, connectedness can explain values underpinning economic transactions in the value chains that may have social and environmental implications (Dicken, 2015, pp. 58-60). With greater availability of transparency regarding value chain transactions and the resulting oversight, the environmental and social performance resulting from value chain transactions has elevated the importance of concepts such as connectedness.

While natural disasters inflict increasingly severe global consequences, the economic effects from the recent natural disasters may only be outward symptoms of more systemic sustainability issues. With globalization, value chains are an indispensable tool for connecting global transactions across disparate geographies, cultures and business climates. As such, they act as an indicator of environmental, social and economic sustainability. Malik *et al.* (2011, p. 6) suggest that "the ability of supply chains to withstand a variety of different, complex scenarios could influence the profitability, and even viability, of organizations in the not too distant future". They note how the rapid commercialization of technology and communication techniques in supporting economic aspects of globalization has spawned complex environmental and social interconnections. These interconnections pose greater risks for organizations as technology, especially provenance (source of production) capabilities, support greater transparency, or the ability to track, analyze and evaluate the performance of value chain participants. For example, where retailers previously could source products through opaque transactions from contractors in countries with lax environmental and labour practices, third party entities can now track entire transactions across global value chains with greater efficiency and accuracy. This allows NGOs to assign responsibility for social and environmental performance to the lead firms in value chains, as well as contractors in developing countries.

While the terms "supply chain" and "value chain" are often used interchange-ably, they differ in that a supply chain involves transferring products or materials to a final point without value add, while a value chain adds value at various points (Gereffi *et al.*, 2005). The value add in value chains underscores its growing com-plexity, which implies increased risk in terms of environmental, social and eco-nomic performance. With globalization and the intense competitive pressures it entails, firms have increasingly externalized transactions and outsourced produc-tion and service requirements to disparate geographies. As more capabilities and requirements are outsourced, the risk of performance shortcomings has increased, particularly with greater transparency and expectations for social and environ-mentally-responsible performance. The increased risk necessitates governance involving coordination between parties often distant geographically, culturally and financially. Governance in this context defined as the "organization of ties between various actors engaged in a global value chain (GVC)" (Seuring and Müller, 2008). This lends urgency to a strategic focus by managers given the indispensability of GVCs, the accessibility of technology to measure performance and the increased acceptance of standards such as ISO 14001 and ISO 26000, all of which elevate the relevance of triple bottom line performance (Humphrey and Schmitz, 2004). While this increased focus relates to various categories of GVCs, this chapter considers the buyer-driven GVC, more specifically the ready made garment (RMG) industry, thereby building on Gereffi's (1999) detailed analysis of value chains in the textile industry.

The RMG industry exemplifies the challenges involved in pursuing the finan-cial rewards offered in locating production in developing countries with low labour costs and lax safety and environmental regulation, while also risking damage to retailer brand reputation should social and environmental problems get publi-cized. The value chain in the RMG industry typically involves a lead firm, such as a global retailer headquartered in a developed country, and suppliers in low wage, developing countries. Seuring and Müller (2008, p. 1,699) define lead companies as usually:

- Governing the supply chain

- Providing direct contact to the customer, and

- Designing the product or service offered.

This chapter examines the relationships in GVCs between lead firms and suppli-ers in the buyer-driven model by focusing on the 2013 Rana Plaza tragedy in Bang-ladesh in which 1,100 garment workers perished when the factory they worked in collapsed. The Bangladesh tragedy underscores how arm's length, third-party contracts characteristic of the garment industry often lack the involvement of the major retailers who tend to be the buying firms. In the case of the Bangladesh trag-edy, several global firms submitted orders for garments through arm's length trans-actions to third-party contractors, some of whom reportedly responded to urgent delivery requirements by using unapproved factories. One commentator observed that, as tragic as the accident was, it was not unexpected, given the more than 1,000 deaths over the previous decade in the booming RMG sector (Tripathi, 2013).

This tragic outcome illustrates the risks inherent in arm's length, third-party transactions in value chains characterized by asymmetric power relationships between the retailers and the contractors (Table 15.1). In the RMG value chain, contractors in low-wage countries, such as Bangladesh, Cambodia and Vietnam, are on the receiving end of a market-based governance process involving large, rush orders in response to the "fast fashion" phenomenon among retailers emphasizing fashion-trendy, price-conscious clothing. Because the contractors do not add value beyond basic production in fulfilling their orders, retailers typically can shift production easily to alternate contractors willing to accept responsibility for meeting short production deadlines.

While the power asymmetry in the RMG value chain imposes the immediate risk to the contractor of either losing a large order or accepting an order that cannot be fulfilled in the stipulated lead time without involving subcontractors who may not be approved by the retailer, the retailer also faces increased risk in the market-based approach. When the interdependent relationships in the value chain are primarily transactional, as in the power dominant connectedness model (see Table 15.1), lead firms lack either the relational dominant or structural dominant connectedness with value chain partners to receive competitive intelligence and respond proactively to potential threats or opportunities. While a value chain approach based on third-party contractors may provide access to low-cost, lightly regulated production, the resulting lack of relationship development through either repetitive transactions (relational dominant) or strong partnering (structural dominant) limits the lead firm's ability to manage the GVC. Thus, from a strictly transactional and financial perspective, lead firms using arm's-length contracting with third parties (i.e. power dominant) in the RMG industry offers access to low wage labour which allows for high profits and low retail pricing, yet it has the consequence of posing unmanaged risk to the brand reputation of the firm.

Table 15.1 Taxonomy of value chain connectedness models

| Constructs | Type of connectedness | | |
	Power dominant	Relational dominant	Structural dominant
Trust	Calculative	Prediction	Intentionality
Governance	Transactions are discrete, market based	Transactions are recurrent, knowledge based	Transactions are relational, values based
Power	Asymmetrical	Symmetrical	Informal contracting
Dependence-interdependence	Asymmetric dependence	Mutual dependence	Strategic interdependence

In addition to examining the role of lead firms in GVCs in this chapter, three models are developed to examine how firms connect in value chains (Table 15.1). The purpose of these models is to enable managers of lead firms to better understand the ramifications of different types of coordination and connectedness in GVCs. By viewing decision-making and strategy from a value chain perspective, managers can better understand the strategic implications of different types of value chain connectedness as an alternative to more traditional, firm-centric strategies. Overall, the objective is for managers to better understand how to deal proactively with global environmental and social outcomes, as the increasing use of provenance allows "customers, governments, and NGOs to demand greater transparency and accountability regarding environmental and social performance" (Andersen and Skjoett-Larsen, 2009, p. 77).

15.2 Factors influencing value chains

Information and communication technology makes sourcing of supplies from different firms in multiple jurisdictions possible, including countries with lower environmental standards (Lang, 2002, p. 177). However, with this global technological reach have come increasing demands from consumers, governments and firms regarding provenance and the technology to track the origin of products. As New (2010, p. 76) observes "consumers, governments, and companies are demanding details about the systems and sources that deliver the goods. Farsighted organizations are directly addressing new threats and opportunities presented by the question, 'Where does all this stuff come from?'"

Essentially, value chain transparency can fill gaps which governments, bound by geography, cannot, or will not, address globally. Transparency and the growing stakeholder focus on social and environmental performance may ultimately inflict discipline on firms more effectively than government regulation by impacting on the reputation of firms and the value of their brand. Information and communications technology has informed societal consciousness about the environmental and social consequences of globalization's excesses. Natural disasters have illuminated societal and environmental degradation and forced humanity to recognize that these disasters do not discriminate among developed and developing countries, or rich and poor. Thus, while typhoons in Asia may have once been a distant problem when communication lacked the immediacy of today, the connection between natural disasters and environmental, social and economic consequences is now transparent and an undisputable reality.

In general, value chains based on short-term transactional relationships (i.e. power dominant connectedness) lack the end-to-end visibility needed to support shifts in the domain environment and inevitably lead to product and project imitation due to a lack of continued innovation and forward thinking. The result is commoditization and transactional, instead of strategic, competition. More broadly, Porter and Kramer (2011, p. 64) bemoan the fact that firms "continue to view value creation narrowly [...] optimizing short-term financial performance in a bubble while missing the most important customer needs and ignoring the broader influences that determine their longer-term success." They conclude that most firms remain stuck in a "social responsibility" mind-set in which societal issues are at the periphery, not the core.

15.3 Value chain connectedness models

Driven by rising costs, shorter life-cycles and intensified international competition, the focus for creating dynamic capabilities among many lead firms has narrowed to product and brand development, while outsourcing other functions to suppliers. In the RMG industry, developing country suppliers have been limited to low-skill production (power dominant connectedness), which creates barriers for developing country firms seeking to upgrade skills and production through the relational dominant or structural dominant connectedness models (Table 15.1) (Gereffi *et al.*, 2001, p. 8).

As mentioned previously, Table 15.1 entails three types of connectedness which differentiate relationships among participants in GVCs based on trust, interdependence and power. Trust characterizes the interaction among value chain participants. Governance is differentiated by the three types of trust in Table 15.1 and defined by Doney *et al.* (1998, p. 604) as calculative, prediction and intentionality. Calculative trust involves opportunism and maximizing self-interest, while prediction trust assumes consistent and predictable behaviour. Intentionality trust requires an overriding focus on collective efforts and a motivation to seek joint gain.

The governance constructs in Table 15.1 utilize Gereffi *et al.* (2005, p. 83) and are defined as follows:

- Market based (lead firm sets supplier standards and can utilize substitute suppliers because of low switching costs)

- Modular networks (lead firm focuses on value-add activities but involves a limited number of suppliers producing commoditized aspects of products), and

- Relational networks (lead firm and key suppliers jointly innovate and one or both may make asset-specific investments).

Kaplinsky and Morris (2002, p. 32) refer to market-based transactions as a "low-trust chain in which suppliers are frequently changed to pursue short-term price advantages" in which failure to perform leads to rapid exclusion from the value chain. In contrast, high-trust relationships, more common in relational approaches, "tend to be associated with long-lived relationships".

To further define value chain connectedness, power and dependence–interdependence constructs (Table 15.1) interact in that the less dependent a lead firm is on other firms in a value chain, the greater its power to control inter-firm actions in the value chain. Lead firms favour developing their core competences around intangibles in the value chain, which then become a source of power. In addition to imposing sanctions on value chain participants for non-performance, they can also decide to withhold or share intangibles with their suppliers. The denial or access to intangibles influences the degree of connectedness and the ability of partner firms to upgrade production capabilities and skills (Gereffi *et al.*, 2001, p. 8). The RMG industry typically is controlled by large retailers who respond to the "fast fashion" dictates of rapid style changes by directing large orders with short lead times to suppliers in Bangladesh or other developing countries, such as Cambodia or Vietnam. In response to the transactional, calculating trust nature of the relationship with retailers, Huq *et al.* (2014) found that suppliers in Bangladesh have engaged in "mock" compliance in safety audits following the Rana Plaza tragedy by keeping two sets of books for auditors.

Related to the power construct, asymmetric dependent relationships in value chains tend to involve a power-dominant firm, such as a lead firm, which exercises influence based on an authority relationship or through other forms of influence, such as the power to exercise sanctions. For example, following the Rana Plaza tragedy, Walmart adopted a zero tolerance policy in which any supplier found in violation of safety or labour regulations would no longer be eligible for Walmart contracts. However, mutual dependence assumes that firms in a value chain are dependent on one another and the relationship is generally symmetrical (Pfeffer and Salancik, 1978). Firms connect where there is mutual dependence because they need each other and cheating on one value chain partner will harm both firms and perhaps others in the value chain. With mutual dependence, firms often express their commitment by making mutual investments in their relationship. In contrast to Walmart's zero-tolerance policy, a group of European retailers, including H&M, agreed to work with suppliers found to be non-compliant with safety and labour requirements and pledged funding to assist suppliers in achieving compliance. Strategic interdependence is based on the relational contracting model, in which exchange relationships evolve based on shared values and informal contracting approaches (Frazier, 1983; Dwyer *et al.*, 1987; Heide and John, 1992). In the RMG industry, strategic interdependence would involve retailers in joint product and marketing development with suppliers and other participants in the GVC. With mutual dependence and strategic interdependence, power is based on embeddedness concepts rather than on authority, as is the case with asymmetric dependence (Hess, 2008, p. 455).

In terms of the power construct, the lead firm uses authority-based power in the power dominant model to control contractors and suppliers, which are dependent on the lead firm for access to value chain participation. The lead firm has access to multiple suppliers, possesses asymmetric power and utilizes calculative trust. This model typifies third-party transactions as in the case of the RMG industry.

In the relational dominant model, the lead firm recognizes the value of limited joint planning and investing in relationship-specific assets. The parties involved have a "trust but verify" approach through the use of formal and informal controls, as well as knowledge-based trust.

In the structural dominant model, the relationship involves high risk and vulnerability. However, the lead firm and other partners in the value chain accept this condition because the collective interests available through relational contracting exceed those available individually. The relationship involves an intentional strategy of interdependence based on informal (social) controls which support embedded relationships among the lead firm and upstream and downstream value chain participants.

15.4 Context, culture and communication: contingency factors

While there could be many contingency factors selected to explain value chain connectedness, in this chapter three factors are selected for further discussion: context (turbulence), culture and communication (Heuer, 2001). The global context of the world economy involves increasing complexity with unintended consequences environmentally, socially and economically. This results in turbulence and dynamic change which imposes risk and uncertainty in decision making and strategy. In a turbulent environment, modular and relational networks would tend to be more resilient than market-based relationships. Where value chain participants can predict performance and there is a commitment, or intention, to support other participants based on trust, performance will tend to exceed market-based, or contractual, relationships. Relational networks should be the most reliable value chain relationship in a turbulent environment because investments have been made in the relationship and, thus, there is commitment. Differences in organizational and national culture among value chain participants may also pose significant connectedness challenges in a turbulent context. While lead firms in the RMG industry rely on market-based, contractual relationships, turbulent conditions may result in less contractual compliance due to a lack of trust-based relationships with other value chain participants. Indeed, Huq *et al.* (2014) found instances of "mock compliance" among suppliers in Bangladesh following the Rana Plaza tragedy. When suppliers lack relationships, or at least a history of repeat orders, lead firms imposing tight deadlines for high street "fast fashions" may encounter shipping problems or quality defects. This may be the case particularly when firms from developed and developing countries with different national cultures (e.g., individualistic versus collectivist) are aligned in a value chain. Overall, partners with congruent national cultures are more likely to have relationships based on trust (Johnson *et al.*, 1996, p. 1,000), while Whitener *et al.* (1998, p. 524) found that managers from less individualistic countries might be more able to initiate trusting relationships than managers from more individualistic countries.

As noted previously, information and communication technology make sourcing of supplies from different firms in multiple jurisdictions possible. In value chains, where arm's length, third-party contracts are in effect, a lack of communication connectedness appears to be the norm. The Bangladesh tragedy highlighted the communication barriers among lead firms, contractors, NGOs, subcontractors and government. In that case, the lack of connectedness can be explained by the asymmetric power of lead firms as purchasing departments dispatched large "fast fashion" orders to contractors who, unable to meet the deadlines for the orders, sent them to unapproved subcontractors working in unsafe environments. A mix of self-interest, opportunism, and lack of trust occurred at each level, resulting in a lack of bilateral communication and information exchange.

To sum up, Dwyer *et al.* (1987, p. 17) found that exchange relationships seem unlikely to form without bilateral [or multilateral] communication of wants, issues, inputs and priorities. Starik (1991, p. 59) found that effective communication between firms and stakeholders requires that an organization allows, even assists, stakeholders in meeting their goals, by actively and frequently staying in touch. Similarly, Freeman (1984, p. 167) noted that communication processes with stakeholders must be bilateral, if the results are to be meaningful. The further apart an organization is from its stakeholders in terms of shared values, the harder truly bilateral communication will be (Freeman, 1984, p. 167).

The influence of context, culture and communication on value chain connectedness will depend on a variety of factors, including the intensity of competition, the availability of substitute suppliers and products and the length of the product life-cycle. External change, such as globalization and technology, can result in turbulence and increased risk and uncertainty. Attempts by individual organizations to manage turbulence are often unsuccessful because the turbulence exceeds the resources and capabilities of the individual firms. Turbulence in the environment is prompting firms to seek cooperative relationships to a greater degree. The expectation is that recurrent and relational transactions would have greater resilience than discrete transactions in accommodating sudden environmental changes, which could range from natural disasters to environmental reporting requirements. In either case, the greater durability of these transactional approaches lends itself to better communication and connectedness in responding to turbulence than discrete contracting approaches, which have short-term, transaction-based relationships and shallow commitments.

The ability of lead firms in value chains to manage externalities as a core competence also relates to the ability to manage and nurture culture. In an inter-organizational context, informal, or social, control is an important aspect of governance. Inter-organizational culture, which can be defined as the collective culture of participants in a network (Abrahamson and Fombrun, 1992, p. 185), recognizes that firms participate in value chains because of at least one other entity initially. Moreover, the ability to adapt to the culture of the network influences how connected a firm will be in the value chain. Following Abrahamson and Fombrun (1992, p. 185), this chapter assumes that more than economic interests alone shape the culture of a value chain. Indeed, social factors, such as trust and the ability and willingness to build long-term relationships based on informal (social) controls, influence culture in value chains. Relational norms based on informal (social) controls influence culture in value chains. In sum, to the extent relational norms are of larger importance to an exchange relationship than transaction-based connections, organizational culture has a greater influence on value chain connectedness.

15.5 Implications

Firms face turbulence, uncertainty and increasing demands from shareholders and stakeholders alike. Against the backdrop of increasing global integration, greater transparency and awareness encourage not only more intense competition but also heightened expectations. Shareholders demand financial performance, while many consumers, governments and NGOs expect firms to be responsible for environmental safety, fair labour practices and ethical business practices. Where opaque, thinly connected global supply chains once allowed firms to cut corners unnoticed, greater transparency is illuminating the connection between financial short cuts and disconnects in value chain performance, environmentally, socially and economically. The implications of this interconnectedness for management involve increased risk and the importance of sustainable supply chain management.

How many firms have systems implemented to identify when an upstream supplier has substituted an inferior product? The well-documented problems with auto part suppliers producing defective parts that result in safety problems is but one example of this gap in product quality. A sudden safety problem due to an inferior product can force a firm into crisis management mode and cause lasting damage to the brand and firm reputation. When such a crisis occurs, managers need to understand how their value chain operates and how to reconfigure the value chain to avoid future problems. When performance shortfalls occur, many firms and its managers understand well enough their firm's organizational structure and strategy to determine if the competitive advantage of the firm is at risk. Indeed, many firms and their managers have evaluated processes and performance with enough precision to determine proactively if adjustments are needed. However, because value chains are external to the firm, often complex and may possess unfamiliar operating procedures, many firms lack the same degree of understanding regarding their value chains.

With technology as an enabler of the relentless growth in globalization, firms face increased economic risk due to environmental and social vulnerabilities in their value chains, which could result in a highly publicized crisis. This has particular implications for Anglo-based firms in developed countries in which corporate governance rules grant primacy to shareholders. The increasing economic risk and vulnerability due to environmental and social performance in value chains could hasten the focus on measuring not just economic performance but also environmental and social performance, as part of the core performance of the firm.

While significant progress has been made in developing value chain scorecards and other measurement systems, there remains a gap in terms of understanding the types of relationships that should be developed and managed based on the type of transactions involved in the value chain. Value chain connectedness models provide a framework for managers to evaluate proactively if their value chain relationships are sustainable.

Thus, for senior management, effective responses to reputational and financial risk involve shifting the strategic focus beyond traditional strategy–structure relationships to conceptualizing the entire value chain as a relevant structure. In this context, managing external relationships from a value chain perspective is a core competence managers must develop in order to manage the risk and vulnerability inherent in a global context in which environmental and social performance have much greater implications than even ten years ago.

15.6 Limitations

By limiting value chain connectedness to three heuristic models, there may be a perception that these models exhaust the possibilities for value chain connectedness. As a result, there may be a tendency to force fit existing value chains into the three models provided. Managers and others using these models should recognize that there are many variants of value chains. For example, a manager in the logistics department of a retailer may determine that certain materials and production techniques are found in Sumatra and "fast fashion" oriented consumers are willing to pay a premium for that material and style. A hybrid approach to the market-based model with repeat purchases with only a limited group of Sumatra-based textile producers could result. Partially completed garments could be shipped from Sumatra to factories elsewhere for final production. In this case, the logistics manager would need to work cross-functionally with purchasing and marketing to understand the need for longer lead times and smaller quantities to accommodate the customization needed but for which customers will pay a premium.

Given the objective of providing models simple enough for managers to use in operational discussions, it is the author's experience that beyond three models it becomes too complex and unwieldy for practical applications, which could reduce adoption by managers. The common use of "low", "medium" and "high" in measuring performance scorecards is one example of this. The value of models increases as managers and others adopt the terminology in models and apply it to their strategy and tactics. For example, when managers and others can refer to a certain strategy as "power dominant" and understand its meaning and implications, the strategies gain currency and have a stronger likelihood of becoming integrated into the daily execution of strategy and tactics.

On the topic of user friendliness in an operational context, many corporate managers find the complexity of concepts about sustainability somewhat bewildering. Confronted with many competing priorities, managers may not understand how to operationalize sustainability to the firm's advantage. Nadvi and Waltring (2004) speak of the bewilderment many line managers face regarding sustainability in noting the collection of "company specific codes of conduct, sector specific standards and labels, and generic international standards that apply to product specifications, safety concerns, and issues of process organization covering social, environmental and ethical concerns" which managers need to address operationally.

The ISO standards touched upon in this chapter, for example, are fertile ground, potentially, for a management team to seize upon for strategic advantage but if offered without the proper context and implementation tools, are likely to confuse more than help. This chapter is a conceptual map to assist managers in understanding where to position social and environmental performance to enhance the financial performance of the firm. It does not offer implementation tools for achieving this performance. The RMG industry was selected for this chapter because it has been studied by leading value chain scholars previously and also because it illustrates the interconnections between the sustainability orientations of global firms and the execution of value chain strategy. In developing this linkage, there could have been more focus on the broader network of stakeholders in the value chain, especially governments and NGOs. As a whole, the role of governments in dealing with environmental and social aspects of global commerce remains a conundrum. Some experts have voiced scepticism about any plans that "depend on the actions of the Bangladesh government whose members include factory owners that have resisted such changes before" (Kapner and Banjo, 2013, B1).

15.7 Conclusion

Value chain connectedness provides models and conceptual tools for managers to use in assessing value chain performance in the face of increasing risk and vulnerability in the face of relentless global competition and increasing demands for provenance and transparency. Power dominant connectedness offers the market-based model of focusing on short-term gains through a lowest cost transaction-based approach. This approach continues to drive the buyer-driven model in the

RMG industry as some retailers, stung by financial and reputational costs following the Bangladesh tragedy, have sought out lower wages and lightly regulated factories in Africa, Cambodia and elsewhere. However, the total cost of performance, including economic costs, as well as social and environmental risk and vulnerability, may not support a decision to pursue a power-dominant connectedness model in the future. The Wall Street Journal (Cheng, 2015, p. 15) reports that "two years after the garment factory collapse in Bangladesh, Fair Trade apparel is gaining ground. Fair Trade USA's apparel certification now appears on 20 brands, up from just a handful before the Rana Plaza factory collapse in Bangladesh". Thus, a response to the social and environmental shortcomings of "fast fashion" may be the next most chic fashion statement. It would take a massive culture and quality management shift for a firm committed to "fast fashion" and the market-based model to become a relation-based retailer!

Value chain connectedness is a response to the premise offered by Gimenez and Tachizawa (2012, p. 533) that "the buying [often the lead] firm in a value chain invests personnel, time and resources to increase the performance and/or capabilities of suppliers to enhance sustainability". Given the ongoing turbulence in the global economy, it is likely that management in lead firms will consider reconfiguring their value chains. The value chain connectedness models provide a context for managers to address questions such as:

- What capabilities can my firm develop through our GVCs to enhance our competitive advantage?

- What are the potential environmental and social risks and vulnerabilities in our GVCs, given the turbulence in the global economy and the rapid advances in technology, especially in terms of provenance?

- How can my firm, as the lead in its GVCs, protect, and even enhance, its reputation through greater connectedness along the entire value chain? Or, where could an additional value chain be developed to reduce risk of a supply disruption?

Based on the recent issues in the garment industry, inaction on environmental and social performance can increase vulnerability to loss of market share and brand equity. Environmental and social vulnerabilities are often too diffuse to evaluate from an internal firm-based perspective. A value chain perspective can provide more concrete insights in understanding these risks and in adjusting external relationships appropriately.

The potential of value chain connectedness lies in firms viewing the value chain as a source of competitive advantage. This requires an intentional strategy to conceptualize how the value chain should be constructed, measured and managed as a source of innovation and value creation over an extended lifecycle. This includes the intangible benefits of reputation enhancement. It also includes a mid- to long-term vision of nurturing relationships with suppliers in developing countries and providing the resources to enable upgrading. It can involve efforts to assist suppliers and NGOs in applying sustainable technologies to conserve the use of natural resources needed by the firms in the value chain. In the process, firms in the value chain can develop innovative practices that enhance sustainable competitive advantage environmentally, socially and economically. In sum, realizing positive outcomes as a participant in value chains requires understanding how to manage external relationships strategically as an important part of achieving competitive advantage.

References

Abrahamson, E., & Fombrun, C. (1992). Forging the iron cage: Interorganizational networks and the production of macrocultures. *Journal of Management Studies*, 29(2), 175-194.

Andersen, M., & Skjoette-Larsen, T. (2009). Corporate social responsibility in global supply chains. *Supply Chain Management: An International Journal*, 14(2), 75-86.

Cheng, A. (2015,). "Fair trade" becomes a fashion trend. *Wall Street Journal*, July 8, 2015, B7.

Dicken, P. (2015). *Global Shift: Mapping the Changing Contours of the World Economy*. New York: The Guilford Press.

Doney, P.M., Cannon, J.P., & Mullen, M.R. (1998). Understanding the influence of national culture on the development of trust. *Academy of Management Review*, 23(3), 601-620.

Dwyer, F., Schurr, P.H., & Oh, S. (1987). Developing buyer-seller relations. *Journal of Marketing*, 51,11-28.

Frazier, G.L. (1983). On the measurement of inter-firm power in channels of distribution. *Journal of Marketing Research*, 20 (May), 158-166.

Freeman, R.E. (1984). Strategic Management: A Stakeholder Approach. Boston, MA: Pitman.

Gereffi, G. (1999). International trade and industrial upgrading in the apparel commodity chain. *Journal of International Economics*, 48, 37-70.

Gereffi, G., Humphrey, J., & Kaplinsky, R. (2001). Introduction: Globalisation, value chains and development. *IDS bulletin*, 32(3), 1-8.

Gereffi, G., Humphrey, J., & Sturgeon, T. (2005). The governance of global value chains. *Review of International Political Economy*,12(1), 78-104.

Gimenez, C., & Tachizawa, E. (2012). Extending sustainability to suppliers: A systematic literature review. *Supplier Chain Management: An International Journal*,17(5): 531-543.

Heide, J.B., & John, G. (1992). Do norms matter in marketing relationships? *Journal of Marketing*, 56 (April), 32-44.

Hess, M. (2008). Governance, value chains and networks: An afterword. *Economy and Society*, 37(3). doi: 10.1080./03085140802172722.

Heuer, M. (2001). Firm–stakeholder connectedness in the deregulating electric utility business: Exchange relationships in a network context. Unpublished dissertation. Washington, DC: George Washington University.

Humphrey, J., & Schmitz, H. (2004). Governance in global value chains. In H. Schmitz (Ed.), *Local Enterprises in the Global Economy: Issues of governance and Upgrading* (pp. 95-109). Cheltenham, UK: Edward Elgar.

Huq, F.A., Stevenson, M., & Zorzini, M. (2014). Social sustainability in developing country suppliers: An exploratory study in the ready made garments industry of Bangladesh. *International Journal of Operations & Production Management*, 34(5), 610-638.

Johnson, J.L., Cullen, J.B., Sakano, T., & Takenouchi, H. (1996). Setting the stage for trust and strategic integration in Japanese–U.S. cooperative alliances, 981-1.003 (Special Issue). *Journal of International Business Studies*.

Kaplinsky, R., & Morris, M. (2002). *A Handbook for Value Chain Research*. Prepared for the IDRC.

Kapner, S., & Banjo, S. (2013). Plan B for Bangladesh. *The Wall Street Journal*, 27 June 2013, B1.

Lang, C.L. (2002). Information and communication technologies: Boon or bane to sustainable development? In J. Park and N. Roome (Eds.), *The Ecology of the New Economy: Sustainable Transformation of Global Information, Communications and Electronics Industries*, (pp. 174-182). Sheffield, UK: Greenleaf Publishing.

Malik, Y., Niemeyer, A., & Ruwadi, B. (2011). Building on the supply chain of the future. *McKinsey Quarterly*, 1, 62-71.

Mattioli, D. (2012). Year of the oops: 2011 spent in reverse. *Wall Street Journal*, A1.

Nadvi, K., & Waltring, F. (2004). Making sense of global standards. In H. Schmitz (ed.), *Local Enterprises in the Global Economy*. Cheltenham, UK: Edward Elgar.

New, S. (2010). The transparent supply chain. *Harvard Business Review*, 88(10), 76-82.

Pfeffer, J., & Salancik, G. (1978). *The External Control of Organizations: A Resource Dependence Perspective*. New York: Harper & Row.

Porter, M.E., & Kramer, M.R. (2011). The big idea: Creating shared value. *Harvard Business Review*, January–February 2011, 62-77.

Seuring, S., & Müller, M. (2008). From a literature review to a conceptual framework for sustainable supply chain management. *Journal of Cleaner Production*, 26, 1,699-1,710.

Starik, M. (1991). Stakeholder management and firm performance: Reputation and financial relationships to U.S. electric utility consumer-related strategies. Unpublished dissertation, Athens, GA: University of Georgia.

Tripathi, S. (2013). *Bangladesh: Society of fabric*. Retrieved from: http://www. ethicalcorp.com (3 June 2015)

Whitener, E.M., Brodt, S.E., Korsgaard, M.A., & Werner, J.M. (1998). Managers as initiators of trust: An exchange relationship framework for understanding managerial trustworthy behavior. *Academy of Management Review*, 23(3), 513-530.

Mark Heuer is an Associate Professor of Management at the Sigmund Weis School of Business at Susquehanna University. He teaches the senior business capstone course, as well as business and social responsibility. Professor Heuer earned an MBA from The Smith School of Business at the University of Maryland and a PhD from George Washington University. He previously held positions in the governmental, non-profit and private sectors for over 30 years. His research interests include sustainability, social issues management and national culture.

16

Sustainable bio-based supply chains in light of the Nagoya Protocol

Freedom-Kai Phillips

University of Ottawa, Canada

The sustainable management of supply chains in bio-based industries (e.g. agriculture, botanicals, cosmetics, industrial biotechnology and pharmaceuticals) must now incorporate account for the access and benefit-sharing (ABS) measures envisaged by the Nagoya Protocol on Access to Genetic Resources and the Fair and Equitable Sharing of Benefits Arising from their Utilization, which has 70 parties and entered into force at the international level on 12 October 2014. The Protocol, a sub-treaty of on Biological Diversity, establishes governing norms and obligations for the access and use of genetic resources and associated traditional knowledge in member jurisdictions. In the Nagoya era, proactive organizations are capitalizing on legislative developments to enhance global supply chain integrity, security and functional equity, and do so in an economically, socially and environmentally sound manner. This chapter will explore the impact of national legal, regulatory and policy measures on ABS as they impact global supply chains in bio-based industries, first by outlining the CBD and the Nagoya Protocol, then surveying legislation in key user and provider jurisdictions to highlight recent developments. Next, effects on global supply chains are outlined, followed by a discussion on challenges and opportunities pertaining to Nagoya era sustainable supply chain management. Equitable sourcing in bio-based industries is an increasing compliance challenge which requires active engagement in ABS regardless of perceived complexities and allows for the establishment of secure and ethically sourced supply chains.

16.1 Introduction

In the Nagoya era, proactive organizations are capitalizing on legislative developments to enhance global supply chain integrity, security and functional equity, and do so in an economically, socially and environmentally sound manner. Organizations like Yves Rocher—which actively partners with villagers in Madagascar for the harvest and distillation of an essential oil derived from saro leaves—have developed guidelines which ensure responsible sourcing. Beraca of Brazil, which has developed independently certified sustainability criteria which support ecosystem conservation and empowerment of local communities in developing marketable bio-based ingredients, are illustrative of this trend (UNCTAD, 2013; CBD, 2014). This chapter explores the impact of national legal, regulatory and policy measures on access and benefit sharing (ABS) on global supply chains within bio-based industries. For the purposes of this chapter, "ABS" refers to the procedure of negotiating, securing and maintaining access to biodiversity components and derivatives in an equitable manner based on prior informed consent and the establishment of mutually agreed terms as envisioned by the proceeding legal regimes, and "bio-based industries", including agriculture, botanicals, cosmetics and fragrances, industrial biotechnology, food and beverage and pharmaceuticals (UNEP, 2012, p. 6.3.6).

First, a brief history is provided of the Convention on Biological Diversity (CBD, 1992) and the Nagoya Protocol on Access to Genetic Resources and the Fair and Equitable Sharing of Benefits Arising from their Utilization (Nagoya Protocol, 2010), followed by a substantive overview of key provisions with a focus on measures relating to ABS. Second, selected legal measures are surveyed across key user and provider jurisdictions—Australia, India, EU, South Africa, Brazil and Peru—to highlight synergies, commonalities and divergence in implementation of the Nagoya Protocol at the national level. Third, effects on global supply chains are outlined including multi-jurisdictional compliance, security of intellectual property rights, benefit-sharing and required collaboration. Finally, challenges and opportunities pertaining to Nagoya era sustainable supply chain management, in terms of sustainable sourcing and compliance, are discussed, and a way forward provided. Bio-based organizations, which are forecasted to contribute a minimum of 2.7% of GDP in OECD countries by 2030 (OECD, 2009), are challenged to actively engage in ABS as a means to facilitate a functional and competitive transition to Nagoya-compliant supply chains by positively incentivizing conservation and sustainable use of national resources. While the Protocol does interject additional administrative and compliance burdens, sustainability in supply chains is no longer about simply balancing people, the planet and profit but has transgressed into a set of strategic drivers which require an equally strategic response.

An example to be considered throughout, which illustrates how an ABS agreement can foster bio-discovery and broad social benefits, is Coartem, the artemisinin-based combination treatment for uncomplicated malaria, which was collaboratively developed based on Chinese traditional medicine by Novartis and Chinese partners through the Institute of Microbiology and Epidemiology and the Academy of Military Medical Sciences of the government of China. Under the agreement, which resulted in co-owned patents in roughly 50 countries and a MoU with the World Health Organization, Novartis reportedly provided technology transfer, roughly US$150 million for sourcing of raw materials, in addition to various royalty payments made to the Chinese partners and continues to provide the drug at a not-for-profit price to public health organizations (UNEP, 2012). The ability to develop the highly effective Coartem, based on Artemether and Lumefantrine two active components utilized in Chinese Traditional Medicine, would not have been possible without the ABS agreement established between the collaborating parties.

16.2 A brief history of access and benefit sharing under the CBD and Nagoya Protocol

16.2.1 Development of the CBD and Nagoya Protocol

The Convention on Biological Diversity (CBD) was adopted in 1992 as one of the three "Rio Treaties" coming into force a year later. It currently has 196 Parties[1] and is arguably the paramount international environmental treaty body. The CBD is based in a broad ecosystem approach and aims to ensure conservation and sustainable use of biodiversity and the fair and equitable sharing of benefits from utilization (CBD, Article 1), ensuring that, while states have sovereign right to govern the use of domestic resources, utilization of biodiversity may not cause undue domestic or extraterritorial environmental damage (CBD, Article 3).

The CBD addresses conservation of biodiversity and related socio-economic aspects (Greiber *et al.*, 2012). In the discussions that preceded the creation of the CBD, the conservation obligations desired by developed countries were included in the text contingent upon the developing country prioritizing sustainable use of biodiversity and receiving equitable benefit sharing. ABS was conceptually developed in the CBD as a means to disseminate both the costs and benefits of biodiversity conservation between developed and developing countries, while positively incentivizing sustainable practices and innovations for indigenous and local communities (ILCs) (Greiber *et al.*, 2012). Due principally to the challenges experienced by CBD Parties in implementation of the ABS provisions of the Convention, a collection of decisions were adopted by the Conference of the Parties (COP) aimed towards encouraging the development of an internationally binding legal regime on ABS (Greiber *et al.*, 2012).

---

1   CBD Secretariat, "List of Parties to the Convention on Biological Diversity" (Montreal, CBD), accessed 30 June 2015; http://www.cbd.int/information/parties.shtml

The progression towards a binding protocol on ABS began with the voluntary, non-legally binding Bonn Guidelines adopted at COP 6 (2002), followed by a call at the World Summit on Sustainable Development for an international regime on ABS. An ad hoc working group (AHWG) on ABS was established at COP 7 (2004) to review and manage negotiations on a binding protocol. Negotiations were conducted over the third and fourth meetings of the AHWG in Bangkok (2005) and Granada (2006), concluding at COP 10 (2010) in Nagoya, Japan, where the Protocol was adopted (CBD, 2010). The Nagoya Protocol on Access to Genetic Resources and the Fair and Equitable Sharing of Benefits Arising from their Utilization (Nagoya Protocol) elaborates upon the pre-existing ABS obligations under the CBD and establishes a legal regime for governance of access and equitable sharing of benefits derived from use of genetic resources (GR) and traditional knowledge (TK) (Nagoya Protocol, Article 1) The Protocol entered into force on October 12, 2014, and currently has 70 Parties.[2] Collectively, the CBD and the Nagoya Protocol provide a sound legal basis for the implementation of sustainable development principles and practices.

16.2.2 Substantive overview

16.2.2.1 CBD

The CBD is grounded in the twin objectives of conservation and sustainable use of biological diversity and ensuring fair and equitable benefit-sharing arising out of utilization of GR (CBD, Article 1; Phillips and Perron-Welch, 2015). Article 2 of the Convention defines "biological diversity" to include terrestrial, marine and other aquatic species and ecosystems, included in a broad set of definitions including; country of origin, in-situ conservation and sustainable use (CBD, Article 2). Article 3 establishes sovereign rights over domestic resources and a responsibility on states to ensure transboundary environmental protection, and refrain from causing undue adverse environmental impacts to other states or areas outside their national jurisdiction (CBD, Article 3).

Article 8 establishes various measures relating to in-situ conservation and the establishment and management of protected areas (CBD, Article 8(a-b)), with parties further obliged to:

- Regulate and manage biological resources with a view of ensuring conservation and sustainable use (CBD, Article 8(c))

- Promote protection of ecosystems and maintenance of viable populations of species (CBD, Article 8(d))

- Rehabilitate degraded ecosystems (CBD, Article 8(f))

---

2   CBD Secretariat, "List of Parties to Nagoya Protocol" (Montreal, CBD), accessed 25 October 2015; https://www.cbd.int/abs/nagoya-protocol/signatories

- Preserve knowledge and practices of indigenous and local communities (ILCs) relating to biodiversity conservation and sustainable use (CBD, Article 8(j))

- Maintain necessary legislation to govern protection of threatened species (CBD, Article 8(k)) and per Article 9 adopt measures relating to the establishment, maintenance and regulation of ex situ collections (CBD, Article 9).

Article 10 aims to implement the second pillar of the Convention, ensuring sustainable use of biodiversity, with parties required to integrate sustainable-use considerations into national decision-making, adopt measures to minimize adverse impacts, support customary use and practices relating to conservation of biodiversity, support local remedial actions in degraded areas and encourage cooperation among public and private stakeholders in development of methods of sustainable use (CBD, Article 10). Article 15 establishes provisions relating to access to genetic resources (GR), recognizing the sovereign right of states over national resources (CBD, Article 15(1)). Parties are required to establish measures to facilitate access to GR for environmentally sound uses (CBD, Article 15(1-2), based on prior informed consent (PIC) and mutually-agreed terms (MAT) (CBD, Article 15(4-5)) and shall aim to share benefits equitably from non-commercial or commercial utilization of GR (CBD, Article 15(7)).

16.2.2.2 Nagoya Protocol

The Nagoya Protocol is a specialized instrument aimed at implementation of the third objective of the Convention: facilitating fair and equitable benefit-sharing arising from access to genetic resources (Nagoya Protocol, Article 1; Phillips and Perron-Welch, 2015). Article 3 establishes the scope of the Protocol to apply to GR as provided for in Article 15 of the CBD, TK associated to such resources and the fair and equitable sharing of benefits arising from utilization (Nagoya Protocol, Article 3). Implementation of the Protocol is to be done in a mutually supportive manner with other international instruments, such as the International Treaty on Plant Genetic Resources for Food and Agriculture (Nagoya Protocol, Article 4.3; Cabrera *et al*, 2013).

Parties to the Protocol, while holding sovereign rights over GR, are required to establish an appropriate legal framework ensuring:

- Access to GR is based on PIC and where applicable approval and involvement of ILCs (Nagoya Protocol, Article 6)

- Access to TK associated with GR held by ILCs accessed based on PIC (Nagoya Protocol, Article 7), and

- Utilization of both GR or TK is based on MAT and results in equitable benefit-sharing with providers including ILCs (Nagoya Protocol, Article 5).

Benefit-sharing options include a non-exhaustive list of both monetary and non-monetary benefits as envisioned originally under the 2002 Bonn Guidelines (Greiber *et al.*, 2012). In establishing measures relating to TK associated with GR, Parties shall take into account the customary laws of ILCs, cooperate with ILCs in establishing information sharing mechanisms to users of GRs, provide support for development of community ABS protocols and may not restrict customary use and exchange of GR and TK amongst ILCs (Nagoya Protocol, Article 12).

Parties are further obliged to designate a National Focal Point (NFP) and at least one Competent National Authority (CNA) on ABS (Nagoya Protocol, Article 13), with the NFP acting as a liaison at the national and local level on ABS, while the CNA provides governance over GR and TK with responsibilities including processing of ABS permits and ongoing monitoring and compliance (Greiber *et al.*, 2012. Parties are further obliged to establish effective measures to ensure the access and use of GR and associated TK in the jurisdiction is done with PIC and on MAT (Nagoya Protocol, Article 15-16), and with proportionate enforcement and monitoring measures in place, including checkpoints (Nagoya Protocol, Article 17).

16.3 Survey of legal measures supporting implementation of the Nagoya Protocol

This section provides a survey of selected legal measures—generally taken from mega or highly diverse regions—which support the implementation of the Nagoya Protocol. Measures developed prior to and following the passing of the Nagoya Protocol have been selected to illustrate differential and complementary approaches to ABS intended to exemplify legal trends and inform identification of impacts, challenges and opportunities for proactive action. The method used for implementing domestic ABS reforms depends heavily on the existing domestic legal framework, political initiatives, priorities of domestic stakeholder groups (e.g. private sector or ILCs) and the desired pace of reform, with measures taking multiple forms including comprehensive legislation, ad-hoc reforms to existing legislation, regulatory measures under environmental legislation and administrative measures or guidelines on ABS.

16.3.1 Australia

Environment Protection and Biodiversity Conservation Act (1999) and Environment Protection and Biodiversity Conservation Regulations (2000)

Australia centralizes authority over genetic resources at the National Ministry of Environment, but takes a decentralized approach to administration, processing and monitoring of access permits. Specialized governmental divisions and regional organizations were established and empowered to administer access to genetic resources within their region or protected area. Organizations like the Great Barrier Reef Marine Park Authority (Australia, 1975; 1983, Rule 2.6.3(d)), and the Australian Government Antarctic Division (Australia, 1999, Section 197(p)) facilitate access leveraging specialized technical expertise about the genetic resource under their management. Permit allocation and processing is delegated to similar authorities across jurisdictions including protected areas. Australia requires commercial applicants to enter into a benefit-sharing agreement with each relevant Access Provider, based on prior informed consent, to obtain a permit for access to genetic resources (Australia, 2000, Rule 8A.07(1)), or traditional knowledge (Australia, 2000, Rule 8A.08). Non-commercial applicants must obtain written permission from each Provider to (a) enter the area, (b) take samples of biological resources and (c) to remove these samples (Australia, 2000, Rule 8A.12(1)). The prior informed consent of ILCs is not required where indigenous knowledge is accessed for non-commercial research and not in relation to resources accessed on indigenous land (Hawke, 2009, paragraph 5.127). In practice, a primary provider is the Genetic Resource Management Section in the Department of Environment on behalf of the Commonwealth. With the sharp commercial/non-commercial divide it has become increasingly difficult to pinpoint distinctions between research and commercial intent (Prip *et al.*, 2014; Cabrera *et al.*, 2014).

16.3.2 India

Biological Diversity Act (2002) and Biological Diversity Rules (2004)

India requires that all parties accessing GR/TK for commercial proposes inform the State Biodiversity Board and receive approval from the National Biodiversity Authority (NBA) prior to access (India, 2002, Article 3, 7). The NBA, in granting approval, ensures that the terms of access secure equitable sharing of benefits arising from use of GR/TK, as determined between benefit claimers, local bodies and the party seeking access (India, 2002, Article 21). Mutually-agreed terms are established between the party applying for access and the NBA in consultation with local community bodies and benefit claimers (India, 2004, Rule 20(5)). The process of consultation facilitated and governed by the NBA includes issuing a public notice in local languages, discussion of the proposal with the general assembly of the local community and gaining their formal consent after being provided adequate information by the accessing party regarding the scope and the socio-economic/cultural implications of the proposed project (India, 2011, Rule 17). An exemption for collaborative research projects conducted through government sponsored or government approved institutions is provided. While a simplified process, governmental approval is also available (India, 2002, Article 5). Approval procedures which require prior approval by the national authority are established for:

- Access to GR or TK

- Transfer of research results internationally

- Filing of patent applications, and

- Third party transfers (India, 2004, Rule 14, 17-19).

India has developed Biodiversity Management Committees (BMC) as local coordination and management bodies tasked with promoting and supporting sustainable use and documentation of biodiversity, and associated cultural practices and traditional knowledge (India, 2002, Article 41(1); 2004, Rule 22). BMCs are empowered at the local level to initiate and document available biological diversity including cultivation and breeding practices, and chronicling related traditional knowledge through the use of registers and electronic databases (India, 2002, Article 41). BMCs collaborate with state and national biodiversity bodies to establish a People's Biodiversity Registers (PBRs) intended to form a system of comprehensive information on availability and associated knowledge relating to the traditional uses of biological resources (India, 2004, Rule 22(6), (9); Cabrera *et al.*, 2014a). National and state bodies must leverage these registers when reviewing decisions related to access to ensure that prior informed consent of the local communities is obtained before commercial utilization of these resources (India, 2002, Article 41(2-3); 2004, Rule 22(11)). At present, PBRs are being developed in seventeen states (National Biodiversity Authority of India, 2014), with specialized guidelines established and a Technical Support Group to providing expert guidance (National Biodiversity Authority of India, 2013; Cabrera *et al.*, 2014).

16.3.3 South Africa

Biodiversity Act (2004), Amendments to the Patents Act (2005), Bioprospecting and ABS Regulations (2008), and Bioprospecting Guidelines (2012).

South Africa has an ABS framework made up of multiple legal instruments, including the Biodiversity Act (2004), Amendments to the Patents Act (2005), Bioprospecting and ABS Regulations (2008), and Bioprospecting Guidelines (2012). The Minister of Water and Environmental Affairs, under the national Department of Environmental Affairs (DEA) is designated as the Competent National Authority (South Africa, 2004, Article 1; 2008, Section 6; ABS Initiative, 2014a). A bioprospecting permit is required for use or export of a biological resource (South Africa, 2004, Article 81(1), 82(1)(b)(i)), with permit eligibility contingent upon: complete disclosure of scope of the access and intend use (South Africa, 2008, Section 8(2)), the PIC granted by the provider (South Africa, 2004, Article 82(2)(a), 82(3)(a); 2008, Section 8(1)(d)), an established benefit-sharing agreement based on MAT governing the transfer (South Africa, 2004, Article 82(2)(b)(i-ii), 82(3)(b), 84(1)(b)(i-vi); 2008, Section 8(1) (c)) and granting of ministerial approval (South Africa, 2004, Article 83(2), 84(2)). The benefit-sharing agreement must include specifics regarding the characteristics of the biological resource, scope of intended use, established review intervals and modalities for benefit sharing (South Africa, 2004, Article 83(1)(b)(i-v), 83(1)(c-g)). Ministerial approval is granted based on determinations of sufficient disclosure to stakeholders and equitable benefit-sharing, and may include technical advice procured by the minister, or have terms included to align more truly with the framework (South Africa, 2008, Section 17(3-4)). The Patents Amendment Act of 2005 integrates protection for biological resources and TK into pre-existing patent legislation, with the inclusion of definitions for "indigenous biological resources" and traditional use (South Africa, 2005, Section 1). The Amendment Act also requires patent applicants to disclose if the patent is based on TK or biological resources, and to demonstrate proper title as required by the Biodiversity Act, which includes a material transfer and benefit-sharing agreement in place (South Africa, 2005, Section 2; Cabrera *et al.*, 2014).

16.3.4 European Union

Regulation (EU) No 511/2014 on compliance measures for users from the Nagoya Protocol

The European Union, through Regulation No 511/2014, has implemented "user measures" relating to genetic resources and traditional knowledge across the EU. Individuals and organizations which use GRs are required to exercise due diligence in determining that the genetic resources and traditional knowledge which are being utilized were accessed, where applicable, in accordance with domestic ABS legislation or regulations, and that benefits are being equitably shared based on mutually agreed terms (EU, 2014, Article 4(1)). Transfer of genetic resources and traditional knowledge must be done in accordance with terms established by the parties and any applicable legislative or regulatory requirements (EU, 2014, Article 4(1a)). Users must retain all internationally-recognized certificates of compliance for access to GR/TK, in addition to all documentation pertaining to the establishment of consent and mutually agreed terms (EU, 2014, Article 4(2)(a)). Where no such certificate is available, users must retain record of:

- The date and place of access
- A description of the resources utilized (GR/TK)
- The source where it was obtained
- Any rights and/or obligations associated with access including benefit sharing, subsequent applications and commercialization
- All permits where applicable, and

- All mutually agreed terms, including benefit-sharing (EU, 2014, Article 4(2)(b)).

If the information held by the user is insufficient to determine the legality of access and utilization persists, the user must obtain a new permit for access, and establish mutually agreed terms, or discontinue use, with users required to keep records of benefit sharing for twenty years following the end of utilization (EU, 2014, Article 4(2b), 4(3)).

Checkpoints are required to be established in each EU Member State to verify compliance with domestic disclosure requirements and to dissuade non-compliance (EU, 2014, Article 9(1–1a), All recipients of research funding involving the utilization of genetic resources and traditional knowledge must declare that due diligence was exercised in regards to access, and that the resources were obtained legally (EU, 2014, Article 7(1). During the final stages of development of a product which uses GR or TK, users must declare conformity and provide certificate(s) of compliance, and/or disclose all required access information, and applicable mutually-agreed terms (EU, 2014, Article 4, 7(2)). A Register of Trusted Collections is also established and intended to simplify access, with membership requiring demonstration of detailed exchange procedures for transfer of genetic material including issuance of compliance documentation and, where possible, use of unique identifiers (EU, 2014, Article 5(1), 5(3)).Where genetic material is obtained from a recognized collection as listed in the Register of Collections within the EU, the user is considered to have fulfilled the due diligence requirement (EU, 2014, Article 4(4)).

16.3.5 Brazil

Provisional Measure n. 2.186-16/2001(MP) and Law No. 13,123 (2015)

Brazil was one of the first countries to ratify the Convention on Biological Diversity (CBD), and in 2001 Provisional Measure n. 2.186-16/2001(MP) was passed to implement measures relating to ABS obligations under Article 15 of the CBD and to provide an interim response to concerns over misappropriation of GR (Brazil, 2001; Cabrera *et al.*, 2014). Under the provisional regime the Genetic Heritage Management Council (Conselho de Gestão do Patrimônio Genético—CGEN) was designated as the domestic authority over ABS, who has issued 41 resolutions since its inception refining the system and clarifying various problems (ABS Initiative, 2014b, In 2014, Bill 7735-2014 (Draft) on ABS was presented to the Congress which was adopted in 2015 through Law No. 13,123 and brings several alterations to the current framework. The proposed scope of the new regime includes genetic resources and traditional knowledge found in situ, including products and proceeds arising out of use, and remittance abroad with the inclusion of derivatives (Brazil, 2015, Article 1). Commercial access and transfer abroad of GR or TK is functionally preferential to nationals or foreign institutions in collaboration with a national institution (Brazil, 2015, Article 11). To minimize bureaucracy, the proposed framework substitutes a permit for commercial access with an online registration system containing the essential data of the research, without the need of previous approval by CGEN (Brazil, 2015, Article 12, 2(XII)). Access to GR or TK is denied to foreign nationals, with prior authorization required for shipments of samples to companies situated overseas, with approval highly dependent upon the intended use (Brazil, 2015, Article 11(§1-2), 13(§1-2), 15). Commercial application requires notification to be provided to CGEN, along with the establishment of a Benefit-Sharing Agreement with set modes of monetary or non-monetary benefit sharing to be filed within one year of notification (Brazil, 2015, Article 16). Producers of the commercial product arising from access to GR and associated TK shall distribute benefits (both monetary and non-monetary) in a fair and equitable manner, regardless of who carried out access previously (Brazil, 2015, Article 17) and where the final product has not been produced domestically, then subsidiaries, affiliates and intermediaries involved and linked to the producer are jointly liable for sharing benefits (Brazil, 2015, Article 17(§7)). Contravention carries broad consequences, ranging from significant fines and seizure of instruments, samples and products derived from GR/TK (Brazil, 2015, Article 27). The new ABS system provides an intriguing model to observe in practice, as it purports to streamline the access process with a considerable focus of encouraging domestic commercialization, establishment of accurate benefit-sharing terms and broad liability for compliance.

16.3.6 Peru

Law No 27811, Law Introducing a Protection Regime for the Collective Knowledge of Indigenous Peoples Derived from Biological Resources (2002) and Law No 28216, Act on the Protection of Access to Peruvian Biological Diversity and the Collective Knowledge of Indigenous Peoples (2008)

Peru has strong protection over TK derived from biological resources, which relates to properties, uses and characteristics of biological diversity, and with a collective origin which has been developed and maintained by Peruvian indigenous peoples groups (Peru, 2002, Article 3). Access requires the prior informed consent of the representatives of ILCs, with PIC needing to be respectful of socio-cultural interests (Peru, 2002, Article 6). Access to TK for commercial purposes requires establishment of License Contracts with ILCs which authorizes third parties access and use of TK that is under their control. The period of validity of these contracts is three years and they require, among others points, a statement of compensation which must include a down payment and royalties of not less than 5% of total gross sales before taxes (Peru, 2002, Article 27), with an additional royalty of 10% of gross sales before taxes required to be paid to the fund for the development of ILCs of the country (Peru, 2002, Article 8).

Three declaratory registers are leveraged, the Public Registry of Collective Knowledge of Indigenous Peoples, the National Confidential Registry of Collective Knowledge of Indigenous Peoples and the Local Registry of Collective Knowledge of Indigenous Peoples, to record TK and ensure PIC (Peru, 2002, Article 17-18, 24). Members of ILCs may bring actions against uses which are an infringement upon their TK, or when their TK is in imminent danger, with the accused having the burden to provide evidence demonstrating the legality of use (Peru, 2002, Article 43-44; Cabrera *et al.*, 2014). A National Commission for the Protection of Access to Peruvian Biological Diversity and to the Collective Knowledge of Indigenous Peoples was established in Law 28216 as an interdisciplinary technical body made up of representatives of various impacted ministries and national institutes, civil society stakeholders and ILCs (Peru, 2008, Article 3). The commission is empowered to, among other things:

- Manage the register of biological resources and collective knowledge
- Protect against acts of misappropriation or "biopiracy"
- Investigate patent applications filed or granted abroad relating to GR/TK of Peru
- Review granted patents and lodge objections for misappropriation (Peru, 2008, Article 4).

Biopiracy for enforcement purposes includes physical control of a biological resource or related TK based on unauthorized and unremunerated access, but also extends to ownership of rights relating to products which illegally incorporate such elements (Peru, 2008, Supplementary and Final Provisions, paragraph 3).

16.4 Nagoya era supply chain considerations

With the entry into force of the Nagoya Protocol and ongoing development or reform of domestic ABS regimes, the legal landscape for access and utilization of genetic resources and associated traditional knowledge is gaining increased consistency across jurisdictions but is also growing in complexity and subsequently changing the degree, frequency and significance of impacts on the research and commercial communities. Operating principles and compliance challenges of bio-based industries, which underpin best practices in biodiscovery and supply chain management, are forced to account for and adaptively respond to these legal changes. Effects of the Nagoya Protocol on global supply chains which will be discussed include:

- Multi-Jurisdictional Compliance Risks
- Security of Intellectual Property Rights

- Complexity of Benefit-Sharing, and

- Requirement for Collaborative Access.

The Nagoya Protocol has direct relevance in Party jurisdictions and potential relevance based on jurisdictions of operation, bioprospecting, research and development (R&D), trade or registration of intellectual property (IP) rights. For example, while the United States has neither signed nor ratified the Nagoya Protocol or the CBD, key trading partners include Canada, who is a party to the CBD and the EU who ratified the Protocol with regulation 511/2014, both of whom influence R&D practices in the US to differing degrees. The risk remains for organizations and researchers in non-Protocol jurisdictions which are utilizing genetic resources and/or associated traditional knowledge occurring in, or originating from, foreign jurisdictions to be subject to Nagoya Protocol compliant requirements and enforcement measures. An international regulatory scheme for ABS is being developed through mutually supportive legislative measures developed in party jurisdictions, which places significant emphasis on disclosure of the country of origin at various checkpoints, restricts access and transfer of resources and, increasingly, derivatives but under specific terms including PIC/MAT, and increases the compliance challenges of biodiscovery. These developments have the potential to increase the overall complexity, cost and time required for compliance clearance prior to market entry. Organizations in bio-based industries, particularly in the pharmaceutical and botanical sectors, that either directly, or indirectly through third parties, utilize genetic resources, biological derivatives, active biological components, or traditional knowledge should understand and strategically respond to Nagoya era supply chain impacts to mitigate any potential additional costs or inhibiting effects.

16.4.1 Multi-jurisdictional compliance risks

A primary effect of the Protocol on global supply chains is the ever evolving, multi-jurisdictional compliance risks, with organizations in party jurisdiction—particular the EU—holding a higher degree of relevance. Depending upon the industry and jurisdictions of key operations such as bioprospecting, R&D, manufacturing and go-to-market, and registration of intellectual property rights, organizations will find multiple, overlapping and often differential regulatory procedures and requirements for due diligence in sourcing, disclosure of country of origin and modalities for negotiation of mutually-agreed terms (MAT). While the temporal scope of the Protocol inhibits retroactive application to samples acquired pre-Nagoya, there is nothing explicit which precludes a party from focusing on the timing of utilization alone in domestic legislation subsequently triggering inclusion under the scope of the ABS framework (UNCTAD, 2014).

If the EU "user measures" seen in harmonization with domestic measures from India, South Africa, Australia, Peru and Brazil, are to be used as a benchmark, multiple compliance challenges can be noted. First, commercial access and utilization of biological resource or traditional knowledge will require PIC and MAT of the provider(s), with some provider jurisdictions not differentiating procedurally between commercial or non-commercial access. Second, utilization of unlawfully sourced genetic resources, including through biotechnology, is subject to various enforcement actions including significant fines and potential imprisonment. Third, users must demonstrate and certify that due diligence in access and sourcing of genetic and biological resources was done through PIC and MAT, including equitable benefit sharing at various stages of development including requests for research funds, registration of IP rights and pre-market approval. Fourth, transfer and utilization of genetic resources will be subject to the terms of the PIC/MAT agreement, with expanded use requiring renegotiation of terms. Fifth, measures relate to "utilization" of genetic resources, with genetic resources currently being utilized in R&D or sourced from an ex situ collection still potentially subject to ABS legislation. Finally, disclosure of the country of origin of genetic or biological resources and associated TK in patent applications is a requirement in a growing number of jurisdictions, including the European Patent Office, requiring disclosure of the use of biological material and/or traditional knowledge in the description phase of the patent application where the patent is based on the resource (EPO, 2013, Article 83; EPO, 2012, Rules 26–27 and Rule 31) and demonstration of legality of access and utilization (EU, 2014, Article 4). Organizations in bio-based industries must cautiously navigate the evolving compliance landscape, often intersecting multiple jurisdictions, to proactively identify and mitigate potential inhibitors to adequate disclosure—such as limited, spurious or non-existent documentation on country of origin—to ensure that new product market access is not restricted or delayed.

16.4.2 Security of intellectual property rights

As noted above, a growing number of jurisdictions require disclosure of use of biological or genetic resources and traditional knowledge at the time of registration of patent, including the EU, Switzerland, India, South Africa and Peru. While the EU and Switzerland require disclosure of source of origin where the patent is based directly on the resource (EPO, 2013, Rule 26(3); Switzerland, 2012, Article 49a), or even if unknown (Switzerland, 2012, Article 49a(2)), variation regarding disclosure of country of origin exists in patent laws across jurisdictions (UNCTAD, 2014). India requires a description for patents including complete specifications of the components, including the "source and geographic origin" of biological material used in an invention (India, 2015, Section 10). Furthermore, proper prior approval must be provided by the National Biodiversity Authority for registration of a patent in a foreign jurisdiction utilizing GR/TK from India (India, 2004, Rule 19). South Africa requires patent applicants to submit a declaration certifying whether or not a patent is based on or derived from indigenous biological or genetic resource, or traditional knowledge and where the patent is based on such resources, evidence of legal right to utilize as prescribed (i.e. PIC/MAT) must be included (South Africa, 2005, Section 30(3A)). The proscribed scope of disclosure under each of these regimes is differentiated on depth, breadth and inclusiveness, with the based on jurisdictions having reduced scope in comparison to jurisdictions using the broader used in or derived from model. Absence of an obligation in the IP regime requiring demonstration of legal access as a component of disclosure, lack of legality of access would not invalidate submission of a patent application, but could result in it being invalidated in the future (UNCTAD, 2014). Organizations must be aware of the variance of disclosure and procedural requirements across jurisdictions and the interface of domestic IP law and ABS requirements in patent jurisdictions to ensure that patent applications are approved and endure.

Disclosure aside, some jurisdictions have adopted aggressive protective measures relating to domestic biological resources and traditional knowledge including the use of digital registers or databases to chronicle biodiversity information and traditional practices, creation of national commissions and proactive collaboration with patent offices in foreign jurisdictions to address misappropriation, including seeking foreign judgments. Both India and Peru have established various digital declaratory registers at the state and local level to record biodiversity and associated knowledge and practices to ensure that upon examination of a patent application the proper indigenous authorities were consulted (India, 2002, Article 41(2–3); 2004, Rule 22(11); Peru, 2002, Article 17–18, 24). Peru has created an inter-ministerial national commission to review patent applications and initiated actions to enforce misappropriated patents aboard, which are based on indigenous biological resources or knowledge (Peru, 2008, Article 3–4). India, has taken a strong stance against misappropriation in recent years seeking judgments in multiple jurisdictions to challenge the validity of patents, including: turmeric in the US, Neem tree or Azadirachta indica, a medicinal plant with the active compound Azadirachtin, in the US, Basmati rice in 15 countries (UK, Australia, France, UAE, etc.), and Atta Chakkis, a traditional grain originally patented by Monsanto, in the EU (Bhattacharya, 2014; EPO, Patent EP0445929B1). India has further established a Traditional Knowledge Digital Library, with national authorities working in collaboration with global patent offices to share information relating to examination and to discuss the development of similar libraries (WIPO, 2011). The above approaches illustrate a trend towards mandatory disclosure and digital collaboration among patent offices to verify and validate novelty in patent applications (UNCTAD, 2014, p. 73). Organizations must proactively ensure the sustainability of their supply chains through the adoption of sound policy measures to ensure patentable products which utilize bio-based compounds or derivatives are based on legally obtained samples and are accompanied by appropriate documentation. Where a benefit sharing agreement is established, ownership of intellectual property rights are in practice often outlined as a component of the mutually agreed terms (Australia, 2012, Section 7.1). With the advent of increased collaboration of patent offices across jurisdictions, due diligence should be exercised to review all previously sourced samples to ensure compliance with applicable legislative regimes in the source jurisdiction or country of origin and jurisdiction(s) of operations, regulatory review and registration of IP rights.

16.4.3 Complexity of benefit sharing

Establishment and administration of benefit-sharing agreements (BSAs) as envisioned under the Protocol present a wide range of additional legal, logistical and administrative complexities to the ongoing management of global bio-based supply chains. BSAs establish the contractual terms governing the transfer/utilization of the genetic or biological resource including potential triggers for commercial intent, the subsequent monetary and non-monetary benefits which will be shared, the timing of payment disbursements and any dispute settlement or review/renegotiation modalities. Depending upon the legal requirements of the jurisdiction, the BSA must be negotiated with the competent national authority, and/or the provider or ILCs with review by the competent national authority. Organizations which utilize bio-based components in their product portfolio must be aware of:

- The particular ABS requirements for each operative jurisdiction, bearing in mind the differential triggers across jurisdictions deeming a change from non-commercial to commercial intent

- Mandatory benefit-sharing requirements or royalty rates, and

- Potential checkpoints relating to auditing, reporting or review of benefit sharing terms.

Australia, a relatively advanced ABS jurisdiction (Prip *et al.*, 2014), provides a model BSA for commercial utilization of samples sourced from the Commonwealth which establishes mandatory terms to standardize the procedure (see Table 16.1).

Table 16.1 Australia model BSA (Australia, 2012)

A 2 year renewal requirement, with an option for an independent review of the terms	Section 3.2.1, 3.2.4
Benefit-sharing threshold criteria, annual payment percentages and example monetary and non-monetary benefits derived from the Bonn Guidelines	Section 5.1, Schedule 3-4
Requirements relating to use of TK and engagement with indigenous peoples	Section 6.1
A full grant of IP rights resulting from research and development	Section 7.1
A restriction on the transfer of samples, products or assignment IP rights to third parties but under an agreement which ensures that the Commonwealth continues to receive an equitable share of the benefits	Section 7.2
Record keeping and reporting requirements, including a detailed annual progress report	Section 11-12, 15
Criteria and consequences of termination, with default resulting in destruction or confiscation of samples and products and reassignment of remuneration rights under third party agreements relating to the samples to the Commonwealth	Section 17

Dispute settlement procedures including negotiation and mediation, and where needed legal proceedings under the governing law of Australia	Section 16

The challenge of accurately valuing particular samples to quantify the timing and delivery of proposed monetary and non-monetary benefits is addressed in multiple ways, with Australia utilizing user investment or "exploitation revenue" threshold amounts as strata indicating the applicable payment percentages based on type and significance of investment in utilization of the biological or resources (Australia, 2012, Section 5.1, Schedule 3). Peru, alternatively, has a mandatory benefit-sharing royalty percentage of 15% of gross profits before tax for access to indigenous traditional knowledge, with two-thirds going to the providing ILCs and one-third going to a state-administered fund for conservation and sustainable use of biodiversity and traditional knowledge (Peru, 2002, Article 8, 27). Finally Brazil, in Law No. 13,123 of May 20, 2015 suggests 1% of annual net revenue as a minimum standard for royalties with the ability for a ministry to reduce that percentage to ensure the competitiveness of the sector and further extends joint liability for benefit-sharing to domestic subsidiaries, affiliates and intermediaries involved and linked to the producer (Brazil, 2015, Article 20-21, 17.7). The approach adopted by Brazil to extend joint liability to domestic partners raises larger impacts on contractual and vendor relations relating to such liability across applicable bio-based supply chains likely requiring establishment of specific insurance and potential for renegotiation of existing agreements. Overall, benefit-sharing while carrying inherent technical and administrative complexities, aims to establish equitable partnerships throughout supply chains which positively incentivizes the conservation and sustainable use of biological resources. Organizations should proactively engage benefit-sharing modalities, rather than attempting to circumvent the need through forum shopping, utilizing them as a means to secure legitimate access to GR and TK in support of compliance requirements and expand supply chain relationships for bio-based components.

16.4.4 Requirement for collaborative access

Access in some jurisdictions is being limited or procedurally favoured to domestic institutions and foreign institutions in collaboration with a domestic institution. Brazil, in Law No. 13,123 (2015), requires applications for commercial use of genetic resources including derivatives and traditional knowledge, to be provided by nationals, or in limited circumstances foreign institutions in collaboration with a nation institution (Brazil, 2015, Article 1(I-VI), 11). India provides for a less onerous process for collaborative research projects with government sponsored or approved institutions, which still requires governmental approval but is less onerous (India, 2002, Article 5(1)). While limited to a set of jurisdictions globally, requirements for collaborative access are becoming increasingly common and tend to be found in developing or transitioning economies as a means to ensure domestic capacity is not subordinated to foreign biodiscovery.

Collaboration with a domestic partner throughout the biodiscovery process provides a wide spectrum of benefits to both partnering organizations. With the domestic organization receiving technology/knowledge transfer and capacity building, in return for a collaborative partner with unique expertise about the domestic biodiversity and, together, reduced costs of biodiscovery operations across the two organizations is possible. It must be noted that while non-monetary benefits included in the BSA may be provided throughout the collaborative relationship to the partner organization, this fact does not negate the need to share benefits, monetary or non-monetary, equitably with the providing authorities. Organizations in bio-based industries should view collaborative access requirements as opportunities to build enduring domestic partnerships, gain hard-to-obtain knowledge on the regional resources and potentially simplify access requirements while defusing costs of penetration into new markets across the domestic value chain.

16.5 Conclusion: Nagoya era challenges, opportunities and recommendations

16.5.1 Challenges and opportunities in global supply chains

With the entry into force of the Nagoya Protocol, and the ongoing development of Protocol compliant legislation in various jurisdictions, addressing Nagoya era effects on global supply chains demands foresight and an understanding of key challenges to effectively capitalize on opportunities presented by the Protocol. Challenges for bio-based industries in adapting to the Nagoya era include:

- Understanding "utilization" of genetic or biological resources and derivatives and accounting for the subsequent compliance requirements which arise in each jurisdiction of operation

- Operationalizing and optimizing prior informed consent (PIC) and collaborative access pathways within the organization

- Monitoring the status of non-commercial research for triggers transitioning into commercialization, notifying the appropriate authority following a change of intent and establishing new mutually agreed terms

- Ensuring traceability and appropriate reporting for each sample accessed and utilized to remain in compliance with applicable legislative regimes, and

- Developing effective internal controls and guidelines which accurately account for cross-jurisdictional compliance requirements.

Opportunities presented by the Nagoya Protocol, which are often overshadowed by the perceived complexity of compliance and operationalization, provide visionary bio-based organizations unique avenues to establish supply chain stability by positively incentivizing conservation and the sustainable use of natural resources through equitable benefit-sharing. First, while the Protocol continues to be implemented at the national level, bio-based organizations operating in those jurisdictions gain increased clarity, legal certainty and predictability in bioprospecting, biodiscovery and regulatory approval to support actualization of investments. Second, with the development of enhanced capacity among domestic authorities and institutions, new or otherwise unattainable opportunities to further strengthen research and development on genetic and biochemical resources may be made available through collaboration and access to TK. Third, participation of ILCs in a sound, transparent and equitable access process establishes trust, increases the potential for future collaboration, and enhances local knowledge of the economic value and importance of conservation practices discouraging overexploitation of resources in the informal sector. Fourth, development of internal or consortium guidelines for bioprospecting proactively addresses challenges raised by operations in jurisdictions lacking effective ABS legislation. Finally, benefit-sharing requirements provide a platform for sound integration of corporate social responsibility (CSR) aspects into business operations in a manner which rewards ethical sourcing.

16.5.2 Recommendations to move ahead

For organizations working in bio-based industries, the Nagoya Protocol provides increased legal clarification on which activities fall within the scope of the ABS regime and the concurrent legal obligations, while questions regarding the operationalization of such obligations persist. In the Nagoya era, R&D on the biochemical composition of biodiversity and identification of bioactive compounds for commercial use requires prior informed consent of the providers and sharing of benefits based on mutually agreed terms. Patent registration is increasingly requiring disclosure of country of origin and demonstration of legal access (PIC/MAT) to claim IP rights, with ongoing debate relating to a change in Article 29 of the Agreement on Trade-Related Aspects of Intellectual Property Rights (TRIPS) requiring mandatory disclosure of origin (UNCTAD, 2014). Organizations should review internal practices and collections to determine relevant risk exposure and adopt bioprospecting guidelines to assist in governing bio-discovery, with early examples of such being the Biotechnology Industry Organization (BIO), or the International Federation of Pharmaceutical Manufacturers Associations (IFPMA) guidelines to govern bioprospecting or utilization of genetic resources (BIO, 2006; IFPMA, 2015). Equitable sourcing in bio-based industries is no longer just a market differentiator, but increasingly an outright compliance requirement. By actively engaging access and benefit-sharing requirements, bio-based industries can concurrently remain compliant, avoid applicable punitive measure, support positive incentives relating to conservation and sustainable use of natural capital and establish secure and ethically sourced supply chains.

References

ABS Initiative (2014a). *National Study on ABS Implementation in South Africa* (Workshop 30–31 January 2014, Cape Town, South Africa). Retrieved from http://www.abs-initi-ative.info/fileadmin/media/Knowledge_Center/Pulications/ABS_Dialogue_042014/National_study_on_ABS_implementation_in_South_Africa_20140716.pdf

ABS Initiative (2014b). *National Study on the Implementation of ABS in Brazil* (Workshop 30–31 January 2014, Cape Town, South Africa). Retrieved from http://www.abs-initi-ative.info/fileadmin/media/Knowledge_Center/Pulications/ABS_Dialogue_042014/National_study_on_ABS_implementation_in_Brazil_20140716.pdf

Australia (2012). *Model Access and Benefit Sharing Agreement between Australian Government and Access Party*. Retrieved from http://laptop.deh.gov.au/biodiversity/science/access/permits/pubs/benefit-sharing-model.pdf

Australia (2000). *Environment Protection and Biodiversity Conservation Regulations*. Retrieved from http://www.comlaw.gov.au/Details/F2011C00848

Australia (1999). *Environment Protection and Biodiversity Conservation Act*. Retrieved from http://www.comlaw.gov.au/Details/C2013C00301

Australia (1983). *Great Barrier Reef Marine Park Regulations*. Retrieved from http://www.comlaw.gov.au/Details/F2013C01014

Australia (1975). *Great Barrier Reef Marine Park Act* (Cth). Retrieved from http://www.comlaw.gov.au/Details/C2011C00149

Bhattacharya, S. (2014). Bioprospecting, biopiracy and food security in India: The emerging sides of neoliberalism. *International Letters of Social and Humanistic Sciences*, 23, 49-56.

BIO (Biotechnology Industry Organization) (2005). *Guidelines for BIO Members Engaging in Bioprospecting*. Retrieved from https://www.bio.org/articles/guidelines-bio-members-engaging-bioprospecting (4 July 2015)

Brazil (2015). *Law No. 13,123* (20 May 2015) [unofficial translation]. Retrieved from http://www.planalto.gov.br/CCIVIL_03/_Ato2015-2018/2015/Lei/L13123.htm

Brazil (2001). *Provisional Measure* n. 2.186-16/2001. Retrieved from http://www.farm-ersrights.org/pdf/americas/Brazil/Brazil-access01.pdf

Cabrera, J., Phillips, F.K., & Perron-Welch, F. (2014a). *Biodiversity Legislation Study: A Review of Biodiversity Legislation in 8 Countries*. Hamburg, Germany: World Future Council. Retrieved from http://www.worldfuturecouncil.org/fileadmin/user_upload/PDF/BIO-DIVERSITY_master.pdf

Cabrera, J., Perron-Welch, F., & Phillips, F.K. (2014b). *Overview of National and Regional Measures on Access and Benefit Sharing: Challenges and Opportunities in Implementing the Nagoya Protocol* (3rd ed.). Montreal, Canada: CISDL. Retrieved from http://www.cisdl.org/aichilex/files/Global%20Overview%20of%20ABS%20Measures_FINAL_SBS11A18.pdf

Cabrera, J., Tvedt, M.W., Perron-Welch, F., Jørem A., & Phillips, F.K. (2013). *The Interface between the Nagoya Protocol on ABS and the ITPGRFA at the International Level: Potential Issues for Consideration in Supporting Mutually Supportive Implementation at the National Level*, FNI Report 1/2013. Oslo, Norway: Fridtjof Nansen Institute. Retrieved from http://www.fni.no/doc&pdf/FNI-R0113.pdf

CBD (Convention on Biological Diversity) (2014). *COP12 Business and Biodiversity Forum* (12–14 October 2014) Pyeongchang, South Korea. Retrieved from https://www.cbd.int/business/GP%20meeting%20doc/Full%20Agenda--COP%2012%20Business%20and%20Biodiversity%20Forum%20(FINAL).pdf

CBD (Convention on Biological Diversity) Secretariat. *List of Parties to Nagoya Protocol* (Montreal: CBD). Retrieved from https://www.cbd.int/abs/nagoya-protocol/signatories (October 25, 2015)

CBD (Convention on Biological Diversity) Secretariat. *List of Parties to the Convention on Biological Diversity* (Montreal: CBD). Retrieved from http://www.cbd.int/information/parties.shtml (25 October 2015)

CBD (Convention on Biological Diversity) (1992). 31 I.L.M. 822. Retrieved from http://www.cbd.int/doc/legal/cbd-en.pdf

EC (European Commission) (2014). *Regulation (EU) No 511/2014 of the European Parliament and of the Council of 16 April 2014 on compliance measures for users from the Nagoya Protocol on Access to Genetic Resources and the Fair and Equitable Sharing of Benefits Arising from their Utilization in the Union*, OJ L 150, 20.5.2014, at pp. 59-71. Retrieved from http://eur-lex.europa.eu/legal-content/EN/TXT/PDF/?uri=CELEX:32014R0511&from=EN

EPO (European Patent Office) (1973, updated 2013). *Convention on the Grant of European Patents and Implementing Regulations to the Convention on the Grant of European Patents* (15th ed.). Retrieved from http://documents.epo.org/projects/babylon/eponet.nsf/0/00E0CD7FD461C0D5C1257C060050C376/$File/EPC_15th_edition_2013.pdf (27 June 2012)

Greiber, T., Moreno, S.P., Åhrén, M., Carrasco, J.N., Kamau, E.C., Cabrera, J., Oliva, M.J., Perron-Welch, F., Ali, N., & Williams, C. (2012). *An Explanatory Guide to the Nagoya Protocol on Access and Benefit-sharing.* IUCN Environmental Policy and Law Paper, 83, Bonn: IUCN-ELC, 2012. Retrieved from https://cmsdata.iucn.org/downloads/an_explanatory_guide_to_the_nagoya_protocol.pdf

Hawke, A. (2009). *Independent Review of the Environment Protection and Biodiversity Conservation Act 1999*, Australian Government Department of the Environment, Water, Heritage and the Arts. Retrieved from http://www.environment.gov.au/system/files/resources/5d70283b-3777-442e-b395-b0a22ba1b273/files/interim-report.pdf

India (2011). *Arunachal Pradesh State Biodiversity Rules.* Retrieved from http://nbaindia.org/uploaded/pdf/notification/Arunachal_pradesh_Rules.pdf

India (2004). *Biological Diversity Rules.* Retrieved from http://www.wipo.int/wipolex/en/text.jsp?file_id=200357

India (2002). *Biological Diversity Act.* Retrieved from http://www.wipo.int/wipolex/en/text.jsp?file_id=185798

India (1970 as amended 2015). *Patent Act.* Retrieved from http://www.ipindia.nic.in/ipr/patent/Patent_Act_1970_11March2015.pdf

IFPMA (International Federation of Pharmaceutical Manufacturers Associations) (2015). *Guidelines for IFPMA Members on Access to Genetic Resources and Equitable Sharing of Benefits Arising out of their Utilization.* Retrieved from http://www.ifpma.org/fileadmin/content/Innovation/Biodiversity%20and%20Genetic%20Resources/IFPMA_Guidelines_Access_to_Genetic_Resources.pdf (July 4, 2015)

Nagoya Protocol on *Access to Genetic Resources and the Fair and Equitable Sharing of Benefits Arising from their Utilization to the Convention on Biological Diversity.* UNEP/CBD/COP/DEC/X/1 (2010). Retrieved from http://www.cbd.int/abs/doc/protocol/nagoya-protocol-en.pdf (29 October 2015)

National Biodiversity Authority of India (2014). *Peoples Biodiversity Register.* Retrieved from http://nbaindia.org/content/105/30/2/pbr.html (July 4, 2015)

National Biodiversity Authority of India (2013). *Peoples Biodiversity Register: Revised PBR Guidelines*. Retrieved from http://nbaindia.org/uploaded/pdf/PBR%20Format%202013.pdf

OECD (Organisation for Economic Co-operation and Development) (2009). *Bioeconomy to 2030: Designing a Policy Framework, Main Findings and Policy Conclusions* (Paris, France: OECD, 2009). Retrieved from http://www.oecd.org/futures/long-termtechnologicalsocietalchallenges/42837897.pdf

Peru (2008). Law No 28216, *Act on the Protection of Access to Peruvian Biological Diversity and the Collective Knowledge of Indigenous Peoples*. Retrieved from http://www.wipo.int/edocs/lexdocs/laws/en/pe/pe013en.pdf

Peru (2002). Law No.27811 of 24 July 2002, *Introducing a Protection Regime for the Collective Knowledge of Indigenous Peoples derived from Biological Resources*, El Peruano, 227953. Retrieved from http://www.wipo.int/wipolex/en/text.jsp?file_id=179597

Phillips, F.K., & Perron-Welch, F. (2015). *The Interface of CITES, the CBD, and the Nagoya Protocol: Issues to Consider for Mutually Supportive Domestic Implementation and Sustainable Development*. Presented at CITES as a Tool for Sustainable Development Conference, Cambridge, UK (20–21 February 2015).

Prip, C., Rosendal, G.K., Andresen, S., & Tvedt M.W. (2014). *The Australian ABS Framework: A Model Case for Bioprospecting?* (FNI Report 1/2014). Retrieved from http://www.fni.no/doc&pdf/FNI-R0114.pdf

South Africa (2012). *South Africa's Bioprospecting, Access and Benefit-Sharing Regulatory Framework: Guidelines for Providers, Users and Regulators*. Retrieved from https://www.environment.gov.za/sites/default/files/legislations/bioprospecting_regulatory_framework_guideline.pdf

South Africa (2008). National Environmental Management: Biodiversity Act 2004 (Act No.10 2004) *Regulations on Bioprospecting and Access and Benefit Sharing 2008*. Retrieved from http://www.wipo.int/wipolex/en/text.jsp?file_id=179663

South Africa (2005). Act No.20 of 2005: Patents Amendment Act, 2005, *Government Gazette* 486(28319). Retrieved from http://www.accu.or.jp/ich/en/training/national_law_pdf/national_law_southafrica_02.pdf

South Africa (2004). *National Environmental Management: Biodiversity Act*, (Act no 10 of 2004). Retrieved from http://faolex.fao.org/docs/pdf/saf45083.pdf

Switzerland (2012). *Loi fédérale du 25 juin 1954 sur les brevets d'invention (état le 1er janvier 2012)* 232.14. Retrieved from https://www.admin.ch/opc/fr/classified-compilation/19540108/201201010000/232.14.pdf

UNCTAD (United Nations Conference on Trade and Development) (2014). *The Convention on Biological Diversity and the Nagoya Protocol: Intellectual Property Implications: A Handbook on the Interface between Global Access and Benefit Sharing Rules and Intellectual Property*, (UN Conference on Trade and Development). Retrieved from http://unctad.org/en/PublicationsLibrary/diaepcb2014d3_en.pdf

UNCTAD (United Nations Conference on Trade and Development) (2013). *Report of the I Biotrade Congress: Biodiversity, the Life of the Green Economy*. UNCTAD/DITC/TED/2012/6 (UN Conference on Trade and Development). Retrieved from http://unctad.org/en/PublicationsLibrary/UNCTAD_DITC_TED_2012_6.pdf

UNEP (United Nations Environment Programme) (2012). *TEEB for Business*, (Bonn: IUCN), Retrieved from http://www.teebweb.org/media/2012/01/TEEB-For-Business.pdf

WIPO (World Intellectual Property Organization) (2011). *International Conference on the Utilization of the Traditional Knowledge Digital Library as a Model for Protection of Traditional Knowledge*, (22–24 March 2011, New Delhi, India).

Freedom-Kai Phillips, MA (Seton Hall), LLB (Dalhousie), is currently undertaking an LLM at the University of Ottawa focusing on IP Law and is a member of the research teams supporting the ABS Canada and Open AIR projects. Additionally, he is a legal consultant and a legal research fellow with the Biodiversity and Biosafety Law Research Program for the Centre for International Sustainable Development Law (CISDL) where he works as the legal researcher in support of the Ramsar Convention Secretariat. He has done work with the International Development Law Organization (IDLO), the Ramsar Convention Secretariat, the Swiss FOEN and the ABS Capacity Development Initiative. His professional work focuses on analyzing, assessing, and implementing access and benefit sharing regimes, bioprospecting and biodiscovery compliance planning, intellectual property rights relating to bio-based products and developing strategies to integrate biodiversity and sustainability goals into organizational risk frameworks.

Part IV
Directions for future research

17

Promoting socially responsible purchasing (SRP)

The role of transaction cost economics dimensions

Simon Bartczek, Janjaap Semeijn and Lieven Quintens
Maastricht University School of Business and Economics, The Netherlands

We investigate the mechanism of socially responsible purchasing (SRP), the consideration of both environmental and social criteria in corporate purchasing decisions, its transfer between buyers and suppliers and the role of transaction cost economic theory (TCE) in this context. Using a dyadic perspective, we develop a conceptual model to investigate the role of supplier behavioural uncertainty, buyer-specific investments and transaction frequency for buyer and supplier SRP. We empirically validate our model using Structural Equation Modelling, based on a sample of 137 firms involved in 89 dyadic supply chain relationships. Focusing on the textile industry, our results show the presence of an underlying mechanism governing buyer SRP vis-à-vis supplier SRP. This chapter illustrates the special nature of TCE dimensions: they appear almost non-relevant as antecedents, rather they act as moderators for the SRP relationship. We find that buyer investments and transaction frequency positively moderate the SRP relationship, while supplier behavioural uncertainty has a negative impact. From a practical perspective, we identify TCE-related conditions for buyers' and suppliers' increased engagement in socially responsible firm behaviour. Our paper gives guidance on how buyers could take TCE dimensions into account for managing upstream Corporate Social Responsibility (CSR) behaviour.

17.1 Introduction

Socially responsible purchasing (SRP) initiatives play a fundamental role in the establishment of a supply chain that employs corporate social responsibility (CSR) practices (Ferrari *et al.*, 2010), covering both environmental and social values. Through its organizational boundary-crossing occupation, the purchasing function is well positioned to transmit these values across organizational boundaries (Krause *et al.*, 2009; Pullman *et al.*, 2009). While the involvement of the purchasing function in CSR logistics activities can lead to significantly improved supplier CSR performance (Carter and Jennings, 2002; Carter, 2005), the underlying mechanisms on a transactional basis remain unclear. To what extent is buyer SRP instrumental in the CSR behavioural alignment among immediate vertical business partners in a supply chain (Krause *et al.*, 2009) and which factors influence this effect?

We rely on the transaction cost economics (TCE) literature, previously shown to be an effective theory to explain and predict corporate and inter-organizational behaviour and related managerial decisions (Heide and John, 1990; Noordewier *et al.*, 1990; Rindfleisch and Heide, 1997; Stump *et al.*, 2002). Recent studies indicate that TCE appears relevant for studying the adoption of environmental practices by suppliers (Tate *et al.*, 2011; Tate *et al.*, 2014). TCE even appears promising for evaluating the effectiveness of the diffusion of voluntary CSR initiatives and standards across a supply chain depending on the transaction costs of the underlying relationship (Rosen *et al.*, 2002). For instance, asset specificity, as one of the elements of transaction cost economics, has been linked to CSR commitment (Simpson *et al.*, 2007). Delmas and Montiel (2009) stress the importance of organizational action and asset specificity as explanatory dimensions of TCE in CSR initiatives as well. So far, the use of transaction cost analysis in supply chain management remains limited despite multiple calls for its application (Grover and Malhotra, 2003; Hobbs, 1996; Williamson, 2008). Also, Sarkis *et al.* (2011) encourage the investigation of TCE dimensions in a CSR supply chain management context.

This study contributes to the emerging, but limited, body of research on transaction-related conditions for buyers' and suppliers' increased engagement in socially responsible firm behaviour. Specifically, we look at the relationship between buyer and supplier SRP and how this relationship is affected by different TCE dimensions. From a theoretical perspective, we expand the TCE literature by investigating to what extent TCE dimensions act as antecedents and/or moderators to the buyer and supplier SRP relationship. We complement research on CSR by examining the implications of buyer CSR activities on the upstream supply chain, beyond the direct supplier (Carter *et al.*, 2000; Kovács, 2008) by investigating the role of TCE dimensions for CSR in a dyadic setting (i.e. buyer–supplier). From a practical perspective, we identify TCE-related conditions for buyers' and suppliers' increased engagement in environmentally and socially responsible firm behaviour.

The remainder of this study is structured as follows: after an introduction of TCE analysis, hypotheses are introduced and the methodology is described, followed by the presentation of the results. Finally, we discuss the implications of our findings, from both a theoretical and managerial perspective.

17.2 Literature review and hypothesis development

We start with a brief discussion of TCE which is essential for the model we propose. We then formulate hypotheses using literature from different areas, including the supply chain collaboration literature.

17.2.1 Transaction cost economics (TCE)

TCE assumes markets to be inefficient, forcing clients to conduct transactional activities that do not occur without friction (Coase, 1937) and to bear the related costs. The expenses stemming from engaging in these transaction-related activities have been termed transaction costs (Arrow, 1970). Search and information costs, bargaining (the costs stemming from the negotiation of individual contracts for every exchange transaction) and contracting costs (the costs of specifying the conditions of a transaction in a long-term contract in detail) as well as costs related to the management of the ongoing transaction process (i.e. monitoring and enforcement costs) may serve as examples of transaction costs.

Transactions are presumed to be conducted in such a way that the costs stemming from these transaction-related activities are minimized (Lai *et al.*, 2005; Williamson, 1991a). TCE theory advocates the efficient governance of transaction relationships to provide the potential for competitive advantage (Williamson, 1991b; Dyer, 1996), where governance efficiency depends heavily on the transactional attributes of asset specificity and uncertainty (Dyer, 1996; Rindfleisch and Heide, 1997). We refer to Williamson (1975, 1981, 1985, and 1991) for an elaborate discussion on the central propositions of TCE, to Shelanski and Klein (1995), David and Han (2004) and Macher and Richman (2008) for comprehensive reviews and to Perrow (1981), Granovetter (1985), and Ghoshal and Moran (1996) for criticism of TCE.

TCE can provide new insights into a supply chain context (Maloni and Carter, 2006; Wallenburg, 2009; Williamson, 2008) as well as specifically for CSR and sourcing activities (Carter and Easton, 2011; Carter and Rogers, 2008; Pagell *et al.*, 2010): detailed frameworks specifying supplier CSR conduct tend to simplify and routinize interfirm transactions based on specific environmental and social supply chain programs. The underlying transaction costs of a relationship can thus have a significant impact on diffusion levels of voluntary CSR standards within supply chains (Rosen *et al.*, 2002). In particular, asset specificity (and resulting degrees of inter-organizational dependencies) have been related to supplier environmental commitment (Simpson *et al.*, 2007) and the adoption of CSR in supply chains previously (Delmas and Montiel, 2009; Vachon and Klassen, 2006).

17.2.2 Conceptual model

According to TCE, specific assets, uncertainty and frequency constitute the core factors that evoke shifts in bilateral governance (Heide and John, 1990). Authors adopting a TCE perspective have consistently shown the effectiveness of the TCE mechanism in explaining the control of a relationship (i.e. supply chain) partner's behavioural uncertainty (e.g. Heide and John, 1992; Ring and Van De Ven, 1994; Coles and Hesterly, 1998). Our model thus uses the core dimensions of transactions (uncertainty, asset specificity and transaction frequency; Rindfleisch and Heide, 1997). Table 17.1 provides an overview of the different TCE constructs used and their definitions.

Table 17.1 Terms used and definitions

Construct	Definition	Construct measured based on data obtained from
Buyer and supplier SRP	Buyer/supplier SRP refers to the combination of buyer/supplier contents and practices that form a dynamic firm capability "to reduce potential risk exposure by prescribing a set of CSR standards that suppliers must meet to win their business" (Keating *et al.*, 2008, p. 175)	Buyer and supplier
Supplier CSR behavioural uncertainty	Supplier CSR behavioural uncertainty constitutes "the inability to predict (...) [upstream] partner (...) [CSR] behaviour or changes in the external environment" (Joshi and Stump, 1999, p. 293)	Buyer
Buyer asset specificity	Asset specificity refers to the extent to which buyer-specific investments have been made by the buyer in a given exchange relationship (Heide and John, 1990)	Buyer
Transaction frequency	"Transaction frequency refers to the number of individual elements that make up the transaction under consideration" (Klein, 1989, p. 256).	Buyer

Figure 17.1 shows the hypothesized relationships between buyer SRP and supplier SRP and the role of TCE. We propose that the TCE dimensions supplier behavioural uncertainty, buyer asset specificity and transaction frequency act as antecedents to and moderate the relationship between buyer and supplier SRP.

Figure 17.1 Hypothesized relationships

Source: authors

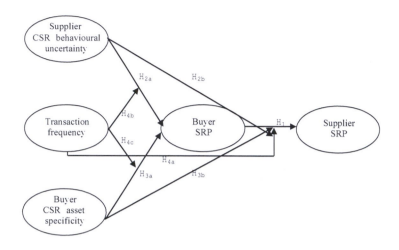

17.2.2.1 Socially responsible purchasing

Corporate CSR performance is inherently dependent on suppliers conforming to the CSR practices of a given supply chain (Krause *et al.*, 2009). Europe's 2013 meat adulteration scandal, that found processed and unprocessed beef to contain considerable amounts of undeclared or improperly declared horse meat, resulted in a significant decrease in customer trust in hamburger fast food restaurants and supermarket chains (The Telegraph, 2013). Boundary-spanning activities, such as purchasing, have been linked to environmental initiatives by both buyers and suppliers (Bowen *et al.*, 2001; Carter and Carter, 1998; Klassen and Vachon, 2003; Vachon and Klassen, 2006). Socially responsible purchasing (SRP), which embraces both environmental and social criteria in corporate purchasing decisions, plays a fundamental role in the establishment of CSR in a supply chain (Ferrari *et al.*, 2010): the involvement of the purchasing function in CSR logistics activities can lead to significantly improved supplier CSR performance (Carter and Jennings, 2002; Carter, 2005) as well as the supply chain's overall efficiency and performance (Corbett and Klassen, 2006; Pagell and Wu, 2009). By employing CSR measures in their supplier evaluation and development activities, buyers can have a leading role in affecting supplier SRP (Walker *et al.*, 2008). CSR behavioural alignment in the supply chain can thus be achieved through SRP decisions of single actors (Krause *et al.*, 2009). Hence,

Hypothesis 1: *Buyer SRP behaviour has a positive effect on supplier SRP behaviour.*

17.2.2.2 CSR-related supplier behavioural uncertainty

Supplier behavioural uncertainty, "the inability to predict [...] [upstream] partner [...] behaviour or changes in the external environment" (Joshi and Stump, 1999, p. 293), originates from "the behavioural uncertainty arising from the (strategic) actions of an exchange partner firm" (Sutcliffe and Zaheer, 1998, p. 4) and thus from difficulties in monitoring compliance with contractual arrangements of exchange partners (Son *et al.*, 2005; Williamson, 1985) including CSR requirements. Purchasing's role as a critical link between the focal firm's manufacturing and its supply base reduces inter-organizational uncertainties and opportunism (Das *et al.*, 2006). Thus, we expect buyers to engage in SRP activities to mitigate perceived supplier CSR-related behavioural uncertainties.

As the extent to which firms engage in cooperative CSR supply chain management depends on pro-active, values-based CSR initiatives (Sharfman *et al.*, 2009), we expect the perceived degree of supplier CSR behaviour to strengthen the relationship between buyer SRP and supplier SRP. Thus, the more CSR pro-active and prominent the supplier (i.e. the less ambiguity in supplier CSR behaviour), the stronger the connection between buyer SRP and supplier SRP. We expect:

Hypothesis 2a: *Supplier CSR-behavioural uncertainty, as perceived by buyers, has a positive effect on buyer SRP.*

Hypothesis 2b: *The weaker supplier CSR behavioural uncertainty, as perceived by buyers, the stronger the relationship between buyer SRP and supplier SRP.*

17.2.2.3 Asset specificity

Integrative forms of governance and bilateral dependence counteract potential opportunistic behaviour or specific assets becoming sunk costs and contribute to supplier commitment and reliability (Williamson, 2008). Asset specificity is the extent to which buyer-specific investments have been made by the buyer and the supplier in a given exchange relationship. Asset specificity can manifest as site specificity, physical asset specificity (e.g. investment in joint or customized equipment), human asset specificity (e.g. possession of unique knowhow), brand name capital and dedicated assets (i.e. special investments made in the supplier's facilities for one particular client (Williamson, 1991a). Asset specificity is negatively related to asset redeploy-ability, which results in sunk costs in the case of the termination of the underlying relationship (Klein *et al.*, 1978); we expect a positive relationship between buyer asset specificity and buyer SRP.

Rising levels of relationship-specific investments by buyers can increase suppliers' responsiveness to a customer's CSR performance requirements (Simpson *et al.*, 2007). These requirements include codes of conduct, CSR programmes, guidelines, monitoring, internal and external certification schemes, knowledge transfer and education (Hughes, 2001; Handfield and Bechtel, 2002; Mayer *et al.*, 2004; King *et al.*, 2005; Baden *et al.*, 2009). Also, the adoption of ISO 14001 has been related to asset specificity (Delmas and Montiel, 2009). We expect buyer CSR asset specificity to increase CSR-alignment between buyers and suppliers.

Hypothesis 3a: *Buyer asset specificity has a positive effect on buyer SRP.*

Hypothesis 3b: *The higher CSR buyer asset specificity, the stronger the relationship between buyer SRP and supplier SRP.*

17.2.2.4 Transaction frequency

Transaction frequency entails "the cost of specialized internal governance" (Williamson, 2002, p. 175). Setup costs of specialized governance structures vary with the relative frequency with which particular transactions recur. For infrequent transactions, losses originating from opportunism and inflexibility are likely to undercut the company's incremental business expenditure (Anderson and Schmittlein, 1984). Specialized governance structures are easier to justify for recurrent transactions compared to identical transactions taking place occasionally (Williamson, 1979). Scale economies stemming from the management and acquired experience and background knowledge on the definition, implementation and monitoring of several upstream CSR initiatives are expected to tip the scales in favour of the continued implementation of upstream CSR activities. In addition, transactions that occur with higher frequencies among the same supply chain partners are expected to cause the benefits of upstream CSR activities to become more apparent and the efforts in the implementation of upstream CSR initiatives to be more appealing. Thus, we expect transaction frequency to strengthen all hypothesized relationships in the model.

Hypothesis 4a: *The higher the transaction frequency between buyer and supplier, the stronger the relationship between buyer SRP and supplier SRP.*

Hypothesis 4b: *The higher transaction frequency between buyer and supplier, the stronger the relationship between supplier CSR behavioural uncertainty and buyer SRP.*

Hypothesis 4c: *The higher the transaction frequency between buyer and supplier, the stronger the relationship between CSR buyer asset specificity and buyer SRP.*

17.3 Research method

17.3.1 Sample

Consistent with Pullman *et al.*'s (2009) expectation that CSR research is likely not to generalize between different industries, we carry out industry=-specific CSR research, namely in the textile industry. Our choice of the garment industry stems from observations that established supplier monitoring practices—manifested in comprehensive codes of conduct, monitoring and auditing activities—repeatedly fail to deliver adequate CSR results (Welford and Frost, 2006; Reynolds and Bowie, 2004). Recurrent ethical scandals detected in the supply chains of global fashion retailers like Gap, Nike, Marks and Spencer and Zara (BBC, 2011; Chamberlain, 2010), the collapse of a supplying garment factory complex in an industrial suburb of Dhaka, Bangladesh, which took the lives of 1,133 people and caused more than 2,000 to be injured (Bhasin, 2013; Zeit Online, 2013), or the fatal fire in 2012 at Ali Enterprises, a Pakistani garment factory resulting in some 300 deaths, unveil severe deficits in the field of working conditions in their upstream production chains. Apparently, fashion producers struggle to create conditions that assert an effective application and enforcement of a set of minimal social and environmental standards.

We selected organizations that claim to be leaders in CSR practices (Pagell and Wu, 2009; Sharfman *et al.*, 2009; Tate *et al.*, 2010) which have taken the initiative to extend their CSR activities across corporate boundaries; the comparatively high mean values of the sampled constructs confirm the claim of superior CSR performance among the sampled firms. Thus, this paper presents industry-specific data on what we believe to be a commercially, environmentally and ethically sensitive industrial branch. Our targeted sampling approach (Eisenhardt and Graebner, 2007; Sharfman *et al.*, 2009) allows for systematic case selection with rich, informative content and facilitates a root cause analysis.

Consistent with the recommendations of Kumar *et al.* (1993) on the use of key informants, we selected respondents with substantial knowledge of their firm's extent of CSR, its supply chain practices and policies, and its competitive environment. Thus, we chose executives whose understanding and areas of expertise pertain to the organization as a whole, most notably managing directors (59%) and senior managers (37%) in the field of CSR, purchasing and supply chain management. To address the key respondent issue, we asked respondents how knowledgeable they were with the survey questions and how confident they were in answering the survey; we only included responses of professionals who demonstrated proficiency in the field of interest. To minimize social desirability bias, we employed the technique of "projective questioning" (Armacost et al., 1991) and asked respondents to answer questions concerning the corporate or purchasing department's position as opposed to their personal perceptions (Rudelius and Buchholz, 1979).

Prior to data collection, in line with Dillman et al. (2009), we pre-tested our survey instrument through preliminary interviews with buyer and supplier representatives to ensure adequacy of the research design as well as face and content validity of the scales. The TCE questionnaire was then tested and adapted in terms of wording and layout.

We collected our primary data through online surveying. Online surveys allow for the collection of large-scale data in a time- and cost-effective manner. They contribute to overcoming respondent's unwillingness to disclose information perceived to be sensitive in nature (Schillewaert and Meulemeester, 2005). At the same time, online surveys yield equally reliable and valid analytical results when compared to mail surveys (Deutskens et al., 2004).

The data was collected in 2011; 214 firms were approached. E-mail invitations and repeated reminders ultimately resulted in a sample of 137 companies (response rate: 64%) that were involved in 89 pairs of dyadic supply chain relationships (please refer to Table 17.2 for demographic information). We tested for, but detected no, non-response bias (Armstrong and Overton, 1977).

Table 17.2 Sample demographics

Industrial field	N	Percentage	<100 FTEs	Firm size 100–200 FTEs	Firm size >200 FTEs
Textile retail	39	28.5	18	9	12
Dying and fabric finishing	38	27.7	9	14	15
Yarn production	34	24.8	13	17	4
Plant color pigments	12	8.8	7	3	2
Fashion accessories	9	6.6	5	4	0
Agriculture	5	3.6	5	0	0

17.3.2 Construct measures

Consistent with prior research, we drew upon research from Carter and Jennings (2004), who operationalize SRP as a second-order construct with environmental and social first-order dimensions (please refer to Section 17.4.1 for a detailed description). TCE constructs play a central role in our model. Behavioural uncertainty stems from difficulties in monitoring supplier performance. We adapted

Grover and Malhotra's (2003) five-item scale to evaluate supplier performance. Asset specificity refers to the extent to which buyer-specific investments have been made by the buyer and the supplier in a given exchange relationship. We used Heide and John's (1990) two-item scale to measure buyer's specific investments. Transaction frequency refers to the relative number of (purchase) transactions (adapted from Klein, 1989).

We controlled for intercorrelations among the items on each scale and eliminated those with high correlations. Principal components factor analysis, which aims to preserve as much of the original measures' total variance as possible, indicated the scales' unidimensionality and discriminant validity. Subsequently, we rotated the factor model for analysis. We employed Varimax rotation to differentiate the original variables by extracted factor. Next, we conducted confirmatory factor analyses on the scale items. Based on structural equation modelling and in line with Gerbing and Anderson's (1988) recommendations for scale development, we tested our measurement model in search of factor loadings permitting an analysis of relationships between observed and unobserved variables. The obtained loadings of observed variables on the latent variables (factors), as well as the correlation between the latent variables support our confidence in the quality of the identified factors.

17.4 Data analysis

We utilized partial least square (PLS) path modelling with latent variables using the SmartPLS 2.0 software to attain the parameter estimates in the measurement and structural models (Chin, 1998; Ringle, 2006; Ringle *et al.*, 2010). In line with Hulland (1999), we analyzed and interpreted our model in two steps: First, we assessed the reliability and validity of the measurement model and then assessed the structural model. Although we used the PLS algorithm to obtain the paths, outer loadings, outer weights and the quality criteria, we relied on the bootstrap functionality to obtain the t-values and to determine the significance levels of structural paths and item loadings. To obtain the desired output, a bootstrap with 1,000 resamples was employed. The psychometric properties of the measurement instruments, as assessed by SmartPLS, included reliability, convergent validity and discriminant validity (Tenenhaus *et al.*, 2005).

The standardized loadings are reported in Table 17.3; all CRs exceed the threshold of 0.7 (Gefen *et al.*, 2000). We measured discriminant validity, the degree to which items from one construct differ from items denoting a different construct, by comparing the magnitude of the square root of the average variance extracted (AVE) in comparison to the value of the correlations; the former should be higher than the latter (Chin, 1998; Fornell and Larcker, 1981). As shown in table 17.3, with the exception of supplier environmental SRP, all AVEs exceeded the recommended cut-off value of 0.5 (Fornell and Larcker, 1981). A composite reliability value exceeding 0.6 reinforced our confidence in the convergent validity of our supplier environmental SRP construct (Fornell and Larcker, 1981) support.

17.4.1 Measurement model

To assess partial model structures and evaluate the adequacy of the measurement model and the structural model (Chin, 1998), we relied on the two-stage process suggested by Henseler *et al.* (2009) to evaluate the model fit (Schepers *et al.*, 2005). To assess reliability, we measured internal consistency reliability, composite reliability and AVE. The measures of the constructs exceed the recommended thresholds of 0.7 for internal consistency and composite reliability and 0.5 for AVE. All measured constructs are above 0.7 (Hair, Anderson *et al.*, 1998) with the exception of supplier environmental SRP ($\alpha = 0.67$). Composite reliability scores of 0.75 or higher for all constructs provide a measure of confidence in the used scales.

Table 17.3 Summary of reliability measurements (n=89)

Construct	Construct mean	Cronbach's Alpha	Composite reliability	AVE	Factor loading (range)
Buyer SRP					
Environmental	5.95	0.96	0.97	0.79	0.86-0.90
Philanthropy and human rights	4.99	0.96	0.97	0.83	0.86-0.92
Ethics	5.00	0.99	0.99	0.91	0.94-0.97
Supplier CSR behavioural uncertainty	2.54	0.97	0.98	0.91	0.94-0.96
Buyer CSR asset specificity	5.42	0.94	0.70	0.93	0.96-0.97
Transaction frequency	5.62	n.a.	n.a.	n.a.	n.a.
Supplier SRP					
Environmental	5.54	0.67	0.75	0.40	0.51-0.88
Philanthropy and human rights	4.64	0.81	0.87	0.57	0.69-0.80
Ethics	5.01	0.77	0.84	0.52	0.66-0.79

We found evidence for discriminant validity, which was assessed with the Fornell-Larcker criterion (Fornell and Larcker, 1981), as the correlations among the all corresponding formative constructs do not exceed the square-roots of AVE scores. These correlations are shown in Table 17.4.

Table 17.4 Correlation table

	1	2	3	4	5	6	7	8	9
Buyer SRP Environmental (1)	0.89								
Buyer SRP Human rights (2)	0.71	**0.91**							
Buyer SRP Ethics (3)	0.17	0.46	**0.96**						
Supplier CSR Behavioural Uncertainty (4)	0.59	0.56	0.19	**0.95**					
Buyer CSR asset Specificity (5)	0.62	0.53	0.16	0.70	**0.97**				
Transaction Frequency (7)	0.61	0.53	0.19	0.68	0.60	**1.00**			
Supplier SRP Environmental (8)	0.41	0.32	0.08	0.38	0.46	0.46	**0.63**		
Supplier SRP Human rights (9)	0.55	0.53	0.38	0.65	0.60	0.57	0.11	**0.76**	
Supplier SRP Ethics (10)	0.25	0.38	0.34	0.32	0.30	0.25	0.01	0.71	**0.72**

Figure 17.2 Measurement model: buyer and supplier SRP

Source: authors

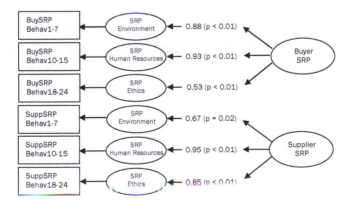

17.4.2 Structural model

The results for the main direct effects model support three of our hypotheses. We find a strong positive direct link among buyer and supplier SRP (b=0.91, t=12.66). Buyer CSR asset specificity (b=0.36, t=1.82) and transaction frequency (b=0.24, t=2.00, not hypothesized) are positively related to buyer SRP. The direct effects model does not find support for supplier CSR behavioural uncertainty as an antecedent for buyer and supplier SRP. Also, buyer CSR asset specificity and transaction frequency (not hypothesized) do not serve as explanatory factors of supplier SRP. The results for the direct effects models are provided in Table 17.5, along with the R2 for each endogenous construct.

Table 17.5 Direct effects: beta coefficients and t-values (in parenthesis)

	Buyer SRP	Supplier SRP
Buyer SRP		0.91 (12.66)***
Supplier CSR behavioural uncertainty	-0.23 (1.00)	0.07 (0.71)
Buyer CSR asset specificity	0.36 (1.82)*	-0.13 (0.85)
Transaction frequency	0.24 (2.00)*	0.06 (0.44)
Construct R2	0.65	0.82

Key: ***p<0.001; ** p<0.01; * p<0.05

With our moderating effects model, we found support for four of our eight hypotheses (please refer to Table 17.5). In contrast to our direct effects model, it should be noted that no direct relationship between buyer SRP and supplier SRP was observed, as the size of the scores, as well as the correlations among the respective formative constructs of buyer and supplier SRP, appear to support the absence of a direct relationship among buyer and supplier SRP. Instead, buyer asset specificity strengthens the relationship between buyer and supplier SRP (b=1.8, t=6.10). Not hypothesized, buyer asset specificity was also found to be a direct antecedent of supplier SRP (b=1.27, t=5.31). Contrary to our expectations, supplier CSR behavioural uncertainty strengthens the relationship between buyer and supplier SRP (b=0.43, t=3.72). Transaction frequency strengthens the relationship between buyer asset specificity and buyer SRP (b=0.41, t=2.09), but fails to display such an effect among the relationships of supplier CSR behavioural uncertainty and buyer SRP.

Table 17.6 Moderating effects: beta coefficients and t-values (in parenthesis)

	Buyer SRP	Supplier SRP
Buyer SRP		0.23 (1.24)
Supplier CSR Behavioural uncertainty	0.32 (1.45)	0.16 (1.56)
Buyer CSR Asset specificity	0.06 (0.26)	1.27 (5.31)***
Transaction Frequency	0.18 (1.41)	0.09 (0.89)
Transaction frequency x supplier CSR behavioural uncertainty	0.11 (0.54)	
Transaction frequency x buyer CSR asset specificity		0.41 (2.09)*
Supplier CSR behavioural uncertainty x buyer SRP		1.80 (6.10)***
Buyer CSR asset specificity x buyer SRP		1.80 (6.10)***
Transaction frequency x buyer SRP		0.18 (1.52)
Construct R2	0.66	0.90

Key: ***p<0.001; ** p<0.01; * p<0.05

17.5 Discussion and conclusions

17.5.1 Summary of findings

Focusing on the textile industry, our direct model indicates that firms appear to be in the position to directly exert influence on upstream dyadic supply chain SRP behaviour through the finding that buyer SRP seems to have a considerable direct impact on supplier SRP. This finding is in line with previous literature, which has long regarded purchasing to be an effective—direct—governance mechanism of supply chain partners (e.g. Heide and John, 1990; Stump, 1995). We interpret this finding as a form of mimicking behaviour of CSR purchasing activities among agents within a supply chain. The results of our first models appear to support the view that SRP decisions constitute a driving force for CSR-related behavioural alignment among the single actors of a supply chain (Krause et al., 2009).

However, appearances can be deceptive: while our results emphasize the importance of SRP in the establishment of CSR in supply chains (Ferrari et al., 2010), buyer SRP practices alone appear insufficient. Instead, the results of our moderated effects model clearly demonstrate that the success of such an endeavour depends on a set of underlying conditions under which supplier SRP behaviour is likely to occur. Understanding these conditions is key to success.

Giving due respect to TCE is helpful in managing upstream relations for increased CSR. We find a strengthening effect of buyer asset specificity on the relation between buyer SRP and supplier SRP. We attribute the moderating effect to a supportive role of relationship-specific CSR procedures and routines in achieving SRP compliance. Readily established CSR requirements, such as codes of conduct and certification schemes, support knowledge transfer and learning. We also find a significant direct effect of buyer asset specificity and supplier SRP. Constraints in the form of complex networks of several actors and operating standards require significant investments in firm resources to define, implement and monitor CSR activities in the upstream supply chain. Buyer asset specificity can affect supplier SRP directly, for example by employing CSR measures in supplier evaluation and development activities (Walker *et al.*, 2008), or when established procedures and rules facilitate the supplier's mimicking behaviour. Both findings are in line with several previous studies (Clark *et al.*, 1995; Shelanski and Klein, 1995; Rindfleisch and Heide, 1997) and the general perception that asset specificity is regarded as the most influential transaction cost construct (David and Han, 2004; McIvor, 2009).

We observe a strengthening, moderating effect of transaction frequency on the relation between buyer asset specificity and buyer SRP. Potentially relevant in terms of setup costs (Williamson, 2008), buyer SRP appears to stimulate stable transactional relationships, as illustrated by an increased number of transactions. CSR behavioural uncertainty and asset specificity appear stronger than transaction frequency. This finding is also in line with several studies that find transaction frequency to be the least influential element among the key attributes of TCE theory for bilateral dependence of transactional actors (Williamson, 1979).

Interestingly, and contrary to our expectations, we find that supplier CSR behavioural uncertainty strengthens the relationship between buyer and supplier SRP. As supplier CSR-related behavioural uncertainty increases, the impact of buyer SRP on supplier SRP increases. Apparently, suppliers' opportunistic behaviour in terms of CSR behaviour is less likely when supplier behavioural uncertainty is higher. It shows the importance of purchasing in alleviating the impact of supplier behavioural uncertainty in a CSR context (Sharfman *et al.*, 2009). Corporate SRP appears to be an important tool to reduce upstream opportunistic behaviour (Rao and Holt, 2005; Koplin *et al.*, 2007; Reuter *et al.*, 2010; Wolf and Moeller, 2011).

Our semi-structured in-depth interviews give us reason to believe that such effects are neither a one-time occurrence nor inherent in our specific sample. Our respondents, who stem from a diverse set of industrial fields (life sciences, cellulose and paper, and insulation), uniformly stress the importance of environmental uncertainty in terms of CSR. In light of renewed public interest in product sources and manufacturing conditions, supplier CSR and SRP commitment and behaviour increasingly demand corporate attention: given close interdependencies among supply chain actors, successful true CSR implementation is perceived to be real-istic only in cooperation with suppliers. In response, firms appear to be in search for mechanisms to bind and contain suppliers to reduce uncertainty in terms of supplier CSR and SRP behaviour. Such inter-firm mechanisms can be found in the underlying transaction, such that the underlying transaction costs of a relationship can have a significant impact on diffusion levels of voluntary CSR standards within supply chains (Rosen *et al.*, 2002).

17.5.2 Theoretical contribution

The originality of this research lies conceptually in extending a TCE perspective to adoption of CSR practices upstream in the supply chain. Empirically, the study presents new insights into strategic CSR foci of the textile industry and its supply chain. Our study makes several contributions. First, we reinforce findings from previous studies that demonstrate empirically that investments in specialized assets create a safeguard that may have a positive effect on the performance of buyer-supplier exchanges in supply chain settings (Zaheer and Venkatraman, 1995) and validate them empirically in an SRP context. Second, we find empirical support for the relevance of TCE in the extension of CSR behavioural practices among supply chain partners (Vachon and Klassen, 2006; Sarkis, Zhu, and Lai 2011). As a result, this study contributes to our understanding of how SRP behaviour relates to adjacent supply chain relations by demonstrating that TCE provides a solid explanation in the context of SRP mimicking effects. Third, we reinforce views on the effectiveness of buyer SRP as an important (Heide and John, 1992; Ring and Van De Ven, 1994; Coles and Hesterly, 1998), yet indirect mechanism driving supplier SRP. Transaction costs, which stem from specific assets (particularly in the presence of significant levels of unpredictability in the business environment) and monitoring activities inherent in the transaction and activities of the upstream supply chain actors involved, act as moderators. Studies relating buyer and supplier SRP directly appear to be a too simplified perception of corporate realities. Instead, there is much more nuance to the theory and the conditions under which it holds.

17.5.3 Managerial implications

Supplier management often requires substantial resources to identify and negotiate with relevant suppliers and to monitor and enforce agreement compliance. We argue that giving due respect to TCE is helpful in managing upstream relations for increased CSR. SRP constitutes a driving force for CSR-related behavioural alignment among the single actors of a supply chain—given a set of underlying conditions under which supplier SRP behaviour is likely to occur. We stress the role of SRP to reduce upstream opportunistic behaviour. The implementation of CSR requirements such as codes of conduct and certification schemes are recommended to support supplier's mimicking behaviour through knowledge transfer and learning. Also, investments in buyer–supplier specific assets, manifested in relationship-specific CSR procedures and routines in achieving SRP compliance, tend to facilitate the supplier's mimicking behaviour. Requiring significant investments in firm's resources to define, implement and monitor CSR activities in the upstream supply chain, they tend to create a lock-in effect by enhancing mutual firm dependencies.

Additionally, an increased number of transactions suggest that buyer SRP appears to stimulate stable transactional relationships. Such information on frequency of transactions and the enhanced degrees of inter-firm communication entailed may be relevant information for new or extended set of indicators to monitor the buyer-supplier relationship. Including "communication" as a KPI may prove to be a valuable diagnostic tool for managers to assess:

- The quality of relationship, and

- Give guidance on what to communicate and how to communicate to external supply chain partners.

Awareness of the importance of inter-firm communication and its potential implications could be raised during trainings and workshops for key-account managers. In the long run, CSR-related activities have the potential to increase trust and thereby reduce transaction costs related to the activities described above (Hosmer, 1995).

17.5.4 Limitations and suggestions for further research

In our study we made efforts to take a supply chain oriented approach by studying the underlying mechanisms and effect of SRP in dyadic (buyer–supplier) settings. For feasibility reasons, we simplified reality and studied supply chain relationships in isolated, unconnected supply chains. Even though our approach seems superior to most studies of supply chain relationships, we may not have captured the full dynamics of interconnected, real-life supply chain networks. We recommend that future studies in this area take a network perspective.

Our study is limited to dyadic relationships. We are also curious how far upstream in the supply chain the effects of TCE governance mechanisms hold. Thus, an approach that looks at multiple tiers could extend the understanding of these relationships.

The implementation of CSR measures in a supply chain setting may take some time to show an effect, as supply chain actors must respond to evolving (quasi-) standards (Campbell, 2007). We therefore recommend conducting a longitudinal study. We also recommend broadening the investigation to industries other than the textile industry and potentially incorporating different cultural contexts as well to increase the external validity of the study.

References

Anderson, E., & Schmittlein, D.C. (1984). Integration of the sales force: An empirical examination. *The RAND Journal of Economics*, 15(3), 385-395.

Armacost, R.L., J.C. Hosseini, S.A. Morris and K.A. Rehbein (1991), "An empirical comparison of direct questioning, scenario, and randomized response methods for obtaining sensitive business information," *Decision Sciences*, 22(5): 1073-1090.

Armstrong, J.S. and T.S. Overton (1977), "Estimating nonresponse bias in mail surveys," *Journal of Marketing Research*, 14(3): 396-402.

Arrow, K.J. (1970). The organization of economic activity: Issues pertinent to the choice of market versus nonmarket allocation. In R.H. Haveman and J. Margolis (Eds.), *Public Expenditure and Policy Analysis*, Chicago, IL: Markham Publishing.

Baden, D.A., Harwood, I.A., & Woodward D.G. (2009). The effects of buyer pressure on suppliers SMEs to demonstrate CSR practices: An added incentive or counterproductive? *European Management Journal*, 27(6), 429-441.

BBC (2011), *Fashion chain Zara acts on Brazil sweatshop conditions*, available at: www.bbc.co.uk/news/world-latin-america-14570564 (accessed 26 August 2012).

Bhasin, K. (2013), *In First Interview Since Bangladesh Factory Collapse, Benetton CEO Confirms Company's Tie To Tragedy*, available at: http://www.huffingtonpost.com/2013/05/08/benetton-bangladesh-factory-collapse_n_3237991.html (accessed 26 Mai 2013).

Bowen, F.E., Cousins, P.D., Lamming, R.C., & Faruk A.C. (2001). The role of supply management capabilities in green supply. *Production and Operations Management*, 10(2), 174-189.

Campbell, J.L. (2007). Why would corporations behave in socially responsible ways? An institutional theory of corporate social responsibility. *The Academy of Management Review*, 32(3), 946-967.

Carter, C.R. (2005). Purchasing social responsibility and firm performance: The key mediating roles of organizational learning and supplier performance. *International Journal of Physical Distribution and Logistics Management*, 35(3), 177-194.

Carter, C.R., & Carter, J.R. (1998). Interorganizational determinants of environmental purchasing: Initial evidence from the consumer products industries. *Decision Sciences*, 29(3), 659-684.

Carter, C.R., & Easton, P.L. (2011). Sustainable supply chain management: evolution and future directions. *International Journal of Physical Distribution and Logistics Management*, 41(1), 46-62.

Carter, C.R., & Jennings, M.M. (2004). The role of purchasing in corporate social responsibility: A structural equation analysis. *Journal of Business Logistics*, 25(1), 145-186.

Carter, C.R., & Jennings, M.M. (2002). Social responsibility and supply chain relationships. *Transportation Research Part E: Logistics and Transportation Review*, 38(1), 37-52.

Carter, C.R., Kale, R., & Grimm, C.M. (2000). Environmental purchasing and firm performance: An empirical investigation. *Transportation Research Part E: Logistics and Transportation Review*, 36(3), 219-228.

Carter, C.R., & Rogers, D.S. (2008). A framework of sustainable supply chain management: Moving toward new theory. *International Journal of Physical Distribution and Logistics Management*, 38(5), 360-387.

Chamberlain, G. (2010), *Gap, Next and MandS in new sweatshop scandal*, available at: www.guardian.co.uk/world/2010/aug/08/gap-next-marks-spencer-sweatshops (accessed 26 August 2012).

Chin, W.W. (1998). Commentary: Issues and opinion on structural equation modeling. *Management Information Systems Quarterly*, 22(1), vii-xvi.

Clark, T., Zmud, R.W., & McCray, G.E. (1995). The outsourcing of information services: Transforming the nature of business in the information industry. *Journal of Information Technology*, (10), 221-238.

Coase, R.H. (1937). The nature of the firm. *Economica*, 4(16), 386-405.

Coles, J.W., & Hesterly, W.S. (1998). The impact of firm-specific assets and the interaction of uncertainty: An examination of make or buy decisions in public and private hospitals. *Journal of Economic Behavior and Organization*, 36(3), 383-409.

Corbett, C.J., & Klassen, R.D. (2006). Extending the horizons: Environmental excellence as key to improving operations. *Manufacturing and Service Operations Management*, 8(1), 5-22.

Das, A., Narasimhan, R., & Talluri, S. (2006). Supplier integration: Finding an optimal configuration. *Journal of Operations Management*, 24(5), 563-582.

David, R.J., & Han, S.-K. (2004). A systematic assessment of the empirical support for transaction cost economics. *Strategic Management Journal*, 25(1), 39-58.

Delmas, M., & Montiel, I. (2009). Greening the supply chain: When is customer pressure effective? *Journal of Economics and Management Strategy*, 18(1), 171-201.

Deutskens, E., de Ruyter, K., Wetzels, M., and P. Oosterveld (2004), Response Rate and Response Quality of Internet-Based Surveys: An Experimental Study, *Marketing Letters*, 15(1): 21-36.

Dillman, D.A., Smyth, J.D., and L. M. Christian (2009), *Mail and internet surveys: the tailored design method*, (3rd ed.), New York, NY: John Wiley and Sons, Inc.

Dyer, J.H. (1996). Does governance matter? Keiretsu alliances and asset specificity as sources of Japanese competitive advantage. *Organization Science*, 7(6), 649-666.

Eisenhardt, K. and M. Graebner (2007), "Theory building from cases: opportunities and challenges," *Academy of Management Journal*, 50(1): 25-32.

Ferrari, I., Luzzini, D., & Spina, G. (2010). Sustainable purchasing practices. *Conference Proceedings of the 19th Annual IPSERA Conference*. Lappeenranta, Finland.

Fornell, C., & Larcker, D.F. (1981). Evaluating structural equation models with unobservable variables and measurement error. *Journal of Marketing Research*, 18(1), 39-50.

Gefen, D., Straub, D.W., & Boudreau, M.-C. (2000). Structural equation modeling and regression: Guidelines for research practice. *Communications of the Association for Information Systems*, 4(7), 1-76.

Gerbing, D.W., & Anderson, J.C. (1988). An updated paradigm for scale development incorporating unidimensionality and its assessment. *Journal of Marketing Research*, 25(2), 186-192.

Ghoshal, S. and P. Moran (1996), Bad for practice: critique of the transaction cost theory, *Academy of Management Review*, 21(1): 13-47.

Granovetter, M. (1985), Economic Action and Social Structure: The Problem of Embeddedness, *The American Journal of Sociology*, 91(3): 481-510.

Grover, V., & Malhotra, M.K. (2003). Transaction cost framework in operations and supply chain management research: Theory and measurement. *Journal of Operations Management*, 21(4), 457-473.

Hair, J., Anderson, R.E., Tatham, R.L., & Black, W.C. (1998). *Multivariate Data Analysis* (5th ed.), Upper Saddle River, NJ: Prentice Hall.

Handfield, R.B., & Bechtel, C. (2002). The role of trust and relationship structure in improving supply chain responsiveness. *Industrial Marketing Management*, 31(4), 367-382.

Heide, J.B., & John, G. (1992). Do norms matter in marketing relationships? *Journal of Marketing*, 56(2), 32-44.

Heide, J.B., & John, G. (1990). Alliances in industrial purchasing: The determinants of joint action in buyer–supplier relationships, *Journal of Marketing Research*, 27(1), 24-36.

Henseler, J., Ringle, C.M., & Sinkovics, R.R. (2009). The use of partial least squares path modelling in international marketing. *Advances in International Marketing*, 20, 277-319.

Hobbs, J.E. (1996). A transaction cost approach to supply chain management. *Supply Chain Management Decision*, 1(2), 15-27.

Hosmer, L.T. (1995). Trust: The connecting link between organizational theory and philosophical ethics. *Academy of Management Review*, 20(2), 379-403.

Hughes, A. (2001). Multi-stakeholder approaches to ethical trade: Towards a reorganisation of UK retailers' global supply chains? *Journal of Economic Geography*, 1(4), 421-437.

Hulland, J. (1999). Use of partial least squares (PLS) in strategic management research: A review of four recent studies, *Strategic Management Journal*, 20(2), 195-204.

Joshi, A.W., & Stump, R.L. (1999). The contingent effect of specific asset investments on joint action in manufacturer–supplier relationships: An empirical test of the moderating role of reciprocal asset investments, uncertainty, and trust. *Journal of the Academy of Marketing Science*, 27(3), 291-305.

Keating, B., Quazi, A., Kriz, A., & Coltman, T. (2008). In pursuit of a sustainable supply chain: Insights from Westpac Banking Corporation. *Supply Chain Management: An International Journal*, 13(3), 175-179.

King, A.A., Lenox, M.J., & Terlaak, A. (2005). The strategic use of decentralized institutions: Exploring certification with the ISO 14001 management standard. *Academy of Management Journal*, 48(6), 1,091-1,106.

Klassen, R.D., & Vachon, S. (2003). Collaboration and evaluation in the supply chain: The impact on plant-level environmental investment. *Production and Operations Management*, 12(3), 336-352.

Klein, B., Crawford, R.G., & Alchian, A.A. (1978). Vertical integration, appropriable rents, and the competitive contracting process. *Journal of Law and Economics*, 21(2), 297-326.

Klein, S. (1989). A transaction cost explanation of vertical control in international markets. *Journal of the Academy of Marketing Science*, 17(3), 253-260.

Koplin, J., Seuring, S., & Mesterharm, M. (2007). Incorporating sustainability into supply management in the automotive industry: The case of the Volkswagen AG. *Journal of Cleaner Production*, 15(11–12), 1,053-1,062.

Kovács, G. (2008). Corporate environmental responsibility in the supply chain. *Journal of Cleaner Production*, 16(15), 1,571-1,578.

Krause, D.R., Vachon, S., & Klassen, R.D. (2009). Special topic forum on sustainable supply chain management: Introduction and reflections on the role of purchasing management. *Journal of Supply Chain Management*, 45(4), 18-25.

Kumar, N., Stern, L.W., and J.C. Anderson (1993), Conducting Interorganizational Research Using Key Informants, *The Academy of Management Journal*, 36(6): 1633-1651.

Lai, K.-H., Cheng, T.C.E., & Yeun, A.C.L (2005). Relationship stability and supplier commitment to quality. *International Journal of Production Economics*, 96(3), 397-410.

Macher, J.T. and B.D. Richman (2008), Transaction costs economics: An assessment of empirical research in the social sciences, *Business and Politics*, 10(1): 1-43.

Maloni, M.J., & Carter, C.R. (2006). Opportunities for research in third-party logistics. *Transportation Journal*, 45(2), 23-38.

Mayer, K.J., Nickerson, J.A., & Owan, H. (2004). Are supply and plant inspections complements or substitutes? A strategic and operational assessment of inspection practices in biotechnology. *Management Science*, 50(8), 1,064-1,081.

McIvor, R. (2009). How the transaction cost and resource-based theories of the firm inform outsourcing evaluation. *Journal of Operations Management*, 27(1), 45-63.

Noordewier, T.G., John, G., & Nevin, J.R. (1990). Performance outcomes of purchasing arrangements in industrial buyer–vendor relationships. *Journal of Marketing*, 54(4), 80-93.

Pagell, M., & Wu, Z. (2009). Building a more complete theory of sustainable supply chain management using case studies of ten exemplars. *Journal of Supply Chain Management*, 45(2), 37-56.

Pagell, M., Wu, Z., & Wasserman, M.E. (2010). Thinking differently about purchasing portfolios: An assessment of sustainable sourcing. *Journal of Supply Chain Management*, 46(1), 57-73.

Perrow, C. (1981), Markets, hierarchies, and hegemony. In A. van de Ven, and W. Joyce (Eds.), *Perspectives on Organization Design and Behavior*, Wiley, New York.

Pullman, M.E., Maloni, M., & Carter, C.R. (2009). Food for thought: Social versus environmental sustainability practices and performance outcomes. *Journal of Supply Chain Management*, 45(4), 38-54.

Rao, P., & Holt, D. (2005). Do green supply chains lead to competitiveness and economic performance? *International Journal of Operations and Production Management*, 25(9), 898-916.

Reuter, C., Foerstl, K., Hartmann, E. and Blome, C. (2010). Sustainable global supplier management: The role of dynamic capabilities in achieving competitive advantage. *Journal of Supply Chain Management*, 46(2), 45-63.

Reynolds, S. J. and N. E. Bowie (2004), A Kantian perspective on the characteristics of ethics programs, *Business Ethics Quarterly*, 14(2), 275-292.

Rindfleisch, A., & Heide, J.B. (1997). Transaction cost analysis: Past, present, and future applications. *Journal of Marketing*, 61(4), 30-54.

Ring, P.S., & Van De Ven, A.H. (1994). Developmental processes of cooperative interorganizational relationships. *Academy of Management Review*, 19(1), 90-118.

Ringle, C.M. (2006). Segmentation for path models and unobserved heterogeneity: The finite mixture partial least squares approach, *Research Papers on Marketing and Retailing at the University of Hamburg*, No. 35, Hamburg.

Ringle, C.M., Wende, S., & Will, A. (2010). Finite mixture partial least squares analysis: Methodology and numerical examples, *Handbook of Partial Least Squares*. Heidelberg: Springer.

Rosen, C.M., Beckman, S.L., & Bercovitz, J. (2002). The role of voluntary industry standards in environmental supply-chain management. *Journal of Industrial Ecology*, 6(3–4), 103-123.

Rudelius, W. and R.A. Buchholz (1979), What industrial purchasers see as key ethical dilemmas, *Journal of Purchasing and Materials Management*, 15(4): 2-10.

Sarkis, J., Zhu, Q., & Lai, K.-H. (2011). An organizational theoretic review of green supply chain management literature. *International Journal of Production Economics*, 130(1), 1-15.

Schepers, J., Wetzels, M., & De Ruyter, K. (2005). Leadership styles in technology acceptance: Do followers practice what leaders preach? *Managing Service Quality*, 15(6), 496-508.

Schillewaert, N. and P. Meulemeester (2005), Comparing response distributions of offline and online data collection methods, *International Journal of Market Research*, 47(2): 163-178.

Sharfman, M.P., Shaft, T.M., & Anex, R.P.J. (2009). The road to cooperative supply-chain environmental management: Trust and uncertainty among pro-active firms. *Business Strategy and the Environment*, 18(1), 1-13.

Shelanski, H.A., & Klein, P.G. (1995). Empirical research in transaction cost economics: A review and assessment. *Journal of Law, Economics, and Organization*, 11(2), 335-361.

Simpson, D., Power, D., & Samson, D. (2007). Greening the automotive supply chain: A relationship perspective. *International Journal of Operations and Production Management*, 27(1), 28-48.

Son, J.-Y., Narasimhan, S., & Riggins, F.J. (2005). Effects of relational factors and channel climate on EDI usage in the customer–supplier relationship. *Journal of Management Information Systems*, 22(1), 321-353.

Stump, R.L. (1995). Antecedents of purchasing concentration: A transaction cost explanation. *Journal of Business Research*, (34), 145-157.

Stump, R.L., Athaide, G.A., & Joshi, A.W. (2002). Managing seller–buyer new product development relationships for customized products: A contingency model based on transaction cost analysis and empirical test. *Journal of Product Innovation Management*, 19(6), 439-454.

Sutcliffe, K.M., & Zaheer, A. (1998). Uncertainty in the transaction environment: An empirical test. *Strategic Management Journal*, 19(1), 1-23.

Tate, W.L., Dooley, K.J., & Ellram, L.M. (2011). Transaction cost and institutional drivers of supplier adoption of environmental practices. *Journal of Business Logistics*, 32(1), 6-16.

Tate, W.L., Ellram, L.M., & Dooley, K.J. (2014). The impact of transaction costs and institutional pressure on supplier environmental practices. *International Journal of Physical Distribution & Logistics Management*, 44(5), 353-372.

Tenenhaus, M., Vinzi, V.E., Chatelin, Y.-M., & Lauro, C. (2005). PLS path modeling. *Computational Statistics and Data Analysis*, 48, 159-205.

The Telegraph (2013, 7 February). *Findus beef lasagne was up to 100 per cent horse meat.* Retrieved from http://www.telegraph.co.uk

Vachon, S., & Klassen, R.D. (2006). Extending green practices across the supply chain: The impact of upstream and downstream integration. *International Journal of Operations and Production Management*, 26(7), 795-821.

Walker, H., Di Sisto, L., & McBain, D. (2008). Drivers and barriers to environmental supply chain management practices: Lessons from the public and private sectors. *Journal of Purchasing and Supply Management*, 14(1), 69-85.

Wallenburg, C.M. (2009). Innovation in logistics outsourcing relationships: Proactive improvement by logistics service providers as a driver of customer loyalty. *Journal of Supply Chain Management*, 45(2), 75-93.

Welford, R. and S. Frost (2006), Corporate social responsibility in Asian supply chains, *Corporate Social Responsibility and Environmental Management*, 13(3): 166-176.

Williamson, O. E. (2008). Outsourcing: Transaction cost economics and supply chain management. *Journal of Supply Chain Management*, 44(2), 5-16.

Williamson, O.E. (2002). The theory of the firm as governance structure: From choice to contract. *The Journal of Economic Perspectives*, 16(3), 171-195.

Williamson, O.E. (1991a). Comparative economic organization: The analysis of discrete structural alternatives. *Administrative Science Quarterly*, 36(2), 269-296.

Williamson, O. E. (1991b).Strategizing, economizing, and economic organization. *Strategic Management Journal*, 12(2), 75-94.

Williamson, O.E. (1985) T*he Economic Institutions of Capitalism: Firms, Markets, Relational Contracting*. New York: Free Press.

Williamson, O.E. (1981). The economics of organization: The transaction cost approach. *American Journal of Sociology*, 87(3), 539-577.

Williamson, O.E. (1979). Transaction cost economics: The governance of contractual relations. *Journal of Law and Economics*, 22(2), 233-262.

Williamson, O.E. (1975). *Markets and Hierarchies: Analysis and Antitrust Implications*. New York: Free Press.

Wolf, J., & Moeller, S. (2011). Sustainable supply chains: Consumers' reaction to lacking sustainability in supply chains. *Proceedings of the 20th International Purchasing and Supply Education and Research Association (IPSERA) Conference*, 1-7.

Zaheer, A., & Venkatraman, N. (1995). Relational governance as an interorganizational strategy: An empirical test of the role of trust in economic exchange. *Strategic Management Journal*, 16(5), 373-392.

Zeit Online (2013), *Kik-Lieferant produzierte in eingestürzter Fabrik,* available at: http://www.zeit.de/gesellschaft/2013-05/kik-fabrik-einsturz-produktion (accessed 8 May 2013).

Simon Bartczek is a lecturer and PhD candidate in the department of Marketing and Supply Chain Management at Maastricht University School of Business and Economics. His PhD project explores how CSR commitment and practices spread upstream in supply chains with an emphasis on the factors and conditions facilitating supplier compliance.

Janjaap Semeijn (ASU 1994) is Professor of Supply Chain Management Strategy at the Department of Marketing and Supply Chain Management at Maastricht University School of Business and Economics. His research focuses on International Transport and Logistics, Supply Chain Management, One-Stop Shopping and 3D Printing.

Lieven Quintens is senior lecturer in supply chain management at Maastricht University School of Business and Economics. His research focuses on global sourcing strategies, buyer-supplier relationships and global supply chains.

Appendix 17.1: Constructs, item measures, and sources

Construct	Item	Mean	α	CR	AVE
Buyer SRP Environmental (Carter and Jennings, 2004)		5.95	0.96	0.97	0.79
BuySRP Behav1	Currently, our purchasing function uses a life cycle analysis to evaluate the environmental friendliness of products and packaging.				
BuySRP Behav2	Currently, our purchasing function participates in the design of products for disassembly.				
BuySRP Behav3	Currently, our purchasing function asks suppliers to commit to waste reduction goals.				
BuySRP Behav4	Currently, our purchasing function participates in the design of products for recycling or reuse.				
BuySRP Behav5	Currently, our purchasing function reduces packaging material.				
BuySRP Behav6	Currently, our purchasing function purchases recycled packaging.				
BuySRP Behav7	Currently, our purchasing function purchases packaging that is lighter in weight.				
Buyer SRP Human Rights and Philanthropy (Carter and Jennings, 2004)		4.99	0.96	0.97	0.83
BuySRP Behav8	Currently, our purchasing function purchases from minority-/women-owned business enterprise suppliers.*				
BuySRP Behav9	Currently, our purchasing function has a formal minority/women owned business enterprise supplier purchase programme.*				
BuySRP Behav10	Currently, our purchasing function visits suppliers' plants to ensure that they are not using sweatshop labour.				
BuySRP Behav11	Currently, our purchasing function ensures that suppliers comply with child labour laws.				
BuySRP Behav12	Currently, our purchasing function asks suppliers to pay a "living wage" greater than a country's or region's minimum wage.				
BuySRP Behav13	Currently, our purchasing function volunteers at local charities.				
BuySRP Behav14	Currently, our purchasing function donates to philanthropic organizations.				
BuySRP Behav15	Currently, our purchasing function helps to increase the performance of suppliers in the local community.				

Construct	Item	Mean	α	CR	AVE
Buyer SRP Ethics (Carter and Jennings, 2004)		5.00	0.99	0.99	0.91
BuySRP Behav18	Currently, our purchasing function invents (makes up) a second source of supply to gain competitive advantage ("DPI", reverse coded).				
BuySRP Behav19	Currently, our purchasing function exaggerates the seriousness of a problem to gain concessions (reverse coded).				
BuySRP Behav20	Currently, our purchasing function deliberately misleads a salesperson in a negotiation (reverse coded).				
BuySRP Behav21	Currently, our purchasing function uses obscure contract terms to gain an advantage over suppliers (reverse coded).				
BuySRP Behav22	Currently, our purchasing function accepts meals from a supplier even if it is not possible to reciprocate (reverse coded).				
BuySRP Behav23	Currently, our purchasing function shares information about suppliers with their competitors.				
BuySRP Behav24	Currently, our purchasing function shows favouritism when selecting suppliers.				
Supplier CSR Behavioural Uncertainty (Grover and Malhotra, 2003)		2.54	0.97	0.98	0.91
SuppBeh Unc1	In terms of corporate social responsibility, it takes significant effort to detect whether the supplier conforms to specifications and quality standards.				
SuppBeh Unc2	In terms of corporate social responsibility, we are in a good position to evaluate how fairly the supplier addresses us. (reverse scored)				
SuppBeh Unc3	In terms of corporate social responsibility, accurately evaluating the supplier requires a lot of effort.				
SuppBeh Unc4	In terms of corporate social responsibility, there is not much concern about the supplier taking advantage of this relationship. (reverse scored).				
SuppBeh Unc5	In terms of corporate social responsibility, it is costly in terms of time and effort to effectively monitor the performance of the supplier.				
Buyer Asset Specificity (Heide and John, 1990)		5.42	0.94	0.97	0.95
BuyAss Spec1	In terms of corporate social responsibility, the procedures and routines developed as part of their relationship with our company are tailored to our particular situation.				

Construct	Item	Mean	α	CR	AVE
BuyAss Spec2	In terms of corporate social responsibility, our company has some unusual technological standards and norms that have required extensive adaptation by the buyer.				
Transaction Frequency (Klein, 1989)					
TransFrequ	The customer frequently purchases products or services at our company.	5.62	n.a.	n.a.	n.a.
Supplier SRP Environmental (Carter and Jennings, 2004)		5.54	0.96	0.97	0.81
SuppSRP Behav1	Currently, our purchasing function uses a life-cycle analysis to evaluate the environmental friendliness of products and packaging.				
SuppSRP Behav2	Currently, our purchasing function participates in the design of products for disassembly.				
SuppSRP Behav3	Currently, our purchasing function asks suppliers to commit to waste reduction goals.				
SuppSRP Behav4	Currently, our purchasing function participates in the design of products for recycling or reuse.				
SuppSRP Behav5	Currently, our purchasing function reduces packaging material.				
SuppSRP Behav6	Currently, our purchasing function purchases recycled packaging.				
SuppSRP Behav7	Currently, our purchasing function purchases packaging that is of lighter weight.				
Supplier SRP Human Rights and Philanthropy (Carter and Jennings, 2004)		4.64	0.89	0.94	0.74
SuppSRP Behav8	Currently, our purchasing function purchases from minority/women owned business enterprise suppliers.*				
SuppSRP Behav9	Currently, our purchasing function has a formal MWBE supplier purchase programme.*				
SuppSRP Behav10	Currently, our purchasing function visits suppliers' plants to ensure that they are not using sweatshop labour.				
SuppSRP Behav11	Currently, our purchasing function ensures that suppliers comply with child labour laws.				
SuppSRP Behav12	Currently, our purchasing function asks suppliers to pay a "living wage" that is greater than a country's or region's minimum wage.				
SuppSRP Behav13	Currently, our purchasing function volunteers at local charities.				
SuppSRP Behav14	Currently, our purchasing function donates to philanthropic organizations.				

Construct	Item	Mean	α	CR	AVE
SuppSRP Behav15	Currently, our purchasing function helps to increase the performance of suppliers in the local community.				
Supplier SRP Safety (Carter and Jennings, 2004)					
SuppSRP Behav16	Currently, our purchasing function ensures that suppliers' locations are operated in a safe manner.*				
SuppSRP Behav17	Currently, our purchasing function ensures the safe delivery of products to our facilities.*				
Supplier SRP Ethics (Carter and Jennings, 2004)		5.01	0.98	0.98	0.87
SuppSRP Behav18	Currently, our purchasing function invents (makes up) a second source of supply to gain competitive advantage ("DPI", reverse coded).				
SuppSRP Behav19	Currently, our purchasing function exaggerates the seriousness of a problem to gain concessions (reverse coded).				
SuppSRP Behav20	Currently, our purchasing function deliberately misleads a salesperson in a negotiation (reverse coded).				
SuppSRP Behav21	Currently, our purchasing function uses obscure contract terms to gain an advantage over suppliers (reverse coded).				
SuppSRP Behav22	Currently, our purchasing function accepts meals from a supplier even if it is not possible to reciprocate (reverse coded).				
SuppSRP Behav23	Currently, our purchasing function shares information about suppliers with their competitors.				
SuppSRP Behav24	Currently, our purchasing function shows favouritism when selecting suppliers.				

*Item omitted.

18

Sustainable business model and supply chain conceptions

Towards an integrated perspective

Florian Lüdeke-Freund
Faculty of Business, Economics & Social Sciences, University of Hamburg, Germany

Stefan Gold
International Centre for Corporate Social Responsibility, Nottingham University Business School, UK

Nancy Bocken
TU Delft, Industrial Design Engineering, The Netherlands

Supply chains and business models are of general importance for any company. Due to these concepts' overarching and interlinking nature, they are of particular importance for companies engaging in sustainable entrepreneurship and sustainability management. These companies look over the rim of their organizations' boundaries—motivating research and practice dealing with sustainable supply chains (SSCs) and sustainable business models (SBMs). SSCs and SBMs come from different origins and use, but are highly interrelated, both in theory and practice, one building in part on the other often without recognition by scholars and practitioners in both fields. Therefore, this chapter compares the main characteristics of SSCs and SBMs as discussed in current academic literature and investigates the conceptual similarities, differences and areas where both can complement each other. Sustainability-oriented extensions of supply chain and business model concepts are meant to bring together multiple stakeholders, their needs and perceptions of value, going beyond suppliers and customers and including local communities (e.g. in the case of social business models) or post-consumer actors (e.g. in the case of closed-loop supply chains). Because of their shared potential to foster multi-stakeholder perspectives on value creation, particular analogies between supply chains and business models can be discerned. A framework is introduced comparing both concepts, highlighting their complementary and distinguishing characteristics. The resulting integrated perspective on value creating activities provides more clarity for those engaging in conceptual and practical SSC and SBM design and management.

18.1 Introduction

> The suppliers work with the buying firm to design the production facility, deliver the chemical, deploy the chemical as indirect production material and finally handle waste treatment. The buying firms pay the suppliers based on a value-added service instead of tonnage of chemicals bought. Furthermore, in this new relationship, the suppliers actually are motivated to reduce chemical usage. (Pagell and Wu, 2009, p. 39)

Reading this description of a chemical product service-system, supply chain experts would probably agree that this is a good example of sustainable supply chain innovation. However, we assume that business model experts would also see this as a good example of sustainable business model innovation. Who is (more) wrong, who is (more) right? Neither, would be our answer since both perspectives overlap to a certain degree. But they also differ in some key aspects. The purpose of this chapter is to take a closer look at current conceptions of sustainable supply chains on the one hand and sustainable business models on the other. Both concepts have risen to some prominence within the last decade, as documented by a growing range of theoretical and conceptual frameworks (Carter and Rogers, (2008); Bocken *et al.* (2014)). Pagell and Wu (2009), for example, define a sustainable supply chain as: "... [a] supply chain ... that performs well on both traditional measures of profit and loss as well as on an expanded conceptualization of performance that includes social and natural dimensions" (Pagell and Wu, 2009, p. 38).

Sustainable business models—here used synonymously with "business models for sustainability"—have recently been defined as follows:

> A business model for sustainability helps describing, analyzing, managing, and communicating (i) a company's sustainable value proposition to its customers, and all other stakeholders, (ii) how it creates and delivers this value, (iii) and how it captures economic value while maintaining or regenerating natural, social, and economic capital beyond its organizational boundaries (Schaltegger *et al.*, 2016, p. 4).

While obvious complementarities between SSC and SBM conceptions exist—e.g. the common objective to contribute to sustainable development, stakeholder integration, as well as their focus on value creation—we see an urgent need to deliberately compare, distinguish and (re-) integrate the perspectives on SSCs and SBMs. Currently, they rather tend to remain in their disciplinary "silos". Rare exceptions represent the study by Matos and Silvestre (2013) who link sustainable supply chains, "base of the pyramid" (BoP) settings and stakeholder theory to sustainable business models, or Wells and Seitz's (2005) typology of closed-loop supply chains and their implications for the value-added business structures in which they are embedded. The discourse on SSCs and sustainable supply chain management (SSCM), respectively, is rooted in the combination of operations management (Gold, 2014) and corporate sustainability with some ties to overarching issues such as global sustainable development (Wolf, 2014). Scholars in the field of sustainable business models often build on the intersections of innovation, strategic management and corporate sustainability (Boons and Lüdeke-Freund, 2013; Schaltegger *et al.*, 2012).

Our discussion builds on two major propositions:

- First, both SSC and SBM concepts regularly refer to one another but mostly without paying sufficient attention to the other concept's nature and characteristics, which leads to a superficial treatment of supply chains in the business model literature and vice versa.

- Second, both concepts share the vision of sustainable value creation, defined as creating triple bottom line value through supply chain and business model innovation and design (Hassini *et al.*, 2012; Bocken *et al.*, 2014), and thus provide two fundamental levers for companies to improve their sustainability performance.

The identification of conceptual dissimilarities, similarities and complementarities might thus also strengthen the practice of both SSC and SBM management. If supply chain and business model managers both understand the interrelations between their respective fields of work, this could lead to new forms of cooperation between operational and strategic management that is currently being hindered by too narrowly defined concepts.

Our methodological approach, therefore, is conceptual theory building, based on a comparison of the major features of SSCs and SBMs as described in chosen academic publications. In a second step, we discuss the differences and similarities of the two concepts so as to provide a more nuanced perspective on both and to build ground for their conceptual integration. The third step is to derive theoretical and practical implications from this integrated perspective. Our overall assumptions are that both streams have more in common than the currently separated bodies of literature suggest and that an integrated view can provide a bridge between the dominant operations management and strategic management perspectives underlying SSCs and SBMs, respectively.

We expect to provide the following conceptual contributions:

- **A clearer view on supply chains as distinct business model elements**: Most business model concepts mention supply chains as core elements without further elaborating on their complexities. That is, we have to "zoom-in" and try to understand the role and functioning of supply chains as a complex system in a similarly complex business model context. Such close-ups should extend SBM approaches towards paying more attention to specific supply chain actors and related sustainability problems.

- **A better understanding of SSC implications for SBM development**: Since supply chains are a crucial lever for corporate (un-)sustainability, supply chain design and management fundamentally influence the functioning and development of SBMs. As supply chains cannot be quickly changed altogether, they limit the range of feasible SBMs, at least in the short term.

- **Business model implications for SSC development**: While supply chains can impact SBMs, the opposite holds true as well. In order to tap the full potential of sustainable value creation, supply chains need to be adapted to the requirements of SBMs, i.e. if a business model is changed towards a potentially more sustainable model this has implications for the underlying supply chain. For example, if a company moves from selling products to leasing them, the sales channels and physical flows of products will need to change dramatically. In this respect, business model management and innovation constitute important sources of supply chain innovation.

These clarifications should be of particular relevance for researchers and practitioners dealing with companies and business models that are strongly influenced by their supply chains, such as most industrial enterprises and companies with global supply chains that connect sensitive and vulnerable input markets (e.g. biomass and minerals from developing countries) with aggressive, high-end product markets (e.g. fuels, automotive and high-technology markets). Clarity of how business models and supply chains support and restrict each other can present new perspectives on operational and strategic performance and point more clearly to causes of (un-)sustainability.

18.2 Overview: conceptions of sustainable business models and supply chains

The Brundtland report defines sustainable development as "a development that meets the needs of the present without compromising the ability of future generations to meet their own needs" (WCED, 1987, p. 8). It specifies the idea that technology and social organization restricts the environment's capacity to fulfil human needs in the long term. Furthermore, special emphasis is put on the needs of the global poor. Dyllick and Hockerts (2002) transfer this definition of sustainable development to the business level, hence "corporate sustainability can [...] be defined as meeting the needs of a firm's direct and indirect stakeholders (such as shareholders, employees, clients, pressure groups, communities etc.), without compromising its ability to meet the needs of future stakeholders as well" (Dyllick and Hockerts, 2002, p. 131). Sustainability-oriented business models and supply chain conceptions integrate the idea of "sustainable development", as popularly disseminated by the Brundtland commission, into the fields of business model and supply chain management.

According to the World Bank, 2.2 billion people lived on less than US$2 a day in 2011 (World Bank, n.d.), which is only a slight improvement compared to the situation in the early 1980s. As many business models and supply chains are developed to benefit from global sourcing and market opportunities (Mollenkopf et al., 2010) they often tap developing countries where most of the world's poor and vulnerable people live. This demonstrates the challenge that business model and supply chain management faces globally, especially with regard to social issues. While in the field of sustainable supply chain management emphasis was traditionally given to environmental aspects, where win–wins in terms of eco-efficiency and eco-effectiveness could be realized more easily (Gold et al., 2010), the reviewed literature suggests that environmental and social issues, although addressed from different perspectives and in different disciplinary contexts, were of equal interest from the beginning of the sustainable business model discourse (Boons and Lüdeke-Freund, 2013).

18.2.1 Current sustainable business model conceptions

Business models are conceptual representations of organizational value creation. While some authors focus on the value-creating activities of an organization and its partners (Zott and Amit, 2010), others conceptualise business models as entity-relationship diagrams (Osterwalder et al., 2005), or as integrated frameworks consisting of different sub-models, such as manufacturing, procurement or financial models (Wirtz et al., 2015). Despite differences in conceptual representations, there seems to be agreement on major functions of this particular class of models: to help describe, analyze, communicate, manage and design the value creation of a particular organization. However, these model functions also apply to larger scales such as whole industries (Hemphill, 2013) and smaller scales such as individual entrepreneurs (Svejenova et al., 2010).

Value creation can be subdivided into value creation in a narrow sense (how value propositions are made), value delivery (how value propositions reach and unfold for respective customers) and value capture (how the focal company, its customers and further stakeholders obtain net value from their interaction). This view on value creation resonates with the work of authors such as Osterwalder (Osterwalder et al., 2005; Osterwalder and Pigneur, 2009), Chesbrough (Chesbrough, 2010;

Chesbrough and Rosenbloom, 2002), Teece (2010) or Zott *et al.* (2011). The presumably most influential business model definition (in terms of uptake by academics and practitioners) has been put forward by Osterwalder and Pigneur (2009, p. 14): "A business model describes the rationale of how an organization creates, delivers, and captures value." This rationale is generally built around a value proposition, i.e. a product or service-based offering made by an organization.

Figure 18.1 shows that an organization creates value (based on own and partner resources and capabilities), offers a value proposition (based on products and services), delivers the value proposition through customer interfaces (based on customer relationships and channels) all the time trying to capture some of the value as financial surplus (based on revenue streams and costs) (modified from Bocken *et al.*, 2014; Osterwalder and Pigneur, 2009). Value capture is required to maintain and improve an organization's value creation activities. Therefore, Figure 18.1 suggests a quasi-circular relationship between value creation, proposition, delivery and capture (Lüdeke-Freund *et al.*, 2016).

Figure 18.1 Business models describe how organizations create value

Source: authors

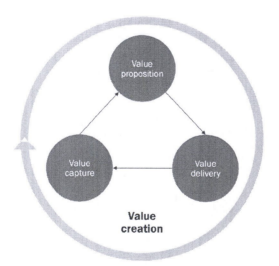

An increasing number of publications discuss the linkages between business models and positive contributions to a sustainable development of nature, society and economy (Rauter *et al.*, 2015; Schaltegger *et al.*, 2012; Stubbs and Cocklin, 2008; Wells, 2013a; for an overview see a recent Organization & Environment special issue on "Business Models for Sustainability"[1]), the earliest dating back more than ten

---

1   Schaltegger *et al.*, 2016, http://oae.sagepub.com/content/29/1.toc

years (Wells and Nieuwenhuis, 2004). However, research in this field is still rather limited with regard to both rigorous theoretical frameworks and empirical analyses (Bocken *et al.*, 2014; Boons *et al.*, 2013; Boons and Lüdeke-Freund, 2013; Schaltegger *et al.*, 2016). Prominent practical examples of potentially sustainable business models often refer to the automotive industry and mobility concepts (Abdelkafi *et al.*, 2013; Cohen and Kietzmann, 2014; Johnson and Suskewicz, 2009; Wells, 2013b), renewable energies (Loock, 2012; Lüdeke-Freund, 2014; Richter, 2012; Wüstenhagen and Boehnke, 2008) and social enterprises (Seelos and Mair, 2005, 2007; Yunus *et al.*, 2010).

In these contexts, the effect of sustainability-oriented business models is often described as the breakup of dominant and purely financially-oriented paradigms of value creation. This can be achieved, for example, through establishing closed-loop and zero-waste production models (McDonough and Braungart, 2013), which replace linear "fire and forget" models and allow for the creation of ecological value (Wells, 2008; Wells and Seitz, 2005). Another effect is the introduction of new ways of value delivery and capture. For example, some social enterprises distinguish between those who pay for a product or service, such as nutrition, health care or education, and those who benefit from it, thus expanding the range of value delivery and capture to poor and neglected social groups (Grassl, 2012; Seelos, 2014; Yunus *et al.*, 2010). With regard to changing the ways of producing and consuming goods and services that are culturally and economically embedded and institutionalized, Wells argues that only radical and sustainability-driven innovations are capable of challenging the persistent and continuously self-reinforcing status quo (Wells 2008, 2013a, 2013b; Hansen *et al.*, 2009). However, radical sustainability innovations often start in niches and struggle to either create new markets or penetrate existing mass markets—e-mobility is a prime example (Bidmon and Knab, 2014; Hockerts and Wüstenhagen, 2010; Schaltegger and Wagner, 2011; Tukker *et al.* 2008). Creating business models based on radical, sustainability-driven innovations, that not only bridge the gap between niches and mass markets but also deliver ecological and social benefits in an economically viable way, is **the** major challenge when developing sustainable business models (Bocken *et al.*, 2014; Lüdeke-Freund, 2013).

There are, however, examples of companies that have managed to create such business models. Stubbs and Cocklin (2008), for example, analyze the Australian Bendigo Bank as well as the famous carpet tile maker Interface Inc. and describe their structural and cultural attributes in relation to their socio-economic contexts and their inter-organizational capabilities. Based on the analysis of both firms' exceptional leadership styles and ability to provide positive external effects to the natural environment and society, Stubbs and Cocklin (2008) propose key characteristics of "sustainability business models" including, inter alia, adopting a stakeholder view of the firm and promoting environmental stewardship.

Having introduced the business model concept in general, and current approaches to extending it towards an inclusion of sustainability aspects, such as reducing environmental harm through improved value creation processes or providing social value propositions through new pricing and financing models, we present selected definitions for sustainable business model concepts in Table 18.1. These were chosen due to:

- Their clarity in extending the general business model notion towards sustainability, and

- Their usefulness in highlighting various conceptual aspects, such as innovation (Bocken *et al.*, 2014), an emphasis on structural aspects (Stubbs and Cocklin, 2008) or underlying normative values and ideals (Stirling, 2014).

Table 18.1 Selected definitions of sustainable business models

Definition	Source
"We define a sustainable business model as the rationale of how an organization creates, delivers and captures economic, environmental and social forms of value simultaneously."	Joyce *et al.*, 2015, p. 3
"Business leaders should develop alternative business models that incorporate a broader range of values and ideals than those associated with traditional economic modelling. Explicit inclusion of a firm's social responsibilities can be implemented via social accounting procedures and its mission statement."	Stirling, 2014, p. 812
"Business model innovations for sustainability are defined as: Innovations that create significant positive and/or significantly reduced negative impacts for the environment and/or society, through changes in the way the organization and its value-network create, deliver value and capture value (i.e. create economic value) or change their value propositions."	Bocken *et al.*, 2014, p. 44
"...a business model for sustainability can be defined as supporting voluntary, or mainly voluntary, activities which solve or moderate social and/or environmental problems. By doing so, it creates positive business effects which can be measured or at least argued for. A business model for sustainability is actively managed in order to create customer and social value by integrating social, environmental, and business activities."	Schaltegger *et al.*, 2012, p. 112
"A business model for sustainability is the activity system of a firm which allocates resources and coordinates activities in a value creation process which overcomes the public/private benefit discrepancy. That is, a business model for sustainability is the structural template of a business logic which creates the business case for sustainability."	Lüdeke-Freund, 2009, p. 56
"An organization adopting an SBM develops internal structural and cultural capabilities to achieve firm-level sustainability and collaborates with key stakeholders to achieve sustainability for the system that the organization is part of."	Stubbs and Cocklin, 2008, p. 123

18.2.2 Major characteristics of sustainable business model conceptions

This section summarizes the major characteristics of current sustainable business model conceptions as found in the above discussion and selected definitions. These definitions highlight various, teleological, subject-related and functional characteristics (Wirtz, 2011). Functional characteristics describe which strategic, operational or conceptual functions are primarily supported. The subject relation describes how a business model conception serves as a frame of reference for representing a business' value creation approach in which contents, components and relations are considered. The subject-related and functional characteristics serve particular goals that are associated with business models, such as creating competitive advantage and securing the financial success of a company. This goal orientation is expressed by a conception's teleological characteristics.

18.2.2.1 Teleological dimension—goals of using SBM conceptions

The teleological dimension asks for the overall goals to be supported by business model conceptions, such as value creation for the organization and its customers, achieving a strategic market position, competitive advantage and profit potential as well as exploiting business opportunities (Al-Debei and Avison, 2010; Wirtz *et al.*, 2016). Acknowledging these fundamental goals, the definitions of sustainable business models presented above clearly exceed their scope. The main theme that most definitions have in common is the goal to create ecological and social value— sometimes in concert, sometimes open to either an ecological or a social emphasis. While Joyce *et al.* (2015) see a simultaneous creation of ecological, social and economic value, Bocken *et al.* (2014) leave the emphasis on one or the other rather open and also include the reduction of negative effects as a valid goal. Schaltegger *et al.* (2012, 2016; Lüdeke-Freund, 2009) define the purpose of a sustainable business model as integrating ecological and social activities into an organization's core business so that business success is achieved **through** solving sustainability problems. Further goals such as building businesses based on leaders' normative values and principles such as stakeholder inclusion are also highlighted (Stubbs and Cocklin, 2008; Stirling, 2014).

18.2.2.2 Subject-related dimension: elements and contents covered by SBM conceptions

In general, most business model conceptions serve as frames of reference to describe an organization's value creation rationale. Component-based frameworks are very common (Wirtz *et al.*, 2016), i.e. frameworks of different conceptual elements and their relationships, such as resources, value proposition, customers or financial model (Osterwalder and Pigneur, 2009). However, other approaches that define business model activities, instead of elements, are also found in the literature (Zott and Amit, 2010). Some authors also see market or pricing strategies and market positions as business model elements, thus also taking a market perspective (Morris *et al.*, 2005; Wirtz *et al.*, 2016).

Figure 18.2 Example of an extended SBM conception, the "flourishing business canvas"

Source: http://www.flourishingbusiness.org; © Antony Upward, 2014, used with permission

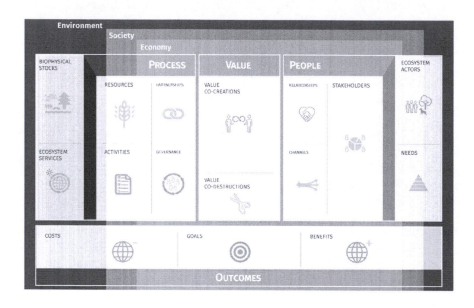

To our knowledge, the most radical extension of the most popular framework, i.e. Osterwalder and Pigneur's "business model canvas" (BMC), is the "strongly sustainable business model canvas" (SSBMC) developed by Upward and Jones (2016).[2] Its coverage of elements and contents has been extended to not only include the elements proposed by the BMC but to also represent an organization's contexts (natural environment, society and financial economy), its stakeholders and their needs. The SSBMC suggests working with actor-specific questions, such as "Who are the human and non-human actors who may choose to engage with the business?" or "Which human and non-human actors' fundamental needs is the organization intending to satisfy?" Consequently, this leads to an extended notion of performance based on a definition of value in alignment with fundamental human needs: "How does the organization define success environmentally, socially and economically (from the perspective of all actors in all their various stakeholder roles)?" (Jones and Upward, 2014) Moreover, the SSBMC proposes extended concepts of resources (e.g. to include bio-physical stocks) and performance metrics reflecting a form of triple bottom line approach.

---

2   The original "strongly sustainable business model ontology" (SSBMO) and its visual representation, "strongly sustainable business model canvas" (SSBMC), were further developed to the "flourishing business canvas" which is currently being tested in business practice (http://www.flourishingbusiness.org).

18.2.2.3 Functional dimension—functions supported by SBM conceptions

Finally, the functional dimension refers to management tasks that can be improved with business model conceptions, such as describing, analyzing, managing and communicating organizational value creation (Osterwalder *et al.*, 2005). This includes functions such as defining the goals of a business (see teleological dimension), describing the major components and contents of respective activities (see subject-related dimension), specification of strategy and strategic positions or the estimation of profit potential. When it comes to tasks such as innovation and modelling, but also investor communications or patenting of specific business model features (Doganova and Eyquem-Renault, 2009), such as a unique pricing mechanism, more detailed definitions and frameworks are required; component-based approaches and visual and design-oriented tools come into play (Wirtz *et al.*, 2016), e.g. to conduct interdisciplinary workshops (Breuer, 2013). Sustainable business model conceptions are expected to support the integration of multiple goals related to organizational value creation and the development of respective stakeholder networks which exceed traditional business relationships (Bocken *et al.*, 2013; Breuer and Lüdeke-Freund, 2014; Rohrbeck *et al.*, 2013). Another crucial function beyond describing, analyzing etc. is to facilitate innovation processes that balance ecological, social and economic stakeholders' needs and value perceptions.

18.2.3 Current sustainable supply chain conceptions

Regarding supply chains and their management, we refer to the seminal paper by Mentzer *et al.* (2001) who proposed a rather broad and inclusive definition. They define the supply chain as "a set of three or more entities (organizations or individuals) directly involved in the upstream and downstream flows of products, services, finances and/or information from a source to a customer" (Mentzer *et al.*, p. 4f). Figure 18.3 depicts a generic model of a supply chain from raw material extraction to end use, with associated flows. Supply chain management is defined as "the systemic, strategic coordination of the traditional business functions and the tactics across these business functions within a particular company and across businesses within the supply chain", aiming for particular purposes, namely "improving the long-term performance of the individual companies and the supply chain as a whole" (ibid., 2001, p. 18). Main characteristics of the philosophy of supply chain management is a systems approach that encompasses the entire supply chain, a strategic orientation towards intra-firm and inter-firm cooperation, and a distinct focus on customer value and customer satisfaction (ibid., p. 7).

Figure 18.3 A generic forward supply chain model from raw material to end use

Source: authors

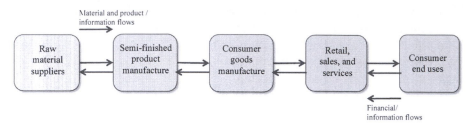

In the last 15 years, research on sustainable supply chains has developed rapidly. It may, however, still be considered to be in a pre-paradigmatic state, featuring low levels of conceptual coherence and integration (Chicksand *et al.*, 2012; Gold, 2014). This general heterogeneity is reflected in a variety of definitions of the overall concept of SSCs and SSCM, respectively.

Ahi and Searcy (2013) point out that SSCM has first concentrated on environmental, i.e. "green", issues and later opened up to a more comprehensive consideration of sustainability, building on the triple bottom line approach (Dyllick and Hockerts, 2002). Although the reviewed definitions refer consistently to all three dimensions of sustainability, i.e. environmental, social and economic aspects, there is little consensus with regard to further characteristics of SSCM. While Pagell and Wu (2009) as well as Carter and Rogers (2008) emphasize the long-term perspective of sustainable supply chain management, Seuring and Müller (2008) explicitly refer to a stakeholder perspective. Carter and Rogers (2008), Seuring and Müller (2008) as well as Badurdeen *et al.* (2009) all highlight the need for collaboration and coordination of processes and activities, including information sharing and common visions, across the supply chain and even across the product life-cycle (Badurdeen *et al.*, 2009). Based on their analysis, Ahi and Searcy (2013) attempt to condense the main features of definitions of SSCM into a more comprehensive definition. Hence, SSCM is:

> [...] the creation of coordinated supply chains through the voluntary integration of economic, environmental, and social considerations with key inter-organizational business systems designed to efficiently and effectively manage the material, information, and capital flows associated with the procurement, production, and distribution of products or services in order to meet stakeholder requirements and improve the profitability, competitiveness, and resilience of the organization over the short- and long-term (Ahi and Searcy, 2013, p. 339).

As with the notion of sustainable business models, we summarize selected definitions of sustainable supply chains and their management in Table 18.2. These were chosen due to:

- Their clarity in extending the general supply chain concept to include sustainability aspects, and

- Their usefulness to highlight different conceptual aspects, such as management functions (Hassini *et al.*, 2012), product life cycle orientation (Badurdeen *et al.*, 2009) or inter-organizational coordination and cooperation (Carter and Rogers, 2008; Seuring and Müller, 2008).

Table 18.2 Selected definitions of sustainable supply chains and their management

Definition	Source
"Sustainable SCM is the management of supply chain operations, resources, information, and funds in order to maximize the supply chain profitability while at the same time minimizing the environmental impacts and maximizing the social well-being."	Hassini *et al.*, 2012, p. 70
"Involvement of the planning and management of sourcing, procurement, conversion and logistics activities involved during pre-manufacturing, manufacturing, use and post-use stages in the life cycle in closed-loop through multiple life-cycles with seamless information sharing about all product life-cycle stages between companies by explicitly considering the social and environmental implications to achieve a shared vision."	Badurdeen *et al.*, 2009, p. 57
"To be truly sustainable a supply chain would at worst do no net harm to natural or social systems while still producing a profit over an extended period of time; a truly sustainable supply chain could, customers willing, continue to do business forever."	Pagell and Wu, 2009, p. 38
"Sustainable SCM is the strategic, transparent integration and achievement of an organization's social, environmental, and economic goals in the systemic coordination of key interorganizational business processes for improving the long-term economic performance of the individual company and its supply chains."	Carter and Rogers, 2008, p. 368
"Sustainable SCM is the management of material, information and capital flows as well as cooperation among companies along the supply chain while taking goals from all three dimensions of sustainable development, i.e. economic, environmental and social, into account which are derived from customer and stakeholder requirements."	Seuring and Müller, 2008, p. 1700

18.2.4 Major characteristics of sustainable supply chain conceptions

In the following, we summarize the main characteristics of current conceptions of sustainable supply chains and their management, again using the above introduced conceptual dimensions: intended ends (teleological), covered phenomena (subject-related) and supported functions (functional).

18.2.4.1 Teleological dimension: goals of using SSC conceptions

SSCM can be seen as a management philosophy that aims at increasing operational performance—quality, speed, flexibility, cost or dependability, for example—for the focal company and across its supply chain (Gunasekaran *et al.*, 2004), aligned with social and environmental goals (Dyllick and Hockerts, 2002). According to the business case, which dominates SSCM so far, this is done for the sake of business performance—e.g., profits, efficiency gains, brand reputation, control of risks, market share, customer satisfaction and loyalty (Schaltegger *et al.*, 2012)—which ultimately is supposed to lead to competitive advantage. It may be noted that the customer focus of traditional supply chain management (Mentzer *et al.*, 2001) can be seen to be replaced by a more comprehensive stakeholder perspective (Seuring and Müller, 2008), thus substantially extending performance dimensions to account for companies' environmental and social effects. Going beyond the business case towards the idea of stakeholder accountability (Brown and Fraser, 2006), fringe stakeholders may also be taken into account by companies and supply chains, such as the global poor, future generations or animals (Anderson *et al.*, 2012).

In the teleological dimension, SSC conceptions aim for an integration of traditional and sustainability performance goals while striving for enhanced competitive advantage for the organizations within a supply chain. At the extreme, sustainable supply chains transcend the business case and respond to stakeholders regardless of their power and instrumental leverage for enhancing a firm's traditional performance goals, thus creating stakeholder accountability along the supply chain.

18.2.4.2 Subject-related dimension: elements and contents covered by SSC conceptions

Supply chain management covers diverse business functions across the members of a supply chain e.g. purchasing, production, marketing and transport. When considering SSCM, the natural and social environment of supply chains is accentuated and conceptually integrated, with stakeholders going beyond internal stakeholders, economic actors and customers. Broadly speaking, SSCM investigates:

- Flows
- Relationships, and
- The embeddedness of supply chains.

In terms of flows, capital, information and material flows are of interest, both as forward and reverse flows (Mentzer *et al.*, 2001; Seuring and Müller, 2008). Furthermore, the relationships across supply chains are examined, looking at issues such as agency, trust, dependence or power (Handfield and Bechtel, 2004). Finally, supply chains are embedded in nature and society, which adds a wide variety of moral, sociological, psychological, ethical and political aspects (Gold, 2014), requiring a significant extension of the phenomena covered.

18.2.4.3 Functional dimension: functions supported by SSC conceptions

Sustainable supply chain management aims at identifying pre-conditions, practices and facilitators that lead to performance and value creation on the triple bottom line, thereby referring to the single companies and the supply chain as a whole. In this respect, the functions of SSCM can be conceptualized as a five-step-model (Fig. 18.4). Awareness of the institutional embeddedness of the supply chain facilitates orientation towards sustainability on an individual and organizational level, which leads to the implementation of a set of managerial practices. These practices are translated into facilitators of SSCM which in turn generate performance and value creation on the triple bottom line (economic, social and environmental).

Effective management of sustainable supply chains requires that managers take their supply chains' specific institutional setting into account such as socio-economic context, traditions, laws and norms (Gold, 2014; Silvestre, 2015). Orientation towards sustainability on the individual level means ensuring the support and commitment of all employees (including the top management); on the organizational level it comprises company values (translated in policies and routines), reward and incentive systems and an integrative view on performance targets aligning social, economic and environmental objectives (Gold *et al.*, 2013). SSCM practices comprise the extension of the supply chain towards non-economic actors (Stiller and Gold, 2014), de-commoditization of suppliers (Pagell *et al.*, 2010), standards and third-party certification (Müller *et al.*, 2009; Ciliberti *et al.*, 2009), as well as information sharing and shared visions (Chen and Paulraj, 2004). These practices are supposed to support facilitators of SSCM, such as traceability, transparency (Mol, 2015), cultural alignment, risk sensitivity (Carter and Rogers, 2008), collaborative attitude and systems thinking (Mentzer *et al.*, 2001), which are preconditions of performance and of value creation on the triple bottom line.

Figure 18.4 A five-step model of sustainable supply chain management functions
Source: authors

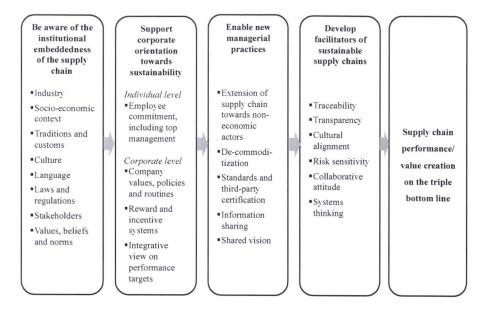

18.3 Comparison and towards perspectival integration

Based on the above discussion of sustainable business model and supply chain conceptions, we summarize their specific characteristics. We propose that their complementary and distinguishing features can be summarized as follows (see also Table 18.3 below):

- Both SBM and SSC conceptions aim at integrating traditional business and sustainability performance **goals** with a view to the needs and value perceptions of multiple stakeholders. However, SBMs focus rather on single organizations' goals of value creation, while SSCs address complex, multi-organizational and thus multi-actor goal systems, although a strong predominance of the focal firm perspective still prevails in research and business practice. SSCs are organized as chains of connected businesses, where one will fail without the delivery of the other (in the case of single sourcing). SBMs have a higher level of abstraction and do not describe (yet) in detail each step in delivering and creating value. Whereas the traditional business model perspective may have focused on the firm as the focal point, it should be noted that the SBM literature increasingly recognizes the business model as a concept that allows businesses to think beyond their boundaries, all the more because global sustainability challenges transcend business boundaries (Stubbs and Cocklin, 2008; Bocken *et al.*, 2013; Bocken *et al.*, 2015). Still, the SBM view typically takes one business as the starting point for systems-level, sustainable value creation (Stubbs and Cocklin, 2008) and lacks the detail and complexity of SSCs. This might be the case because of the difference in **goals**: SSCM as a "tool" covers strategic, tactical and operational levels, i.e. also day-to-day business (Gunasekaran *et al.*, 2004), whereas SBM conceptions as "tools" are typically applied at a higher-abstraction level, the strategic level, to guide decision-making.

- Both SBM and SSC conceptions contain similar **elements and contents**. Both concepts share the idea of embedding business models and supply chains respectively in their wider ecological, social and economic contexts, which requires adding further dedicated conceptual elements and relationships. However, while SBMs focus on the value-creating elements of a single organization, with some attempts to go beyond its boundaries, SSCs by nature conceptualize inter-organizational flows (e.g. products, money and information) and relationships to create and deliver value (Mentzer *et al.*, 2011; Carter and Rogers, 2008).

- The **functions** supported are, in both cases, extensions of traditional entrepreneurial and managerial functions, in other words business model development and supply chain management. However, SBM conceptions are rather devices to develop, describe and communicate value creation rationales, while SSC and respective management conceptions rather support management and governance functions such as developing shared visions and incentive systems across the organizations in a supply chain. It should also be noted that in large multi-national organizations the function of "supply chain expert" is omnipresent and clearly understood, whereas the function of "business model expert" has not yet reached that level of familiarity. This might be the case because of the higher level of abstraction of the concept of the "business model" and the different organizational functions it might potentially cross (finance, marketing, logistics, etc.).

Making use of both conceptions in an integrated manner can offer an extended perspective on value creation from a focal organization's perspective in relation to its position in the supply chain and the relationships with other organizations positioned on upstream or downstream segments (Schweizer, 2005 and his approach to deriving business models from value chain configurations[3]). This integrated perspective also provides more clarity in terms of business model changes due to

---

3   The concepts of value chain and supply chain are often used interchangeably. However, depending on the particularities of disciplines such as operations management or strategy, some authors also highlight differences between both. For the sake of clarity, this chapter builds on an understanding of the supply chain concept as broadly defined by the authors mentioned in Table 18.2 and does not address similarities or differences to value chain conceptions.

variations of the degree of horizontal or vertical integration along the supply chain (Bresser *et al.*, 2000 on the deconstruction of value chains). These variables, i.e. position on the supply chain and the degree of horizontal and vertical integration, extend the range of business model development by helping to better understand how their variation affects an organization's value creation rationale.

Figures 18.5a and 18.5b use the examples of a consumer goods manufacturer and a waste management provider to illustrate some of the connections and differences between supply chains and business models. These figures present both the supply chain and the business model perspective. Whereas materials in a supply chain typically "flow" downstream (e.g. from raw material suppliers to semi-finished product manufacturer), money gets passed upstream (e.g. from consumer to retailer); information flows in both directions are essential for coordinating these processes (See Fig. 18.3 above). In a high-level view of the business model the detail of the supply chain is typically not stipulated. However, the conceptualization of a business model focuses on value proposition, value creation, value delivery and value capture (See Fig. 18.1 above).

Table 18.3 Conceptual comparison of SBM and SSC

Dimensions	SBM	SSC
Teleological (goals of using SBM and SSC conceptions)	· Traditional business goals, such as competitive advantage and financial value	· Enhanced competitive advantage for the organizations within a supply chain
	· Joint creation of ecological, social and economic value is the central goal	· Integration of traditional and sustainability performance goals
	· Inclusion of an organization's leadership values and stakeholders' value perceptions	· Stakeholder management, inclusion and even accountability along the supply chain
	· Strategic decision-making	· Strategic as well as tactical and operational decision-making
	Extension of a single-organization's goals in terms of value creation, performance and accountability towards its ecological, social and economic contexts	**Extension of a multi-organization system's goals** towards triple bottom line performance and accountability for its ecological, social and economic impacts
Subject-related (elements and contents covered)	· Elements of value creation and their relations	· Different kinds of material and immaterial flows, both forward and reverse flows
	· Organization-centred, but extending core concepts such as resources, customer, value and performance	· Relationships between different organizations, including non-business actors
	· Embeddedness in wider environmental, societal and economic contexts	· Embeddedness within nature and society, leading to moral, sociological etc. issues
	Coverage of an organization's value creation elements and conceptualization of contextual embeddedness	**Coverage of multiple organizations' (im-)material flows and relationships** and conceptualization of contextual embeddedness

Dimensions	SBM	SSC
Functional (functions of SBM and SSC conceptions)	· Supporting the development, description and communication of organizational value creation	· Supporting the extension of traditional management functions by providing an orientation towards sustainability
	· Bringing together multiple stakeholders, their particular needs and value perceptions	· Implementing respective incentive and governance systems and practices
	· Supporting the facilitation of multi-stakeholder and interdisciplinary innovation	· Developing central facilitators of sustainable supply chains
	Supporting the development of business models while considering multiple stakeholders' needs and value perceptions	**Supporting the development of management/governance systems** and facilitators of sustainable supply chains

In Figure 18.5a for instance the consumer goods manufacturer, the focal actor (bold-framed) in this case, has a particular value proposition in mind for the end-consumer (bold/dashed-framed): delivering "refreshment through delivering a thirst-quenching drink in a can". The manufacturer expects the drink to be sold at a certain price point and receives part of the profits of the sales to capture value from the delivered value proposition. This is the picture that a marketer might have in mind. However, it can only be put in practice through lining up a full supply chain to create and deliver value to the consumer. The start of a new business (idea) most likely starts with the drawing up of a business model, which provides the initial template of the business. With this broad business template, the detailed supply chain can then be mapped out.

Figure 18.5a Supply chain position and value creation rationale of consumer goods producer

Source: authors

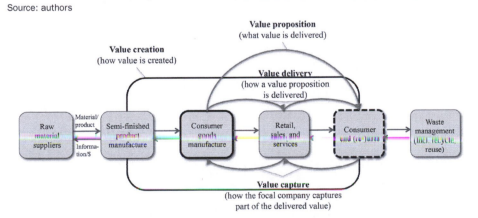

In the case of a waste management provider (Fig. 18.5b), "waste" becomes a form of raw material and offers a new value proposition (i.e., waste as a resource) for the set up of new waste management business models. The integrated view on supply chain and business models helps in understanding the different, but interrelated, value propositions that even a very simple waste management business model can deliver. The focal actor, the waste management company (bold-framed), offers a value proposition to consumers (bold/dashed-framed): to take care of their waste that results from use and consumption of products and services. That is, consumers do not have to be concerned about what to do with their daily litter, they simply put it to their waste bin or bring it to some waste management centre and pay for its disposal, which could also be financed publicly (here, business model variations come into play).

This consumer-focused business model is, however, embedded in an overarching model which is about the relationship between the waste management provider and, for example, a raw material supplier (bold/dashed-framed). Primary raw materials such as copper or wolfram, but also secondary materials such as paper and glass, are becoming increasingly valuable due to reducing natural reserves, the need for efficient logistics and continuously improving recycling technologies that help closing material flows and at the same time stimulate new policy and business models based on "urban mining" (Krook *et al.*, 2015; Zaman, 2015) and "cradle–to–cradle" approaches (McDonough and Braungart, 2013). The overarching model is based on a value proposition for raw material suppliers, i.e. access to secondary resources that were already processed by some form of metabolism of production and consumption. In return, the waste management company gets paid by the raw material supplier. Again, there is also space for model variations: the waste management company could also deliver to semi-finished product manufacturers in case they have integrated the step of secondary material re-processing. This relationship between the waste management company and the raw material supplier, however, depends directly on the business model that builds on consumers and their waste.

Figure 18.5b Supply chain position and business models of a waste management
provider

Source: authors

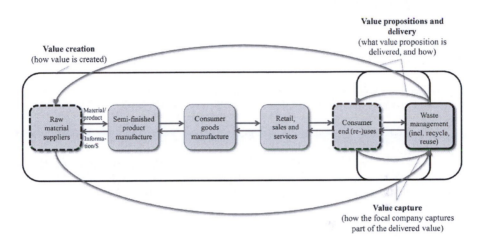

We see that multiple and interrelated business models can build on one supply chain, even from the perspective of only one actor (e.g. a waste management company). Using both perspectives, supply chain and business model, in an integrated manner helps in untangling and creating potential business models, which becomes increasingly important in complex cases such as multi-loop models around resource use and the reduction of environmental impacts. The above introduced perspective, which only scratched the surface of analytical and creative possibilities, can be used in the future to continue the work of authors such as Wells and Seitz (2005) who began discussing closed-loop supply chains from a business model perspective. Another important task for future research is the conceptualization of the above discussed multi-stakeholder perspective as a core element of an integrated perspective, which would inevitably lead to the question of how different forms of ecological, social and economic value can be represented and managed.

18.4 Implications for future research and practice

The relationships between business model and supply chain conceptions are mostly rather implicit, as in Osterwalder and Pigneur's (2009) linear framework from inputs to customers, but sometimes they are made very explicit, as in Schweizer's (2005) approach of deriving different types of business model from different types of value chain configuration. We argue that clarity about the major characteristics of business model and supply chain conceptions helps in understanding their respective foci and strengths, and identifying synergies in terms of analysis, development and management. Along the three conceptual dimensions of goals aimed for (teleological), elements and contents represented (subject-related), and the entrepreneurial and managerial functions to be supported (functional), we found some similarities, such as an extension of goals and stakeholder perspectives towards more inclusiveness to non-economic aspects, but also fundamental differences, such as a tendency to a single-actor perspective on the side of SBM conceptions and a multi-actor perspective on the side of SSC and SSCM conceptions.

Broadly speaking, sustainability integration is the issue which provides for a strong conceptual and maybe philosophical link between both:

> To create a sustainable supply chain then seems to require proactive top management that understands that sustainability is an organizational commitment. This understanding may be evidenced by redesigning products and/or processes, which can only occur if all employees including the designers are properly motivated and rewarded (Pagell and Wu, 2009, p. 39).

This not only holds for supply chains, but also for business models, particularly opportunities for innovation of sustainable practices which often need more radical change: "… TQM and other continuous improvement-focused operational philosophies may be most useful for making an existing supply chain **more** sustainable. However, the same operational philosophy may become a hindrance when the organization needs to radically change what they do to become **truly** sustainable." (Pagell and Wu, 2009, p. 39, original emphasis) The tension between incremental and radical innovation has also been found for business models (Smith *et al.*, 2010). The magnitude of this innovation management challenge multiplies in cases where radical changes of a supply chain are needed but hindered by a business model's inability to absorb and mirror these changes, and vice versa (Wüstenhagen and Boehnke, 2008). Energy utilities' search for radically-innovative business models for solar and other forms of renewable energy is an example to illustrate this aspect. Their traditional business models, often based on historically grown monopolies, are based on large-scale production and sale of kilowatt hours, which makes them struggle to capitalize on the decentralized supply networks through wind parks, solar farms or biomass power stations (e.g. Richter, 2012; 2013).

In consequence, a potentially truly sustainable supply chain (or business model) cannot fully unfold in the case of business model (supply chain) innovation inertia; this becomes even more critical when the purpose of a business model and/or supply chain is to be completely redefined: "There is also literature that examines innovation at a scale that redefines what the entire supply chain does. For instance, rather than just redesigning products and/or processes, sustainable organizations could move to a service oriented strategy" (Pagell and Wu, 2009, p. 39). Issues of product-service-system (PSS) based business models have some "tradition" in the SBM discourse (Charter *et al.*, 2008; Reim *et al.*, 2015). Here, strong synergies between both conceptions are to be expected. Future research should therefore study respective cases to understand these dynamics and offer managerial advice. Reverse logistics and closed-loop supply chains and business models are additional topics which need further research, especially due to the increasing attention policy makers and companies pay to the idea of a circular economy.

The proposed integrated perspective might also support a conceptual and practical shift to the level of value networks (Peppard and Rylander, 2006)—on this level SBM and SSC could merge to a consistent and integrated field of research and practice. Network collaboration, including the education and certification of supply chain members, are exemplary best practices of SSCM (Pagell and Wu, 2009), pointing to the need for collaboration and mutual coordination. Collaboration is a rather new issue in the SBM discourse (Breuer and Lüdeke-Freund, 2014; Rohrbeck *et al.*, 2013). Boons and Lüdeke-Freund (2013) point to the importance of collaborative and responsible supplier and customer management, but provide no further details as to how this could be achieved. Here, the SBM perspective must be explicitly extended towards SSCs and their management. However, approaches such as certification as a means to develop sustainable business model ecosystems are not addressed, at least to our knowledge. The importance of a broader stakeholder approach is increasingly understood in SBM research and practice, but not yet sufficiently resolved, an issue that, according to our review, is traditionally at the heart of sustainable supply chain management. Therefore, an integrated perspective on SBMs and SSCs might help to develop clear and operable approaches to turn business models into real platforms for multi-stakeholder integration and value creation.

References

Abdelkafi, N., Makhotin, S., & Posselt, T. (2013). Business model innovations for electric Mobility: What can be learned from existing business model patterns? *International Journal of Innovation Management*, 17(01), Article ID 1340003.

Ahi, P., & Searcy, C. (2013). A comparative literature analysis of definitions for green and sustainable supply chain management. *Journal of Cleaner Production*, 52, 329-341.

Al-Debei, M., & Avison, D. (2010). Developing a unified framework of the business model concept. *European Journal of Information Systems*, 19(03), 359-376.

Anderson, M.W., Teisl, M., & Noblet, C. (2012). Giving voice to the future in sustainability: Retrospective assessment to learn prospective stakeholder engagement. *Ecological Economics*, 84, 1-6.

Badurdeen, F., Iyengar, D., Goldsby, T.J., Metta, H., Gupta, S., & Jawahir, I.S. (2009). Extending total life-cycle thinking to sustainable supply chain design. *International Journal of Product Lifecycle Management*, 4(1/2/3), 49-67.

Bidmon, C., & Knab, S. (2014): The three roles of business models for socio-technical transitions. In K. Huizingh, S. Conn, M. Torkkeli & I. Bitran (Eds.), *The Proceedings of XXV ISPIM Conference: Innovation for Sustainable Economy and Society*, 8–11 June 2014, Dublin, Ireland.

Bocken, N.M.P., Rana, P., & Short, S.W. (2015). Value mapping for sustainable business thinking. *Journal of Industrial and Production Engineering*, 32(1), 67-81.

Bocken, N.M.P., Short, S., Rana, P., & Evans, S. (2014). A literature and practice review to develop sustainable business model archetypes. *Journal of Cleaner Production*, 65, 42-56.

Bocken, N.M.P., Short, S., Rana, P., & Evans, S. (2013). A value mapping tool for sustainable business modelling. *Corporate Governance: The International Journal of Business in Society*, 13(5), 482-497.

Boons, F., & Lüdeke-Freund, F. (2013). Business models for sustainable innovation: State-of-the-art and steps towards a research agenda. *Journal of Cleaner Production*, 45, 9-19.

Bresser, R., Heuskel, D., & Nixon, R. (2000). The deconstruction of integrated value chains: Practical and conceptual challenges. In R. Bresser, M. Hitt, R. Nixon & D. Heuskel (Eds.), *The Strategic Management Series. Winning Strategies in a Deconstructing World*, (pp. 1-22). Chichester, UK: Wiley.

Breuer, H. (2013). Lean venturing: Learning to create new business through exploration, elaboration, evaluation, experimentation, and evolution. *International Journal of Innovation Management*, 17(3), doi: 10.1142/S1363919613400136.

Breuer, H., & Lüdeke-Freund, F. (2014). Normative innovation for sustainable business models in value networks. In K. Huizingh, S. Conn, M. Torkkeli & I. Bitran (Eds.), *The Proceedings of XXV ISPIM Conference: Innovation for Sustainable Economy and Society*, 8–11 June 2014, Dublin, Ireland.

Brown, J., & Fraser, M. (2006). Approaches and perspectives in social and environmental accounting: An overview of the conceptual landscape. *Business Strategy and the Environment*, 15(2), 103-117.

Carter, C.R., & Rogers, D.S. (2008). A framework of sustainable supply chain management: Moving towards new theory. *International Journal of Physical Distribution & Logistics Management*, 38(5), 360-387.

Charter, M., Gray, C., Clark, T., & Woolman, T. (2008). Review: The role of business in realising sustainable consumption and production. In A. Tukker, M. Charter, C. Vezzoli, E. Stø, & M.M. Andersen (Eds.), *System Innovation for Sustainability: Vol. 1. Perspectives on Radical Changes to Sustainable Consumption and Production*, (pp. 46-69). Sheffield, UK: Greenleaf Publishing.

Chen, I.J., & Paulraj, A. (2004). Towards a theory of supply chain management: The constructs and measurements. *Journal of Operations Management*, 22(2), 119-150.

Chesbrough, H. (2010). Business model innovation: Opportunities and barriers. *Long Range Planning*, 43(2/3), 354-363.

Chesbrough, H., & Rosenbloom, R. (2002). The role of the business model in capturing value from innovation: Evidence from Xerox Corporation's technology spin-off companies. *Industrial & Corporate Change*, 11(03), 529-555.

Chicksand, D., Watson, G., Walker, H., Radnor, Z., & Johnston, R. (2012). Theoretical perspectives in purchasing and supply chain management: An analysis of the literature. *Supply Chain Management: An International Journal*, 17(4), 454-472.

Ciliberti, F., De Groot, G., De Haan, J., & Pontrandolfo, P. (2009). Codes to coordinate supply chains: SMEs' experiences with SA8000. *Supply Chain Management*, 14(2), 117-127.

Doganova, L., & Eyquem-Renault, M. (2009). What do business models do? Innovation devices in technology entrepreneurship. *Research Policy*, 38(10), 1,559-1,570.

Dyllick, T., & Hockerts, K. (2002). Beyond the business case for corporate sustainability. *Business Strategy and the Environment*, 11(2), 130-141.

Gold, S. (2014). Supply chain management as Lakatosian research program. *Supply Chain Management: An International Journal*, 19(1), 1-9.

Gold, S., Hahn, R., & Seuring, S. (2013). Sustainable supply chain management in "Base of the Pyramid" food projects: A path to triple bottom line approaches for multinationals? *International Business Review*, 22(5), 784-799.

Gold, S., Seuring, S., & Beske, P. (2010). The constructs of sustainable supply chain management: A content analysis based on published case studies. *Progress in Industrial Ecology*, 7(2), 114-137.

Grassl, W. (2012). Business models of social enterprise: A design approach to hybridity. ACRN *Journal of Entrepreneurship Perspectives*, 1(1), 37-60.

Gunasekaran, A., Patel, C., & McGaughey, R.E. (2004). A framework for supply chain performance measurement. *International Journal of Production Economics*, 87(3), 333-347.

Handfield, R.B., & Bechtel, C. (2004) Trust, power, dependence, and economics: Can SCM research borrow paradigms? *International Journal of Integrated Supply Management*, 1(1), 3-30.

Hansen, E.G., Große-Dunker, F., & Reichwald, R. (2009). Sustainability innovation cube: A framework to evaluate sustainability-oriented innovations. *International Journal of Innovation Management*, 13(4), 683-713.

Hassini, E., Surti, C., & Searcy, C. (2012). A literature review and a case study of sustainable supply chains with a focus on metrics. *International Journal of Production Economics*, 140(1), 69-82.

Hemphill, T. (2013). The global food industry and "creative capitalism": The partners in food solutions sustainable business model. *Business and Society Review*, 118(04), 489-511.

Hockerts, K., & Wüstenhagen, R. (2010). Greening Goliaths versus emerging Davids: Theorizing about the role of incumbents and new entrants in sustainable entrepreneurship. *Journal of Business Venturing*, 25(5), 481-492.

Johnson, M.W., & Suskewicz, J. (2009). How to jump-start the clean tech economy. *Harvard Business Review*, 87(11), 52-60.

Jones, P., & Upward, A. (2014). Caring for the future: The systemic design of flourishing enterprises. In Proceedings of RSD3, *Third Symposium of Relating Systems Thinking to Design*, *Oslo School of Architecture and Design*, 15–17 October 2014, Oslo, Norway.

Krook, J., Svensson, N., & Wallsten, B. (2015). Urban infrastructure mines: On the economic and environmental motives of cable recovery from subsurface power grids. *Journal of Cleaner Production*, 104, 353-363.

Loock, M. (2012). Going beyond best technology and lowest price: On renewable energy investors' preference for service-driven business models. *Energy Policy*, 40, 21-27.

Lüdeke-Freund, F. (2014). BP's solar business model: A case study on BP's solar business case and its drivers. *International Journal of Business Environment*, 6(3), 300-328.

Lüdeke-Freund, F. (2013). *Business Models for Sustainability Innovation: Conceptual Foundations and the Case of Solar Energy*. Lüneburg: Leuphana University.

Lüdeke-Freund, F. (2009). *Business Model Concepts in Corporate Sustainability Contexts: From Rhetoric to a Generic Template for "Business Models for Sustainability"*. Lüneburg: Centre for Sustainability Management.

Lüdeke-Freund, F., Massa, L., Bocken, N., Brent, A., & Musango, J. (2016). *Business Models for Shared Value: How Sustainability-Oriented Business Models Contribute to Business Success and Societal Progress*. Cape Town: Network for Business Sustainability South Africa.

Matos, S., & Silvestre, B.S. (2013). Managing stakeholder relations when developing sustainable business models: The case of the Brazilian energy sector. *Journal of Cleaner Production*, 45, 61-73.

McDonough, W., & Braungart, M. (2013). *The Upcycle*. New York: North Point Press.

Mentzer, J.T., DeWitt, W., Keebler, J.S., Min, S., Nix, N.W., Smith, C.D., & Zacharia, Z.G. (2001). Defining supply chain management. *Journal of Business Logistics*, 22(2), 1-25.

Mol, A.P.J. (2015). Transparency and value chain sustainability. *Journal of Cleaner Production*, 107, 154-161.

Mollenkopf, D., Stolze, H., Tate, W.L., & Ueltschy, M. (2010). Green, lean, and global supply chains. *International Journal of Physical Distribution and Logistics Management*, 40(1–2), 14-41.

Müller, M., Gomes dos Santos, V., & Seuring, S. (2009). The contribution of environmental and social standards towards ensuring legitimacy in supply chain governance. *Journal of Business Ethics*, 89(4), 509-523.

Osterwalder, A., & Pigneur, Y. (2009). *Business Model Generation: A Handbook for Visionaries, Game Changers, and Challengers*. Amsterdam (published by the author).

Osterwalder, A., Pigneur, Y., & Tucci, C. (2005). Clarifying business models: Origins, present and future of the concept. *Communications of the Association for Information Systems*, 16, Article 1.

Pagell, M., & Wu, Z. (2009). Building a more complete theory of sustainable supply chain management using case studies of ten exemplars. *Journal of Supply Chain Management*, 45(2), 37-56.

Pagell, M., Wu, Z., & Wasserman, M.E. (2010). Thinking differently about purchasing portfolios: An assessment of sustainable sourcing. *Journal of Supply Chain Management*, 46(1), 57-73.

Peppard, J., & Rylander, A. (2006). From value chain to value network. *European Management Journal*, 24(2–3), 128-141.

Rauter, R., Jonker, J., & Baumgartner, R. (2015). Going one's own way: Drivers in developing business models for sustainability. *Journal of Cleaner Production*, online first 4 May 2015.

Reim, W., Parida, V., & Örtqvist, D. (2015). Product-Service Systems (PSS) business models and tactics: A systematic literature review. *Journal of Cleaner Production*, 97, 61-75.

Richter, M. (2013). Business model innovation for sustainable energy: German utilities and renewable energy. *Energy Policy*, 62, 1,226-1,237.

Richter, M. (2012). Utilities' business models for renewable energy: A review. *Renewable and Sustainable Energy Reviews*, 16(5), 2,483-2,493.

Rohrbeck, R., Konnertz, L., & Knab, S. (2013). Collaborative business modelling for systemic and sustainability innovations. *International Journal of Technology Management*, 63(1/2), 4-23.

Schaltegger, S., Hansen, E.G., & Lüdeke-Freund, F. (2016). Business models for sustainability: Origins, present research, and future avenues. *Organization & Environment*, 29(1), 3-10.

Schaltegger, S., Lüdeke-Freund, F., & Hansen, E.G. (2012). Business cases for sustainability: The role of business model innovation for corporate sustainability. Int. J. *Innovation and Sustainable Development*, 6(2), 95-119.

Schaltegger, S., & Wagner, M. (2011). Sustainable entrepreneurship and sustainability innovation: Categories and interactions. *Business Strategy and the Environment*, 20(4), 222-237.

Schweizer, L. (2005). Concept and evolution of business models. *Journal of General Management*, 31(2), 37-56.

Seelos, C. (2014). Theorizing and strategizing with models: Generative models of social enterprises. *International Journal of Entrepreneurial Venturing*, 6(1), 6-21.

Seelos, C., & Mair, J. (2007). Profitable business models and market creation in the context of deep poverty: A strategic view. *Academy of Management Perspectives*, 21(4), 49-63.

Seelos, C., & Mair, J. (2005). Social entrepreneurship: Creating new business models to serve the poor. *Business Horizons*, 48(3), 241-246.

Seuring, S., & Müller, M. (2008). From a literature review to a conceptual framework for sustainable supply chain management. *Journal of Cleaner Production*, 16(15), 1,699-1,710.

Silvestre, B.S. (2015). Sustainable supply chain management in emerging economies: Environmental turbulence, institutional voids and sustainability trajectories. *International Journal of Production Economics*, 167, 156-169.

Smith, W.K., Binns, A., & Tushman, M.L. (2010). Complex business models: Managing strategic paradoxes simultaneously. *Long Range Planning*, 43(2/3), 448-461.

Stiller, S., & Gold, S. (2014). Socially sustainable supply chain management practices in the Indian seed sector: A case study. *Supply Chain Forum*, 15(1), 52-67.

Stirling, K. (2014). Buddhist wisdom as a path to a new economic enlightenment. *Journal of Management Development*, 33(8/9), 812-823.

Stubbs, W., & Cocklin, C. (2008). Conceptualizing a "sustainability business model". *Organization & Environment*, 21(2), 103-127.

Svejenova, S., Planellas, M., & Vives, L. (2010). An individual business model in the making: A chef's quest for creative freedom. *Long Range Planning*, 43(2/3), 408-430.

Teece, D.J. (2010). Business models, business strategy and innovation. *Long Range Planning*, 43(2-3), 172-194.

Tukker, A., Emmert, S., Charter, M., Vezzoli, C., Stø, E., Andersen, M., & Lahlou, S. (2008). Fostering change to sustainable consumption and production: An evidence based view. *Journal of Cleaner Production*, 16(11), 1,218-1,225.

Upward, A., & Jones, P. (2016). An ontology for strongly sustainable business models: Defining an enterprise framework compatible with natural and social science. *Organization & Environment.* 29(1), 97-123.

WCED (World Commission on Environment and Development) (1987). *Our Common Future.* Oxford, UK: Oxford University Press.

Wells, P. (2013). *Business Models for Sustainability.* Cheltenham, UK: Edward Elgar Publishing.

Wells, P. (2013). Sustainable business models and the automotive industry: A commentary. *IIMB Management Review*, 25(4), 228-239. doi: 10.1016/j.iimb.2013.07.001.

Wells, P. (2008). Alternative business models for a sustainable automotive industry. In A. Tukker, M. Charter, C. Vezzoli, E. Stø & M.M. Andersen (Eds.), *System Innovation for Sustainability: Vol. 1. Perspectives on Radical Changes to Sustainable Consumption and Production* (pp. 80-98). Sheffield, UK: Greenleaf Publishing.

Wells, P., & Nieuwenhuis, P. (2004). Business models for relocalisation to deliver sustainability. *Greener Management International*, 47, 89-98.

Wells, P., & Seitz, M. (2005). Business models and closed-loop supply chains: A typology. *Supply Chain Management: An International Journal*, 10(3–4), 249-251.

Wirtz, B.W. (2011). *Business Model Management: Design, Instruments, Success Factors.* Wiesbaden: Gabler.

Wirtz, B.W., Pistoia, A., Ullrich, S., & Göttel, V. (2016). Business models: Origin, development and future research perspectives. *Long Range Planning*, 49, 36-54.

Wolf, J. (2014). The relationship between sustainable supply chain management, stakeholder pressure and corporate sustainability performance. *Journal of Business Ethics*, 119(3), 317-328.

World Bank (n.d.). Poverty Overview. Retrieved from http://www.worldbank.org/en/topic/poverty/overview (June 9, 2015)

Wüstenhagen, R., & Boehnke, J. (2008). Business models for sustainable energy. In A. Tukker, M. Charter, C. Vezzoli, E. Stø & M. M. Andersen (Eds.), *System Innovation for Sustainability: Vol. 1. Perspectives on Radical Changes to Sustainable Consumption and Production* (pp. 70-79). Sheffield, UK: Greenleaf Publishing.

Yunus, M., Moingeon, B., & Lehmann-Ortega, L. (2010). Building social business models: Lessons from the Grameen experience. *Long Range Planning*, 43(2/3), 308-325.

Zaman, A.U. (2015). A comprehensive review of the development of zero waste management: Lessons learned and guidelines. *Journal of Cleaner Production*, 91, 12-25.

Zott, C., & Amit, R. (2010). Business model design: An activity system perspective. *Long Range Planning*, 43(2/3), 216-226.

Zott, C., Amit, R., & Massa, L. (2011). The business model: Recent developments and future research. *Journal of Management*, 37(04), 1,019-1,042.

Florian Lüdeke-Freund is Senior Research Associate at the University of Hamburg and a research fellow at the Centre for Sustainability Management (CSM), Leuphana University, Germany. He is a member of the Strongly Sustainable Business Model Group at OCAD University, Toronto, Canada. His main research interests are sustainable entrepreneurship, business models and sustainability innovations. Florian is convening www.SustainableBusinessModel.org as a community platform to support exchange within the growing community of sustainability-oriented business model researchers.

Stefan Gold is Assistant Professor at the International Centre for Corporate Social Responsibility (ICCSR) of Nottingham University Business School, UK. He received his doctoral degree from the Faculty of Business and Economics of the University of Kassel, Germany. His research interests comprise sustainability, supply chain and operations management and strategic management.

Nancy Bocken is Associate Professor at TU Delft, Industrial Design Engineering. She was awarded the TU Delft Technology Fellowship to research sustainable business models, design and innovation. Nancy also has a position as a Senior Research Associate at the University of Cambridge and is a Fellow at the Cambridge Institute for Sustainability Leadership. Nancy has held positions in logistics, banking and consulting. Originally from the Netherlands, she has lived and worked in France, the UK and USA. Nancy holds a PhD from the University of Cambridge (Engineering), which was funded by Unilever.

19

A network perspective on the TBL in global supply chains[1]

Lance W. Saunders
Virginia Commonwealth University, USA

Wendy L. Tate
University of Tennessee, USA

Joe Miemczyk
Audencia Nantes School of Management, France

George A. Zsidisin
Virginia Commonwealth University, USA

This chapter discusses the emerging importance being placed on analysing global supply chains from a network perspective. This perspective is especially important for sustainability, as non-economic outcomes introduce stakeholders outside of the typical supply chain that have an important impact on triple bottom line (TBL) outcomes. This chapter will illustrate these impacts by using common social network variables to explain their impact on TBL outcomes in global supply chains. The chapter concludes with two illustrative examples to demonstrate how these variables interact in the networks of large multi-national organizations.

1   The authors would like to thank the Global Education Office at VCU for a grant helping to support this study

19.1 Introduction

Sustainability issues in the supply chain can become very complex due to the diversity of stakeholders (e.g. focal organization work groups, suppliers, customers, government entities at various levels, non-governmental organizations (NGOs) and the local community) that are involved in implementing and managing sustainable programmes across a global network. Another degree of complexity in these global networks comes from how many multi-national entities (MNEs) (e.g. Apple or Ford Motor Company) develop corporate social responsibility (CSR) programmes that are appropriate for a specific geographic location, predominantly the home country, but many times are implemented across the entire global network. As they try to diffuse these programmes to stakeholders or other operational units in disparate geographies, with differing needs and cultural norms, they often experience disappointing TBL results (economic, social and environmental) (Kolk and Van Tulder, 2010) that can be traced back to the complexity inherent in networks surrounding sustainable supply chain issues.

As companies shift their networks to include less developed regions of the world, they need to take a broader perspective towards sustainability that includes social, environmental and economic concerns that can be very different from those developed for their home regions. These types of issues can be difficult to relate to by initiative and policy makers that are in separate and often distant locations from where programmes are implemented (Andersen and Skjoett-Larsen, 2009). Global business is increasingly being conducted in low labour cost areas or emerging nations and thus many CSR initiatives are implemented within networks in less-developed regions of the world by multi-national organizations. There is a lack of understanding regarding the sustainability issues (economic, social and environmental) in these regions largely because they are different or vary in importance from the focal organization's home region (Kolk and Van Tulder, 2010). In some situations, the "good" that a company tries to do for a particular region may have negative sustainability implications unless the MNE can properly balance the needs of network stakeholders. An example that is discussed later in the chapter is the industry groups set up by North American and European retailers to deal with safety issues in Bangladesh garment factories. Accidents kept occurring that these groups were set up to prevent and, as will be discussed, many of the problems that led to these accidents can be traced back to the structure of network relationships.

The awareness of these issues is primarily dependent on stakeholders in the MNE's network that the MNE might not have direct connections with, or even be aware exist. This network includes not just members of the conventional supply chain but all of the stakeholders that influence how the TBL is managed. One method that has been used to gain an understanding of how information and knowledge is diffused through a network is social network analysis. Social network analysis uses variables describing the configuration of a network of stakeholders to understand how focal organizational outcomes are dependent on the social relationships between stakeholders in the network (Wuyts *et al.*, 2004). Common social network variables, such as centrality and density, can be used to determine which stakeholders and relationships most heavily influence information flow, either through resources and information that they possess, or by connecting the focal organization to other stakeholders in the network with which the focal organization is not directly connected (Rowley, 1997). This type of analysis is therefore an opportunity to understand how sustainable supply chain management is implemented across organizational boundaries in multi-national settings (Sarkis *et al.*, 2011).

This chapter addresses issues pertaining to the effect of network theory on TBL outcomes by first describing some common social network variables and how each influences the manner by which sustainable supply chain initiatives are diffused through global networks of stakeholders. These issues are especially relevant to developed or emerging regions, as designing culturally-appropriate sustainability strategies for emerging locations is an issue of importance to many modern organizations as they expand their operations to new markets (Hall and Matos, 2010). The behaviour and relationships discussed are important however for the diffusion of sustainable initiatives in any supply chain regardless of location, as understanding and managing one's network is critical in global supply chains regardless of location. Each of the relevant social network variables is discussed individually using examples to illustrate its importance in understanding how TBL initiatives are diffused in global supply chains.

19.2 The relevance of social network theory in sustainable supply chain management

The diffusion of sustainability initiatives from strategy to operationalization is a complex process, as decisions involve numerous stakeholders, both internal and external, to the organization and a supply chain that can impact on the success or failure of this process. Stakeholders, such as internal focal organization departments, government organizations, NGOs, suppliers, customers, investors and the communities in which the organization operates all influence sustainable practices by MNEs. Coordinating and collaborating among these stakeholders in a complex supply chain that spans national and organizational boundaries can be challenging. All of these groups of stakeholders bring their own set of goals, specialized knowledge and cultures to the network that must be integrated to develop and implement a sustainability initiative that is appropriate for a given location (Jamali, 2010).

An example social network for a hypothetical sustainable supply chain is shown in Figure 19.1. This diagram illustrates the variety, depth and complexity of relationships when analyzing a supply chain from a TBL perspective. For example, as shown in Figure 19.1 many times tier-2 suppliers form the conduit by which sustainability initiatives are transferred from strategy to implementation at the operational level at lower-tier suppliers. This can introduce a great deal of uncertainty surrounding how information is diffused to stakeholders, as the focal organization in the network does not directly communicate with lower-tier suppliers. Social network variables can be used to identify these types of interactions and thus deliver key insights into how sustainable practices are diffused through global networks of interconnected firms by assessing the configuration and quality of relationships within the network.

These relationships are based on the alignment of rules, norms and values between stakeholders. Social network analysis can provide insight into how the closeness of relationships in the network affects sustainable outcomes. For instance, social network analysis can provide understanding into whether the local third party logistics (3PL) firm in Figure 19.1 is more likely to be an aligned supporter for the focal firm or a gatekeeper to the local retailers that the focal firm is trying to diffuse information. This information is critical for the focal firm when developing effective communication strategies for sustainability initiatives in their supply chain.

Figure 19.1 Example sustainable supply chain social network diagram
Source: authors

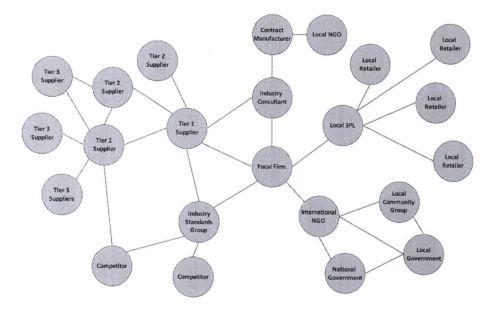

19.3 Social network variables

There are a variety of variables available to analyze a social network. A common viewpoint when using social network analysis is to assume that the network itself should serve as the predictor and to examine the effects on the transfer of knowledge between a focal firm and other organizations in the supply chain. In this view, the network is a resource that can be used by the focal firm and variables must measure the structure of the network itself as well as the focal firm's ability to access the resources provided by the network, based on their location in the network and the quality of relationships available to them. The variables listed in Table 19.1 are discussed in more detail below regarding their impact on the TBL in global supply chains. They are based on the work of Carpenter *et al.* (2012) that define the appropriate variables for conducting social network analysis at the organizational level. The variables discussed below will illustrate a key trade-off that many MNEs must manage in regard to sustainability, which is the trade-off between access to new ideas and the ability to effectively manage the implementation of sustainability initiatives.

Table 19.1 Network-level characteristics

Variable	Description	Sustainable issues
Network size	Extent of membership of supply chain network	Many stakeholders such as NGOs, government entities, suppliers or tiers of suppliers in the supply chain can lead to new ideas but inhibit the focal firm's ability to manage information flow effectively to a large number of stakeholders
Density	Degree of connectivity within a network	Many direct connections between stakeholders can lead to easier implementation of sustainability initiatives because of common connections but can close the focal firm off to new ideas from stakeholders with which the MNE is not directly connected
Cohesion	Strength of the forces acting on a stakeholder in a network to stay in that network	Cohesive networks are generally good at implementing sustainable initiatives but cohesion also impacts ethical issues and can close the MNE off to ideas from outside the stakeholders with which it has cohesive relationships
Centrality	Importance of the focal firm in the dissemination of information in the network	A high degree of centrality makes the firm more powerful and influential in the communication and resulting adoption of TBL initiatives in their supply chain

19.4 Social network variable discussion

The following section includes discussion of the key social network variables that are used to describe how TBL initiatives are diffused, adopted and balanced in a supply chain context. Each variable includes an overview of its relationship with the TBL and why it is important for explaining TBL outcomes.

19.4.1 Network size

The size of a network can have an impact on the ability of an MNE to acquire and transfer knowledge amongst the members of its global supply chain, as network size influences the amount of diverse information available from network stakeholders. The basis of this relationship is that a large number of available relationships increases the probability that required knowledge can be accessed when needed by a focal firm (Reagans and McEvily, 2003). Many times local NGOs or community groups are criticized for promoting awareness of local sustainability issues in emerging economies, as MNEs expanding to these locations have little to no prior experience in these locations. For example, the stringent reporting requirements that MNEs face today regarding conflict minerals are often credited as having been born from local NGOs that raised awareness of the issue. These NGOs were able to raise awareness of local conditions to the point that larger organizations took notice and eventually practices were implemented that helped to decrease the proliferation of these materials (Bieri, 2013).

This highlights the importance of the inclusion of typical non-economic actors in a network for driving awareness to issues that can help properly balance the TBL in a manner that takes into account network level needs (and not just based on focal firm needs). From a purely supply chain perspective, this relates to the degree that the focal firm has relationships over the entirety of the supply chain network. This ability to integrate the knowledge resources of lower-tier suppliers has been shown to be a facilitator of improved outcomes (Fawcett and Magnan, 2002; Zsidisin *et al.*, 2015). A higher number of actors in the network also increases the complexity of management of information flow. This is one of the primary reasons that many MNEs, such as those in the automotive industry, have "tiered" their supply chains so that tier-1 suppliers are responsible for managing the information flow to lower-tier suppliers. Volkswagen for example has used their German first-tier suppliers to implement environmental and social standards to other firms in their global supply network, as it allows Volkswagen to focus their communication efforts on a smaller subset of the overall network (Beske *et al.*, 2008).

19.4.2 Density

The sheer quantity of stakeholders, while important, does not fully explain how TBL information flows in a supply chain. The structure of a network that impacts on how a focal firm and its conduits relay information to indirectly connected stakeholders is also important for explaining how the TBL is managed in a global supply chain. Network density can provide insight in this regard, as density refers to the degree of integration in a social network by measuring the proportion of actual ties in a network divided by the number of potential ties. This measure is an indicator of the degree that stakeholders in the network are directly or indirectly connected with each other.

There is diverging research on the benefits of high density within a network. Autry and Griffis (2008) summarized this topic by concluding that high density can lead to benefits in terms of execution in a supply chain while lower density (less direct connections for the focal firm) has advantages in terms of innovation. The execution argument lies in the fact that direct relationships lead to increased knowledge of values, process and norms that enhance knowledge coordination among firms in a network. This can be thought of as a "learning curve" effect that improves execution of an MNEs sustainable practices over time (Granovetter, 1992). The reverse of this argument is that boundary-spanning relationships that provide (broker) access to indirectly connected stakeholders are important for having access to novel information. Networks in which MNEs have a high number of relationships beyond their firm and industry have been shown to increase the ability of the firm to acquire new information (Burt, 2002).

One key point that Autry and Griffis (2008) make when discussing execution versus innovation is that there is not one correct way to manage the network in this regard. Firms must understand their goals and develop a portfolio of relationships, based on those goals, that properly balances execution of sustainable practices versus access to novel ideas that can be used to properly manage the TBL. Attaining total value from a network lies in the ability of the MNE to manage relationships with the mindset that the stakeholders with which they have connections must either be critical from an execution standpoint or allow the firm to access key information.

This puts a focus on those actors that "bridge" the focal firm to indirectly connected actors, as these are the stakeholders that can provide the proper balance in the portfolio of relationships. MNEs must have efficient knowledge transfer processes with these stakeholders in order to access new information. Fortunately, in most networks a large percentage of the total ties are clustered into sub-groups of stakeholders that are locally dense and separated to some degree from the rest of the network (Scott, 2012). These clusters can be thought of as specialized pools of knowledge that the MNE needs to access, where stakeholders within the same network tend to be more aligned in terms of values and norms than stakeholders in different clusters. The clustering membership of the focal firm, brokering actors (actors in the network that connect the focal firm to others with which it does not have direct ties) and indirectly connected stakeholder(s) therefore can provide valuable insight into how the TBL is managed in global supply chains. Brokering agents can come from within the supply network itself (direct or indirect suppliers) or horizontally through other stakeholders, such as NGOs or governmental organizations. Further, the relationship of the focal firm with these actors should differ depending on the desired outcomes.

An example of the power that bridging relationships can provide can be found within the recent announcement by the World Wildlife Fund (WWF) of new programmes between Apple and local Chinese communities. The plan attempts to reduce the deforestation of local Chinese communities, that are multiple tiers in Apple's supply chain, by producing paper products used for packaging from responsibly-managed forests within China's borders (Schwartz, 2015). The plan balances the needs of the focal firm with local sustainable needs by WWF taking values from both sides and helping to create a plan. The recognition of a local issue could have been difficult for an organization as large as Apple to identify on its own without some type of event to initiate awareness and, thus, the brokering stakeholder in the exchange (WWF) played a pivotal role that is readily evident by taking a network perspective.

19.4.3 Cohesion

Cohesion derives from the forces that keep stakeholders within a network and thus have an impact on the content of knowledge flow (Carpenter *et al.*, 2012). Cohesion is related to the quality of relationships that the focal firm possesses and is commonly associated with tie strength constructs such as communication frequency or perceived quality of content from stakeholders in the network. The level of cohesion required within a network is associated with the type of knowledge transferred within that network. Networks with proprietary information generally require more trust and thus more cohesion within the network (Dhanaraj *et al.*, 2004). However, this must be balanced with over reliance on relationships with strong ties versus weak ones, as ethical issues, such as collusion, can be associated with sub-groups that have high levels of cohesion. Highly cohesive networks can also drive stakeholders to focus mostly on its networks for new knowledge, thereby potentially foregoing opportunities for incorporating new ideas in fostering critical supply chain processes such as innovation.

Cohesion is important in global supply chains in areas such as purchasing where the accumulation of trust with key suppliers can lead to improved buying firm performance (Autry and Griffis, 2008). The general theme within the purchasing area is that positive relationships with suppliers through mechanisms that positively influence knowledge transfer, such as long-term relationships and early supplier involvement, can reduce conflict and facilitate the utilization of supplier knowledge and skillsets that the buying firm does not possess as well as positively impact the diffusion of TBL practices from MNEs to their network (Tate *et al.*, 2013). This principle tends to hold to the point where buyer objectivity is affected and opportunistic behaviour by suppliers tends to increase (the connection between cohesion and ethical behaviour) (Villena *et al.*, 2011).

An example of how highly cohesive networks, in which stakeholders are aligned, can influence TBL outcomes can be seen through an electronics firm in the south-eastern United States that selected the tier-2 corrugated supplier in the supply chain but assigned tier-1 Chinese suppliers responsibility for managing supplier performance. Both the focal firm and the tier-1 supplier work together on design changes with the tier-2 supplier. In one instance, changes were made specifically to reduce the amount of packaging being used to protect the products being shipped from the tier-1 supplier to the focal firm. Adoption of sustainability practices across tiers was facilitated by alignment of expectations between the actors in the exchange and the high levels of trust and aligned expectations between the firms.

19.4.4 Centrality

Social network analysis also allows examination of how the MNE's specific position in the network impacts on its ability to access resources and disseminate information through the network to other actors regardless of the types of ties it possesses. The centrality variable can be used to determine how fundamental the MNE is in the overall flow of information within the network (Brass *et al.*, 2004). A high level of centrality suggests that the MNE mediates the communication between stakeholders in the overall network, while a low level of centrality implies that the focal firm does not have a high level of influence regarding the flow of TBL information. A more central position of the focal firm in the network has been shown to impact its ability to access knowledge, and thus is positively related to a MNEs ability to recognize, influence and respond to sustainable information from within the network (Tsai, 2001). In fact, a highly central location in the network enables a focal firm to access other stakeholder knowledge and puts the firm in a position that increases its power to manage the transfer of knowledge and influence the adoption of sustainable practices by network members (Burt, 2009).

One example related to the power that centrality can play in the diffusion and adoption of TBL information is Samsung. Samsung has been shown to be very centrally located within the South Korean electronics industry, with the ability to act as a "gatekeeper" to firms trying to diffuse knowledge into the South Korean electronics industry due to their influence over this cluster of electronics firms (Spencer, 2003). Samsung has been able to realize this central location due to it accounting for 28.2% of the South Korean gross domestic product as of 2012 (Harlan, 2012). This centrality is a mechanism by which Samsung can both control the flow of information and have power influencing the adoption of TBL initiatives within this group of stakeholders.

19.5 Industry examples

The above describes how specific social network variables can have an important impact on sustainability initiatives by MNEs. These variables can tell an even more complete story of how these outcomes are realized by analysing them as a whole instead of individually. The following examples give a more complete picture of how network variables can help explain TBL outcomes in global supply chains.

19.5.1 Electronics industry citizenship coalition (EICC)

The EICC is a group of large electronics industry manufacturers Dell, Hewlett Packard, and IBM, along with five of their contract manufacturers, that formed in 2004. The purpose for forming this coalition was to coordinate the diffusion of a common code of conduct between the focal firms and tier-1 suppliers in response to targeted reports by NGOs on sustainability issues at the contract manufacturers (tier-2 or -3 suppliers). Other companies have joined this coalition and use the EICC as a consultant to their networks to reduce the complexity created by diffusing separate codes to the same contract manufacturers (Electronic Industry Citizenship Coalition, 2015). This is helpful for the firms in the network because the EICC is the direct connection for the large electronics manufacturers and increases the efficiency of communicating codes of conduct to a large network of suppliers spread out over multiple tiers. The suppliers also see benefits and are aided in their execution of sustainable practices by an outside party that was setup to create standard codes of conduct from multiple electronics manufacturers that do business with these firms. This is helpful because they can concentrate on implementing a single set of practices instead of multiple practices for each manufacturer.

There are however dangers with this type of exchange that can have an impact on achieving more balanced TBL outcomes. The EICC was formed specifically in response to targeted NGO reports on sustainable issues at contract manufacturers for three large electronics companies. The social issues related to work rights and child labour. Initiating these reports became the focus of the consultant's efforts and thus there was an opportunity to overlook other issues that might not have been part of the NGO reports. From a network perspective, the MNEs involved in disseminating sustainable practices to suppliers must ensure that they are not overlooking important TBL issues from stakeholders that are not part of the EICC network.

This example illustrates how analyzing a supply chain from a social network perspective can provide valuable insight into how sustainable practices are disseminated across global supply chains. MNEs, such as Dell and Hewlett Packard, recognized the complexity of communicating and implementing sustainable practices across a large supply chain, as they were having great difficulty managing a large network consisting of primarily direct connections. However, this could have potentially closed them off to acquiring information that might have allowed them to avoid the issues that led to the NGO reports. Condensing all of these direct connections down to one highly cohesive broker (the EICC), that can concentrate on managing these relationships, allowed them to better align the information diffusion process. The suppliers also saw benefits because they were no longer having to manage practices from their customers that at many times could diverge or at least increase the time required to implement multiple practices.

19.5.2 Bangladesh garment industry

The EICC example above shows the power that a broker, aligned with the focal firm and suppliers, can have on sustainable practices in a global supply chain. It can be inferred from this example that the electronics manufacturers and their tier-1 suppliers were in the same cluster, based on them joining together within the same coalition. There are however instances when an MNE is not aligned within the same subgroup as those to which it is trying to transfer TBL information, which can make coordination of supply chain members much more difficult. One well-known example of this type of network is within the Bangladesh garment industry. This industry is very large in Bangladesh and has contracts with major retailers such as Gap and Walmart. It has been plagued by deadly worker safety issues, such as a 2013 building collapse that killed over 1,100 people (Banjo, 2013). Analysing this example from a social network perspective leads to some interesting insights into how direct and indirect connections affected how information was relayed amongst network members.

Major retailers in both the United States and Europe have formed separate partnerships to be their unified representative when dealing with garment suppliers in Bangladesh. The industry groups were formed to diffuse expectations to local clusters of garment manufacturers in Bangladesh in their supply networks due to safety incidents within the country. Studies have found however that many of the practices diffused by the North American and European retailers were not properly implemented within the Bangladesh garment industry (Bhowmick, 2014). The retailers communicated codes of conduct that explicitly stated their expectations of safe working conditions for employees and were aligned through the retailer-funded monitoring groups. However, the government was responsible for inspecting factory conditions, instead of the manufacturers or outside third parties being responsible. Knowing that the inspectors were not centrally located in the network and limited in their ability to routinely inspect the manufacturing facilities drove behaviour that was counter to the expectations of the retailers. The governmental control of the inspectors was a major factor of poor adoption of safety practices by Bangladesh manufacturers (Srivastava, 2013).

These issues in the local Bangladesh sub-group could have been visible to the focal firms and brokers. The stakeholder responsible for communicating the TBL information was tied to an actor in the Bangladesh sub-group (the government) that was not the one where the actual issues were occurring (the factories). The government was not explicitly trying to undermine the intentions of the global retailers but the retailers and their representatives were easily satisfied when the government placated them by agreeing to audit the Bangladesh factories. They were satisfied however without determining what the issues were that would matter to all of the stakeholders in the network. Having access to stakeholders that controlled this information could have led to better TBL outcomes. The "well-meaning but flawed" knowledge transfer process was attributed as a large factor as to why all of the local issues were not discovered, as the representative monitoring groups funded by the retailers were incentivized to cater "more to the brands involved than the workers toiling on the line" (Jamieson and Hossain, 2013, p. 1). This example illustrates how the configuration of a network as described by the variables such as centrality, density and size can have an important effect on TBL outcomes, as the configuration of relationships resulted in a network that did not allow the diffusion and adoption of TBL initiatives in a manner consistent with the goals of the North American and European industry groups.

19.6 Conclusions

This chapter highlights the important role that networks have on TBL outcomes in global supply chains. The benefits of taking a network perspective when managing a supply chain have been discussed previously (Choi and Kim, 2008). This research discussed how an understanding of its position within the overall supply network can allow a firm to be more aware of the value that their connections play in either increasing the effectiveness of implementation of practices within the network, providing access to a wider span of novel information or improving the efficiency of the knowledge dissemination process. This perspective is vitally important when assessing how TBL initiatives are developed and implemented in global supply chains, as non-economic outcomes can introduce many new stakeholders into the network. Social network variables such as size, density, cohesiveness and centrality are measurable and can provide valuable insights into how the structure and quality of relationships a firm possesses impacts on its ability to manage the TBL in its supply chain.

References

Andersen, M., & Skjoett-Larsen, T. (2009). Corporate social responsibility in global supply chains. *Supply Chain Management: An International Journal*, 14(2), 75-86.
Autry, C.W., & Griffis, S.E. (2008). Supply chain capital: The impact of structural and relational linkages on firm execution and innovation. *Journal of Business Logistics*, 29(1), 157-173.
Banjo, S. (2013, October 23). Wal-Mart, Gap Press for Safety in Bangladesh. *Wall Street Journal*. Retrieved from http://www.wsj.com

Beske, P., Koplin, J., & Seuring, S. (2008). The use of environmental and social standards by German first tier suppliers of the Volkswagen AG. *Corporate Social Responsibility and Environmental Management*, 15(2), 63-75.

Bhowmick, N. (2014). Bangladesh's garment factories still unsafe for workers, says report. *Time*. Retrieved from http://www.time.com

Bieri, F. (2013). *From Blood Diamonds to the Kimberley Process: How NGOs Cleaned up the Global Diamond Industry*. Burlington: Ashgate Publishing.

Brass, D.J., Galaskiewicz, J., Greve, H.R., & Tsai, W. (2004). Taking stock of networks and organizations: A multilevel perspective. *Academy of Management Journal*, 47(6), 795-817.

Burt, R.S. (2009). *Structural Holes: The Social Structure of Competition*. Cambridge, MA: Harvard University Press.

Burt, R.S. (2002). The social capital of structural holes. *The New Economic Sociology*, 148-192.

Carpenter, M.A., Li, M., & Jiang, H. (2012). Social network research in organizational contexts: A systematic review of methodological issues and choices. *Journal of Management*, 38(4), 1,328-1361.

Choi, T.Y., & Kim, Y. (2008). Structural embeddedness and supplier management: A network perspective. *Journal of Supply Chain Management*, 44(4), 5-13.

Dhanaraj, C., Lyles, M.A., Steensma, H.K., & Tihanyi, L. (2004). Managing tacit and explicit knowledge transfer in IJVs: The role of relational embeddedness and the impact on performance. *Journal of International Business Studies*, 35(5), 428-442.

Electronic Industry Citizenship Coalition (2015). History. Retrieved from http://www.eiccoalition.org/about/history (June 23, 2015)

Granovetter, M. (1992). *Economic institutions as social constructions: A framework for analysis*. Acta Sociologica, 35(1), 3-11.

Hall, J., & Matos, S. (2010). Incorporating impoverished communities in sustainable supply chains. *International Journal of Physical Distribution and Logistics management*, 40(1/2), 124-147.

Harlan, C. (2012). In South Korea, the Republic of Samsung. *Washington Post*. Retrieved from http://www.washingtonpost.com

Jamali, D. (2010). The CSR of MNC subsidiaries in developing countries: Global, local, substantive or diluted? *Journal of Business Ethics*, 93(2), 181-200.

Jamieson, D., & Hossain, E. (2013). Bangladesh collapse shows safety audit shortcomings. *Huffington Post*. Retrieved from: http://www.huffingtonpost.com

Kolk, A., & Van Tulder, R. (2010). International business, corporate social responsibility and sustainable development. *International Business Review*, 19(2), 119-125.

Reagans, R., & McEvily, B. (2003). Network structure and knowledge transfer: The effects of cohesion and range. *Administrative Science Quarterly*, 48(2), 240-197.

Rowley, T.J. (1997). Moving beyond dyadic ties: A network theory of stakeholder influences. *Academy of Management Review*, 22(4), 887-910.

Sarkis, J., Zhu, Q., & Lai, K.-H. (2011). An organizational theoretic review of green supply chain management literature. *International Journal of Production Economics*, 130(1), 1-15. doi: 10.1016/j.ijpe.2010.11.010.

Schwartz, J. (2015). WWF and Apple Commit to Help Protect China's Forests. Retrieved from http://www.worldwildlife.org

Scott, J. (2012). *Social Network Analysis*. Thousand Oaks, CA: Sage.

Spencer, J.W. (2003). Global gatekeeping, representation, and network structure: A longitudinal analysis of regional and global knowledge-diffusion networks. *Journal of International Business Studies*, 34(5), 428-442.

Srivastava, M. (2013). For Bangladesh factory safety, outside inspectors are still MIA. Bloomberg. Retrieved from http://www.bloomberg.com/bw/articles/2013-10-31/in-bangladesh-new-factory-safety-inspections-are-behind-schedule

Tate, W.L., Ellram, L.M., & Gölgeci, I. (2013). Diffusion of environmental business practices: A network approach. *Journal of Purchasing and Supply Management*, 19(4), 194-275.

Tsai, W. (2001). Knowledge transfer in intraorganizational networks: Effects of network position and absorptive capacity on business unit innovation and performance. *Academy of Management Journal*, 44(5), 996-1,004.

Villena, V.H., Revilla, E., & Choi, T.Y. (2011). The dark side of buyer–supplier relationships: A social capital perspective. *Journal of Operations Management*, 29(6), 561-576.

Wuyts, S., Stremersch, S., Van den Bulte, C., & Franses, P.H. (2004). Vertical marketing systems for complex products: A triadic perspective. *Journal of Marketing Research*, 41(4), 479-487.

Zsidisin, G.A., Hartley, J.L., Bernardes, E.S., & Lance W. Saunders, L.W. (2015). Examining supply market scanning and internal communication climate as facilitators of supply chain integration. *Supply Chain Management: An International Journal*, 20(5), 549-560.

Lance W. Saunders PE, PhD is an Assistant Professor in the Department of Supply Chain Management and Analytics at Virginia Commonwealth University (VCU). He attained his PhD in Industrial and Systems Engineering from Virginia Tech in 2012 and is a registered Professional Engineer of Industrial Engineering. His research has been funded by the Occupational Safety and Health Administration (OSHA), Air Liquide, Proctor and Gamble, Ryder Logistics and Volvo Trucks. He has also published multiple papers surrounding the development of analytical models for improving logistics and distribution performance, as well as how sustainability practices are effectively implemented at the supply chain level using network analysis techniques.

Wendy L. Tate, PhD (Arizona State University, 2006) is an Associate Professor of Supply Chain Management Department of Marketing and Supply Chain Management at the University of Tennessee. She teaches undergraduate, MBA and PhD students Strategic Sourcing and Manufacturing and Service Operations and has an interest in the financial impacts of business decisions across the supply chain.

Joe Miemczyk is an Associate Professor in operations and supply chain management at Audencia Nantes School of Management in the Department of Information Systems and Supply Chains. Previous to this post he was a research fellow at the University of Bath School of Management and Business Process Engineer at Unipart Group of Companies. His research explores responsive and sustainable supply chains and the interaction between the two. In relation to this subject he has researched the role of logistics in build to order in the automotive sector and end of life product strategies. His work is published in the International Journal of Operations and Production Management, International Journal of Production Economics, Journal of Business Logistics, International Journal of Physical Distribution and Logistics Management and Supply Chain Management: An International Journal among others.

George A. Zsidisin, PhD (Arizona State University), CPSM, CPM, is a Professor of Supply Chain Management at Virginia Commonwealth University. Professor Zsidisin has conducted extensive research on various topics in supply chain management, with a focus on how firms assess and manage supply disruptions and commodity price volatility. His research has resulted in publishing over 70 research and practitioner articles that have been extensively cited, attaining various grants from businesses and foundations and receiving numerous awards, such as from the Institute for Supply Management, Deutsche Post, Council of Supply Chain Management Professionals and the Decision Sciences Institute. Professor Zsidisin currently serves as the co-editor of the Journal of Purchasing and Supply Management, is the Director of the Master of Supply Chain Management programme at Virginia Commonwealth University and sits on the Editorial Review Board for several academic supply chain journals.